LISREL® 7
A Guide to the Program and Applications
2nd Edition

JÖRESKOG and SÖRBOM/SPSS Inc.

SPSS Inc.
444 N. Michigan Avenue
Chicago, Illinois 60611
Tel: (312) 329-2400
Fax: (312) 329-3668

T0204583

PREFACES

Preface to Second Edition

In this second edition, new material on the *Completely Standardized Solution* has been added in Sections 1.18 and 9.3, and Sections 1.21 and 2.14 have been rewritten to take into account new developments in the program. The section on growth curves has been expanded and presented with a real worked example (Example 10.4). Several paragraphs and sentences have been rewritten for better clarification, and numerous typographical and other errors have been corrected.

We are grateful to Leo Stam and Werner Wothke for their careful proofreading of the first edition.

Uppsala, Sweden, January 1989
Karl G Jöreskog   Dag Sörbom

Preface to First Edition

Some History of LISREL

The idea of combining features of both *econometrics* and *psychometrics* into a single mathematical model was born in the mind of the first author in the spring of 1970. This idea was inspired by work of Professor Arthur S. Goldberger published in *Psychometrika*, 1971. The first version of LISREL was a *linear structural equation model* for *latent variables,* each with a single observed, possibly *fallible, indicator*. This model was first presented at the conference on *Structural Equation Models in the Social Sciences* held in Madison, Wisconsin, in November 1970. The proceedings of this conference, edited by Professors Goldberger and Duncan, were published in 1973. This LISREL model was generalized in 1971-72 to include models previously developed for *multiple indicators of latent variables*, for *confirmatory factor analysis* (Jöreskog, 1969), for *simultaneous factor analysis in several populations* (Jöreskog, 1971) and more general models for *covariance structures* (Jöreskog, 1970a, 1973b, 1974). The basic form of the LISREL model has remained the same ever since and is still the same model as used today. The general form of the LISREL model, due to its flexible specification in terms of fixed and free parameters and simple equality constraints, has proven to be so rich that it can handle not only the large variety of problems studied by hundreds of social science researchers but also complex models, such as mean structures (Sörbom, 1974, 1976, 1978) and multiplicative models (Kenny and Judd, 1984; Wothke and Browne, 1989), far beyond the type of models for which it was originally conceived.

The first two computer versions of LISREL were written by the first author with assistance of Marielle van Thillo. The program was completely rewritten in 1974-75 by the second author. This version, called LISREL III, was the first made generally available with a written manual. It had fixed column input, fixed dimensions, only the maximum likelihood method, and users had to provide starting values for all parameters. The versions that followed demonstrated an enormous development in both statistical methodology and programming technology:

- LISREL IV (1978) had Keywords, Free Form Input, and Dynamic Storage Allocation

- LISREL V (1981) had Automatic Starting Values, Unweighted and Generalized Least Squares, and Total Effects

- LISREL VI (1984) had Parameter Plots, Modification Indices, and Automatic Model Modification

For the current version of the program - LISREL 7 - to be described in this book, we have again rewritten the program in the light of new statistical developments (Browne, 1984) for *weighted least squares* with general weight matrices. Together with the companion program PRELIS that produces these weight matrices, LISREL 7 provides efficient estimates and correct asymptotic χ^2 and standard errors under non-normality of the observed variables and when some or all of the observed variables are only measured on an ordinal scale. While maintaining compatibility with LISREL 6, with few exceptions, LISREL 7 has many more features and options, runs faster and can handle larger problems than LISREL 6. It also handles most problem cases better.

In addition to the many researchers who have used LISREL to help solve their substantive problems and who have published their findings, many people have studied the behavior and performance of various aspects of the LISREL methodology both by means of theoretical investigations and by means of Monte Carlo simulations. A bibliography of LISREL-related literature is published at the end of this book. In preparing this book and the new version of the program, we have benefited from some of these discussions.

How to Read this Book

This book is *not* written for mathematical statisticians. It is written for graduate students and researchers in the social and behavioral sciences who need to use the LISREL program as a research tool to solve empirical substantive data-analytic problems. It is not necessary to understand the advanced mathematical and statistical theory on which LISREL is based to use the program for this purpose. Nevertheless, in order to give an accurate description of what the program is doing, some statistical concepts, notations and formulas are necessary.

The focus in this book is on

> *What can I do with* LISREL?

and

> *How can I do it?*

For these purposes, we give a large number of typical examples from various disciplines and show in some detail how LISREL is used.

The book proceeds as follows. Chapter 1 defines the general LISREL model and its submodels. It also considers, in general terms, the methods of identification, estimation, and testing used by the program and describes most of the output that can be produced. Because of the general formulation in Chapter 1, the material is rather abstract.

Chapter 2 gives detailed instructions for how to run the program in general terms and Chapters 3-7 give examples with detailed input and output for several single-sample problems. The LISREL Submodels 1 and 2 are defined and illustrated in Chapters 3 and 4, respectively. The full LISREL model is illustrated in Chapter 5. Chapter 6 defines and illustrates the LISREL Submodel 3. A separate chapter (Chapter 7) is devoted to the analysis of ordinal variables and non-normal continuous variables.

Miscellaneous issues are discussed in Chapter 8 such as constraints, hypothesis testing, power calculation, and equivalent models.

Chapter 9 describes and illustrates multi-sample analysis based on covariance matrices and Chapter 10 describes and illustrates models with mean structures and their analysis in several samples.

Chapter 11 explains some technical parameters in LISREL and discusses how to solve problem cases.

A second volume is planned to give a unified comprehensive account of the mathematical and statistical theory and the computational approaches used in the program.

Experienced LISREL users need only browse through Chapters 1, 2, 7, 8, 10 and 11 noting particularly passages about new information.

Beginners and those with just a little experience with LISREL may want to read Chapters 3-6 before they begin with Chapters 1 and 2.

Acknowledgments

Work on LISREL 7 and the preparation of this book has been supported by *The Swedish Council for Research in the Humanities and the Social Sciences* under Research Program *Multivariate Statistical Analysis*.

Our thanks are due to Carina Skoog-Eriksson and Suzanne Lindman for typing the manuscript and to Peter Götlind for expert typesetting with TeX and drawing of the figures.

LISREL 7 vs LISREL 6

Compatibility of Input

An input file prepared for LISREL 6 will run on LISREL 7 with the following exceptions:

- The default value of NO (number of cases, sample size) has been changed from 100 to 0. When a covariance, correlation or other moment matrix is to be read, NO must be specified or the program will stop; see Sections 2.3 and 2.4.2. The new default value agrees with that of PRELIS and SIMPLIS.

- If there are fixed zero elements in the diagonals of $\Phi, \Psi, \Theta_\epsilon$, or Θ_δ, one must set AD=OFF on the OU line. More generally, this must be done for all models which, by definition, prevent these matrices from being positive definite. See Sections 1.11 and 2.15.

- The default value for the *maximum number of iterations* (IT) has been changed to three times the number of parameters in the model. In LISREL 6, this value was 250. Therefore, if a LISREL 6 problem took more than three times the number of parameters to converge, the IT parameter must be set to a large value in LISREL 7. This is specified on the OU line. See Section 2.15 and Chapter 11.

- LISREL 7 handles *missing values by listwise deletion only*. For pairwise deletion or any other raw data problems, the companion program PRELIS produces the relevant covariance or correlation matrix, see Section 1.10. LISREL 7 assumes that there is a global numeric value XM assigned to represent all missing values in the whole data matrix. With PRELIS, one can have different missing value representations for different variables.

The value of XM may be specified on the RA line. The parameters MV and PP of Mainframe LISREL 6 are no longer supported. Use PRELIS to compute polychoric and polyserial correlations.

- LISREL 7 checks that a scale has been defined for each latent variable as described in Section 1.2.1 and 1.12. If a scale for a latent variable has not been specified in this way, the program will stop unless the SO parameter (see Sections 2.15 and 11.7) appears on the OU line. The SO parameter is needed for very special models where scales for latent variables are defined in a different way; see Example 6.1 in Chapter 6. The SO parameter is also needed in models with mean structures when the augmented moment matrix is analyzed. However, such models should no longer be done that way since it is much easier to specify them as an extended LISREL model (see Chapter 10).

Compatibility of Output

The output from LISREL 7 may differ in many ways from that obtained by LISREL 6. The output has been reorganized so that many sections appear in a different order. Also, many sections contain other and/or additional information. Note particularly the following:

- The logical parameters VA, MR, RS, and EF on the OU line have slightly different meanings:

  MR produces covariances between the observed and latent variables. These covariances were previously included in tables produced by the keyword VA. However, variances are no longer included, so VA is not an appropriate keyword, although it can still be used. See Section 1.17.

  EF produces both *total* and *indirect* effects and, when used in combination with SE, it produces *standard errors* of total and indirect effects. See Section 1.16.

  In LISREL 6, the keyword MR was equivalent to VA, RS, and EF. Now MR is only equivalent to VA except as just stated.

  RS still produces matrices of fitted and standardized residuals and a Q-plot of standardized residuals. But stemleaf plots of fitted and standardized residuals are produced *without* RS. This is convenient to avoid large matrices in the output.

- Because of improvements of the iterative algorithm LISREL 7 will successfully run many problems which did not run with LISREL 6.

- New and improved methods of initial estimates (IV and TSLS) may produce different values, especially when equality constraints are imposed. Differences may also result when starting values are explicitly given for free parameters.

- The methods ULS, GLS, and ML produce the same parameter estimates in LISREL 6 and LISREL 7. GLS and ML produce the same standard errors, t-values, and χ^2 in LISREL 6 and LISREL 7. Improved methods of estimating modification indices, in particular in the context of equality constraints, may produce different results in LISREL 6 and LISREL 7.

- An error in GFI for GLS has been corrected so that GFI will differ between LISREL 6 and LISREL 7 for method GLS but not for ULS and ML. As a consequence, AGFI will also differ. See Sections 1.11 and 1.19.

- Standardized residuals (called normalized residuals in LISREL 6) may differ considerably between LISREL 6 and LISREL 7. An oversimplified formula for the asymptotic variances of the residuals was used in LISREL 6. A formula which requires many more computations but yields asymptotically correct variances, is used in LISREL 7. See Section 1.15.

- The parameter plot in LISREL 6 is a plot of the *marginal* fit function against a specified parameter. By contrast, LISREL 7 plots the *concentrated* fit function. This takes much more time but gives a more useful plot. See Section 3.3.

Features Included in LISREL 7 but not in LISREL 6

- A thorough check of the syntax in LISREL input lines in the same way it is done in PRELIS.

- An *admissibility check* of the model with options to stop before iterations begin or after a specified number of iterations if a non-admissible solution is produced. See Sections 1.11 and 2.15.

- Two new estimation methods, WLS and DWLS, have been added to those already available in LISREL 6, and a unified approach to estimation is now taken. WLS requires an asymptotic covariance matrix produced by PRELIS. This method produces asymptotically correct standard errors and χ^2 values under non-normality and when one or more of the observed variables are ordinal. WLS is particularly important when analyzing polychoric and/or polyserial correlations. Note that the computational requirements for WLS become demanding as the number of variables increases. A reasonable compromise between normal theory ML or GLS and non-normal WLS may be DWLS which requires only the asymptotic variances of estimated correlations (or variances and covariances). These asymptotic variances are also obtained by PRELIS.

- Standard errors, *t*-values, standardized residuals, and χ^2 goodness-of-fit values can now be obtained for method ULS. These are correct under standard normal theory.

- The *Ridge Option* is a new feature in LISREL 7. This option handles covariance and correlation matrices which are not positive definite. If the covariance or correlation matrix to be analyzed is not positive definite, a constant times the diagonal is added to the diagonal before iterations begin. This *Ridge Constant* is automatically determined by the program or can be be specified by the user. See Section 2.15.

  The Ridge Option is particularly useful in econometric models containing identities and in regression models with high multicollinearity among the regressors; see Chapter 4.

  The Ridge Option may also be chosen even if the covariance or correlation matrix to be analyzed is positive definite (see Section 2.15). This adds a whole new class of estimation methods. The Ridge Option may be used in combination with all the iterative methods ULS, GLS, ML, WLS, and DWLS. Methods IV and TSLS are not affected by the Ridge Option.

- The modification indices will now work with all iterative estimation methods and have been extended and supplied with tables of the estimated change in each parameter potentially to be relaxed. This indicates how sensitive the model is to changes in each parameter and gives information about the power of the χ^2 measure.

- Stemleaf plots of residuals and standardized residuals are obtained in the standard output. These are useful in the assessment of fit.

- Both *indirect* and total effects are given and *standard errors* of these will be obtained by requesting both SE and EF on the OU line.

- The LISREL model has been extended to include four new parameter matrices (see Chapter 10). Models with mean parameters (intercept terms and mean values of latent variables) can now be specified directly. This makes it much easier to analyze models with mean structures.

Explanation of Notational System

Equations, tables and figures are numbered consecutively within chapters. Matrices and vectors appear in boldface. Matrices are denoted by upper-case letters; vectors are denoted by lower-case letters. The transpose of a matrix is denoted by a prime. For example, $\mathbf{\Gamma}'$ is the transpose of $\mathbf{\Gamma}$. All vectors without a prime are column vectors. A row vector is denoted as a transpose of a column vector. If $\mathbf{S}$ is a matrix we use s_{ij} to denote a typical element of $\mathbf{S}$. The inverse matrix of $\mathbf{\Sigma}$, say, is written $\mathbf{\Sigma}^{-1}$. The determinant of a square matrix $\mathbf{\Sigma}$, say, is denoted $\|\mathbf{\Sigma}\|$ and the trace, or sum of diagonal elements, of a square matrix $\mathbf{\Sigma}$, say, is denoted $\mathrm{tr}(\mathbf{\Sigma})$.

Greek letters are used to denote true population parameters, hypothetical latent (unobservable) random variables, and random error variables. For example, in $\mathbf{x} = \mathbf{\Lambda}_x \mathbf{\xi} + \mathbf{\delta}$, $\mathbf{\xi}$ and $\mathbf{\delta}$ are vectors of random latent and error variables, $\mathbf{x}$ is a vector of observed random variables and $\mathbf{\Lambda}_x$ is a matrix of parameters. Parameter estimates are denoted by a hat (ˆ) above the corresponding parameter. For example, $\hat{\mathbf{\Lambda}}_x$ denotes the estimate of $\mathbf{\Lambda}_x$, regardless of the method of estimation used.

The Greek Alphabet			Other Notation	
			Example	Meaning
α	A	alpha	$\mathbf{x}$	Column vector
β	B	beta	$\mathbf{x}'$	Row vector
γ	Γ	gamma	$\mathbf{X}$	Matrix
δ	Δ	delta	$\mathbf{X}'$	Matrix transpose
ϵ	E	Epsilon	$\mathbf{X}^{-1}$	Matrix inverse
ζ	Z	zeta	x_{ij}	Matrix element
η	H	eta	$\|\mathbf{X}\|$	Determinant of $\mathbf{X}$
θ	Θ	theta	$\mathrm{tr}(\mathbf{X})$	Trace of $\mathbf{X}$
ι	I	iota	Greek letters	Population parameters,
κ	K	kappa		latent random variables
λ	Λ	lambda	Roman letters	Observed random variables
μ	M	mu		
ν	N	nu	Typical LISREL Notation	
ξ	Ξ	xi, ksi	$\mathbf{x}, \mathbf{y}$	Observed variables
o	O	omicron	ξ, η	Latent variables
π	Π	pi	ζ, δ, ϵ	Error variables
ρ	P	rho		
σ	Σ	sigma	Λ_y, Λ_x	Factor loadings
τ	T	tau	$\mathbf{B}, \Gamma$	Structural parameters
υ	Υ	upsilon	Φ, Ψ	Covariance matrices
ϕ	Φ	phi	$\Theta_\epsilon, \Theta_\delta$	Error covariance matrices
χ	X	chi		
ψ	Ψ	psi	$\hat{\Lambda}_x$	Estimate of Λ_x
ω	Ω	omega		

LISREL Examples, Data and Input Files

This book has many examples illustrating most of the common types of models and methods used with LISREL. For beginners of LISREL it is instructive to go over these examples to learn how to set up the input file for particular models and problems. We also suggest using these examples as exercises in the following ways:

- Estimate the same model with a different method of estimation

- Estimate the same model from correlations instead of covariances or vice versa

- Request other options for the output

- Formulate and test hypotheses about the parameters of the model

- Estimate a different model for the same data

- Make deliberate mistakes in the input file and see what happens

Input and data files for these examples are available on diskette. For these files we use the following naming conventions.

The first letters in the file refer to the example in the book. Thus, EX31B means Example 3.1B in Chapter 3. Input files have suffix .LS7 for LISREL 7 and .PRL for PRELIS. The suffix after the period in the name of the data file refers to the type of data it contains:

- LAB for labels

- COV for covariance matrix

- COR for correlation matrix

- RAW for raw data

- DAT for a file containing several types of data

- PML for matrix of polychoric (and polyserial) correlations produced by PRELIS under listwise deletion

- KML for matrix of product-moment correlations (based on raw scores or normal scores) produced by PRELIS under listwise deletion

- ACP for asymptotic covariance matrix of the elements of a PML matrix produced by PRELIS

- ACK for asymptotic covariance matrix of the elements of a KML matrix produced by PRELIS

Example 1:   Hypothetical Model   7-9,73-74
                    Data File: EX1.COV
                    Input File: EX1.LS7

Example 3.1: Reader Reliability in Essay Scoring   79
                    Data File: None
                    Input Files: EX31A.LS7, EX31B.LS7, EX31C.LS7

x

Contacting SPSS Inc.

If you would like to be on our mailing list, write to us at one of the addresses below. We will send you a copy of our newsletter and let you know about SPSS Inc. activities in your area.

SPSS Inc.
444 North Michigan Ave.
Chicago, IL 60611
Tel: (312) 329-2400
Fax: (312) 329-3668

SPSS Federal Systems
12030 Sunrise Valley Dr.
Suite 300
Reston, VA 22091
Tel: (703) 391-6020
Fax (703) 391-6002

SPSS Latin America
444 North Michigan Ave.
Chicago, IL 60611
Tel: (312) 329-3556
Fax: (312) 329-3668

SPSS Benelux BV
P.O. Box 115
4200 AC Gorinchem
The Netherlands
Tel: +31.1830.36711
Fax: +31.1830.35839

SPSS UK Ltd.
SPSS House
5 London Street
Chertsey
Surrey KT16 8AP
United Kingdom
Tel: +44.932.566262
Fax: +44.932.567020

SPSS UK Ltd., New Delhi
No. 3 Business Centre
Ashok Hotel
Chanakyapuri
New Delhi 110 021
India
Tel: +91.11.600121 x1029
Fax: +91.11.6873216

SPSS GmbH Software
Steinsdorfstrasse 19
D-8000 Munich 22
Germany
Tel:+49.89.2283008
Fax: +49.89.2285413

SPSS Scandinavia AB
Sjöängsvägen 21
S-191 72 Sollentuna
Sweden
Tel: +46.8.7549450
Fax: +46.8.7548816

SPSS Asia Pacific Pte. Ltd.
10 Anson Road, #34-07
International Plaza
Singapore 0207
Singapore
Tel: +65.221.2577
Fax: +65.221.9920

SPSS Japan Inc.
Gyoen Sky Bldg.
2-1-11, Shinjuku
Shinjuku-ku
Tokyo 160
Japan
Tel: +81.3.33505261
Fax: +81.3.33505245

SPSS Australasia Pty. Ltd.
121 Walker Street
North Sydney, NSW 2060
Australia
Tel: +61.2.954.5660
Toll-free: +008.024.836
Fax: +61.2.954.5616

Contents

List of Tables

List of Figures

Chapter 1

GENERAL DESCRIPTION OF MODELS AND METHODS

1.1 Structural Equation Modeling

Structural equation models have proven useful in solving many substantive research problems in the social and behavioral sciences. Such models have been used in the study of macroeconomic policy formation, intergenerational occupational mobility, racial discrimination in employment, housing and earnings, studies of antecedents and consequences of drug use, scholastic achievement, evaluation of social action programs, voting behavior, studies of genetic and cultural effects, factors in cognitive test performance, consumer behavior, and many other phenomena.

Methodologically, the models play many roles, including simultaneous equation systems, linear causal analysis, path analysis, structural equation models, dependence analysis, and crosslagged panel correlation technique.

A structural equation model is used to specify the phenomenon under study in terms of putative cause-and-effect variables and their indicators. Because each equation in the model represents a causal link rather than a mere empirical association, the structural parameters do not, in general, coincide with coefficients of regressions among observed variables. Instead, the structural parameters represent relatively unmixed, invariant and autonomous features of the mechanism that generates the observed variables. To serve these purposes, the use of structural equation models requires statistical tools that are based upon, but go well beyond, conventional regression analysis and analysis of variance.

Goldberger (1973) considered three situations in which structural equations are important and regression parameters fail to give the relevant information: (i) when the observed variables contain measurement errors and the interesting relationship is among the true or disattenuated variables, (ii) when there is interdependence or simultaneous causation among the observed response variables, and (iii) when important explanatory variables have not been observed (omitted variables).

Unlike the natural sciences, social and behavioral sciences seldom allow rigorous experimentation under controlled conditions. Instead, causal inference must be based on studies in which causal models and hypotheses are statistically evaluated. Even in these studies, causal relationships cannot be proved; they can only be established as more or less reasonable relative to alternative specifications. These weak inferences often depend upon the direction of causality

1

given by the design of the study. See Heise (1975) and James et al. (1982) for a discussion of causal inference in the social sciences.

Most theories and models in the social and behavioral sciences are formulated in terms of theoretical concepts or constructs, which are not directly measurable or observable. However, often a number of indicators or symptoms of such concepts can be used to study the theoretical variables, more or less well.

Broadly speaking, there are two basic problems for scientific inference in the social and behavioral sciences.

The first concerns measurement: What do the observed measurements really measure? In what way and how well can one measure the kinds of things that need to be measured? How can validities and reliabilities of the measures be expressed?

The second problem concerns causal relationships among the variables and the relative explanatory power of such relationships. How can one infer complex causal relationships among variables that are not directly observable, but are reflected in fallible indicators? How can the strengths of latent relationships be assessed?

To handle these two basic problems of scientific inference, the LISREL model, in its most general form, consists of two parts: the measurement model and the structural equation model. The measurement model specifies how the latent variables or hypothetical constructs are measured in terms of the observed variables, and it describes the measurement properties (validities and reliabilities) of the observed variables. The structural equation model specifies the causal relationships among the latent variables and describes the causal effects and the amount of unexplained variance.

Measurement models are important in the social and behavioral sciences when one tries to measure such abstractions as people's behavior, attitudes, feelings and motivations. Most measures employed for such purposes contain sizable measurement errors and the measurement models allow us to take these measurement errors into account.

The LISREL method estimates the unknown coefficients in a set of linear structural equations. Variables in the equation system may be either directly observed variables or unmeasured latent (theoretical) variables that are not observed but relate to observed variables. The model assumes that there is a "causal" structure among a set of latent variables, and that the observed variables are indicators or symptoms of the latent variables. Sometimes the latent variables appear as linear composites of observed variables, other times as intervening variables in a "causal chain." The LISREL methodology is particularly designed to accommodate models that include latent variables, measurement errors, reciprocal causation, simultaneity, and interdependence.

In addition, LISREL covers a wide range of models useful in the social and behavioral sciences, including confirmatory factor analysis, path analysis, econometric models for time series data, recursive and non-recursive models for cross-sectional and longitudinal data, and covariance structure models.

Background material on structural equation models may be found in Goldberger (1964, Chapter 7), Heise (1975), Duncan (1975), Kenny (1979), and Jöreskog and Sörbom (1979). Several volumes of Blalock (1971, 1974, 1985a-b) contain papers dealing with basic issues and problems at an elementary level. At a more advanced level, the two volumes, Goldberger and Duncan (1973) and Aigner and Goldberger (1977), cover several issues, problems and applications. Bielby and Hauser (1977) review the sociological literature on structural equation models and Bentler (1980) gives a review of the psychological and statistical literature on latent variable models. Recently, several authors have written books on structural equation models and related topics, notably Dwyer (1983), Everitt (1984), Long (1983a-b), Saris and Stronkhorst (1984), Hayduk (1987), Cuttance and Ecob (1987), and Bollen (1989). Books in German include Hodapp (1984), Möbus and Schneider (1986) and Pfeifer and Schmidt (1987). These sources contain numerous applications and methodological discussions of psychological, educational, sociological, business, econometric and other social sciences.

The basic LISREL model was introduced by Jöreskog (1973). More recent descriptions of it are given by Jöreskog (1977, 1978, 1981). The present description of LISREL, however, does not require familiarity with these references but is rather self-contained. Other model formulations for structural equation models have been considered by McDonald (1978), Bentler and Weeks (1980) and McArdle and McDonald (1984). These models can also be handled within the LISREL framework.

Although the LISREL program is specifically designed to deal with models for latent variables and structural equation models for directly observed variables, it can also be used to handle various standard multivariate methods such as regression analysis, analysis of variance, multivariate analysis of variance and various extensions thereof.

The program is usually applied to analyze data from a single sample, but it can also be used to analyze samples from several populations simultaneously. For example, one can test hypotheses of equality of covariance matrices, equality of correlation matrices, equality of regressions, equality of factor patterns, etc. In general, some or all of the parameters can be constrained to be equal in all populations. One can also estimate mean structures. For example, one can estimate constant intercept terms in the measurement model and in the structural equations and mean values of the latent variables.

1.2   The Full LISREL Model

The LISREL model is a formal mathematical model which has to be given substantive content in each application. The meaning of the terms involved in the model varies from one application to another. The formal LISREL model defines a large class of models within which one can work and this class contains several useful subclasses as special cases.

In analysis of a single sample, there is seldom any interest in mean values of latent variables and intercept terms in the equations. Such parameters, however, may be of considerable interest in multi-sample analysis. We shall therefore postpone the discussion of such problems until Chapter 10. Here, in this chapter, we shall assume that all variables, observed as well as latent, are measured in deviations from their means. The full LISREL model can then be defined as follows.

Consider random vectors $\eta' = (\eta_1, \eta_2, \ldots, \eta_m)$ and $\xi' = (\xi_1, \xi_2, \ldots, \xi_n)$ of latent dependent and independent variables, respectively, and the following system of linear structural relations

$$\eta = \mathbf{B}\eta + \mathbf{\Gamma}\xi + \zeta, \tag{1.1}$$

where $\mathbf{B}(m \times m)$ and $\mathbf{\Gamma}(m \times n)$ are coefficient matrices and $\zeta' = (\zeta_1, \zeta_2, \ldots, \zeta_m)$ is a random vector of residuals (errors in equations, random disturbance terms). The elements of $\mathbf{B}$ represent direct effects of η-variables on other η-variables and the elements of $\mathbf{\Gamma}$ represent direct effects of ξ-variables on η-variables. It is assumed that ζ is uncorrelated with ξ and that $\mathbf{I} - \mathbf{B}$ is non-singular.

Vectors η and ξ are not observed, but instead vectors $\mathbf{y}' = (y_1, y_2, \ldots, y_p)$ and $\mathbf{x}' = (x_1, x_2, \ldots, x_q)$ are observed, such that

$$\mathbf{y} = \mathbf{\Lambda}_y \eta + \epsilon, \tag{1.2}$$

and

$$\mathbf{x} = \mathbf{\Lambda}_x \xi + \delta, \tag{1.3}$$

where ϵ and δ are vectors of error terms (errors of measurement or measure-specific components). These equations represent the multivariate regressions of $\mathbf{y}$ on η and of $\mathbf{x}$ on ξ, respectively. It is convenient to refer to $\mathbf{y}$ and $\mathbf{x}$ as the observed variables and η and ξ as the latent variables. The errors ϵ and δ are assumed to be uncorrelated between sets but may be correlated within sets. The assumption that ϵ is uncorrelated with δ can be relaxed (see Chapter 6).

In summary, the full LISREL model is defined by the three equations,

$$\begin{array}{ll}
\text{Structural Equation Model:} & \eta = \mathbf{B}\eta + \mathbf{\Gamma}\xi + \zeta \\
\text{Measurement Model for } \mathbf{y}: & \mathbf{y} = \mathbf{\Lambda}_y\eta + \epsilon \\
\text{Measurement Model for } \mathbf{x}: & \mathbf{x} = \mathbf{\Lambda}_x\xi + \delta
\end{array}$$

with the assumptions,

1. ζ is uncorrelated with ξ

2. ϵ is uncorrelated with η

3. δ is uncorrelated with ξ

4. ζ, ϵ, and δ are mutually uncorrelated

5. $\mathbf{I} - \mathbf{B}$ is non-singular.

1.2.1 Defining the Unit of Measurement for Latent Variables

Since η and ξ are unobserved they do not have a definite scale. Both the origin and the unit of measurement in each latent variable are arbitrary. To define the model properly the origin and the unit of measurement of each latent variable must be assigned. The origin has already been assigned by the assumption that each variable has zero mean. However, in order to interpret the elements of $\mathbf{\Gamma}$, one must also assign units of measurements to the latent variables.

The most useful and convenient way of assigning the units of measurement of the latent variables is to fix a non-zero value (usually one) in each column and in different rows of $\mathbf{\Lambda}_y$ and $\mathbf{\Lambda}_x$. This defines the unit for each latent variable in relation to one of the observed variables. Strictly speaking, the unit of measurement of the latent variable will be equal to the unit of measurement of the observed variable minus its error term. In practice, one should choose the fixed value for the observed variable, which, in some sense, best represents the latent variable.

An alternative way to define the unit of measurement in the latent variables is to assume that they are standardized, i.e., that they have unit variances. This can be done easily for ξ-variables but cannot be done for η-variables, since, as will be seen, the covariance matrix of η is not a free parameter matrix in the model. (The η-variables can be standardized afterwards, if required.)

In every application of a LISREL model, the units of measurement must be assigned in one way or other. Failure to observe this will lead to a model which is not identified and which cannot be estimated. The examples in Chapters 3-7 will clarify how the units of measurement are assigned in practice. See also Section 11.7.

1.2.2 Fixed, Free, and Constrained Parameters

Let $\mathbf{\Phi}(n \times n)$ and $\mathbf{\Psi}(m \times m)$ be the covariance matrices of ξ and ζ, respectively, and let $\mathbf{\Theta}_\epsilon$ and $\mathbf{\Theta}_\delta$ be the covariance matrices of ϵ and δ, respectively. Then it follows, from the above assumptions, that the covariance matrix $\mathbf{\Sigma}[(p + q) \times (p + q)]$ of $\mathbf{z} = (\mathbf{y}', \mathbf{x}')'$ is

$$\Sigma = \begin{pmatrix} \Lambda_y(I-B)^{-1}(\Gamma\Phi\Gamma'+\Psi)(I-B')^{-1}\Lambda_y' + \Theta_\epsilon & \Lambda_y(I-B)^{-1}\Gamma\Phi\Lambda_x' \\ \Lambda_x\Phi\Gamma'(I-B')^{-1}\Lambda_y' & \Lambda_x\Phi\Lambda_x' + \Theta_\delta \end{pmatrix} \qquad (1.4)$$

The elements of Σ are functions of the elements of Λ_y, Λ_x, B, Γ, Φ, Ψ, Θ_ϵ, and Θ_δ. In applications, some of these elements are fixed and equal to assigned values. In particular, this is so for elements of Λ_y, Λ_x, B, and Γ, but it is possible to have fixed values in the other matrices also. For the remaining non-fixed elements, one or more subsets may have identical but unknown values. Thus, the elements in Λ_y, Λ_x, B, Γ, Φ, Ψ, Θ_ϵ, and Θ_δ are of three kinds:

- *fixed parameters* that have been assigned specified values,

- *constrained parameters* that are unknown but equal to one or more other parameters, and

- *free parameters* that are unknown and not constrained to be equal to any other parameter.

1.3 From Path Diagrams to Equations

In presenting and discussing a LISREL model it is often useful to draw a path diagram. The path diagram effectively communicates the basic conceptual ideas of the model. However, the path diagram can do more than that. If the path diagram is drawn correctly and includes sufficient detail, it can represent exactly the corresponding algebraic equations of the model and the assumptions about the error terms in these equations.

Here and throughout this chapter we use an hypothetical model to illustrate the general LISREL model and its basic ingredients. The path diagram for this hypothetical model is given in Figure 1.1. If certain rules are followed in the path diagram, it is possible to derive the model equations from the path diagram and to derive the LISREL parameter matrices. The following conventions for path diagrams are assumed.

- Observed variables such as x- and y-variables are enclosed in squares or rectangles. Latent variables such as ξ- and η-variables are enclosed in circles or ellipses. Error variables such as δ-, ϵ-, and ζ-variables are included in the path diagram but are not enclosed.

- A one-way arrow between two variables indicate a postulated direct influence of one variable on another. A two-way arrow between two variables indicates that these variables may be correlated without any assumed direct relationship.

- There is a fundamental distinction between independent variables (ξ-variables) and dependent variables (η-variables). Variation and covariation in the dependent variables is to be accounted for or explained by the independent variables. In the path diagram this corresponds to the statements

  – no one-way arrows can point to a ξ-variable

  – all one-way arrows pointing to an η-variable come from ξ- and η-variables

- Coefficients are associated to each arrow as follows:

  – An arrow from ξ_i to x_b is denoted $\lambda_{bi}^{(x)}$

  – An arrow from η_g to y_a is denoted $\lambda_{ag}^{(y)}$

   – An arrow from η_h to η_g is denoted β_{gh}

   – An arrow from ξ_i to η_g is denoted γ_{gi}

   – An arrow from ξ_j to ξ_i is denoted ϕ_{ij}

   – An arrow from ζ_h to ζ_g is denoted ψ_{gh}

   – An arrow from δ_b to δ_a is denoted $\theta_{ab}^{(\delta)}$

   – An arrow from ϵ_d to ϵ_c is denoted $\theta_{cd}^{(\epsilon)}$

The last four arrows are always two-way arrows.

Each coefficient has two subscripts, the first being the subscript of the variable where the arrow is pointing to and the second being the subscript of the variable where the arrow is coming from. For example, γ_{23} corresponds to the arrow from ξ_3 to η_2. For two-way arrows the two subscripts may be interchanged so that $\phi_{21} = \phi_{12}$ in Figure 1.1. Arrows which have no coefficient in the path diagram are assumed to have a coefficient of one.

- All direct influences of one variable on another must be included in the path diagram. Hence the non-existence of an arrow between two variables means that it is assumed that these two variables are not directly related. (They may still be indirectly related, however; see Section 1.16.)

If the above conventions for path diagrams are followed it is always possible to write the corresponding model equations by means of the following general rules:

- For each variable which has a one-way arrow pointing to it there will be one equation in which this variable is a left-hand variable.

- The right-hand side of each equation is the sum of a number of terms equal to the number of one-way arrows pointing to that variable and each term is the product of the coefficient associated with the arrow and the variable from which the arrow is coming.

Following these rules, we can now write the equations for the path diagram in Figure 1.1. There are seven x-variables as indicators of three latent ξ-variables. Note that x_3 is a complex variable measuring both ξ_1 and ξ_2. There are two latent η-variables each with two y-indicators. The five latent variables are connected in a two-equation interdependent system. The model involves both errors in equations (the ζ's) and errors in variables (the ϵ's and δ's).

The structural equations are

$$\begin{aligned} \eta_1 &= \beta_{12}\eta_2 + \gamma_{11}\xi_1 + \gamma_{12}\xi_2 + \zeta_1 \\ \eta_2 &= \beta_{21}\eta_1 + \gamma_{21}\xi_1 + \gamma_{23}\xi_3 + \zeta_2 \end{aligned}$$

or in matrix form

$$\begin{pmatrix} \eta_1 \\ \eta_2 \end{pmatrix} = \begin{pmatrix} 0 & \beta_{12} \\ \beta_{21} & 0 \end{pmatrix} \begin{pmatrix} \eta_1 \\ \eta_2 \end{pmatrix} + \begin{pmatrix} \gamma_{11} & \gamma_{12} & 0 \\ \gamma_{21} & 0 & \gamma_{23} \end{pmatrix} \begin{pmatrix} \xi_1 \\ \xi_2 \\ \xi_3 \end{pmatrix} + \begin{pmatrix} \zeta_1 \\ \zeta_2 \end{pmatrix}$$

This corresponds to the structural equation model (1.1).

The measurement model equations for y-variables are

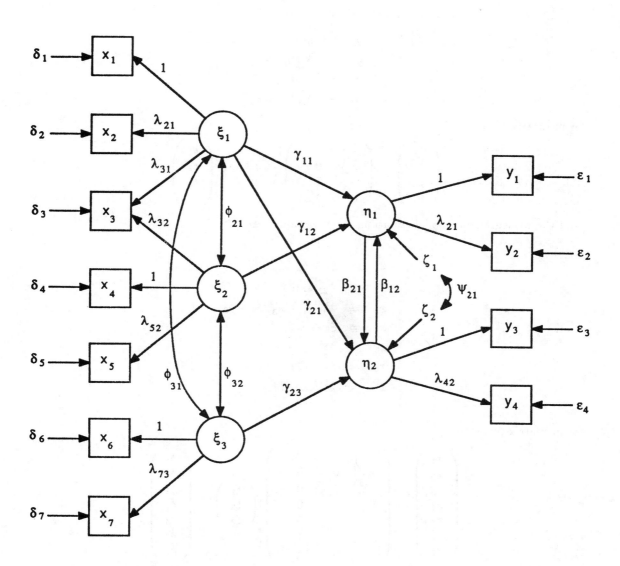

Figure 1.1: Path Diagram for Hypothetical Model

$$
\begin{aligned}
y_1 &= \eta_1 + \epsilon_1 \\
y_2 &= \lambda_{21}^{(y)}\eta_1 + \epsilon_2 \\
y_3 &= \eta_2 + \epsilon_3 \\
y_4 &= \lambda_{42}^{(y)}\eta_2 + \epsilon_4
\end{aligned}
$$

or in matrix form

$$
\begin{pmatrix} y_1 \\ y_2 \\ y_3 \\ y_4 \end{pmatrix} =
\begin{pmatrix} 1 & 0 \\ \lambda_{21}^{(y)} & 0 \\ 0 & 1 \\ 0 & \lambda_{42}^{(y)} \end{pmatrix}
\begin{pmatrix} \eta_1 \\ \eta_2 \end{pmatrix} +
\begin{pmatrix} \epsilon_1 \\ \epsilon_2 \\ \epsilon_3 \\ \epsilon_4 \end{pmatrix}
$$

and the measurement model equations for x-variables are

$$
\begin{aligned}
x_1 &= \xi_1 + \delta_1 \\
x_2 &= \lambda_{21}^{(x)}\xi_1 + \delta_2 \\
x_3 &= \lambda_{31}^{(x)}\xi_1 + \lambda_{32}^{(x)}\xi_2 + \delta_3 \\
x_4 &= \xi_2 + \delta_4 \\
x_5 &= \lambda_{52}^{(x)}\xi_2 + \delta_5 \\
x_6 &= \xi_3 + \delta_6 \\
x_7 &= \lambda_{73}^{(x)}\xi_3 + \delta_7
\end{aligned}
$$

or in matrix form

$$
\begin{pmatrix} x_1 \\ x_2 \\ x_3 \\ x_4 \\ x_5 \\ x_6 \\ x_7 \end{pmatrix} =
\begin{pmatrix}
1 & 0 & 0 \\
\lambda_{21}^{(x)} & 0 & 0 \\
\lambda_{31}^{(x)} & \lambda_{32}^{(x)} & 0 \\
0 & 1 & 0 \\
0 & \lambda_{52}^{(x)} & 0 \\
0 & 0 & 1 \\
0 & 0 & \lambda_{73}^{(x)}
\end{pmatrix}
\begin{pmatrix} \xi_1 \\ \xi_2 \\ \xi_3 \end{pmatrix} +
\begin{pmatrix} \delta_1 \\ \delta_2 \\ \delta_3 \\ \delta_4 \\ \delta_5 \\ \delta_6 \\ \delta_7 \end{pmatrix}
$$

These equations correspond to (1.2) and (1.3), respectively.

One λ in each column of Λ_y and Λ_x has been set equal to 1 to fix the scales of measurement in the latent variables.

In these equations, note that the second subscript on each coefficient is always equal to the subscript of the variable that follows the coefficient. This can serve as a check that everything is correct. Furthermore, in the matrices $\mathbf{B}$, $\boldsymbol{\Gamma}$, Λ_y, and Λ_x, subscripts on each coefficient, which were originally defined in the path diagram, now correspond to the row and column of the matrix in which they appear. Also note that arrows which are not included in the path diagram correspond to zeros in these matrices.

Each of the parameter matrices contain fixed elements (the zeros and ones) and free parameters (the coefficients with two subscripts).

The four remaining parameter matrices are the symmetric matrices

$$\Phi = \begin{pmatrix} \phi_{11} & & \\ \phi_{21} & \phi_{22} & \\ \phi_{31} & \phi_{32} & \phi_{33} \end{pmatrix},$$

the covariance matrix of ξ,

$$\Psi = \begin{pmatrix} \psi_{11} & \\ \psi_{21} & \psi_{22} \end{pmatrix},$$

the covariance matrix of ζ, and the diagonal matrices

$$\Theta_\epsilon = diag(\theta_{11}^{(\epsilon)}, \theta_{22}^{(\epsilon)}, \ldots, \theta_{44}^{(\epsilon)}),$$

the covariance matrix of ϵ and

$$\Theta_\delta = diag(\theta_{11}^{(\delta)}, \theta_{22}^{(\delta)}, \ldots, \theta_{77}^{(\delta)}),$$

the covariance matrix of δ.

1.4   Submodels

The general LISREL model involves four kinds of variables in addition to the error variables ζ, ϵ, and δ, namely y-variables, x-variables, η-variables and ξ-variables. The notation for the number of each of these is given in Table 1.1.

Table 1.1: Notation for Number of Variables

	Mathematical Notation	LISREL Notation
Number of y-variables	p	NY
Number of x-variables	q	NX
Number of η-variables	m	NE
Number of ξ-variables	n	NK

The general model subsumes many models as special cases. A submodel will be obtained when one or more of NY, NX, NE and NK are zero or are not specified, i.e., when one or more of these are default on the MO line (the MO line is explained in Chapter 2). This means that one or more of the four types of variables are not included in the model. Thus each submodel involves only some of the eight parameter matrices. The default values for NY, NX, NE, and NK have been chosen so as to be able to specify the most common submodels with a minimum of input. A user who is only interested in a particular submodel needs only be concerned with a subset of the eight parameter matrices and does not have to understand the full model.

A summary of the different submodels is given in Table 1.2.

Table 1.2: Submodels in LISREL

Type	Specified	Default	Model	Parameters
1	NX,NK	NY,NE	$\mathbf{x} = \mathbf{\Lambda}_x \mathbf{\xi} + \mathbf{\delta}$	$\mathbf{\Lambda}_x, \mathbf{\Phi}, \mathbf{\Theta}_\delta$
2	NY,NX	NE,NK	$\mathbf{y} = \mathbf{By} + \mathbf{\Gamma x} + \mathbf{\zeta}$	$\mathbf{B}, \mathbf{\Gamma}, \mathbf{\Psi}$
3A	NY,NE,NK	NX	$\mathbf{y} = \mathbf{\Lambda}_y(\mathbf{I} - \mathbf{B})^{-1}(\mathbf{\Gamma\xi} + \mathbf{\zeta}) + \mathbf{\epsilon}$	$\mathbf{\Lambda}_y, \mathbf{B}, \mathbf{\Gamma}, \mathbf{\Phi}, \mathbf{\Psi}, \mathbf{\Theta}_\epsilon$
3B	NY,NE	NX,NK	$\mathbf{y} = \mathbf{\Lambda}_y(\mathbf{I} - \mathbf{B})^{-1}\mathbf{\zeta} + \mathbf{\epsilon}$	$\mathbf{\Lambda}_y, \mathbf{B}, \mathbf{\Psi}, \mathbf{\Theta}_\epsilon$

The common types of submodels are as follows.

1.4.1 Submodel 1 or the LISREL model with only x- and ξ-variables

When only NX and NK are specified, the program assumes the model

$$\mathbf{x} = \mathbf{\Lambda}_x \mathbf{\xi} + \mathbf{\delta} \tag{1.5}$$

i.e., a measurement model or a factor analysis model for x-variables. In this case there is no structural equation model of the form (1.1) and there are no y-variables or η-variables and consequently no measurement model of the form (1.2). Only one of the three equations (1.1), (1.2) and (1.3), namely (1.3), is in operation. The only parameter matrices included in this submodel are $\mathbf{\Lambda}_x$, $\mathbf{\Phi}$, and $\mathbf{\Theta}_\delta$. Examples of this are given in Chapter 3.

1.4.2 Submodel 2 or the LISREL model with only y- and x-variables

When only NY and NX are specified, the program assumes the model

$$\mathbf{y} = \mathbf{By} + \mathbf{\Gamma x} + \mathbf{\zeta} \tag{1.6}$$

i.e., a structural equation model or a path analysis model for directly observed variables. If, in addition, $\mathbf{B}=0$, one can have multivariate or univariate regression models and other forms of the multivariate general linear model. Technically, when NE and NK are omitted on the MO line, the program sets NE = NY, NK = NX, $\mathbf{\Lambda}_y = \mathbf{I}$, $\mathbf{\Lambda}_x = \mathbf{I}$, $\mathbf{\Theta}_\epsilon = 0$, $\mathbf{\Theta}_\delta = 0$ and $\mathbf{\Phi} = \mathbf{S}_{xx}$. The only matrices involved in this submodel are $\mathbf{B}$, $\mathbf{\Gamma}$, and $\mathbf{\Psi}$. Examples of this kind of model are given in Chapter 4.

1.4.3 Submodel 3A or the LISREL model with only y-, η-, and ξ-variables

When only NY, NE, and NK are specified, the program assumes the model

$$\mathbf{\eta} = \mathbf{B\eta} + \mathbf{\Gamma\xi} + \mathbf{\zeta} \tag{1.7}$$

$$\mathbf{y} = \mathbf{\Lambda}_y \mathbf{\eta} + \mathbf{\epsilon} \tag{1.8}$$

or equivalently,

$$\mathbf{y} = \mathbf{\Lambda}_y(\mathbf{I} - \mathbf{B})^{-1}(\mathbf{\Gamma\xi} + \mathbf{\zeta}) + \mathbf{\epsilon} . \tag{1.9}$$

When $\mathbf{B} = 0$, this becomes

$$\mathbf{y} = \boldsymbol{\Lambda}_y(\boldsymbol{\Gamma}\boldsymbol{\xi} + \boldsymbol{\zeta}) + \boldsymbol{\epsilon}\,, \tag{1.10}$$

which is a second-order factor analysis model for y-variables with first-order factor loadings given by $\boldsymbol{\Lambda}_y$ and second-order factor loadings given by $\boldsymbol{\Gamma}$. Equation (1.10) is of the form of Jöreskog's (1969, 1970a, 1973b, 1974) ACOVS-model, so that such models can be handled by LISREL in this way. *Note that the model can have ξ-variables even though there are no x-variables.* This model involves the following parameter matrices: $\boldsymbol{\Lambda}_y$, $\boldsymbol{\Gamma}$, $\boldsymbol{\Phi}$, $\boldsymbol{\Psi}$, and $\boldsymbol{\Theta}_\epsilon$.

1.4.4   Submodel 3B or the LISREL model with only y- and η-variables

When only NY and NE are specified, the program assumes the model

$$\mathbf{y} = \boldsymbol{\Lambda}_y\boldsymbol{\eta} + \boldsymbol{\epsilon} \tag{1.11}$$

$$\boldsymbol{\eta} = \mathbf{B}\boldsymbol{\eta} + \boldsymbol{\zeta} \tag{1.12}$$

or equivalently

$$\mathbf{y} = \boldsymbol{\Lambda}_y(\mathbf{I} - \mathbf{B})^{-1}\boldsymbol{\zeta} + \boldsymbol{\epsilon}\,. \tag{1.13}$$

This is just a special case of submodel 3A above. In this case the parameter matrices are $\boldsymbol{\Lambda}_y$, $\mathbf{B}$, $\boldsymbol{\Psi}$, and $\boldsymbol{\Theta}_\epsilon$. When $\mathbf{B} = 0$, this model reduces to

$$\mathbf{y} = \boldsymbol{\Lambda}_y\boldsymbol{\zeta} + \boldsymbol{\epsilon} \tag{1.14}$$

with parameter matrices $\boldsymbol{\Lambda}_y$, $\boldsymbol{\Psi}$, and $\boldsymbol{\Theta}_\epsilon$. This, of course, is a factor analysis model for a set of y-variables, in which the matrix $\boldsymbol{\Psi}$ plays the role of a factor covariance or correlation matrix. To analyze a factor analysis model, one can use either model (1.5) or model (1.14) but, as we shall see, because of an option we have added for the matrix $\boldsymbol{\Phi}$ (see next section), it is slightly more convenient to use model (1.5). Examples of submodels 3A and 3B are given in Chapter 6.

1.5   Default Values for Parameter Matrices

There are eight parameter matrices in LISREL: $\boldsymbol{\Lambda}_y, \boldsymbol{\Lambda}_x, \mathbf{B}, \boldsymbol{\Gamma}, \boldsymbol{\Phi}, \boldsymbol{\Psi}, \boldsymbol{\Theta}_\epsilon$, and $\boldsymbol{\Theta}_\delta$. The LISREL names for these parameter matrices, their possible forms and default values are given in Table 1.3.

One can make any number of specifications of the form

MN = AA,BB

where MN is a matrix name (column 3), AA is a matrix form (column 5) and BB is FR (free) or FI (fixed) (column 7). Either AA or BB may be omitted in which case the defaults of Table 1.3 are used. The order of AA and BB is immaterial so that the above specification can also be written MN=BB,AA.

Table 1.3: Parameter Matrices in LISREL: Their Possible Forms and Default Values

Name	Math Symbol	LISREL Name	Order	Possible Forms	Default Form	Default Mode
LAMBDA-Y	Λ_y	LY	NY×NE	ID,IZ,ZI,DI,FU	FU	FI
LAMBDA-X	Λ_x	LX	NX×NK	ID,IZ,ZI,DI,FU	FU	FI
BETA	$\mathbf{B}$	BE	NE×NE	ZE,SD,FU	ZE	FI
GAMMA	Γ	GA	NE×NK	ID,IZ,ZI,DI,FU	FU	FR
PHI	Φ	PH	NK×NK	ID,DI,SY,ST	SY	FR
PSI	Ψ	PS	NE×NE	ZE,DI,SY	SY	FR
THETA-EPSILON	Θ_ϵ	TE	NY×NY	ZE,DI,SY	DI	FR
THETA-DELTA	Θ_δ	TD	NX×NX	ZE,DI,SY	DI	FR

The meaning of the possible form values are as follows:

- ZE = **0** (zero matrix)

- ID = **I** (identity matrix)

- IZ =(**I** **0**) or $\begin{pmatrix} \mathbf{I} \\ \mathbf{0} \end{pmatrix}$ (partitioned identity and zero)

- ZI = (**0** **I**) or $\begin{pmatrix} \mathbf{0} \\ \mathbf{I} \end{pmatrix}$ (partitioned zero and identity)

- DI = a diagonal matrix

- SD = a full square matrix with fixed zeros in and above the diagonal and all elements under the diagonal free (refers to **B** only)

- SY = a symmetric matrix which is not diagonal

- ST = a symmetric matrix with fixed ones in the diagonal (a correlation matrix)

- FU = a rectangular or square non-symmetric matrix.

The eight parameter matrices are stored in the order Λ_y, Λ_x, $\mathbf{B}$, Γ, Φ, Ψ, Θ_ϵ, Θ_δ, and within each matrix, elements are ordered row-wise. Only the lower triangular parts of the symmetric matrices Φ, Ψ, Θ_ϵ, and Θ_δ are stored in memory and if a matrix is specified to be diagonal, only the diagonal elements are stored. Matrices which are specified to be **I** (ID) or **0** (ZE) are not stored in memory.

1.6   Specification of Fixed and Free Elements

Sections 1.6 - 1.8 give a brief account of how parameters can be specified. The purpose of these sections is only to give the reader the basic idea of how things can be done. More specific details about how it is actually done in the input file are given in Chapter 2.

For each and every element in each of the eight parameter matrices Λ_y, Λ_x, $\mathbf{B}$, Γ, Φ, Ψ, Θ_ϵ, and Θ_δ, one must specify whether it is a fixed, free or constrained parameter. Any element in these matrices can be referred to by its matrix name and row and column index: MN(i,j). For example, γ_{34} is written in LISREL as GA(3,4). One can also use a linear index. If Γ has five columns, say, γ_{34} is the 14-th element in Γ and can therefore be referred to as GA(14).

Section 1.4 described how one can specify an entire matrix to be fixed or free. One can also specify individual elements to be free or fixed.

For example, if Λ_y has been specified as fixed and Λ_y should be

$$\Lambda_y = \begin{pmatrix} x & 0 & 0 \\ x & 0 & 0 \\ x & x & 0 \\ 0 & x & 0 \\ 0 & x & 0 \\ 0 & 0 & x \\ 0 & 0 & x \end{pmatrix}$$

where 0 stands for a fixed element and x for a free element, then one can specify the free elements by the line

FREE LY(1,1) LY(2,1) LY(3,1) LY(3,2) LY(4,2) LY(5,2) LY(6,3) LY(7,3)

Blanks can be used instead of parentheses and commas, so that LY(4,2) can also be written LY 4 2 and the entire line can be written

FREE LY 1 1 LY 2 1 LY 3 1 ...

Using linear indices instead, LY(4,2) can be written LY(11) or LY 11 since it is the eleventh element in Λ_y and the line above can be written

FREE LY 1 LY 4 LY 7 LY 8 LY 11 LY 14 LY 18 LY 21

Another way in which the pattern of fixed and free elements of a matrix may be specified is by reading in an integer matrix with 1's for free and 0's for fixed elements (see Section 2.8). As a second example, consider

$$\mathbf{B} = \begin{pmatrix} 0 & x & x & x & x \\ x & 0 & 0 & 0 & 0 \\ x & 0 & 0 & 0 & 0 \\ 0 & 0 & 0 & 0 & 0 \\ 0 & 0 & 0 & 0 & 0 \end{pmatrix},$$

where the x's represent free parameters. We show three different ways of specifying the pattern by coordinates:

- Since the first five free elements are in consecutive order they can be referred to collectively as BE(1,2)-BE(2,1) (or BE(2)-BE(6)). Thus, all free elements can be defined by

  FREE BE(1,2)-BE(2,1) BE(3,1).

- In the second alternative, the first statement frees β_{12} through β_{31}. The second statement fixes β_{22} through β_{25} thereby overriding the first specification.

  FREE BE(1,2)-BE(3,1)

FIX BE(2,2)-BE(2,5)

- In the third alternative, the first statement frees all elements except β_{11}. The second statement fixes β_{22} through β_{55}. The last statement frees β_{31}. Note that every statement overrides the previous one.

FREE BE(1,2)-BE(5,5)

FIX BE(2,2)-BE(5,5)

FREE BE(3,1)

If a matrix has been specified as diagonal, only the diagonal elements are counted. For example, if $\mathbf{\Psi}$ has been specified as fixed and diagonal and $\mathbf{\Psi}$ is supposed to be

$\mathbf{\Psi}=$ diag (1, x, x, 0, x, x, x)

then one can specify this as

FREE PS(2) PS(3) PS(5)-PS(7)

or alternatively

FREE PS(2)-PS(7)

FIX PS(4)

Here ψ_{ii} can be referred to as either PS(i,i) or PS(i).

When fixing or freeing matrix elements, note particularly the following:

1. *If a matrix has been specified as* **0** *(ZE) or* **I** *(ID), one cannot refer to any element of this matrix as it is not stored in the computer memory.*

2. *Also, if a matrix has been specified as diagonal (DI) one cannot refer to off-diagonal elements of this matrix as only diagonal elements are stored in the computer memory.*

3. *The specification* PH=ST *has a very special meaning. It means precisely that the diagonal elements of* $\mathbf{\Phi}$ *are fixed at one and the off-diagonal elements are free. This specification cannot be overridden by fixing and/or freeing elements of* $\mathbf{\Phi}$. *The specifications* PH=ST,FI *and* PH=ST,FR *are not permitted and are considered contradictory.*

    If one wants something different from PH=ST, one can get this by specifying PH=FI or PH=FR and then freeing and/or fixing elements of $\mathbf{\Phi}$.

4. Special explanation is needed for the specification of Θ_ϵ and Θ_δ. The default for these is that they are diagonal with free diagonal elements. This is the most common specification. However, if one specifies TE = SY, this is taken to mean that Θ_ϵ is symmetric with free diagonal elements and *fixed off-diagonal* elements, and similarly for Θ_δ. We have done it in this way, because when Θ_ϵ, say, is not diagonal, usually only a few of the off-diagonal elements are free and these can be declared free by a FR line. Very rarely is one interested in a model where a majority of the elements of Θ_ϵ, say, are to be free. However, if this is the case, one can specify this most easily by writing TE = SY, FR on the MO line and then specify the fixed elements on a FI line. See Chapter 2.

Summing up the specifications for TE and TD:

- Default means diagonal and free. Off-diagonal elements cannot be relaxed.
- TE = SY or TD = SY means symmetric with free diagonal and fixed off-diagonal elements. Off-diagonal elements can be relaxed.
- TE = SY,FR or TD = SY,FR means that the whole matrix is free.

1.7 Specification of Equality Constraints

To define equality constraints in the model, one specifies a set of equalities, one for each group of parameters which are constrained to be equal. In each set of equalities, one first defines one element which has been defined to be a free parameter, then one defines all other elements in the group.

Suppose in the first example in 1.6, we would like to impose the constraints that

$$\lambda_{21}^{(y)} = \lambda_{31}^{(y)}, \lambda_{42}^{(y)} = \lambda_{52}^{(y)}, \lambda_{63}^{(y)} = \lambda_{73}^{(y)} \ .$$

These constraints are specified as

EQUAL LY(2,1) LY(3,1)

EQUAL LY(4,2) LY(5,2)

EQUAL LY(6,3) LY(7,3)

The constrained elements within a group may be elements of any parameter matrix. For example, $\beta_{35} = \gamma_{41} = \phi_{21}$ is specified as, assuming γ_{41} has been defined as a free element previously,

EQUAL GA(4,1) BE(3,5) PH(2,1)

If a matrix is specified to be symmetric, only elements below and in the diagonal are counted. As far as the program is concerned, the elements in the upper half of the matrix do not exist. Thus, there is no need to treat these elements as constrained parameters. However, if one refers to such an element, it is automatically taken to mean the corresponding element in the lower half. Note also, that if one refers to an element in a symmetric matrix by its linear index, again only the lower half including the diagonal is counted. For example, if Φ is symmetric, PH(5) always refers to the element ϕ_{32} in the third row and second column of Φ.

1.8 Specification of Non-Zero Fixed Parameters

It should be noted that the specification described in Sections 1.6 and 1.7 only concerns whether certain parameters are to be fixed or free and does not specify their actual values. The value of each parameter, whether free or fixed, is zero by default. All *non-zero fixed* parameters must be specified by the user. This will be explained in this section.

The values of non-zero fixed parameters are defined either by reading a matrix of real numbers (see Section 2.10) or by specifying the fixed value and the matrix elements where this value is to be set.

For example, if one wants to specify that $\lambda_{11}^{(y)} = \lambda_{21}^{(y)} = \lambda_{64}^{(y)} = 0.5$, one can write

VALUE 0.5 LY(1,1) LY(2,1) LY(6,4)

Any real number in any format can be used and this number can be set in any position in any matrix. For example, one can write

VALUE 1.47E-6 LY(4,2) BE(6,1) PS(5,4) TE(7,3)

Also, as before, every statement of this type overrides the previous one. Thus, one can first set a group of elements equal to 1 and then set some of these equal to 0.5.

1.9 Identification of Models and Parameters

When the model involves latent variables, there are usually more unobserved variables than observed variables in the model. For example, the model (1.5) involves $n + q$ unobserved variables in ξ and δ but only q observed variables in $\mathbf{x}$. Therefore, the model is not testable or estimable at the level of the variables. However, the model implies that a certain covariance structure, in general given by (1.4), must hold, and this may be testable. By fitting the implied covariance structure to the observed covariance matrix, one can also estimate the parameters of the model. However, before an attempt is made to estimate a model, *the identification problem* must be resolved. A rigorous definition of the identification problem will be given in Volume II. Here we present it in a way which hopefully can be understood by most users of LISREL.

It is assumed that the distribution of the observed variables is sufficiently well described by the moments of first and second order, so that information contained in moments of higher order may be ignored. In particular, this will hold if the distribution is multivariate normal. If the mean vector is unconstrained, the distribution of $\mathbf{z} = (\mathbf{y}',\mathbf{x}')'$ is described by the independent parameters in Λ_y, Λ_x, $\mathbf{B}$, Γ, Φ, Ψ, Θ_δ, Θ_ϵ, generating Σ in (1.4). Chapter 10 generalizes this to general moment structures where the mean vector of $\mathbf{z}$ may also be constrained. Under non-normality of $\mathbf{z}$ or when some or all variables in $\mathbf{z}$ are ordinal, one can use fourth-order moments and other information to form a weight matrix for weighted least squares (WLS) yielding asymptotically efficient estimates (see Section 1.11 and Chapter 7).

Identifiability depends on the choice of model and on the specification of fixed, constrained, and free parameters. Under a given model specification, a given set of values of the independent parameters in Λ_y, Λ_x, $\mathbf{B}$, Γ, Φ, Ψ, Θ_ϵ, Θ_δ, generates one and only one Σ, but there may be several sets of parameter values generating the same Σ. If two or more sets of parameter values generate the same Σ, they are said to be *equivalent*. If a parameter has the same value in all equivalent sets, the parameter is said to be *identified*. If all parameters of the model are identified, *the whole model is said to be identified*.

Let θ be a vector of all the independent parameters, i.e., counting all free parameters and each distinct constrained parameter only once. The identification problem is the problem of whether or not θ is uniquely determined by Σ.

If a parameter is identified, LISREL can determine several consistent estimators of it (see Section 1.10). However, if a parameter is not identified it does not make sense to talk about an estimator of it.

One way to phrase the identification problem is as follows. Suppose the model is correct but we do not know the values of the parameters of the model. Suppose we have data on all individuals in the entire population. The identification problem is concerned with the question: Is there a unique set of parameter values consistent with this data? Some parameters may be *identified*, i.e., uniquely defined in this sense; others may not be so. If all the parameters of the model are identified the whole model is identified. Otherwise, the model is *non-identified*. If the model is non-identified it does not mean that everything is hopeless. In many cases, the parameters which are identified can still be estimated consistently by the program. And for parameters which are not identified, it may be, for example, that the sum or the product of two parameters is identified although each parameter is not separately identified. Although the computer program sometimes can estimate models which are non-identified, it is recommended to deal with such models by adding appropriate conditions so as to make all the parameters identified. For example, if only the sum of two parameters is identified we may fix one and estimate the other or we may assume that the two parameters are equal and estimate the common value. When making arbitrary assumptions of this sort, one must remember, however, that other parameters may be affected and that parameter estimates will be arbitrary to some extent. In interpreting the results of an analysis, it is necessary to have a complete understanding of the identification status of each parameter of the model.

Non-identification is the same thing as insufficient information, not in the sense that the sample size is too small, but in the sense that the model must be more tightly specified or more variables must be added in the model to make the parameters uniquely defined. The additional information needed must come from substantive theory or hypotheses.

Since necessary and sufficient conditions for identification in the full LISREL model are generally not available or not practically useful, it is suggested that the identification problem be studied on a case-by-case basis. Chapters 3-6 give several examples of how the identification problem may be resolved.

In principle, one could resolve the identification problem by examining the equations

$$\sigma_{ij} = f_{ij}(\boldsymbol{\theta}), i \leq j \tag{1.15}$$

defining the σ's as functions of $\boldsymbol{\theta}$.

There are $\frac{1}{2}(p+q)(p+q+1)$ equations in t unknown parameters θ_1, θ_2,..., θ_t, t being the total number of free parameters in the model. Hence, a necessary condition for identification of all parameters is that

$$t \leq \frac{1}{2}(p+q)(p+q+1) \tag{1.16}$$

If a parameter θ can be determined from these equations, this parameter is identified, otherwise it is not. Often some parameters can be determined in different ways. This gives rise to overidentifying conditions on $\boldsymbol{\Sigma}$ which must hold if the model is true. The equations (1.15) are usually non-linear, the solution is often complicated, and explicit solutions for all θ's seldom exist. However, it is not necessary to actually solve the equations, only to determine which of the parameters can be solved and which cannot. Even this is often very difficult to do in practice.

Several necessary and sufficient conditions for identification have been given for some special classes of LISREL models; see Sections 3.1 and 4.1. Unfortunately, however, the sufficient conditions that have been proposed are almost impossible to verify in practice. The practical value of these conditions is very limited.

The LISREL program checks the identification of the model in the following way. The program checks the *positive definiteness* of *the information matrix*. (The information matrix is the probability limit of the matrix of second order derivatives of the fit function used to estimate the model, see Section 1.11.) If the model is identified, the information matrix is almost certainly positive definite. If the information matrix is singular, the model is not identified and *the rank of the information matrix* indicates how many parameters are identified. For an example of how this works, see Section 6.2. One should be aware, however, that this check is not one hundred percent reliable although experience indicates that it is nearly so. The check depends on the data, the estimated point in the parameter space at which the information matrix is evaluated, and on the numerical accuracy by which the information matrix is inverted. The program applies this check of identification after the model has been fitted.

Modification indices can be used to determine whether a parameter, which is held fixed in a model, will be identified if it is set free (see Section 1.19). If a modification index is positive for a fixed parameter, this indicates that this parameter will be identified if it is set free. On the other hand, if the modification index is zero for a fixed parameter, this indicates that the parameter will not be identified if it is set free. For an example of this use of modification indices, see Section 5.3.

Another way to use the program to check the identification status of the model is the following. Choose a set of reasonable values for the parameters and compute Σ. (See Chapter 8 for how the program can do this.) Then run the program with this Σ as data matrix and estimate θ. If this results in the same estimated values as those used to generate Σ, then it is most likely that the model is identified. Otherwise, those parameters which gave a different value are probably not identified.

1.10   Kinds of Input Data and Moment Matrices to be Analyzed

Equations (1.1)-(1.3) represent a model for a population of individuals (observational units). This population is characterized by the mean vector μ and the parameters θ generating the covariance matrix Σ in (1.4). In practice, μ and θ are unknown and must be estimated from data. It is assumed that the data are a random sample of independent cases from the population.

Any number, k, of input variables may be read by the program. From these input variables, the p y-variables and q x-variables to be included in the model are selected and ordered.

Let $\mathbf{Z}$ be a matrix of raw data of order $N \times k$, with N independent cases on k input variables. The program can read the following types of input data:

A The raw data matrix $\mathbf{Z}$ itself.

B The moment matrix $\mathbf{M} = (1/N)\mathbf{Z'Z}$, i.e., the matrix of moments about zero.

C The covariance matrix $\mathbf{S} = [1/(N-1)] \, (\mathbf{Z'Z} - N\bar{z}\,\bar{z}')$, where $\bar{z}$ is the mean vector $(1/N)\mathbf{Z'1}$.

D The correlation matrix $\mathbf{R} = \mathbf{D}^{-1}\mathbf{S}\mathbf{D}^{-1}$, where $\mathbf{D} = (\text{diag } \mathbf{S})^{\frac{1}{2}}$ is a diagonal matrix of standard deviations.

E A correlation matrix consisting of any type of correlations such as tetrachoric, polychoric, biserial, polyserial, canonical or product moment correlations based on raw scores, normal scores or optimal scores. Such correlation matrices may be produced by PRELIS: see below.

One can also read in a vector of means $\bar{z} = (1/N)\mathbf{Z'1}$ and/or a vector of standard deviations $(s_1, s_2,..., s_k)$, where $s_i = \sqrt{s_{ii}}$.

Independently of the kind of data provided, one may choose to analyze

a A moment matrix $\mathbf{M}$.

b An augmented moment matrix.

$$\mathbf{M}_A = \begin{pmatrix} \mathbf{M} & \bar{\mathbf{z}} \\ \bar{\mathbf{z}}' & 1 \end{pmatrix}$$

This can be used if the model includes intercept terms in the equations and/or mean values of latent variables; see Section 2.4.3 and Chapter 10.

c A covariance matrix **S**. This should be used in general.

d A correlation matrix **R**. This could be used if the units of measurements in the observed variables are arbitrary and irrelevant and the model is scale invariant; see Section 1.20.

The program will compute **M** from **S** and $\bar{\mathbf{z}}$ and compute **S** from **M** and $\bar{\mathbf{z}}$ using the formulas

$$\mathbf{M} = [(N-1)/N]\mathbf{S} + \bar{\mathbf{z}}\bar{\mathbf{z}}' \quad \mathbf{S} = [N/(N-1)](\mathbf{M} - \bar{\mathbf{z}}\bar{\mathbf{z}}')$$

Similarly, the program will compute **S** from **R** and **D** and compute **R** from **S** and **D** using the formulas

$$\mathbf{S} = \mathbf{DRD} \quad \mathbf{R} = \mathbf{D}^{-1}\mathbf{SD}^{-1} \ .$$

Default values are zero for means and one for standard deviations. As a consequence, the program can always compute the matrix to be analyzed (**M**, **M**$_A$, **S**, or **R**) regardless of what has been read (**Z**, **M**, **S**, or **R**): i.e., any input A, B, C, or D may be combined with any matrix a, b, c, or d to be analyzed.

From the matrix computed (**M**, **M**$_A$, **S** or **R**), the variables to be included in the analysis are selected and possibly reordered. The p y-variables are selected first and the q x-variables second. After selection and reordering, the resulting matrix is partitioned as

$$\mathbf{S}[(p+q) \times (p+q)] = \begin{pmatrix} \mathbf{S}_{yy}(p \times p) & \mathbf{S}_{yx}(p \times q) \\ \mathbf{S}_{xy}(q \times p) & \mathbf{S}_{xx}(q \times q) \end{pmatrix}$$

This matrix is referred to as the *matrix analyzed* (MA) and is printed in the output file. It may also be saved in a file for further use (see Section 2.15).

When raw data are read, LISREL 7 handles missing observations only by listwise deletion, assuming there is a global missing value code for all variables. The companion program PRELIS (Jöreskog and Sörbom, 1986) handles many other sorts of problems with raw data and computes an appropriate moment matrix to use in LISREL.

PRELIS has the following features:

- PRELIS reads raw data of any numeric form, case after case. As the data are not stored in memory, the number of cases (the sample size) is unlimited. PRELIS can also read grouped data and weighted data where each case carries a weight.

- The scale type of each variable may be declared as ordinal, censored, or continuous. Groups of variables (including all variables) of the same scale type may be declared collectively. Ordinal variables may have up to 15 categories.

- A numeric value may be defined for each variable to represent a missing value. Such a numeric value can also be defined collectively for a group of variables or globally for all variables. Moment matrices may be computed either under listwise deletion or pairwise deletion.

- Continuous variables may be transformed using any one of a large family of transformations. Ordinal variables may be recoded or transformed to normal scores, or they may first be recoded and then transformed to normal scores. Maximum and/or minimum values of censored variables may also be transformed to normal scores.

- In addition to moment and covariance matrices based on raw scores or normal scores, the program can compute a number of different types of correlation coefficients: product moment (Pearson), canonical, polychoric (including tetrachoric), polyserial (including biserial), and product moment correlations based on normal or optimal scores. The program can also estimate correlations between censored variables and ordinal or continuous variables.

- The program saves the computed moment matrix in a file which can be read directly by LISREL.

- PRELIS can produce an estimate of the *asymptotic* (large sample) *covariance matrix* of the estimated sample variances and covariances under arbitrary non-normal distributions (see Browne, 1982, 1984). This can be used to compute a weight matrix for WLS (Weighted Least Squares, equivalent to Browne's ADF) in LISREL 7 (see Chapter 7). PRELIS can also compute estimates of the asymptotic variances and covariances of estimated product moment correlations, polychoric correlations, and polyserial correlations; these can also be used with WLS in LISREL 7. Optionally, PRELIS may be used to compute a diagonal matrix consisting of estimates of the *asymptotic variances* of estimated variances, covariances, or correlations. These diagonal matrices can be used with DWLS (Diagonally Weighted Least Squares) in LISREL 7 (see Chapter 7).

1.11   Estimation of the Model

The term covariance matrix is used here in the general sense of a moment matrix, which may be a matrix of moments about zero, a matrix of variances and covariances, or a matrix of correlations. In the following, the matrix to be analyzed after selection of variables is denoted S regardless of whether it is an M, M_A, S, or R. Here we assume that the mean vector is unconstrained, so the estimation is essentially that of fitting the covariance matrix Σ in (1.4) implied by the model to the sample covariance matrix S. The case of mean structures is considered in Chapter 10.

LISREL can obtain seven kinds of estimates of parameters:

- Instrumental Variables (IV)

- Two-Stage Least Squares (TSLS)

- Unweighted Least Squares (ULS)

- Generalized Least Squares (GLS)

- Maximum Likelihood (ML)

- Generally Weighted Least Squares (WLS)

- Diagonally Weighted Least Squares (DWLS)

Under general assumptions, all seven methods give consistent estimates of parameters. This means that they will be close to the true parameter values in large samples (assuming, of course, that the model is correct). The seven types of estimates differ in several respects. The TSLS and IV methods are procedures which are non-iterative and very fast. They are described in the next section. The ULS, GLS, ML, WLS, and DWLS estimates are obtained by means of an iterative procedure which minimizes a particular fit function by successively improving the parameter estimates. Initial values for the iterative procedures are provided by IV or TSLS.

1.11.1 Specific Fit Functions

The "classical" methods are ULS, GLS and ML. The fit function for ULS is

$$F = \frac{1}{2} tr[(\mathbf{S} - \mathbf{\Sigma})^2] , \qquad (1.17)$$

i.e., half the sum of squares of all the elements of the matrix $\mathbf{S}$ - $\mathbf{\Sigma}$.

The fit function for GLS,

$$F = \frac{1}{2} tr[(\mathbf{I} - \mathbf{S}^{-1}\mathbf{\Sigma})^2] , \qquad (1.18)$$

uses sums of squares weighted by the inverse of the sample covariance matrix $\mathbf{S}$.

Finally, ML minimizes the function

$$F = \log \|\mathbf{\Sigma}\| + tr(\mathbf{S}\mathbf{\Sigma}^{-1}) - \log \|\mathbf{S}\| - (p+q) , \qquad (1.19)$$

where, for a square matrix $\mathbf{A}$, $\|\mathbf{A}\|$ denotes the determinant of $\mathbf{A}$ and $tr(\mathbf{A})$ denotes the sum of the diagonal elements of $\mathbf{A}$. Each of the three equations represents a function of the independent parameters θ, i.e., the free and constrained elements in $\mathbf{\Lambda}_y$, $\mathbf{\Lambda}_x$, $\mathbf{B}$, $\mathbf{\Gamma}$, $\mathbf{\Phi}$, $\mathbf{\Psi}$, $\mathbf{\Theta}_\epsilon$, and $\mathbf{\Theta}_\delta$, and is minimized with respect to these. The fit functions are always non-negative; they are equal to zero only when there is a perfect fit in which case the fitted $\mathbf{\Sigma}$ equals $\mathbf{S}$.

The fit function for ULS is justified when all variables are measured in the same units. The fit function for ML is derived from the maximum likelihood principle based on the assumption that the observed variables have a multinormal distribution (see, e.g., Jöreskog, 1967). The GLS estimator is a straightforward application of Aitken's (1934-35) generalized least-squares principle (cf. Jöreskog and Goldberger, 1972, and Browne, 1974). GLS and ML estimates have similar asymptotic properties. Under the assumption of multivariate normality, both estimators are optimal in the sense of being most precise in large samples. LISREL provides large sample standard errors for ULS, GLS, and ML parameter estimates under normal theory. A standard error is a measure of the precision of each parameter estimate. LISREL does not provide standard errors for IV and TSLS estimates.

The fit function for ML or GLS may also be used to compute parameter estimates even if the distribution of the observed variables deviates from normality. Even standard errors and chi-square goodness-of-fit measures may be used if interpreted with caution. ML and GLS estimates have been found to be robust against non-normality, see e.g. Monte Carlo studies by Boomsma (1983) and Harlow (1985) and theoretical studies by Browne (1987) and Anderson and Amemiya (1985, 1986). However, if the distributions deviate *very* far from normality it *may* be best to use the general WLS method with an asymptotic covariance matrix $\mathbf{W}$ produced by PRELIS. This is particularly important if one wants asymptotically correct standard errors of parameter estimates and chi-square goodness-of-fit measures. The WLS method should also be used when polychoric (tetrachoric) and polyserial correlations are analyzed and when product moment correlations based on normal scores are analyzed. The WLS and DWLS methods will now be explained. These methods will be discussed further in Chapter 7. See also Section 1.21 on special problems associated with analysis of correlation matrices. A complete account of all results on estimation and fit functions will be given in Volume II.

1.11.2   General Fit Function

All fit functions are special cases of a general family of fit functions for analysis of covariance structures which may be written (see, e.g., Browne, 1984)

$$
\begin{aligned}
F(\theta) &= (\mathbf{s} - \boldsymbol{\sigma})' \mathbf{W}^{-1} (\mathbf{s} - \boldsymbol{\sigma}) & (1.20) \\
&= \sum_{g=1}^{k} \sum_{h=1}^{g} \sum_{i=1}^{k} \sum_{j=1}^{i} w^{gh,ij} (s_{gh} - \sigma_{gh})(s_{ij} - \sigma_{ij}) \,,
\end{aligned}
$$

where

$$
\mathbf{s}' = (s_{11}, s_{21}, s_{22}, s_{31}, ..., s_{kk}) \,,
$$

is a vector of the elements in the lower half, including the diagonal, of the covariance matrix $\mathbf{S}$ of order $k \times k$ used to fit the model to the data,

$$
\boldsymbol{\sigma}' = (\sigma_{11}, \sigma_{21}, \sigma_{22}, \sigma_{31}, ..., \sigma_{kk}) \,,
$$

is the vector of corresponding elements of $\boldsymbol{\Sigma}(\theta)$ reproduced from the model parameters θ, and $w^{gh,ij}$ is a typical element of a positive definite matrix $\mathbf{W}^{-1}$ of order $u \times u$, where $u = \frac{1}{2}k(k+1)$. In most cases, the elements of $\mathbf{W}^{-1}$ are obtained by inverting a matrix $\mathbf{W}$ whose typical element is denoted $w_{gh,ij}$. The usual way of choosing $\mathbf{W}$ in weighted least squares is to let $w_{gh,ij}$ be a consistent estimate of the asymptotic covariance between s_{gh} and s_{ij}. If this is the case, we say that $\mathbf{W}^{-1}$ is a *correct weight matrix*. To estimate the model parameters θ, the fit function is minimized with respect to θ.

To obtain consistent estimates, any positive definite matrix $\mathbf{W}$ may be used. Under very general assumptions, if the model holds in the population and if the sample variances and covariances in $\mathbf{S}$ converge in probability to the corresponding elements in the population covariance matrix $\boldsymbol{\Sigma}$ as the sample size increases, any fit function with a positive definite $\mathbf{W}$ will give a consistent estimator of θ. In practice, numerical results obtained by one fit function are often close enough to the results that would be obtained by another fit function to give the same substantive interpretations of the results.

Further assumptions must be made, however, if one needs an asymptotically correct chi-square measure of goodness-of-fit and asymptotically correct standard errors of parameter estimates.

"Classical" theory for covariance structures (see e.g., Browne, 1974, or Jöreskog, 1981), assumes that the asymptotic variances and covariances of the elements of $\mathbf{S}$ are of the form

$$
ACov(s_{gh}, s_{ij}) = (1/N)(\sigma_{gi}\sigma_{hj} + \sigma_{gj}\sigma_{hi}) \,, \tag{1.21}
$$

where N is the total sample size. This holds, in particular, if the observed variables have a multivariate normal distribution, or if $\mathbf{S}$ has a Wishart distribution. The GLS and ML methods and their chi-square values and standard errors are based on (1.21). The GLS method corresponds to using a matrix $\mathbf{W}^{-1}$ in (1.20) whose general element is

$$
w^{gh,ij} = N(2 - \delta_{gh})(2 - \delta_{ij})(s^{gi}s^{hj} + s^{gj}s^{hi}) \,, \tag{1.22}
$$

where δ_{gh} and δ_{ij} are Kronecker deltas. The fit function (1.19) for ML is not of the form (1.20) but may be shown to be equivalent to using a $\mathbf{W}^{-1}$ of the form (1.22), with s replaced by an estimate of σ which is updated in each iteration.

In recent fundamental work by Browne (1982, 1984), this classical theory for covariance structures has been generalized to any multivariate distribution for continuous variables satisfying very mild assumptions. This approach uses a $\mathbf{W}$ matrix with typical element

$$w_{gh,ij} = m_{ghij} - s_{gh}s_{ij} , \tag{1.23}$$

where

$$m_{ghij} = (1/N) \sum_{a=1}^{N} (z_{ag} - \bar{z}_g)(z_{ah} - \bar{z}_h)(z_{ai} - \bar{z}_i)(z_{aj} - \bar{z}_j) \tag{1.24}$$

are the fourth-order central moments. Using such a $\mathbf{W}$ in (1.20) gives what Browne calls "asymptotically distribution free best GLS estimators" for which correct asymptotic chi-squares and standard errors may be obtained. As shown by Browne, this $\mathbf{W}$ matrix may also be used to compute correct asymptotic chi-squares and standard errors for estimates which have been obtained by the classical ML and GLS methods. When $\mathbf{W}$ is defined by (1.23), we call the fit function WLS (Weighted Least Squares), to distinguish it from GLS where $\mathbf{W}$ is defined by (1.22). WLS and GLS are different forms of weighted least squares: WLS is asymptotically distribution free, while GLS is based on normal theory.

While WLS is attractive in theory it presents several difficulties in practical applications. First, the matrix $\mathbf{W}$ is of order $u \times u$ and has $\frac{1}{2}u(u+1)$ distinct elements. This increases rapidly with k, demanding large amounts of computer memory when k is at all large. For example, when $k = 20$, $\mathbf{W}$ has 22,155 distinct elements. Second, to estimate moments of fourth order with reasonable precision requires very large samples. Third, when there are missing observations in the data, different moments involved in (1.23) may be based on different numbers of cases unless listwise deletion is used. When pairwise deletion is used, it is not clear how to deal with this problem.

Browne's (1984) development is a theory for sample covariance matrices for continuous variables. In practice, correlation matrices are often analyzed; i.e., covariance matrices scaled by stochastic standard deviations. The elements of such a correlation matrix do not have asymptotic variances and covariances of the form (1.21), even if $\mathbf{S}$ has a Wishart distribution. In PRELIS, we have extended Browne's (1984) work so that an estimate of the asymptotic covariance matrix of estimated correlations can also be obtained under the same general assumptions of non-normality. This approach can also be used when some or all of the variables are ordinal or censored, if the raw scores are replaced by normal scores. PRELIS can also compute estimates of the asymptotic variances and covariances of estimated polychoric and polyserial correlations. See Section 1.20 and Chapter 7.

Computation of asymptotic covariance matrices of estimated coefficients is very time consuming and demands large amounts of memory when the number of variables is large. An alternative approach, which may be used even when the number of variables is large, is to compute only the asymptotic variances of the estimated coefficients.

Let w_{gh} be an estimate of the asymptotic variance of s_{gh}. These estimates may be used with a fit function of the form

$$F(\theta) = \sum_{g=1}^{k} \sum_{h=1}^{k} (1/w_{gh})(s_{gh} - \sigma_{gh})^2 \tag{1.25}$$

This corresponds to using a diagonal weight matrix $\mathbf{W}^{-1}$ in (1.20). In LISREL 7 we call this DWLS (Diagonally Weighted Least Squares). This does not lead to asymptotically efficient estimates of model parameters but is offered as a compromise between unweighted least squares (ULS) and fully weighted least squares (WLS). DWLS can be used also when correlation matrices are analyzed.

1.11.3   Minimization and the Information Matrix

The fit function $\mathrm{F}(\boldsymbol{\theta})$ is minimized by an iterative procedure which, starting at the initial estimates $\boldsymbol{\theta}^{(1)}$, generates successively new points $\boldsymbol{\theta}^{(2)}$, $\boldsymbol{\theta}^{(3)}$... in the parameter space such that $\mathrm{F}(\boldsymbol{\theta}^{(s+1)}) < \mathrm{F}(\boldsymbol{\theta}^{(s)})$, until convergence is obtained. Details of the iteration algorithm are given in Chapter 11. The minimization method makes use of the first-order derivatives and approximations (probability limits) to the second-order derivatives of F. For the ML and GLS methods, the approximation to the second-order derivatives is the information matrix which is nearly always positive definite if the model is identified. The information matrix is used to compute standard errors for all the parameters. The whole estimated covariance or correlation matrix of all the estimated parameters may also be obtained.

It can happen that there are several local minima of the fit function. The only way to avoid this is to have a model which is appropriate for the data and a large random sample. Experience indicates, however, that multiple solutions very seldom occur, and when they do, it is usually with solutions on the boundary of or outside the admissible parameter space.

1.11.4   Admissibility Test

The computer program does not in general constrain the solution to be admissible. In LISREL 7, however, there is a built-in admissibility check which will stop the iterations after a specified number of iterations (default = 10) if the solution becomes non-admissible. The *admissibility* check is that

  1. $\boldsymbol{\Lambda}_y$ and $\boldsymbol{\Lambda}_x$ have full column ranks and no rows of only zeros.
  2. $\boldsymbol{\Phi}$, $\boldsymbol{\Psi}$, $\boldsymbol{\Theta}_\epsilon$, and $\boldsymbol{\Theta}_\delta$ are positive definite.

There are situations where one wants to have a non-admissible solution intentionally, so there are provisions to set the admissibility check off.

It is often possible, though not always, to use various tricks to force the program to stay within the admissible parameter space. See Rindskopf (1983 a-b, 1984) or for an example, see Jöreskog (1981). See also Chapter 8.

1.11.5   The Fixed-x Case

A special class of LISREL models, not mentioned specifically before, is one in which $\boldsymbol{\xi} \equiv \mathbf{x}$ so that the x-variables themselves influence the η-variables directly. The x-variables are either random variables with an unconstrained covariance matrix or a set of fixed variables. For the estimation of such a model, it is sufficient to consider only the *conditional distribution* of $\mathbf{y}$ for given $\mathbf{x}$. Examples of such models are given in Chapters 4 and 5.

In this kind of a model we have $\boldsymbol{\Lambda}_x = \mathbf{I}$ and $\boldsymbol{\Theta}_\delta = 0$ and $\boldsymbol{\Phi}$ is the covariance matrix of $\mathbf{x}$ which is unconstrained. If $\mathbf{x}$ is random, it can be shown that the minimum of the fit function always occurs when $\boldsymbol{\Phi} = \mathbf{S}_{xx}$, the sample covariance matrix of $\mathbf{x}$. When $\mathbf{x}$ is fixed, of course, $\boldsymbol{\Phi}$ is automatically equal to $\mathbf{S}_{xx}$. Thus, regardless of whether $\mathbf{x}$ is considered fixed or random, we may take $\boldsymbol{\Phi} = \mathbf{S}_{xx}$ and hold $\boldsymbol{\Phi}$ fixed in the minimization.

This kind of model is so common that it is convenient to introduce a special keyword for it. This keyword FI, which stands for Fixed-x, may be given on the MO line; see Chapter 2. The keyword FI automatically implies all of the following

$$NK = NX, \; \mathbf{\Lambda}_x = \mathbf{I}, \Theta_\delta = \mathbf{0}, \mathbf{\Phi} = \mathbf{S}_{xx}(\text{fixed})$$

The program also adjusts the degrees of freedom in the model so that these will be correct regardless of whether **x** is fixed or random.

1.11.6 Ridge Option

The *Ridge Option* is a new feature in LISREL 7. This option handles covariance and correlation matrices which are not positive definite. If the covariance or correlation matrix to be analyzed is not positive definite, a constant times the diagonal is added to the diagonal before iterations begin.

This constant called the *Ridge Constant* is automatically determined by the program but may also be specified by the user (see Section 2.15).

The Ridge Option is particularly useful in econometric models containing identities and in regression models with high multicollinearity among the regressors (see Chapter 4).

The Ridge Option may also be chosen even if the covariance or correlation matrix to be analyzed is positive definite (see Section 2.15). This adds a whole new class of estimation methods. The Ridge Option may be used in combination with all the iterative methods ULS, GLS, ML, WLS, and DWLS. IV and TSLS are not affected by the Ridge Option.

1.12 IV and TSLS Estimates

The iterative methods ULS, GLS, ML, WLS, and DWLS described in the previous section require starting values for all free parameters of a model.

These starting values are obtained by computing *consistent estimates* of all the parameters of the model using *instrumental variables* methods and *two-stage least-squares* methods developed by Hägglund (1982) and Jöreskog (1983).

When the model fits the data well, the starting values produced by the program are often so close to the iterated solution that only a few iterations are necessary to compute these solutions. For some models the estimated starting values are identical to ML and other estimates. To emphasize the fact that the starting values are estimates in their own right we call them *initial estimates* instead of starting values. One can choose to obtain only these initial estimates and not compute ML or other estimates. In particular, this may be used with large models to save computer time especially when the model is only tentative. In such a situation the initial estimates themselves and/or other information in the output may suggest ways to improve the model.

In most cases, one need only specify the non-zero fixed values in each column of $\mathbf{\Lambda}_y$ and $\mathbf{\Lambda}_x$, necessary to fix the scales for η and ξ, and leave it to the program to compute estimates of all the free parameters. However, one *can* specify starting values for any number of free parameters. This is sometimes necessary in non-standard models to give the program some help to start the iterations off.

A key concept in the computation of initial estimates (IV and TSLS) is that of a *reference variable*. A reference variable for a latent variable is an observed variable which represents the latent variable in the sense of being a valid and reliable measure of it. There is one reference variable for each latent variable. The selection of reference variables is done automatically by the program. However, there is a connection between the selection of reference variables and the assignment of scales to the latent variables (see Section 1.2) in the following way. If one assigns scales to the latent variables by fixing a non-zero value in each column of Λ_y and Λ_x, then the variables for which these non-zero values have been fixed will be reference variables. In this way, users can specify the reference variables exactly.

The initial estimates are computed in four steps as follows:

- Step 1: *Reference variables* are determined as follows. If the scales for η and ξ have been fixed by assigning a non-zero fixed value in each column of Λ_y and Λ_x, LISREL will determine non-singular submatrices of Λ_y and Λ_x of m and n rows, respectively, if this is possible. The rows of these submatrices determine the reference variables. In this way $m+n$ reference variables can be determined provided Λ_y and Λ_x contain m and n linearly independent rows, respectively. Note that this requires that $m \leq p$ and $n \leq q$.

  Remember that all parameters are zero by default. This means that, when this process is applied, all elements of Λ_y and Λ_x are zero except those that have been assigned non-zero values by the user. If no non-zero values have been assigned, both Λ_y and Λ_x are zero so that this procedure fails.

  If the scales of ξ have been fixed by standardizing Φ, the program will automatically assign fixed values in the columns of Λ_x, relax the fixed diagonal elements of Φ and use the same procedure as above to determine the reference variables. When the initial estimates for Λ_x have been determined in Step 2 the program will rescale the ξ-variables so that $\mathrm{diag}(\Phi) = \mathbf{I}$.

- Step 2: For each row of Λ (Λ_y or Λ_x), the free parameters, if any, are estimated from the linear relation between each observed variable and the reference variables using all other observed variables as instrumental variables. Details of this procedure will be presented in Volume II.

- Step 3: For given Λ_y and Λ_x, the joint covariance matrix of η and ξ and Θ_ϵ and Θ_δ are estimated by unweighted least squares (ULS) applied to $\mathbf{S} - \mathbf{\Sigma}$. For given Λ_y and Λ_x this leads to a quadratic function which can be minimized easily. Parameters in Φ, Θ_ϵ and Θ_δ which have non-zero fixed values are held fixed during this minimization.

- Step 4: When the joint covariance matrix of η and ξ has been estimated as in Step 3, the structural equation system can be estimated by instrumental variables methods. We estimate each equation separately using all the ξ-variables as instrumental variables. Again, non-zero parameters in $\mathbf{B}$ and $\mathbf{\Gamma}$ are held fixed. The estimates computed in this step are identical to the well-known instrumental variables or two-stage least-squares estimators; see e.g., Goldberger (1964).

The following four examples illustrate how the program selects reference variables for ξ-variables when PH=ST and no non-zero values are set in Λ_x. Here x means a free parameter and 0 means a parameter fixed at zero.

- **Example 1:**

$$\Lambda_x = \begin{pmatrix} x & 0 \\ x & 0 \\ 0 & x \\ 0 & x \end{pmatrix}$$

Reference variables: x_1 and x_3.

- **Example 2:**

$$\Lambda_x = \begin{pmatrix} x & 0 \\ x & x \\ 0 & x \\ x & x \end{pmatrix}$$

Reference variables: x_1 and x_3.

- **Example 3:**

$$\Lambda_x = \begin{pmatrix} x & 0 \\ x & 0 \\ x & x \\ x & x \end{pmatrix}$$

Reference variable for ξ_1 : $x_1 + x_2 + x_3 + x_4$. Reference variable for ξ_2 : $x_3 + x_4$. In this case, no x-variable can serve as reference variable for ξ_2, so sum-variables are used instead as shown. This model is only identified if ξ_1 and ξ_2 are uncorrelated.

- **Example 4:**

$$\Lambda_x = \begin{pmatrix} x & x \\ x & x \\ x & x \\ x & x \end{pmatrix}$$

No reference variable can be found. The procedure fails. The model is not identified unless further conditions are imposed on Λ_x.

The instrumental variables method used in Steps 2 and 4 requires that the number of instrumental variables be at least as large as the number of right-hand variables whose parameters are to be estimated. In general, this does not hold for all models (for example, the model may have no ξ-variables). Whenever this condition fails, or if the instrumental variables procedure fails for any other reason, the linear relation is estimated by ordinary least squares (OLS) instead. This may result in estimates which in some cases may be slightly biased (or inconsistent).

For non-standard types of models, the procedure described here for generating starting values may not work or may lead to unreasonable results. In all such cases, one must provide starting values and tell the program not to use the initial estimates as starting values. How to do this is explained in Chapter 2.

1.13   Parameter Estimates for Hypothetical Model

Parameter estimates for the hypothetical model in Section 1.3 can be obtained by specifying population parameter values and generating a random sample from this population. A random sample covariance matrix based on N = 100 cases is

```
3.204
2.722  2.629
3.198  2.875   4.855
3.545  3.202   5.373   6.315
0.329  0.371  -0.357  -0.471   1.363
0.559  0.592  -0.316  -0.335   1.271   1.960
1.006  1.019  -0.489  -0.591   1.742   2.276   3.803
0.468  0.456  -0.438  -0.539   0.788   1.043   1.953   1.376
0.502  0.539  -0.363  -0.425   0.838   1.070   2.090   1.189   1.741
1.050  0.960   1.416   1.714   0.474   0.694   0.655   0.071   0.104   1.422
1.260  1.154   1.923   2.309   0.686   0.907   0.917   0.136   0.162   1.688   2.684
```

Using this covariance matrix, parameter estimates were computed with methods IV, TSLS, ULS, GLS, and ML. These are shown in Table 1.4 for Λ_y, Λ_x, $\mathbf{B}$, and $\boldsymbol{\Gamma}$. Standard errors of parameter estimates are given in parentheses for GLS and ML. The methods WLS and DWLS are illustrated in Chapter 7.

Table 1.4 gives a rough idea of how much sampling variability one should expect in a sample of size 100 when the variables are multinormal, the model is true, and the model fits the data well. Under these circumstances, differences between methods are rather small. For most practical purposes, the fast methods IV and TSLS would serve as well as the more costly methods GLS and ML. When the models fit the data poorly, however, there will be larger differences between methods.

Table 1.4: Parameter Estimates for Hypothetical Model

Parameter	True	IV	TSLS	ULS	GLS	ML
LY(2,1)	0.90	0.92	0.92	0.91	0.92(0.04)	0.92(0.04)
LY(4,2)	1.10	1.14	1.14	1.14	1.13(0.03)	1.14(0.03)
LX(2,1)	1.30	1.28	1.26	1.31	1.28(0.10)	1.29(0.11)
LX(3,1)	0.90	1.06	0.83	1.10	0.93(0.12)	0.92(0.12)
LX(3,2)	1.20	0.92	1.14	0.93	1.08(0.12)	1.09(0.12)
LX(5,2)	1.10	1.05	1.08	1.05	1.07(0.09)	1.08(0.08)
LX(7,3)	1.40	1.32	1.39	1.32	1.45(0.10)	1.44(0.09)
BE(1,2)	0.49	0.55	0.55	0.55	0.58(0.06)	0.54(0.06)
BE(2,1)	0.60	0.99	0.90	1.01	0.86(0.16)	0.94(0.18)
GA(1,1)	0.40	0.24	0.18	0.24	0.15(0.14)	0.21(0.15)
GA(1,2)	0.40	0.45	0.51	0.46	0.54(0.14)	0.50(0.15)
GA(2,1)	-1.00	-1.22	-1.18	-1.25	-1.20(0.12)	-1.22(0.12)
GA(2,3)	1.20	0.91	1.00	0.89	1.06(0.16)	1.00(0.15)

Standard Errors in Parentheses

1.14 The LISREL Solution

To give a general idea of the kinds of results that LISREL 7 produces and how these results are presented in the output file, we define the results in general and illustrate them with sections of the output for the hypothetical model estimated by ML. How to set up the input file to produce these results is shown in Chapter 2.

The parameter estimates of the independent parameters θ obtained by any of the iterative methods ULS, GLS, ML, WLS or DWLS are denoted $\hat{\theta}$. The parameter matrices with these estimates inserted and with all fixed and constrained elements included are denoted

$$\hat{\Lambda}_y, \hat{\Lambda}_x, \hat{B}, \hat{\Gamma}, \hat{\Phi}, \hat{\Psi}, \hat{\Theta}_\epsilon, \hat{\Theta}_\delta .$$

These matrices are printed in a section called LISREL ESTIMATES. We call them LISREL estimates regardless of what method has been used to produce them, but the method used is specified in parentheses after the header LISREL ESTIMATES.

This section of the output also contains an estimate of the joint covariance matrix of (η, ξ), which is

$$\begin{pmatrix} \hat{A}(\hat{\Gamma}\hat{\Phi}\hat{\Gamma}' + \hat{\Psi})\hat{A}' \\ \hat{\Phi}\hat{\Gamma}'\hat{A}' \qquad \hat{\Phi} \end{pmatrix} \qquad (1.26)$$

where $\mathbf{A} = (\mathbf{I} - \mathbf{B})^{-1}$. This is a symmetric matrix of order $(m + n) \times (m + n)$.

The upper left $m \times m$ part of this matrix is an estimate of the covariance matrix of η and the lower left $n \times m$ part contains estimates of the covariances between ξ and η. These matrices are functions of other parameter matrices in LISREL, unlike the lower right $n \times n$ part which is the estimate of Φ, the covariance matrix of ξ, which is an independent parameter matrix in the LISREL model.

For the hypothetical model, the section LISREL ESTIMATES looks like this.

```
LISREL ESTIMATES (MAXIMUM LIKELIHOOD)
    LAMBDA Y
              ETA 1      ETA 2
    VAR 1     1.000      .000
    VAR 2      .921      .000
    VAR 3      .000     1.000
    VAR 4      .000     1.139
    LAMBDA X
              KSI 1      KSI 2      KSI 3
    VAR 5     1.000      .000       .000
    VAR 6     1.291      .000       .000
    VAR 7      .920     1.092       .000
    VAR 8      .000     1.000       .000
    VAR 9      .000     1.079       .000
    VAR 10     .000      .000      1.000
    VAR 11     .000      .000      1.437
```

```
    BETA
               ETA 1        ETA 2
   ETA 1        .000         .538
   ETA 2        .937         .000
     GAMMA
               KSI 1        KSI 2        KSI 3
   ETA 1        .213         .495         .000
   ETA 2      -1.223         .000         .996
     COVARIANCE MATRIX OF ETA AND KSI
               ETA 1        ETA 2        KSI 1        KSI 2        KSI 3
   ETA 1       2.957
   ETA 2       3.115        4.719
   KSI 1        .482        -.217         .974
   KSI 2        .554        -.312         .788        1.117
   KSI 3        .932        1.402         .525         .133        1.175
     PSI
               ETA 1        ETA 2
   ETA 1        .486
   ETA 2       -.069         .133
     THETA EPS
               VAR 1        VAR 2        VAR 3        VAR 4
                .247         .123         .136         .197
     THETA DELTA
               VAR 5        VAR 6        VAR 7        VAR 8        VAR 9        VAR 10
                .389         .336         .063         .259         .440          .247
     THETA DELTA
               VAR 11
                .259
```

1.15   Residuals and Standardized Residuals

The matrix $\hat{\Sigma}$ computed from (1.4) using the LISREL estimates is called the fitted covariance matrix. This is a covariance matrix or a matrix of moments about zero depending on what type of matrix is being analyzed. If it has ones in the diagonal, it may be interpreted as a correlation matrix. The matrix $\hat{\Sigma}$ may be printed in the output file and saved in a file (see Section 2.15). This matrix may be useful for checking the identification of the model (see Section 1.9) and for making power calculations (see Section 8.2).

The elements of $S - \hat{\Sigma}$, the difference between S and the fitted moment matrix $\hat{\Sigma}$, are called FITTED RESIDUALS. If the fit of the model is good, the fitted residuals should be small relative to the observed moments in S. However, the matrix of fitted residuals may be large and is often difficult to interpret especially if the unit of measurement differs considerably from variable to variable. For the hypothetical model, the fitted residuals are:

```
FITTED RESIDUALS
              VAR 1     VAR 2     VAR 3     VAR 4     VAR 5     VAR 6
VAR  1         .000
VAR  2         .000      .000
VAR  3         .083      .007      .000
VAR  4        -.002     -.064      .000      .000
VAR  5        -.153     -.073     -.140     -.224      .000
VAR  6        -.063      .019     -.036     -.017      .013      .000
VAR  7        -.042      .054      .051      .023     -.015      .007
VAR  8        -.086     -.054     -.126     -.184      .000      .025
VAR  9        -.096     -.011     -.027     -.042     -.013     -.028
VAR 10         .118      .102      .014      .118     -.051      .016
VAR 11        -.079     -.079     -.091      .016     -.068     -.067
FITTED RESIDUALS
              VAR 7     VAR 8     VAR 9     VAR 10    VAR 11
VAR  7         .000
VAR  8         .008      .000
VAR  9        -.009     -.017      .000
VAR 10         .026     -.062     -.040      .000
VAR 11         .014     -.056     -.045      .000      .000
```

Only a statistical summary of this matrix will be given in the standard output. This summary consists of the smallest, median, and largest residuals, and a stemleaf plot of all the residuals.

For the hypothetical model, this set of summary statistics looks like

```
SUMMARY STATISTICS FOR FITTED RESIDUALS

SMALLEST FITTED RESIDUAL =      -.224
  MEDIAN FITTED RESIDUAL =      -.001
 LARGEST FITTED RESIDUAL =       .118

STEMLEAF PLOT
-2|2
-1|85
-1|430
-0|9988777666655
-0|444443322111100000000000000000
 0|111111222233
 0|558
 1|022
```

For those who need to inspect all the fitted residuals, the whole matrix $S - \hat{\Sigma}$ may be printed on request by writing the logical parameter RS on the OU line; see Section 2.15.

Since the fitted residuals are usually difficult to interpret, another set of residuals is computed by the program. These so-called STANDARDIZED RESIDUALS are often very useful in the assessment of model fit. A standardized residual is a fitted residual divided by its asymptotic standard error. The asymptotic standard error of a fitted residual is a very complicated function of the elements of S. This is derived in Volume II. In earlier versions of LISREL, we used a simple formula which gave an overestimate of the asymptotic variance of the fitted residual and therefore an underestimate of the standardized residual. In LISREL 7, the correct formula is used. If standard asymptotic theory (Browne, 1984) is valid, this produces correct standardized residuals in large samples with GLS and ML under normal theory and with WLS if a correct weight matrix is used. In principle, each standardized residual can be interpreted as a standard normal deviate and considered "large" if it exceeds the value 2.58 in absolute value. When interpreting the standardized residuals statistically, one must bear in mind, however, that they are correlated from cell to cell. The true probability level associated with the largest standardized residual, z say, may well be larger than $1 - \Phi(z)$, where $\Phi(z)$ is the standard normal distribution function.

The program gives summary statistics for the standardized residuals in the form of smallest, largest, and median, and a stemleaf plot. The program also lists those standardized residuals which are larger than 2.58 in absolute value and the variables these are associated with. The whole matrix of standardized residuals is printed only if requested by the RS parameter on the OU line; see Section 2.15.

For the hypothetical model, the standardized residuals and their summary statistics look like this:

```
STANDARDIZED RESIDUALS
            VAR 1      VAR 2      VAR 3      VAR 4      VAR 5      VAR 6
 VAR  1      .000
 VAR  2      .000       .000
 VAR  3     1.661       .215       .000
 VAR  4     -.040     -1.665       .000       .000
 VAR  5    -1.500      -.829     -1.143     -1.592       .000
 VAR  6     -.708       .266      -.364      -.144       .584       .000
 VAR  7     -.560      1.269       .929       .346      -.451       .349
 VAR  8    -1.023      -.773     -1.290     -1.633      -.005       .596
 VAR  9     -.863      -.119      -.199      -.274      -.203      -.485
 VAR 10     1.641      1.743       .201      1.447      -.761       .256
 VAR 11    -1.112     -1.576     -1.546       .229      -.839     -1.006
   STANDARDIZED RESIDUALS
            VAR 7      VAR 8      VAR 9     VAR 10     VAR 11
 VAR  7      .000
 VAR  8      .530       .000
 VAR  9     -.372     -1.077       .000
 VAR 10      .351      -.982      -.490       .000
 VAR 11      .249      -.794      -.462       .000       .000
```

SUMMARY STATISTICS FOR STANDARDIZED RESIDUALS

```
SMALLEST STANDARDIZED RESIDUAL =   -1.665
  MEDIAN STANDARDIZED RESIDUAL =    -.023
 LARGEST STANDARDIZED RESIDUAL =    1.743
```

```
STEMLEAF PLOT
-1|766655
-1|3111000
-0|988888765555
-0|4432211000000000000000
 0|222233334
 0|5669
 1|34
 1|677
```

An effective summary of the fit, as judged by all the standardized residuals jointly, is given by the Q-plot of the standardized residuals. For our example this is given in Figure 1.2.

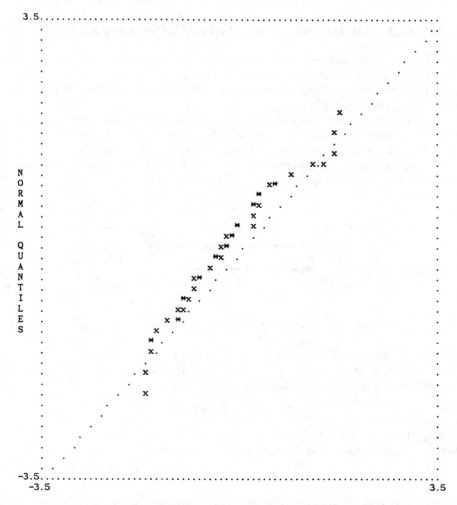

Figure 1.2: The Q-Plot for the Hypothetical Model

The Q-plot is a plot of the standardized residuals against normal quantiles, but for computational reasons we have turned the plot so that the standardized residuals are along the horizontal axis. Each single point is represented by an x and multiple points by an *. The 45-degree line is given by small dots. In most LISREL models, there are a few elements of Σ which fit the data trivially in the sense that there is one free parameter per such element. For example, for every free parameter in Θ_δ the corresponding element of Σ will fit trivially. Elements of Σ which fit the data trivially correspond to zero residuals and zero standardized residuals. Such zero standardized residuals are omitted in the Q-plot.

The Q-plot may be examined as follows. By visual inspection, fit a straight line to the plotted points. If the slope of this line is larger than one, as compared with the 45-degree line, this is indicative of a good fit. Slopes which are close to one correspond to moderate fits and slopes which are smaller than one to poor fits. Non-linearities in the plotted points are indicative of specification errors in the model or of departures from linearity or normality.

1.16   Direct, Indirect, and Total Effects (EF)

It can be seen in the path diagram of Figure 1.1 that there are both direct and indirect effects of ξ_1 on η_2. For example, in addition to the direct effect γ_{21} of ξ_1 on η_2 there is an indirect effect $\beta_{21}\gamma_{11}$ mediated by η_1. Similarly, although there is no direct effect of ξ_3 on η_1, there is an indirect effect $\beta_{12}\gamma_{23}$ mediated by η_2.

There are usually no direct effects of an η on itself, i.e., all diagonal elements of $\mathbf{B}$ are zero. Nevertheless, there may be a total effect of each η on itself. How can this be? This can only occur in non-recursive models and can best be understood by defining a cycle. A cycle is a causal chain going from one η, passing over some other η's and returning to the original η. The two η's in Figure 1.1 are shown in isolation in Figure 1.3.

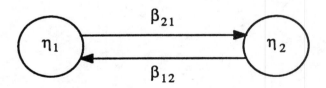

Figure 1.3: Reciprocal Causation Between η_1 and η_2

One cycle for η_1 consists of one path to η_2 and a return to η_1. The effect of one cycle on η_1 is $\beta_{21}\beta_{12}$. After two cycles the effect will be $\beta_{21}^2\beta_{12}^2$, after three cycles $\beta_{21}^3\beta_{12}^3$, etc. The total effect on η_1 will be the sum of the infinite geometric series

$$\beta_{21}\beta_{12} + \beta_{21}^2\beta_{12}^2 + \beta_{21}^3\beta_{12}^3 \cdots$$

which is $\beta_{21}\beta_{12}/(1 - \beta_{21}\beta_{12})$ if $\beta_{21}\beta_{12} < 1$.

In general, the total effect of $\boldsymbol{\eta}$ on itself is

$$\mathbf{B} + \mathbf{B}^2 + \mathbf{B}^3 + ... = (\mathbf{I} - \mathbf{B})^{-1} - \mathbf{I} , \tag{1.27}$$

provided the infinite series converges. Similarly, one finds that the total effect of $\boldsymbol{\xi}$ on $\boldsymbol{\eta}$ is

$$(\mathbf{I} + \mathbf{B} + \mathbf{B}^2 + \mathbf{B}^3 + \cdots)\boldsymbol{\Gamma} = (\mathbf{I} - \mathbf{B})^{-1}\boldsymbol{\Gamma} . \tag{1.28}$$

Table 1.5: Decomposition of Effects

	$\xi \longrightarrow \eta$	$\eta \longrightarrow \eta$
Direct	$\mathbf{\Gamma}$	$\mathbf{B}$
Indirect	$(\mathbf{I} - \mathbf{B})^{-1} \mathbf{\Gamma} - \mathbf{\Gamma}$	$(\mathbf{I} - \mathbf{B})^{-1} - \mathbf{I} - \mathbf{B}$
Total	$(\mathbf{I} - \mathbf{B})^{-1} \mathbf{\Gamma}$	$(\mathbf{I} - \mathbf{B})^{-1} - \mathbf{I}$

	$\xi \longrightarrow \mathbf{y}$	$\eta \longrightarrow \mathbf{y}$
Direct	$\mathbf{0}$	$\mathbf{\Lambda}_y$
Indirect	$\mathbf{\Lambda}_y(\mathbf{I} - \mathbf{B})^{-1} \mathbf{\Gamma}$	$\mathbf{\Lambda}_y(\mathbf{I} - \mathbf{B})^{-1} - \mathbf{\Lambda}_y$
Total	$\mathbf{\Lambda}_y(\mathbf{I} - \mathbf{B})^{-1} \mathbf{\Gamma}$	$\mathbf{\Lambda}_y(\mathbf{I} - \mathbf{B})^{-1}$

A necessary and sufficient condition for convergence of the series in (1.27) and (1.28), i.e., for stability of the system, is that all the eigenvalues of $\mathbf{B}$ are within the unit circle. In general the eigenvalues of $\mathbf{B}$ are complex numbers somewhat difficult to compute. However, a sufficient condition for convergence is that the largest eigenvalue of $\mathbf{BB}'$ is less than one. This is very easy to verify. The program prints the largest eigenvalue of $\mathbf{BB}'$ under the name of STABILITY INDEX.

Several writers (Duncan, 1966; 1975; Finney, 1972; Alwin and Hauser, 1975; Greene, 1977; Graff and Schmidt, 1982, and Bollen, 1987) have proposed definitions of indirect and total effects, discussed their interpretations and provided techniques for estimating specific effects. In LISREL, the definitions given in Table 1.5 are used.

The indirect and total effects will be computed and printed if requested by the EF parameter on the OU line; see Section 2.15. Standard errors of total effects can also be computed (Folmer, 1981; Sobel, 1982). In LISREL 7, these are produced automatically if both EF and SE are included on the OU line.

For the hypothetical model, some of the estimated indirect and total effects and their standard errors are:

```
TOTAL AND INDIRECT EFFECTS
   TOTAL EFFECTS OF KSI ON  ETA
            KSI 1      KSI 2      KSI 3
   ETA 1    -.895       .999      1.080
   ETA 2   -2.062       .936      2.008
   STANDARD ERRORS FOR TOTAL EFFECTS OF KSI ON  ETA
            KSI 1      KSI 2      KSI 3
   ETA 1     .428       .342       .224
   ETA 2     .517       .403       .268
   INDIRECT EFFECTS OF KSI ON  ETA
            KSI 1      KSI 2      KSI 3
   ETA 1   -1.109       .503      1.080
   ETA 2    -.839       .936      1.012
   STANDARD ERRORS FOR INDIRECT EFFECTS OF KSI ON  ETA
            KSI 1      KSI 2      KSI 3
   ETA 1     .340       .240       .224
   ETA 2     .466       .403       .309
```

```
       TOTAL EFFECTS OF ETA ON  ETA
                ETA 1       ETA 2
ETA 1        1.016        1.084
ETA 2        1.890        1.016
LARGEST EIGENVALUE OF B*B' (STABILITY INDEX) IS     .879
       STANDARD ERRORS FOR TOTAL EFFECTS OF ETA ON  ETA
                ETA 1       ETA 2
ETA 1         .410         .282
ETA 2         .717         .410
       INDIRECT EFFECTS OF ETA ON  ETA
                ETA 1       ETA 2
ETA 1        1.016         .546
ETA 2         .953        1.016
       STANDARD ERRORS FOR INDIRECT EFFECTS OF ETA ON  ETA
                ETA 1       ETA 2
ETA 1         .410         .247
ETA 2         .548         .410
       TOTAL EFFECTS OF ETA ON  Y
                ETA 1       ETA 2
VAR 1        2.016        1.084
VAR 2        1.856         .998
VAR 3        1.890        2.016
VAR 4        2.152        2.296
       STANDARD ERRORS FOR TOTAL EFFECTS OF ETA ON  Y
                ETA 1       ETA 2
VAR 1         .410         .282
VAR 2         .384         .259
VAR 3         .717         .410
VAR 4         .817         .471
       INDIRECT EFFECTS OF ETA ON  Y
                ETA 1       ETA 2
VAR 1        1.016        1.084
VAR 2         .936         .998
VAR 3        1.890        1.016
VAR 4        2.152        1.157
       STANDARD ERRORS FOR INDIRECT EFFECTS OF ETA ON  Y
                ETA 1       ETA 2
VAR 1         .410         .282
VAR 2         .380         .259
VAR 3         .717         .410
VAR 4         .817         .468
```

1.17   Miscellaneous Results (MR)

The general form of the LISREL model involves four basic variables: $\mathbf{y}$, $\boldsymbol{\eta}$, $\mathbf{x}$, and $\boldsymbol{\xi}$. By using the model equations (1.1), (1.2) and (1.3) and the associated assumptions one can deduce that the joint covariance matrix of $\mathbf{y}$, $\boldsymbol{\eta}$, $\mathbf{x}$, and $\boldsymbol{\xi}$ is

$$\begin{pmatrix} \boldsymbol{\Lambda}_y(\boldsymbol{\Pi}\boldsymbol{\Phi}\boldsymbol{\Pi}' + \boldsymbol{\Psi}^*)\boldsymbol{\Lambda}_y' + \boldsymbol{\Theta}_\epsilon & & & \\ (\boldsymbol{\Pi}\boldsymbol{\Phi}\boldsymbol{\Pi}' + \boldsymbol{\Psi}^*)\boldsymbol{\Lambda}_y' & \boldsymbol{\Pi}\boldsymbol{\Phi}\boldsymbol{\Pi}' + \boldsymbol{\Psi}^* & & \\ \boldsymbol{\Lambda}_x\boldsymbol{\Phi}\boldsymbol{\Pi}'\boldsymbol{\Lambda}_y' & \boldsymbol{\Lambda}_x\boldsymbol{\Phi}\boldsymbol{\Pi}' & \boldsymbol{\Lambda}_x\boldsymbol{\Phi}\boldsymbol{\Lambda}_x' + \boldsymbol{\Theta}_\delta & \\ \boldsymbol{\Phi}\boldsymbol{\Pi}'\boldsymbol{\Lambda}_y' & \boldsymbol{\Phi}\boldsymbol{\Pi}' & \boldsymbol{\Phi}\boldsymbol{\Lambda}_x' & \boldsymbol{\Phi} \end{pmatrix}$$

where $\boldsymbol{\Pi} = (\mathbf{I} - \mathbf{B})^{-1}\boldsymbol{\Gamma}$ and $\boldsymbol{\Psi}^* = (\mathbf{I} - \mathbf{B})^{-1}\boldsymbol{\Psi}(\mathbf{I} - \mathbf{B}')^{-1}$.

It is possible to obtain estimates of all the submatrices of this large matrix but the various parts will appear in different sections of the output. The y-y, x-y, and x-x parts are contained in the fitted covariance matrix $\hat{\boldsymbol{\Sigma}}$ which will appear in the output if requested by RS on the OU line. This matrix will also be written to a file if requested by SI = filename on the OU line, see Section 2.15. The η-η, η-ξ, and ξ-ξ parts are contained in the joint covariance matrix of η and ξ which is always given in the section LISREL ESTIMATES (see Section 1.14). The covariance parts y-η, y-ξ, x-η, and x-ξ are printed if requested by the logical parameter MR on the OU line. For the hypothetical model these covariance parts are printed as

```
COVARIANCES
    Y - ETA
              VAR 1      VAR 2      VAR 3      VAR 4
    ETA 1     2.957      2.722      3.115      3.547
    ETA 2     3.115      2.868      4.719      5.373
    Y - KSI
              VAR 1      VAR 2      VAR 3      VAR 4
    KSI 1      .482       .444      -.217      -.247
    KSI 2      .554       .510      -.312      -.355
    KSI 3      .932       .858      1.402      1.596
    X - ETA
              VAR 5      VAR 6      VAR 7      VAR 8      VAR 9      VAR 10
    ETA 1      .482       .622      1.048       .554       .598       .932
    ETA 2     -.217      -.280      -.540      -.312      -.336      1.402
    X - ETA
              VAR 11
    ETA 1     1.339
    ETA 2     2.014
    X - KSI
              VAR 5      VAR 6      VAR 7      VAR 8      VAR 9      VAR 10
    KSI 1      .974      1.258      1.757       .788       .851       .525
    KSI 2      .788      1.018      1.945      1.117      1.206       .133
    KSI 3      .525       .678       .629       .133       .144      1.175
    X - KSI
              VAR 11
    KSI 1      .754
    KSI 2      .192
    KSI 3     1.688
```

1.18   Standardized Solutions (SS and SC)

The latent variables in the LISREL solution are generally not standardized. An exception is when the model has only ξ's and when Φ is standardized (PH = ST on the MO line). In LISREL 7 there are two kinds of standardized solutions: SS (Standardized Solution), in which the latent variables are scaled to have variances equal to one and the *observed variables are still in the original metric* and SC (for Completely Standardized), in which both observed and latent variables are standardized.

These standardized solutions can only be computed after the original solution has been computed. As before, let $\hat{\Lambda}_y$, $\hat{\Lambda}_x$, $\hat{\mathbf{B}}$, $\hat{\Gamma}$, $\hat{\Phi}$, $\hat{\Psi}$, $\hat{\Theta}_\epsilon$, $\hat{\Theta}_\delta$ be the original LISREL solution, and let

$$\mathbf{D}_\eta = (diag[(\mathbf{I} - \hat{\mathbf{B}})^{-1}(\hat{\Gamma}\hat{\Phi}\hat{\Gamma}' + \hat{\Psi})(\mathbf{I} - \hat{\mathbf{B}}')^{-1}])^{\frac{1}{2}} , \tag{1.29}$$

$$\mathbf{D}_\xi = (diag\,\hat{\Phi})^{\frac{1}{2}} . \tag{1.30}$$

Furthermore, let

$$\mathbf{D}_y = (diag[\hat{\Lambda}_y(\mathbf{I} - \hat{\mathbf{B}})^{-1}(\hat{\Gamma}\hat{\Phi}\hat{\Gamma}' + \hat{\Psi})(\mathbf{I} - \hat{\mathbf{B}}')^{-1}\hat{\Lambda}_y' + \hat{\Theta}_\epsilon])^{\frac{1}{2}} , \tag{1.31}$$

and

$$\mathbf{D}_x = (diag[\hat{\Lambda}_x\hat{\Phi}\hat{\Lambda}_x' + \hat{\Theta}_\delta])^{\frac{1}{2}} . \tag{1.32}$$

These diagonal matrices define the estimated standard deviations of η, ξ, $\mathbf{y}$, and $\mathbf{x}$, respectively. The standardized solutions SS and SC are computed by applying these standard deviations or their reciprocals as scale factors in the rows and columns of the estimated parameter matrices of the LISREL solution, as shown in Table 1.6. It should be noted that the standard deviations of the observed variables are obtained from the fitted covariance matrix $\hat{\Sigma}$ rather than the observed covariance matrix $\mathbf{S}$, so that estimates are standardized regardless of whether

$$diag(\hat{\Sigma}) = diag(\mathbf{S}) \tag{1.33}$$

or not. Property (1.33) holds for some, *but not all*, models and for some, *but not all*, methods, see also Section 1.21. If (1.33) does not hold, the standardized solutions cannot be obtained by analyzing the sample correlation matrix $\mathbf{R}$ instead of the sample correlation matrix $\mathbf{S}$.

The SS solution corresponds to the LISREL model

$$\eta^* = \mathbf{B}^*\eta^* + \Gamma^*\xi^* + \zeta^* \tag{1.34}$$

$$\mathbf{y} = \Lambda_y^*\eta^* + \epsilon \tag{1.35}$$

$$\mathbf{x} = \Lambda_x^*\xi^* + \delta \tag{1.36}$$

where η^* and ξ^* are standardized to unit variances.

In the printed output, the joint *correlation* matrix of η^* and ξ^* is also given, as well as the regression matrix of η^* on ξ^*, which is

$$\hat{\Pi}^* = (\mathbf{I} - \hat{\mathbf{B}}^*)^{-1}\hat{\Gamma}^* \tag{1.37}$$

Table 1.6: Standardized Solutions

SS	SC
$\hat{\Lambda}_y^* = \hat{\Lambda}_y \mathbf{D}_\eta$	$\hat{\Lambda}_y^{**} = \mathbf{D}_y^{-1} \hat{\Lambda}_y \mathbf{D}_\eta$
$\hat{\Lambda}_x^* = \hat{\Lambda}_x \mathbf{D}_\xi$	$\hat{\Lambda}_x^{**} = \mathbf{D}_x^{-1} \hat{\Lambda}_x \mathbf{D}_\xi$
$\hat{\mathbf{B}}^* = \mathbf{D}_\eta^{-1} \hat{\mathbf{B}} \mathbf{D}_\eta$	$\hat{\mathbf{B}}^{**} = \mathbf{D}_\eta^{-1} \hat{\mathbf{B}} \mathbf{D}_\eta$
$\hat{\boldsymbol{\Gamma}}^* = \mathbf{D}_\eta^{-1} \hat{\boldsymbol{\Gamma}} \mathbf{D}_\xi$	$\hat{\boldsymbol{\Gamma}}^{**} = \mathbf{D}_\eta^{-1} \hat{\boldsymbol{\Gamma}} \mathbf{D}_\xi$
$\hat{\boldsymbol{\Phi}}^* = \mathbf{D}_\xi^{-1} \hat{\boldsymbol{\Phi}} \mathbf{D}_\xi^{-1}$	$\hat{\boldsymbol{\Phi}}^{**} = \mathbf{D}_\xi^{-1} \hat{\boldsymbol{\Phi}} \mathbf{D}_\xi^{-1}$
$\hat{\boldsymbol{\Psi}}^* = \mathbf{D}_\eta^{-1} \hat{\boldsymbol{\Psi}} \mathbf{D}_\eta^{-1}$	$\hat{\boldsymbol{\Psi}}^{**} = \mathbf{D}_\eta^{-1} \hat{\boldsymbol{\Psi}} \mathbf{D}_\eta^{-1}$
$\hat{\boldsymbol{\Theta}}_\epsilon^* = \hat{\boldsymbol{\Theta}}_\epsilon$	$\hat{\boldsymbol{\Theta}}_\epsilon^{**} = \mathbf{D}_y^{-1} \hat{\boldsymbol{\Theta}}_\epsilon \mathbf{D}_y^{-1}$
$\hat{\boldsymbol{\Theta}}_\delta^* = \hat{\boldsymbol{\Theta}}_\delta$	$\hat{\boldsymbol{\Theta}}_\delta^{**} = \mathbf{D}_x^{-1} \hat{\boldsymbol{\Theta}}_\delta \mathbf{D}_x^{-1}$

When equality constraints are imposed on parameters of the model, these will hold in the original solution but not in general in the standardized solutions. However, equality constraints imposed on parameters in the same columns of $\boldsymbol{\Lambda}_y$ and $\boldsymbol{\Lambda}_x$, will hold also in the SS solution.

For the hypothetical model, the SS solution is

```
STANDARDIZED SOLUTION
    LAMBDA Y
                ETA 1       ETA 2
    VAR 1       1.719        .000
    VAR 2       1.583        .000
    VAR 3        .000       2.172
    VAR 4        .000       2.474
    LAMBDA X
                KSI 1       KSI 2       KSI 3
    VAR 5        .987        .000        .000
    VAR 6       1.274        .000        .000
    VAR 7        .908       1.154        .000
    VAR 8        .000       1.057        .000
    VAR 9        .000       1.141        .000
    VAR 10       .000        .000       1.084
    VAR 11       .000        .000       1.557
    BETA
                ETA 1       ETA 2
    ETA 1        .000        .679
    ETA 2        .742        .000
```

```
        GAMMA
                KSI 1      KSI 2      KSI 3
ETA 1           .123       .304       .000
ETA 2          -.556       .000       .497
        CORRELATION MATRIX OF ETA AND KSI
                ETA 1      ETA 2      KSI 1      KSI 2      KSI 3
ETA 1           1.000
ETA 2           .834       1.000
KSI 1           .284      -.101       1.000
KSI 2           .305      -.136       .756       1.000
KSI 3           .500       .595       .491       .117       1.000
        PSI
                ETA 1      ETA 2
ETA 1           .164
ETA 2          -.018       .028
        REGRESSION MATRIX ETA ON KSI (STANDARDIZED)
                KSI 1      KSI 2      KSI 3
ETA 1          -.514       .614       .681
ETA 2          -.937       .455       1.002
```

In the SC solution, only Λ_y, Λ_x, Θ_ϵ, and Θ_δ differ from the SS solution. These are

```
COMPLETELY STANDARDIZED SOLUTION
        LAMBDA Y
                ETA 1      ETA 2
VAR 1           .961       .000
VAR 2           .976       .000
VAR 3           .000       .986
VAR 4           .000       .984
        LAMBDA X
                KSI 1      KSI 2      KSI 3
VAR 5           .845       .000       .000
VAR 6           .910       .000       .000
VAR 7           .465       .592       .000
VAR 8           .000       .901       .000
VAR 9           .000       .864       .000
VAR 10          .000       .000       .909
VAR 11          .000       .000       .950
        THETA EPS
                VAR 1      VAR 2      VAR 3      VAR 4
                .077       .047       .028       .031
        THETA DELTA
                VAR 5      VAR 6      VAR 7      VAR 8      VAR 9      VAR 10
                .285       .171       .017       .188       .253       .174
        THETA DELTA
                VAR 11
                .097
```

1.19 Assessment of Fit

An important part in the application of LISREL is the assessment of fit and the detection of lack of fit of a model. LISREL provides several powerful tools for this purpose. As in all statistical analyses, the assessment of fit must be made with careful subjective judgment based on what is already known about the substantive area and the quality of the data.

The tools for assessment of fit fall naturally into three groups:

- Examination of the solution

- Measures of overall fit

- Detailed assessment of fit

1.19.1 Examination of the Solution

The first and most obvious way of assessing the goodness of a model is to examine the results of an analysis. One should pay careful attention to the following quantities:

- Parameter estimates

- Standard errors

- Correlations of parameter estimates

- Squared multiple correlations

- Coefficients of determination

Parameter Estimates

Parameter estimates should have the right sign and size. Examples of unreasonable values of parameter estimates are negative variances, correlations which are larger than one in magnitude, covariance or correlation matrices which are not positive definite.

Standard Errors

Standard errors are estimates of the precision of each parameter estimate. Small standard errors correspond to good precision and large standard errors to poor precision. What is small or large depends on the units of measurement in observed and/or latent variables and the magnitude of the parameter estimate itself. In practice, t-values are often used, which are independent of the units of measurement. A t-value is defined as the ratio between the parameter estimate and its standard error.

Standard errors and t-values are given for ML, GLS, WLS, ULS, and DWLS. They are not given for IV and TSLS. Standard errors are correct for ML and GLS under multivariate normality of the observed variables and for WLS if a correct weight matrix is used. Standard errors for ML- and GLS-estimates are robust against moderate departures from normality; see Chapter 7. Standard errors for ULS and DWLS are only approximate.

A standard error which is extremely large indicates that the parameter cannot be reasonably determined by the data.

Correlations of Parameter Estimates

An estimate of the asymptotic covariance matrix of the parameter estimates can be obtained from the information matrix. The correlations of parameter estimates are obtained by scaling the asymptotic covariance matrix to a correlation matrix. This may be examined to see if there are any large correlations. If two or more parameters are highly correlated, the model is nearly non-identified and some of these parameters cannot be determined from the data.

Squared Multiple Correlations and Coefficients of Determination

The program gives squared multiple correlations for each observed variable separately and co-efficients of determination for all the observed variables jointly. It also gives squared multiple correlations for each structural equation and coefficients of determination for all structural equations jointly. The squared multiple correlation is a measure of the strength of a linear relationship and the coefficient of determination is a measure of the strength of several relationships jointly.

These coefficients are defined as follows. The *squared multiple correlation* for the i:th observed variable is

$$1 - \frac{\hat{\theta}_{ii}}{\hat{\sigma}_{ii}} \ , \tag{1.38}$$

where $\hat{\theta}_{ii}$ is the estimated error variance and $\hat{\sigma}_{ii}$ is the fitted variance of the i:th variable. The *coefficient of determination* is

$$1 - \frac{\|\hat{\Theta}\|}{\|\hat{\Sigma}\|} \ ,$$

where $\|\hat{\Theta}\|$ is the determinant of $\hat{\Theta}$ and $\|\hat{\Sigma}\|$ is the determinant of the fitted covariance matrix $\hat{\Sigma}$ of the observed variables. These measures show how well the observed variables serve, separately or jointly, as measurement instruments for the latent variables. The measure should be between zero and one, large values being associated with good models.

The squared multiple correlation for the i:th structural equation is defined as

$$1 - \frac{\widehat{Var(\zeta_i)}}{\widehat{Var(\eta_i)}} \ ,$$

where $\widehat{Var(\zeta_i)}$ and $\widehat{Var(\eta_i)}$ are the estimated variances of ζ_i and η_i, respectively.

The total coefficient of determination for all structural equations jointly is defined as

$$1 - \frac{\|\hat{\Psi}\|}{\|\widehat{Cov(\eta)}\|} \ ,$$

where $\|\hat{\Psi}\|$ is the determinant of $\hat{\Psi}$ and $\|\widehat{Cov(\eta)}\|$ is the determinant of the estimated covariance matrix of η obtained from (1.26).

1.19.2 Measures of Overall Fit

The second part of the model evaluation concerns the assessment of the overall fit of the model to the data. The goodness of fit of the whole model may be judged by means of four measures of overall fit:

- Chi-square (χ^2)

- Goodness-of-fit index (GFI)

- Adjusted goodness-of-fit index (AGFI)

- Root mean squared residual (RMR)

Chi-square

For ML, GLS, and WLS, the χ^2-measure is $(N-1)$ times the minimum value of the fit function for the specified model. The χ^2-measure is distributed asymptotically as a chi-square distribution under certain conditions. For ULS and DWLS, certain adjustments are made so as to make the χ^2-measure also asymptotically correct for these methods, see Browne (1984). The χ^2-measure is correct for ULS, ML, GLS, and DWLS under multinormality of the observed variables if a covariance matrix is analyzed. With WLS, the χ^2-measure is correct if a correct weight matrix is used. If a correlation matrix is analyzed with ML, χ^2 is correct only if the model is scale-invariant (Section 1.20) and condition (1.33) holds. For other cases, see Section 1.21.

If the model is correct and the sample size is sufficiently large, the χ^2-measure may be used as a test statistic for testing the model against the alternative that Σ is unconstrained. The degrees of freedom for χ^2 are

$$df = \frac{1}{2}(p+q)(p+q+1) - t \, , \tag{1.39}$$

where $p+q$ is the number of observed variables analyzed and t is the total number of independent parameters estimated. The P-value reported by the program is the probability level of χ^2, that is, the probability of obtaining a χ^2-value larger than the value actually obtained, given that the model is correct.

Although the χ^2-measure may be viewed theoretically as a test statistic for testing the hypothesis that Σ is of the form implied by the model against the alternative that Σ is unconstrained (see Jöreskog, 1977), it should be emphasized that such a use of χ^2 is not valid in most applications. In most empirical work, the model is only tentative and is only regarded as an approximation to reality. From this point of view the statistical problem is not one of testing a given hypothesis (which *a priori* may be considered false), but rather one of fitting the model to the data and to decide whether the fit is adequate or not.

Instead of regarding χ^2 as a test statistic, one should regard it as a goodness (or badness)-of-fit measure in the sense that large χ^2-values correspond to bad fit and small χ^2-values to good fit. The degrees of freedom serve as a standard by which to judge whether χ^2 is large or small. The χ^2-measure is sensitive to sample size and very sensitive to departures from multivariate normality of the observed variables. Large sample sizes and departures from normality tend to increase χ^2 over and above what can be expected due to specification error in the model. One reasonable way to use χ^2-measures in comparative model fitting is to use χ^2-differences in the following way. If a value of χ^2 is obtained, which is large compared to the number of degrees of freedom, the fit may be examined and assessed by an inspection of the fitted residuals, the standardized residuals, and the modification indices (see below). Often these quantities will suggest ways to relax the model somewhat by introducing more parameters. The new model usually yields a smaller χ^2. A large drop in χ^2, compared to the difference in degrees of freedom, indicates that the changes made in the model represent a real improvement. On the other hand, a drop in χ^2 close to the difference in number of degrees of freedom indicates that the improvement in fit is obtained by "capitalizing on chance," and the added parameters may not have real significance and meaning.

Goodness-of-Fit Indices

The other two measures of overall fit are the goodness-of-fit index GFI and the root mean squared residual RMR. Following Tanaka and Huba (1985), the goodness-of-fit index is defined as

$$ \text{GFI} = 1 - \frac{(\mathbf{s} - \hat{\sigma})'\mathbf{W}^{-1}(\mathbf{s} - \hat{\sigma})}{\mathbf{s}'\mathbf{W}^{-1}\mathbf{s}} \; . \tag{1.40} $$

The numerator in (1.40) is the minimum of the fit function after the model has been fitted; the denominator is the fit function before any model has been fitted.

The goodness-of-fit index adjusted for degrees of freedom, or the adjusted GFI, AGFI, is defined as

$$ \text{AGFI} = 1 - \frac{(p+q)(p+q+1)}{2d}(1 - \text{GFI}) \; , \tag{1.41} $$

where d is the degrees of freedom of the model. This corresponds to using mean squares instead of total sums of squares in the numerator and denominator of 1 - GFI. Both of these measures should be between zero and one, although it is theoretically possible for them to become negative. (This should not happen, of course, for it means that the model fits worse than any model at all.) Although GFI does not depend explicitly on sample size, its distribution does.

Root Mean Squared Residual

The root mean squared residual RMR is defined as

$$ \text{RMR} = \left[2\sum_{i=1}^{p+q}\sum_{j=1}^{i}(s_{ij} - \hat{\sigma}_{ij})^2/(p+q)(p+q+1)\right]^{\frac{1}{2}} \; . \tag{1.42} $$

RMR is a measure of the average of the fitted residuals and can only be interpreted in relation to the sizes of the observed variances and covariances in **S**. This measure works best if all observed variables are standardized.

The root mean squared residual can be used to compare the fit of two different models for the same data. The goodness of fit index can be used for this purpose too but can also be used to compare the fit of models for different data.

It should be emphasized that the measures χ^2, GFI, and RMR are measures of the overall fit of the model to the data and do not express the quality of the model judged by any other internal or external criteria. For example, it can happen that the overall fit of the model is very good but with one or more relationships in the model very poorly determined, as judged by the squared multiple correlations, or vice versa. Furthermore, if any of the overall measures indicate that the model does not fit the data well, it does not tell what is wrong with the model or which part of the model is wrong.

For our hypothetical model, the measures of overall fit are listed as

```
CHI-SQUARE WITH  33 DEGREES OF FREEDOM =    29.10 (P = .662)
              GOODNESS OF FIT INDEX = .953
     ADJUSTED GOODNESS OF FIT INDEX = .906
          ROOT MEAN SQUARE RESIDUAL =     .065
```

1.19.3 Detailed Assessment of Fit

If, on the basis of overall measures of fit or other considerations, it is concluded that the model does not fit sufficiently well, one can examine the fit more closely to determine possible sources of the lack of fit.

Standardized Residuals

As we have already seen in Section 1.15, a more detailed assessment of fit can be obtained by an inspection of the standardized residuals. A Q-plot of the standardized residuals gives a very effective summary. Standardized residuals which appear as outliers in the Q-plot are indicative of non-linearity, non-normality, or of a specification error in the model. How standardized residuals and Q-plots can be used in the assessment of fit is discussed further in Chapter 3.

Modification Indices

The modification index is a clever innovation by Sörbom (1989), although it has been included in the program long before this paper was written.

The modification indices are measures associated with the fixed and constrained parameters of the model. For each fixed and constrained parameter, the modification index is a measure of predicted decrease in χ^2 if a single constraint is relaxed and the model is reestimated. For GLS, ML, and WLS, these indices, therefore, may be judged by means of a χ^2-distribution with 1 degree of freedom. The fixed parameter corresponding to the largest such index is the one which, when relaxed, will improve fit maximally. The improvement in fit is measured by a reduction in χ^2 which is expected to be close to the modification index. This procedure seems to work well in practice, but it is recommended to use it only when relaxing a parameter makes sense from a substantive point of view and when the estimated value of this parameter can be clearly interpreted.

A new feature in LISREL 7 is that not only are measures of expected improvement of fit provided but also a prediction of the *estimated change* of each fixed and constrained parameter. This gives useful information about the sensitivity of the measure of fit to changes in parameters. The practical use of modification indices is discussed in Chapters 3 and 8.

Modification indices are useful not only for fixed parameters but also for assessing equality constraints. We use the notation $MI(\theta)$ and $CH(\theta)$ for the modification index of θ and the estimated change in θ. If $\theta_1 = \theta_2$, then $MI(\theta_1) = MI(\theta_2)$. If $\theta_1 = \theta_2 = \theta_3$, there will be three modification indices $MI(\theta_1)$, $MI(\theta_2)$, and $MI(\theta_3)$ which will generally not be equal. $MI(\theta_3)$, say, measures the predicted decrease in χ^2 if θ_3 is freed while the equality constrained $\theta_1 = \theta_2$ is retained and $CH(\theta_3)$ measures the predicted change of θ_3 under this condition.

For the hypothetical model, the modification indices appear in the output as

```
MODIFICATION INDICES AND ESTIMATED CHANGE
    MODIFICATION INDICES FOR LAMBDA Y
              ETA 1        ETA 2
   VAR 1       .000         .990
   VAR 2       .000         .990
   VAR 3      2.115         .000
   VAR 4      2.115         .000
    ESTIMATED CHANGE FOR LAMBDA Y
              ETA 1        ETA 2
   VAR 1       .000         .058
   VAR 2       .000        -.053
   VAR 3       .089         .000
   VAR 4      -.102         .000
    MODIFICATION INDICES FOR LAMBDA X
              KSI 1        KSI 2        KSI 3
   VAR 5       .000         .108        1.049
   VAR 6       .000         .108         .342
   VAR 7       .000         .000        3.376
   VAR 8       .304         .000        1.373
   VAR 9       .304         .000         .241
   VAR 10      .208         .001         .000
   VAR 11      .208         .001         .000
    ESTIMATED CHANGE FOR LAMBDA X
              KSI 1        KSI 2        KSI 3
   VAR 5       .000        -.044        -.082
   VAR 6       .000         .057        -.054
   VAR 7       .000         .000         .148
   VAR 8       .082         .000        -.077
   VAR 9      -.089         .000        -.038
   VAR 10      .034        -.001         .000
   VAR 11     -.048         .002         .000
NO NON-ZERO MODIFICATION INDICES FOR BETA
NO NON-ZERO MODIFICATION INDICES FOR GAMMA
NO NON-ZERO MODIFICATION INDICES FOR PHI
NO NON-ZERO MODIFICATION INDICES FOR PSI
NO NON-ZERO MODIFICATION INDICES FOR THETA EPS
NO NON-ZERO MODIFICATION INDICES FOR THETA DELTA
```

1.20   Scale Invariance

Following Browne (1982), we say that the model $\Sigma(\theta)$ is *scale invariant* if for any diagonal matrix $\mathbf{D}$ of positive scale factors and any parameter vector θ, there exists another parameter vector θ^*, such that

$$\Sigma(\theta^*) = \mathbf{D}\Sigma(\theta)\mathbf{D} \qquad (1.43)$$

Many common types of models have this property. Some do not, however. The scale invariance of the model should be investigated in each particular case. Examples are given in

Chapters 3-5.

Following Krane and McDonald (1978), we say that a parameter θ_i in θ is *scale free* if (i) the model $\Sigma(\theta)$ is scale invariant and (ii) for all choices of $\mathbf{D}$ in (1.43), $\theta_i^* = \theta_i$.

Scale invariance is a property of a model and scale freeness is a property of parameters of a model.

We can also define scale invariance of a fit function. We say that the fit function $F(\mathbf{S}, \Sigma)$ is scale invariant, if for any diagonal matrix $\mathbf{D}$,

$$F(\mathbf{DSD}, \mathbf{D\Sigma D}) = F(\mathbf{S}, \Sigma) . \tag{1.44}$$

The fit functions for ML, GLS, WLS, and DWLS have this property; ULS does not. If the model and the fit function are scale invariant, the analyses of the same variables in different scales will yield results which are properly related, i.e., one can obtain $\hat{\theta}^*$ from $\hat{\theta}$ and the scale factors in $\mathbf{D}$. In these cases, the goodness-of-fit measure χ^2 is invariant (does not change) under different scalings of the observed variables. This holds for modification indices and for standardized residuals as well.

1.21   Problems with Analysis of Correlation Matrices

The general rule is that the covariance matrix should be analyzed. However, in many behavioral sciences applications, units of measurements in the observed variables have no definite meaning and are often arbitrary or irrelevant. For these reasons, for convenience, and for interpretational purposes, the correlation matrix is often analyzed as if it is a covariance matrix. This is a common practice.

The analysis of correlation matrices is problematic in several ways. As pointed out by Cudeck (1989), such an analysis may

(a) modify the model being analyzed,

(b) produce incorrect χ^2 and other goodness-of-fit measures, and

(c) give incorrect standard errors.

Problem (a) can occur when the model includes constrained parameters. For example, if $\lambda_{11}^{(x)}$ and $\lambda_{21}^{(x)}$ are constrained to be equal but the variances $\sigma_{11}^{(xx)}$ and $\sigma_{22}^{(xx)}$ are not equal, then analysis of the correlation matrix will give estimates of

$$\lambda_{11}^{(x)} / \sqrt{\sigma_{11}^{(xx)}} \text{ and } \lambda_{21}^{(x)} / \sqrt{\sigma_{22}^{(xx)}}$$

which are not equal. Correlation matrices should not be analyzed if the model contains equality constraints of this kind.

The main question is whether the standard errors and χ^2 goodness-of-fit measures produced when correlation matrices are analyzed are asymptotically correct. The exact conditions under which this is the case are extremely complicated and give little practical guidance. However, two crucial conditions are

- that the model is scale invariant as defined in (1.43)

- that condition (1.33) holds

Condition (1.33) can be checked by examining the fitted residuals, see Section 1.15. For the ML method, this condition is expected to hold if the diagonal elements of Θ_ϵ and Θ_δ are free parameters and the joint covariance matrix of η and ξ is unconstrained. This holds in Examples 3.2 and 3.3 but it does not hold in Examples 5.5, 6.5, and 6.6. In Examples 5.5 and 6.6, the covariance matrix should be used.

To clarify the issue further, we distinguish between covariance and correlation structures. In principle, all LISREL models are covariance structures, where the variances of Σ as well as the covariances are functions of parameters. By contrast, in a correlation structure, the diagonal elements of Σ are constants independent of parameters. We now distinguish between four possible cases.

A A sample covariance matrix is used to estimate a covariance structure.

B A sample correlation matrix is used to estimate a covariance structure.

C A sample covariance matrix is used to estimate a correlation structure.

D A sample correlation matrix is used to estimate a correlation structure.

Case A is the standard case in LISREL. Because asymptotic variances and covariances of sample variances and covariances often tend to be of the form (1.21), chi-squares and standard errors can be used in most cases to evaluate the model. See also Section 7.4.

Case B is a very common situation. Asymptotic variances and covariances of sample correlations are not of the form (1.21), so standard normal asymptotic theory is not valid. However, if the model is scale invariant and if the ML method produces estimates such that

$$diag(\hat{\Sigma}) = \mathbf{I},$$

then standard errors and χ^2 goodness-of-fit measures *may still be asymptotically correct.* Examples 3.2 and 3.3 in Chapter 3 are typical examples. However, this property does not hold when such models are estimated with GLS.

In case C, if the model is defined as a *correlation structure* $\mathbf{P}(\theta)$, with diagonal elements equal to 1 (i.e., *the diagonal elements are not functions of parameters*), it may be formulated as a covariance structure

$$\Sigma = \mathbf{D}_\sigma \mathbf{P}(\theta) \mathbf{D}_\sigma, \tag{1.45}$$

where $\mathbf{D}_\sigma$ is a diagonal matrix of population standard deviations σ_1, σ_2,..., σ_k of the observed variables, which are regarded as free parameters. The covariance structure (1.45) has parameters σ_1, σ_2,..., σ_k, θ_1, θ_2,..., θ_t. Such a model may be estimated correctly using the sample covariance matrix $\mathbf{S}$. However, the standard deviations σ_1, σ_2,..., σ_k as well as θ must be estimated from data and the estimate of σ_i does not necessarily equal the corresponding standard deviation s_{ii} in the sample. When $\mathbf{P}(\theta)$ is estimated directly from the sample correlation matrix $\mathbf{R}$, standard errors and χ^2 goodness-of-fit values will not in general be correct.

Consider Case D. To obtain correct asymptotic standard errors in LISREL for a *correlation structure* when the correlation matrix is analyzed, the WLS method must be used with a weight matrix $\mathbf{W}^{-1}$, where $\mathbf{W}$ is a consistent estimate of the asymptotic covariance matrix of *the correlations being analyzed.* Such a $\mathbf{W}$ may be obtained with PRELIS under non-normal theory. PRELIS can estimate such a $\mathbf{W}$ also for a correlation matrix containing polychoric and/or polyserial correlations; see Chapter 7.

The asymptotic covariance matrix $\mathbf{W}$ produced by PRELIS is a consistent estimate of the covariance matrix of

$$\mathbf{r} = (r_{21}, r_{31}, r_{32}, r_{41}, r_{42}, r_{43}, \ldots)$$

The diagonal elements of the correlation matrix *are not included* in this vector. The number of distinct elements in $\mathbf{W}$ are

$$(1/2)k(k-1)[(1/2)k(k-1)+1] \,,$$

where $k = p + q$ is the number of observed variables in the model. In fitting a correlation structure $\mathbf{P}(\theta)$ to a correlation matrix using WLS, LISREL minimizes the fit function [cf. (1.20)]

$$
\begin{aligned}
F(\theta) &= (\mathbf{r} - \rho)'\mathbf{W}^{-1}(\mathbf{r} - \rho) \\
&= \sum_{g=2}^{k}\sum_{h=1}^{g-1}\sum_{i=2}^{k}\sum_{j=1}^{i-1} w^{gh,ij}(r_{gh} - \rho_{gh})(r_{ij} - \rho_{ij})
\end{aligned}
\tag{1.46}
$$

where

$$\rho' = (\rho_{21}(\theta), \rho_{31}(\theta), \rho_{32}(\theta), \rho_{41}(\theta), \ldots, \rho_{k,k-1}(\theta)) \,.$$

This approach assumes that the diagonal elements of $\mathbf{P}(\theta)$ are fixed ones and not functions of parameters. Example 7.5 of Chapter 7 illustrates such a model.

WLS may also be used to fit ordinary LISREL models (i.e. *covariance structures*) to sample correlation matrices (Case B). This is especially useful when polychoric and polyserial correlations are analyzed. A small problem arises here because the fit function (1.46) is not a function of the diagonal elements of $\mathbf{P}(\theta)$, and, as a consequence, parameters such as the diagonal elements of Θ_ϵ and Θ_δ cannot be estimated directly. However, they can of course be estimated afterwards. For example, in Submodel 1, one can estimate Θ_δ as

$$\hat{\Theta}_\delta = \mathbf{I} - diag(\hat{\Lambda}_x \hat{\Phi} \hat{\Lambda}_x')$$

A better and more general approach is to add the term

$$\sum_{i=1}^{k}[1 - \sigma_{ii}(\theta)]^2 \tag{1.47}$$

to the fit function (1.46). The program does this automatically when the diagonal elements of Σ are functions of parameters. This corresponds to using

$$\begin{pmatrix} \mathbf{W}^{-1} & \mathbf{0} \\ \mathbf{0} & \mathbf{I} \end{pmatrix}$$

as a weight matrix in (1.20). The advantages of this approach are

- Estimates of all parameters can be obtained directly even when constraints are imposed

- When the diagonal elements of Θ_ϵ and Θ_δ are free parameters, the WLS solution will satisfy

$$diag(\hat{\Sigma}) = \mathbf{I} \,.$$

Examples 7.1, 7.2, and 7.3 in Chapter 7 illustrate this case.

This approach can be generalized further by replacing the 1 in (1.47) by a variance s_{ii} which has been estimated or obtained separately from the correlations. Such variances can be obtained with PRELIS for ordinal variables for which the thresholds are assumed to be equal.

Chapter 2

DETAILED INSTRUCTIONS FOR THE PROBLEM RUN

2.1 LISREL Control Lines, Line Names and Parameter Names

LISREL control lines and data are explained in detail in this chapter. The input for LISREL is controlled by certain two-letter line names and parameter names. The input is actually very easy to set up once certain basic keywords have been learned. General rules for keywords are given in this chapter. The examples in the following chapters will clarify how the rules are applied in practice.

On LISREL control lines, upper-case and lower-case characters may be used interchangeably without any restrictions. Thus, DA, Da, da, and dA all mean the same thing. In this book we use upper-case characters for line names, parameter names and character parameter values.

The input for LISREL falls naturally into three groups:

- Specification of the type of data

- Specification of the type of model

- Specification of the output

The type of data is specified by a DA line, the model is defined by a MO line and the output is specified by a OU line. These lines are required for every problem. Other lines may be required to define the data and the model completely. A typical input for LISREL may be

```
Title line(s)
DA.....(specification of the data)
.......(further specification of the data)
MO.....(specification of the model)
.......(further specification of the model)
OU.....(specification of the output)
```

The term "line" is used here in the sense of an input record from a terminal or a punched card. On a terminal the end of a record is specified by a RETURN character. The physical

51

line length is 127 characters. A LISREL control line ends either with a RETURN character or a semicolon (;). By using a semicolon to end a LISREL control line, several LISREL control lines can be put on a physical line. Thus, for example, the physical line

```
DA NI=6 NOBS=556 MA=KM; LA FI=LABELS; KM SY
```

consists of the three LISREL control lines

```
DA NI=6 NOBS=556 MA=KM
LA FI=LABELS
KM SY
```

The first two non-blank characters on a LISREL control line must be a LISREL line name such as DA, MO or OU. A line name may contain any number of characters but only the first two are significant. Thus

```
DATA
DATAPARAMETERS
DATA-PARAMETERS
DATA-SPECIFICATION
DA
```

are all equivalent as long as they do not contain a blank.

Each LISREL line beginning with a line name may contain parameter names and parameter values. Parameter names may also contain any number of characters but only the first two are significant. Blanks are used to separate different parameter names and thus cannot be used within names. All LISREL parameters have default values which have been defined so that one can specify the common types of problems and models with a minimum of input. Only parameters which differ from their default values must be given. All line names, parameter names, and character parameter values are listed in the Subject Index.

There are three kinds of parameters in LISREL: some parameters require a numeric value; others require a character value; still others are logical parameters, where only the presence or absence of the parameter name is significant.

Parameters which have a numeric value are specified by an equals sign and a number. For example, the parameter NI on the DA line, which specifies the number of input variables (see Section 2.2), can be given as

```
DA NI = 5
```

or as

```
DATA NINPUTVARIABLES = 5
```

Any number of blanks may be used before and after the equal sign.

Character values may also contain any number of characters as long as the first two characters are correct. For example, one of the three alternative values of the parameter MA on the DA line is MM (moment matrix) and this may be given in any of the following ways

```
MA = MM
MATRIX = MM
MA = MMATRIX
```

Logical parameters, i.e., parameters which can take only two "values," are given without an equal sign. The absence of such a parameter name implies the default value and the presence implies the other value. For example, the presence of the parameter SE (standard errors) on the OU line specifies that standard errors should be given in the output. The default is that standard errors will not be given.

If one line of 127 characters is not sufficient for all the parameters, write a C for CONTINUE or COMMENT and continue on the next line. Every character appearing after the C on that line will be ignored by the program. The C must appear in place of a parameter name, not in place of an equal sign or a parameter value.

A description of all LISREL control lines follows. The order among the lines is arbitrary to a certain extent but they will be presented here in the order which seems most natural.

2.2 Title

The first line for each problem should be a title line containing any information used as a heading for this problem. Most users will only use a single title line. However, the program will read any number of title lines which may be used to describe the model and the data. The program will read title lines until it finds a DA line, i.e., a line whose first two non-blank characters are DA. Therefore, one should avoid title lines which begin with the two characters DA. The first line of the title will be printed on every section of the printed output.

Unlike LISREL 6, title lines are optional (but strongly recommended). The input file can begin directly with a DA line. Only title lines can appear before the DA line.

2.3 DA Line (Data Parameters)

The DA line contains the following parameters which determine the data to be used:

- NG = Number of groups (see Chapter 9). Default value = 1

- NI = Number of input variables. This parameter must be specified

- NO = Sample size N or number of cases, i.e., the number of statistical units (e.g. persons) on which the NI variables have been measured or observed; see PRELIS User's Guide for treatment of missing values. Default value = 0

  If a covariance, correlation or moment matrix is to be read, N must be specified or the program will stop. If the covariance, correlation, or moment matrix has been produced by PRELIS under listwise deletion, N should be the total effective (listwise) sample size. If the matrix has been produced by PRELIS under pairwise deletion, N should be a representative average of the pairwise sample sizes.

  If N is unknown and raw data is to be read, leave NO default and the program will compute N (see Section 2.4.2), using listwise deletion if there are missing values in the raw data.

  Note: Unlike LISREL 6, LISREL 7 does not handle missing values by pairwise deletion. Use the LISREL pre-processor PRELIS for handling missing values. PRELIS also handles transformation and recoding of variables and provides options for handling ordinal and censored variables. PRELIS will compute and save an appropriate moment matrix (moment, covariance or correlation matrix) which can be read by LISREL; see Section 2.4.3.

- MAtrix Type of matrix to be analyzed

    = MM for a matrix of moments about zero

    = AM for an augmented moment matrix; see Section 2.4.3

    = CM for a covariance matrix

    = KM for a matrix of product moment correlations based on raw scores or normal scores

    = OM for a correlation matrix of optimal scores produced by PRELIS

    = PM for a matrix which includes polychoric or polyserial correlations

If MA is not specified, CM will be used.

Note: The MA parameter specifies the *kind of matrix* to be analyzed. It *does not* specify the *kind of data* to be read. The program will use the data in whatever form it is provided to compute the kind of matrix specified by MA; see Section 1.10. The matrix analyzed will be this matrix after selection and reordering of variables, if this has been specified by an SE line; see Section 2.5.

2.4 Input Data

After the DA line one usually enters various kinds of input data. This is done in the following way. First enter a line with a line name specifying the kind of data to be read, then a line specifying a format and then a number of lines containing data given in this format. If the data are in free format, with blanks or commas separating the data values, the line containing the format may be omitted.

The different line names for reading data are:

LA for labels

RA for raw data

MM for a moment matrix

CM for a covariance matrix

KM for a correlation matrix based on raw or normal scores

OM for a correlation matrix based on optimal scores

PM for a matrix of polychoric, polyserial and product moment correlations

ME for means

SD for standard deviations

AC for asymptotic covariance matrix of covariance or correlation matrix

AV for asymptotic variances of the elements of the covariance or correlation matrix

DM for user-defined diagonal weight matrix

Except for AC, AV, and DM, which are explained in Sections 2.4.5 - 2.4.7, these lines may contain three parameters FI, FO and RE:

FIle = *filename*   FOrmat-in-input-file   REwind

where *filename* is the name of the file where the data is stored if it is not in the input file and where FO and RE are logical parameters. Normally the format and the data will be read from an external file specified by FI = *filename*. However, if FO appears, the format is given in the immediately following line in the input file. If the format and the data are in the input file, along with the other control lines, the line need only contain the line name. If RE appears, the file containing the specified data will be rewound after the data has been read. Otherwise it is not rewound.

For compatibility with LISREL 6, one can also use

UN = logical unit number (not number 5 or 6; these are reserved for the input and output files)

Use this if the data will be read from some external file identified by a logical unit number. The file must be opened and assigned to this logical unit number before LISREL is run. (Note: In the PC-version of LISREL 7, if a logical unit number is specified, the program will stop during execution and ask for a filename. To avoid this delay, always specify FI = *filename* when entering data from external files.)

The lines MM, CM and KM may contain one additional parameter explained in Section 2.4.3.

The line after the line with the line name for input data contains *either* a specified FORTRAN format beginning with a left parenthesis and ending with a right parenthesis *or* an * (asterisk) in column 1. In the first case, the entries will be read according to this format; in the second case the entries may be in free form and are separated by blanks or commas. If the data is in free format, the line containing the * may be omitted. The *-line is included as an option only for compatibility with LISREL 6.

A FORTRAN format in LISREL 7 may be up to 5 lines of 128 characters each.

2.4.1 Labels (LA)

A label (a name) may be assigned to each observed variable, to make the printed output easier to read. The number of labels to be entered is NI, the value given on the DA line. Each label may consist of any number of characters, but only the first eight characters will be retained and printed by the program.

To enter labels, write an LA line followed by a new line containing either a user-specified FORTRAN format specifying A-format or an * in column 1 specifying free format. Then the labels begin on a new line after the format line. Thus

LA line
Format line (optional if labels are in free format)
Labels

When entering labels in free format, the format line containing the * in column 1 may be omitted. When labels are read with a user-specified A-format, the labels must strictly follow that format. When labels are read in free format, blanks, commas and return characters (carriage returns or line feeds) are used as delimiters. Therefore, blanks and commas cannot be used within labels unless the label is enclosed between single quotes. In free format, the return character is ignored until all labels have been read or a / (forward slash) is encountered. If a

/ is found, the remaining labels are set equal to the corresponding default labels. The default labels for observed variables are VAR 1, VAR 2, VAR 3, ...

Labels will be right-adjusted within a field of eight characters; blanks will be filled in before the label if it contains fewer than eight characters. But there is no need to take these blanks into account when referring to labels.

- **Example 1:** The following ways of entering labels are all equivalent:

```
LA
(6A8)
VIS PERC    CUBESLOZENGESPAR COMPSEN COMPWORDMEAN

LA
*
'VIS PERC' CUBES LOZENGES 'PAR COMP' 'SEN COMP' WORDMEAN

LA
'VIS PERC'      CUBES    LOZENGES 'PAR COMP','SEN COMP', WORDMEAN

LA
'VIS PERCEPTION' CUBES LOZENGES 'PAR COMP' 'SEN COMPLETION'
WORDMEANING
```

- **Example 2:** Suppose that NI = 4 and we read

```
LA
FAEDUC MOEDUC/
```

Variables 3 and 4, with no labels specified, will then be labeled VAR 3 and VAR 4 by default.

- **Example 3:** Suppose instead that we want to assign the labels FAEDUC and MOEDUC to variables 1 and 3 and that we do not care about labels for variables 2 and 4. This can be done as follows

```
LA
FAEDUC,,MOEDUC/
```

Note the two commas in the middle for variable 2. Ending the line with no label specified for variable 4 requires no commas.

In general, the effect of two consecutive commas is that one default label will be inserted. Three consecutive commas will result in two default labels being inserted, etc. The following three examples illustrate the use of the FI and FO parameters.

- **Example 1:**

```
LA
'VIS PERC' CUBES LOZENGES ...
```

The labels are read from the input file.

- **Example 2:**

`LA FILE = LABELS`

The labels are read from a file called LABELS. If the labels are to be read by a fixed A-format, that format must precede the labels in this file.

- **Example 3:**

`LA FI = LABELS FO`
`(10A8)`

The labels are read in format 10A8 from the file LABELS. In this example, the format line is in the input file and not in the file LABELS.

2.4.2 Raw Data (RA)

To specify that raw data is to be read, write an RA line and follow with a format line. The format line contains either a user-specified format for reading floating point decimal numbers or an * in column 1 to specify free format reading. When reading raw data in free format, the format line containing the * may be omitted. This option is included only for compatibility with LISREL 6.

The format for the raw data, if any, may precede the raw data in the same file or may be included in the input file. In the latter case, the FO parameter must appear on the RA line.

The raw data are read one case after another. Each case must begin on a new line. There must be NI data values for each case. Cases are read until NO cases have been read or an end-of-file is encountered. If NO = 0, the program will determine the sample size, and the number of cases read will be given in the output and will be used as NO in subsequent computations.

If the number of cases, NO, is erroneously set too large, the program will terminate input when an end-of-file is encountered and will use the correct case count in the computations. If NO is set too small, only NO cases will be read, regardless of how many more cases exist.

When reading a case of raw data in free format, blanks and commas are used as delimiters, return characters are ignored and the following options are available:

- Ending a case with a / (forward slash) may be used to indicate that all remaining data values for this case are the same as the corresponding data values for the previous case.

- Two consecutive commas may be used to specify that the corresponding data value for the previous case should be inserted between the commas. Three consecutive commas imply that two data values from the previous case will be inserted, etc.

- Repetitions of the same data value can be specified by an * preceded by a repeat factor. For example, 4*1 means 1 1 1 1.

- LISREL interprets all data values as floating point decimal numbers. However, for data values which are integers, the decimal point may be omitted.

LISREL 7 handles *missing values by listwise deletion only*. For pairwise deletion or any other raw data problems, use PRELIS to produce the relevant covariance or correlation matrix; see Section 1.10. LISREL 7 assumes that there is a global numeric value XM assigned to represent all missing values in the whole data matrix. With PRELIS, one can have different missing value representations for different variables. The value of XM is specified on the RA line.

2.4.3   Covariance, Correlation and Moment Matrices (CM, KM, MM)

All matrices are read row-wise. When reading a symmetric matrix, one may choose to read it in three alternative ways. To read the full matrix, i.e., the elements of the matrix above as well as below the diagonal, enter the logical parameter FUll on the first line and read one line for each row of the matrix, i.e., each row begins on a new line. To read only the lower half of the matrix, enter the logical parameter keyword SYmmetric and read each row up to and including the diagonal element, beginning each row on a new line. In the default option, i.e., when neither FU or SY is given, enter the lower half of the matrix row-wise as one long line.

The following example illustrates the three alternatives. Suppose one wants to read the covariance matrix

$$\mathbf{S} = \begin{pmatrix} 1.13 & -0.87 & 1.08 \\ -0.87 & 2.17 & 1.83 \\ 1.08 & 1.83 & 3.25 \end{pmatrix}$$

using the format F5.2. Then the input in the three alternatives will be (note the blanks)

```
CM FU
(16F5.2)
   113   -87   108
   -87   217   183
   108   183   325

CM SY
(16F5.2)
   113
   -87   217
   108   183   325

CM
(16F5.2)
   113   -87   217   108   183   325
```

Another possibility is to read the matrix with a free format. If blanks are used as delimiters, there is no distinction between starting a new line for each row of the matrix and reading all elements as one long line. When reading only the lower half of the matrix, the parameter SY is redundant. For example, one can read the full matrix by giving

```
CM FU
1.13 -.87 1.08
-.87 2.17 1.83
1.08 1.83 3.25
```

and one can read the lower half as

```
CM
1.13 -.87 2.17 1.08 1.83 3.25
```

or equivalently as

```
CM
1.13
-.87   2.17
1.08   1.83   3.25
```

Augmented Moment Matrix

Suppose one reads NI = k and MA = AM (Augmented Moment Matrix) on the DA line (see Section 2.3). Let $z_{i1}, z_{i2},..., z_{ik}$ denote the input variables for the i:th unit in the sample, i = 1, 2,..., N. Then the program will compute the augmented moment matrix **M** of order (k + 1) x (k + 1), defined as

$$\mathbf{M} = \begin{pmatrix} m_{11} & & & \\ m_{21} & m_{22} & & \\ \vdots & \vdots & & \\ m_{k1} & m_{k2} & \cdots & m_{kk} \\ \bar{z}_1 & \bar{z}_2 & \cdots & \bar{z}_k & 1 \end{pmatrix}$$

where

$$m_{jk} = (1/N) \sum_{i=1}^{N} z_{ij} z_{ik} \text{ and } \bar{z}_j = (1/N) \sum_{i=1}^{N} z_{ij}$$

This is the sample moment matrix when the variable which is equal to 1 for every sample unit has been added as the last variable. This variable will be given the default label 'CONST.' The program also automatically updates NI from NI $= k$ to NI $= k + 1$.

As shown in Chapter 10, the augmented moment matrix is really not necessary, as mean structures can be specified directly. The option of analyzing the augmented moment matrix (MA=AM) is provided for compatibility with LISREL 6 for those who prefer to specify mean structures the old way, i.e., by translating the mean structure into a moment structure; see Chapter 10.

Note that the program can compute the augmented moment matrix regardless of what kind of input data is actually read in (raw data, covariance matrix, correlation matrix, means and standard deviations) provided, of course, that information about both means and standard deviations are obtainable from the input.

2.4.4   Means and Standard Deviations (ME, SD)

The means or the standard deviations of the input variables may be given by first entering an ME or SD line, then a format line and then on a new line the means or standard deviations as one long vector. The vector must contain NI data values.

Some of the control lines for input data considered so far will now be illustrated by means of a small but fairly typical example. Suppose the three variables are denoted Y, X1 and X2 and their covariance matrix is given by **S** in the previous subsection. The means are 1.051, 2.185 and 3.753. The covariance matrix **S** and the means are stored in the file COVMEANS, say. The format for the covariance matrix is also in that file but not the format for the means. The file COVMEANS contains the following

```
(16F5.2)                          Format for covariance matrix
  113
 -87   217                        Covariance matrix
 108   183   325
1051  2185  3753                  Means
```

The input may then be

```
LISREL Model for Y, X1 and X2      Title
DA NI=3 MA=MM                       DA line
LA                                  LA line
Y X1 X2                             Labels
CM FI=COVMEANS                      CM line
ME FI=COVMEANS FO RE                ME line
(16F5.3)                           Format for means
```

The file COVMEANS will be rewound after the means have been read so that this data may be used immediately in another problem in a stacked input.

2.4.5 Asymptotic Covariance Matrix (AC)

The use of the WLS method in LISREL 7 (see Section 1.11) requires a consistent estimate of the asymptotic covariance matrix of the elements in the covariance or correlation matrix to be analyzed. This asymptotic covariance matrix is produced by PRELIS and is available only for MA = CM, KM, and PM. To read the asymptotic covariance matrix, include a line

AC FI = *filename*,

where *filename* is the name of the file in which PRELIS saved the asymptotic covariance matrix. FO and RE are not allowed on the AC line. The asymptotic covariance matrix must be read from an external file. No format is necessary if the file is produced by PRELIS. Otherwise, specify the format in the first line of the external file if the elements of the asymptotic covariance matrix are in fixed format.

If NI = k, the number of independent elements in the asymptotic covariance matrix is

$$(1/2)k(k + 1)[(1/2)k(k + 1) + 1] \quad \text{if MA = CM}$$
$$(1/2)k(k - 1)[(1/2)k(k - 1) + 1] \quad \text{if MA = KM or MA = PM}$$

These are huge numbers if k is at all large.

In the WLS method, the asymptotic covariance matrix is the matrix $\mathbf{W}$ in (1.20), i.e., the weight matrix $\mathbf{W}^{-1}$ in (1.20) is the *inverse* of the asymptotic covariance matrix.

An AC line in the input file changes the default method of estimation from ML to WLS; see Section 2.15. If ULS, GLS or ML is requested, the information provided by the asymptotic covariance matrix is ignored. If DWLS is requested, only the diagonal elements of the asymptotic covariance matrix will be used (see next section).

See Section 2.5 about the selection of variables and its effect on the asymptotic covariance matrix.

2.4.6 Asymptotic Variances (AV)

The use of the DWLS method in LISREL 7 (see Section 1.11) requires consistent estimates of the asymptotic variances of the elements of the covariance or correlation matrix to be analyzed. These asymptotic variances are produced by PRELIS and are only available for MA = CM, KM, and PM. To read the asymptotic variances, include a line

AV FI = *filename*,

where *filename* is the name of the file in which PRELIS saved the asymptotic variances. FO and RE are not allowed on the AV line. The asymptotic variances must be read from an external file. No format is necessary if the file is produced by PRELIS. Otherwise, specify the format in the first line of the external file if the asymptotic variances are in fixed format.

If NI = k, the number of elements in this file is

$(1/2)k(k+1)$ if MA = CM
$(1/2)k(k-1)$ if MA = KM or MA = PM.

In the DWLS method, the asymptotic variances are the terms w_{gh} in (1.25), i.e., the weights are the reciprocals of the asymptotic variances.

An AV line in the input file makes DWLS the default method of estimation. If ULS, ML or GLS are chosen, the asymptotic variances are ignored and the choice of WLS leads to an error message.

See Section 2.5 on selection of variables and its effect on the asymptotic variances.

2.4.7   User-Specified Diagonal Weight Matrix (DM)

Suppose we want to minimize the fit function (1.25) for DWLS, which we now write

$$F(\boldsymbol{\theta}) = \sum_{g=1}^{k} \sum_{h=1}^{g} d_{gh}(s_{gh} - \sigma_{gh})^2.$$

where d_{gh} is a non-negative weight applied to $(s_{gh} - \sigma_{gh})^2$.

The DM option allows users to specify the weights d_{gh} directly. DM is similar to AV. However, while an asymptotic variance must be positive, a weight read by DM can be zero.

To read the weights, include a line

    DM FI = *filename*,

where *filename* is the name of the file, where the d_{gh} are stored. FO and RE are not allowed on the DM line. The weights must be read from an external file. No format is necessary if the weights are in free format. Otherwise, specify the format in the first line of the external file if the elements are in fixed format.

If NI = k, the number of elements in this file should be
$(1/2)k(k+1)$ if MA = CM or MA = MM
$(1/2)k(k-1)$ if MA = KM or MA = PM.

Example:

Suppose $k = 3$ and we wish to give the diagonal elements of **S** half as much weight in the fitting process as the off-diagonal elements and we do not want to use s_{21} at all. This can be done by reading a file containing the following numbers:

d_{11}	d_{21}	d_{22}	d_{31}	d_{32}	d_{33}
0.5	0	0.5	1	1	0.5

The fit function will then be:

$$(1/2) \sum_{i=1}^{3} (s_{ii} - \sigma_{ii})^2 + (s_{31} - \sigma_{31})^2 + (s_{32} - \sigma_{32})^2 \ .$$

A DM line included in the input file makes DWLS the default method of estimation. No standard errors, *t*-values, chi-squares, etc., can be obtained.

2.5   SE Line (Selection of Variables)

Any number of the NI input variables may be selected to be included in the model and the order in which these variables should appear may be specified.

To select variables, write the line SE and then on a new line a list of selected variables. The selected variables should be listed either by numbers or by labels in the order one wants them in the model and *the y-variables should be listed first*. The list of selected variables are read in free format and the entries are separated by blanks or commas. *No format line is required.* A /(slash) signals the end of the list of selected variables and must be included regardless of whether the selected variables are listed by numbers or by labels. If all variables are selected, the /(slash) is not required.

The list of variables can also be in an external file specified on the SE line as

SE FI = *filename*,

If no selection line is included in the input file it means that all the input variables should be used in the analysis and that they are already in the correct order.

The selection and reordering of variables specified by the SE line will also automatically select and order the asymptotic covariance matrix (Section 2.4.5) and the asymptotic variances (Section 2.4.6) if these have been entered.

The SE line is of great practical usefulness as it enables users to start with a given covariance or correlation matrix for many variables (and the asymptotic covariance matrix of the elements of this matrix) and then do many analyses of subsets of these variables. Example 7.2 in Chapter 7 illustrates this.

2.6   MO Line (Model Parameters)

The MO line is used to specify the model to be estimated. To begin with, the following parameters may be given on the MO line:

NY = number of y-variables in the model (p)
NX = number of x-variables in the model (q)
NE = number of η-variables in the model (m)
NK = number of ξ-variables in the model (n)

When one or more of these are default on the MO line, a submodel of the general model is obtained (see Section 1.3 and Table 1.2). For example, if NY and NE are default, one obtains Submodel 1:

$$\mathbf{x} = \mathbf{\Lambda}_x \boldsymbol{\xi} + \boldsymbol{\delta}$$

involving only the three parameter matrices $\mathbf{\Lambda}_x$, $\mathbf{\Phi}$, and $\mathbf{\Theta}_\delta$. If NE and NK are default, one obtains Submodel 2:

$$\mathbf{y} = \mathbf{B}\mathbf{y} + \mathbf{\Gamma}\mathbf{x} + \boldsymbol{\zeta}$$

which involves only the parameter matrices $\mathbf{B}$, $\mathbf{\Gamma}$, and $\mathbf{\Psi}$.

For each parameter matrix involved in the model (submodel) one can write a specification of the form

MN = MF,FF

where MN is a *name of a parameter matrix*, i.e., LY, LX, BE, GA, PH, PS, TE, and TD, MF is a *matrix form* ZE, ID, IZ, ZI, DI, SD, ST, and FU, and FF is either FI (fixed) or FR (free) (see Section 1.4 and Table 1.3). For example,

LX = DI,FR

implies that Λ_x is diagonal with free diagonal elements. The order of MF and FF may be interchanged so that this specification can also be written

LX = FR,DI

Either MF or FF may be omitted in which case the default values given in Table 1.3 will be used. For example,

LX = DI

means that Λ_x is a fixed diagonal matrix, and

LX = FR

means that Λ_x is a full matrix with all elements free. Also, LX may be default entirely on the MO line which implies that Λ_x is a full fixed matrix.

One should make a specification of the form

MN = MF,FF

for each matrix in the model (submodel) whose form and/or fixed-free status differs from the default. Study the default values in Table 1.3 carefully. They have been chosen so that most of the commonly used models require a minimum of specifications on the MO line.

Important Note: The specification PH=ST on the MO line has a very special meaning. It means precisely that the diagonal elements of Φ are fixed at one and the off-diagonal elements are free. This specification cannot be overridden by fixing and/or freeing elements of Φ on FI or FR lines; see Section 2.8. The specifications PH=ST,FI and PH=ST,FR are not permitted.

If one wants something different from PH=ST, one can get this by specifying PH=FI or leaving PH default on the MO line and then specifying the fixed-free status of each element of Φ on FI or FR lines. For example, suppose we want Φ to be

$$\Phi = \begin{pmatrix} 1 & & & \\ x & 1 & & \\ 0 & 0 & x & \\ 0 & 0 & 0 & x \end{pmatrix},$$

where x's are free parameters and 0's and 1's are fixed parameters. This can be specified as

```
MO ... PH=FI ...
FR PH(2,1) PH(3,3) PH(4,4)
VA 1 PH(1,1) PH(2,2)
```

In this case it is absolutely essential for the program to work properly that a scale has been defined for ξ_3 and ξ_4 by fixing a non-zero value in columns 3 and 4 of Λ_x.

One additional parameter may be given on the MO line, namely the logical parameter FIxed-x (see Section 1.11.5). This signifies that the x-variables are unconstrained fixed or random variables. If FI is given on the MO line, the program *automatically* sets NK = NX, Λ_x = I, Θ_δ = 0, $\Phi = S_{xx}$ (fixed), i.e., $\xi \equiv x$. The FI specification is automatically included if both NE and NK are default on the MO line, i.e., for submodel 2, the program *automatically* takes x to be a set of unconstrained variables (predetermined or exogenous).

2.7   LK and LE Lines (Labels for Latent Variables)

One can use labels for latent variables as well. This is recommended as it makes the printed output more readable.

To read labels for ξ-variables one uses an LK line and to read labels for η-variables one uses an LE line. The syntax for both is the same as for the LA line (Section 2.4.1). The number of ξ-labels must be equal to NK and the number of η-labels must be equal to NE, where NK and NE are specified on the MO line; see Section 2.6.

Default labels for ξ-variables are KSI 1, KSI 2, ... Default labels for η-variables are ETA 1, ETA 2, ... These will be used if no labels for latent variables are specified.

2.8   FR and FI Lines (Fixed and Free Matrix Elements)

On the MO line, one can specify that an entire parameter matrix is to be fixed or free, i.e., that *all* the elements of the matrix are fixed or free. The FR and FI lines can be used to define the fixed-free status of *single matrix elements*. For example, if Λ_x has been declared free on the MO line by the specification LX=FR, the elements $\lambda_{12}^{(x)}$, $\lambda_{22}^{(x)}$, $\lambda_{31}^{(x)}$, and $\lambda_{41}^{(x)}$ can be declared fixed by the line

FI LX(1,2) LX(2,2) LX(3,1) LX(4,1)

Here blanks are used as delimiters between the matrix elements. Blanks may also be used *instead of* the parentheses and the comma. Thus, the above line can also be written

FI LX 1 2 LX 2 2 LX 3 1 LX 4 1

Any specification on a FR or FI line overrides any previous specification made for the elements listed on that line. Thus, for example,

FR BE(2,1) LY(5,2) LX(4,1) PS(1,1)

declares the elements β_{21}, $\lambda_{52}^{(y)}$ $\lambda_{41}^{(x)}$, and ψ_{11} to be free regardless of their previous fixed-free status. Similarly,

FI LX(2,1) LX(3,1) GA(1,1) PS(2,1)

declares the elements $\lambda_{21}^{(x)}$, $\lambda_{31}^{(x)}$, γ_{11}, and ψ_{21} to be fixed regardless of their previous fixed-free status.

If one wants to declare a range of parameters which are in consecutive order (see Section 1.4) to be free or fixed, one can use a hyphen or minus sign (-). For example,

FR BE(1,2) GA(1,1) GA(2,2)-GA(2,5)

defines β_{12}, γ_{11}, γ_{22}, γ_{23}, γ_{24}, and γ_{25} to be free.

There are three important rules which one must remember in FR and FI lines:

- If a matrix has been specified as ZE or ID on the MO line, one cannot refer to any element of this matrix since this is not stored in the computer memory.

- If a matrix has been specified as DI on the MO line, one cannot refer to any off-diagonal element of this matrix since only the diagonal elements are stored in memory.

- If one specifies PH=ST on the MO line, one cannot refer to any elements of Φ on FI or FR lines; see Section 2.6.

2.9 PA Line (Pattern Matrix)

When a matrix contains many fixed and free elements, the method of specifying their fixed-free status by means of a FR or a FI line is inconvenient. In this case one can use a PA line instead. A PA line tells the program to read a pattern matrix of zeros and ones, where a zero means a fixed element and a one means a free element.

To read a pattern matrix, enter a line:

PA MN

where MN is the name of the matrix, LY, LX, BE, GA, PH, PS, TE, or TD. This is followed by a format line specifying an *integer* format or an optional * for free format and then, beginning on a new line, a pattern matrix of zeros and ones. The pattern matrix is read as one long vector reading row-wise, but, by specifying the format properly, one can arrange to read the pattern as a matrix.

- **Example 1:** The following are four alternative ways of reading the pattern matrix for

$$\Gamma = \begin{pmatrix} free & fixed & fixed \\ fixed & free & free \end{pmatrix}$$

```
PA GA
(6I1)
100011


PA GA
(3I1)
100
011


PA GA
*
1 0 0 0 1 1
```

```
PA GA
*
1 0 0
0 1 1
```

As before, the line containing the * may be omitted.

- **Example 2**: If a matrix is symmetric, only the elements in the lower half, including the diagonal, should be read. If a matrix is specified to be diagonal, only the diagonal elements should be read. For example, if $\Phi(4 \times 4)$ is symmetric with fixed diagonal elements and free off-diagonal elements, and if $\Psi(4 \times 4)$ is diagonal, with elements ψ_{11} and ψ_{33} fixed and ψ_{22} and ψ_{44} free, the pattern matrices are read as

```
PA PH
*
0 1 0 1 1 0 1 1 1 0
```

```
PA PS
*
0 1 0 1
```

- **Example 3**: Suppose one wants to read the following pattern matrix for Λ_x.

$$\begin{pmatrix} 1 & 0 & 0 \\ 1 & 0 & 0 \\ 1 & 0 & 0 \\ 0 & 1 & 0 \\ 0 & 1 & 0 \\ 0 & 1 & 0 \\ 0 & 0 & 1 \\ 0 & 0 & 1 \\ 0 & 0 & 1 \end{pmatrix}$$

This can be read as

```
PA LX
3*(1 0 0) 3*(0 1 0) 3*(0 0 1)
```

or even more simply (by omitting the asterisks) as

```
PA LX
3(1 0 0) 3(0 1 0) 3(0 0 1)
```

Pattern matrices can also be read from an external file by specifying FI = filename on the PA line.

2.10 EQ Line (Equality Constraints)

The EQ line is used to specify equality constraints; see Section 1.6. One simply lists those elements which are supposed to be equal. Each group of parameters constrained to be equal must be defined on a separate EQ line. The first parameter listed in each group is usually defined as a free parameter separately. If one line is not sufficient to list all the constrained parameters in a group put a C in place of a matrix name and continue on the next line. For example,

```
EQ LY(3,4) LY(4,4) BE(2,2)-BE(2,4) GA(4,6) TE(5,2)
```

defines

$$\lambda_{34}^{(y)} = \lambda_{44}^{(y)} = \beta_{22} = \beta_{23} = \beta_{24} = \gamma_{46} = \theta_{52}^{(\epsilon)}$$

One can also use an EQ line to fix parameters. If λ_{34} is a fixed parameter in the example above, then all the other parameters will be fixed and equal to the value set for λ_{34}.

2.11 VA and ST Lines (Fixed Values and Starting Values)

FR and FI lines defined in Section 2.8 specify whether elements are to be fixed or free and EQ lines defined in Section 2.10 specify whether or not elements are to be equal. *These lines do not specify the actual values of matrix elements. All elements, whether fixed, free, or constrained are zero by default. All non-zero fixed values must be specified.* In most cases, non-zero values for free parameters, so-called *starting values*, need not be specified. However, if good starting values, i.e., good guesses of what the parameter estimates might be, are available, these may be specified, thereby giving the program some help in computing the LISREL solution.

The VA and the ST lines are used to define non-zero values for fixed parameters and starting values for free parameters, respectively, see Sections 1.7 and 1.11. Each line reads a number and inserts it in the locations given by a list of matrix elements.

For example,

```
VA 1.5 LX(2,1) LY(6,2) GA(1,2)
```

assigns the value 1.5 to $\lambda_{21}^{(x)}$, $\lambda_{62}^{(y)}$, and γ_{12}.

As a second example, suppose that $\mathbf{B}$ is subdiagonal, $\boldsymbol{\Psi}$ is symmetric and $\boldsymbol{\Theta}_\epsilon$ is diagonal with the following starting values for the free parameters:

$$\mathbf{B} = \begin{pmatrix} 0 & 0 & 0 \\ 0.5 & 0 & 0 \\ 0.5 & 0.5 & 0 \end{pmatrix} \qquad \boldsymbol{\Psi} = \begin{pmatrix} 1.5 & & \\ 0.5 & 1.9 & \\ 0.7 & 0.5 & 1.5 \end{pmatrix}$$

$$\boldsymbol{\Theta}_\epsilon = diag(1.5, 1.5, 1.5)$$

The starting values for the free parameters can then be set by the following ST lines:

```
ST  0.5 BE(2,1) BE(3,1)-BE(3,2) PS(2,1) PS(3,2)
ST  1.5 PS(1,1) PS(3,3) TE(1)-TE(3)
ST  1.9 PS(2,2)
ST  0.7 PS(3,1)
```

A hyphen (or minus sign) may be used for a range of elements in consecutive order, but the meaning of this is different on the two lines. *Whenever a range of elements is specified on an ST line, only those elements in this range which have been specified as non-fixed (free or constrained) elements will be set. For a range on a VA line, however, all elements in the range will be set.*

Thus, the first of the ST lines above can also be written

```
ST 0.5 BE(1,1)-BE(3,3) PS(2,1) PS(3,2)
```

with the same effect.

All non-fixed elements in all parameter matrices can be set at the same starting value, 0.5 say, by

```
ST 0.5 ALL
```

The word ALL must be entered with three characters. This is an exception to the general rule that only the first two characters of parameter names are significant.

2.12   MA Line (Matrix)

If there are many *different* non-zero fixed values in a matrix, using VA lines to specify them will be inconvenient. In that case, one can use a MA line instead. The MA line tells the program to read a matrix of real numbers. The elements of this matrix provide fixed values for fixed parameters and starting values for free and constrained parameters.

To read a matrix of values, enter first a line

```
   MA MN
```

where MN is the name of the matrix and then a format line or a line with an * in column 1. The matrix is then read row-wise as one long vector. For the matrices Λ_y, Λ_x, $\mathbf{B}$, and Γ one can, by specifying the format properly, arrange to read it so that each row begins on a new line and this can also be done when the matrix is in free format. If the matrix is symmetric, the lower half, including the diagonal, should be entered as one long vector reading row-wise. If the matrix has been specified as diagonal, only the diagonal elements should be entered.

- **Example** 1: Using the last example of the previous section, the matrices $\mathbf{B}$, $\mathbf{\Psi}$, and Θ_ϵ could be read as

```
MA BE
(3F1.1)
000
500
550
MA PS
*
1.5 0.5 1.9 0.7 0.5 1.5
MA TE
*
1.5 1.5 1.5
```

- **Example** 2: Suppose the symmetric matrix Φ is of order 10 x 10 and partitioned as

$$\Phi = \begin{pmatrix} \mathbf{I} & \\ \mathbf{0} & \mathbf{0} \end{pmatrix}$$

where $\mathbf{I}$ is an identity matrix of order 5 x 5, say. One can read this matrix as

```
MA PH
1
0 1
0 0 1
0 0 0 1
0 0 0 0 1/
```

The / implies that the remaining elements will all be zero. Data containing repetitions of the same number or group of numbers can be read very conveniently. For example, the matrix Φ can also be read as

```
MA PH
1 0 1 2*0 1 3*0 1 4*0 1/
```

Here 3*0 is equivalent to 0 0 0.

These matrices can also be read from an external file by adding FI = filename and possibly FO and RE on the MA line.

Using free format (*) it is possible to read only a leading subset of elements in a matrix by terminating the list with a / (slash).

As before, the line containing the * may be omitted.

2.13   PL Line (Parameter Plots)

For any given solution, one may choose to plot the fit function (ULS, GLS, ML, WLS or DWLS) against any parameter, whether fixed or free. Up to ten such plots may be requested in each run. For free parameters, the range of the abscissa in the plot is chosen to correspond to an approximate 95% confidence interval. For fixed parameters the range of the abscissa is chosen to be the predicted estimated change in the parameter when it is set free. Alternatively, the interval for the abscissa may be specified directly to be $a \leq \theta \leq b$, where a and b are two given numbers. In each case, 11 equidistant points are plotted.

The syntax for the PL line is

PL parameterlist FROM a TO b

where a and b have the default values specified above. For example, to plot the parameters LX(2,1), LY(4,3), TD(1,1), write

```
PL LX(2,1) LY(4,3) TD(1,1)
```

and to plot TD(1,1) and TD(2,2) from 0.4 to 0.5, write

```
PL TD(1,1) TD(2,2) FROM 0.4 TO 0.5
```

Several PL lines may be included in the input file but at most ten parameters can be plotted in each run.

   Important note: The parameter plots in LISREL 6 and LISREL 7 differ. The plot in LISREL 7 is a plot of the *concentrated* fit function, i.e., for each value of θ, the *minimum* of the fit function with respect to all other free parameters is plotted. For further information, see Section 3.3.

2.14   NF Line (Never Free These Parameters)

If modification indices (see Section 1.19.3) are requested by MI on the OU line, the program will compute a modification index for all fixed and constrained parameters. Each such modification index is rather time consuming to compute. Many of these modification indices may not be of any interest because it may be meaningless to have these as parameters of a model. Recall that one should only relax a parameter if it makes sense in the model. The NF line provides the possibility of specifying fixed parameters for which modification indices should not be computed. For example, if LX is specified as ID or IZ or ZI, modification indices for Λ_x are usually of no interest. This can be specified as

```
NF LX(1,1) - LX(10,4)
```

if Λ_x is of order 10 × 4, say. Similarly, if **B** must be subdiagonal by definition, modification indices for elements of **B** in and above the diagonal are of no interest. If $m = 4$, say, this can be specified as

```
NF BE(1,1) - BE(1,4) BE(2,2) - BE(2,4) BE(3,3) BE(3,4) BE(4,4)
```

   The syntax for the NF line is the same as that of the FR and FI lines. A hyphen (or minus sign) may be used for a range of parameters in consecutive order. *Only fixed parameters will be affected by the NF line. Free parameters on the NF line are ignored.* Therefore, if BE is specified as SD in the second example, the NF line can be written more conveniently as

```
NF BE(1,1) - BE(4,4)
```

   Modification indices and estimated changes for elements specified on NF lines will appear as 0.000 in the output. In the parameter specifications such elements appear as -1.

   It is particularly important to use NF lines with the *automatic model modification* procedure. This option is available to let the program automatically modify the model sequentially, by freeing in each step that fixed parameter or that equality constraint which corresponds to the largest modification index and continuing to do so for as long as this index is statistically significant. The user can specify the significance level.

   One should use automatic model modification with careful judgment. Only such parameters and constraints that make sense from a substantive point of view should be relaxed. See section 4.2.2 for how the automatic model modification procedure could be used. See section 8.3 for the dangers involved.

   To use the automatic model modification, write the logical parameter AM on the OU line (see Section 2.15). The significance level for the modification index may also be specified on the OU line as SL = 5, i.e., 5%. The default value is SL = 1. Parameters which *must not* be set free are specified on one or more NF lines.

   It should be noted that only fixed and constrained parameters included in the original model will be relaxed during the automatic model modification. For example, if Θ_δ is diagonal, no off-diagonal elements of Θ_δ will be relaxed. If one wants to have the possibility of relaxing off-diagonal elements of Θ_δ, one must specify TD = SY on the MO line even if Θ_δ is diagonal in the original model, see Section 1.6.

2.15 OU Line (Output Requested)

The OU line is used to specify the output requested. The output line may contain many parameters most of which are logical parameters.

Some parameters have to do with the kinds of estimates to be computed. These are specified by assigning character values to the ME parameter, ME for MEthod (For compatibility with LISREL, they can also be written without the ME =):

IV for Instrumental variables method

TS for Two-stage least-squares method (TSLS)

UL for Unweighted least-squares method (ULS)

GL for Generalized least-squares method (GLS)

ML for Maximum likelihood method

WL for Generally weighted least-squares (WLS)

DW for Diagonally weighted least-squares (DWLS)

If ME is not specified, ML will be used, unless an AC, AV or DM line is included in the input file; see Sections 2.4.5-2.4.7. WL requires an asymptotic covariance (AC) matrix produced by PRELIS (see Section 1.11.2). All methods except the first two (IV and TS) are iterative and require starting values for all independent free parameters. These are produced by IV for UL and by TS for GL, ML, WL and DW, unless one specifies

NS Do not compute starting values; start iterations from the starting values given by the user.

Two parameters that can affect *parameter estimates* in addition to those already mentioned are

RO Use Ridge Option

RC Ridge Constant c (Default value = 0.001)

The Ridge Option means that the matrix

$$\mathbf{S} + c(diag\mathbf{S})$$

will be analyzed instead of $\mathbf{S}$. This option will be invoked automatically if $\mathbf{S}$ is not positive definite. Otherwise, it will only be used if RO is present on the OU line.

If the matrix $\mathbf{S} + c(diag\mathbf{S})$ is not positive definite, the Ridge Constant c will be multiplied repeatedly by 10 until this matrix becomes positive definite.

Other parameters on the OU line determine the output requested. The standard output is always obtained. This consists of a list of the control lines in the input file, the title with parameter listing, the parameter specifications, the matrix to be analyzed, the IV or TS estimates, the LISREL estimates (ULS, GLS, ML, WLS, DWLS) and the overall goodness-of-fit measures. Summary statistics for fitted and standardized residuals are also in the standard output. All other output is controlled by the following parameters:

SE Print standard errors

TV Print t-values

PC Print correlation matrix of parameter estimates

RS Print estimated covariance matrix, residuals, standardized residuals, and Q-plot

EF Print total effects and indirect effects

MR Print covariances

MI Print modification indices

FS Print factor scores regression

SS Print standardized solution

ALL Print everything

TO Print with 80 characters/record. TO is default in PC-version

WP Print with 132 characters/record. WP is default in mainframe versions

ND =number of decimals (0-8) on the printed output (Default is ND = 3)

The meaning and interpretation of most standard and optional output is discussed in Chapter 1 and in Chapters 3-10 in connection with real examples.

In addition, the following technical parameters may be specified to control the program (other technical parameters are defined in Chapter 11):

TM = Maximum number of CPU-seconds allowed for this problem. Default value varies from 172 800 seconds (2 days) for PC-version to 60 seconds for most mainframe versions

IT = Maximum number of iterations allowed (default value = three times the number of independent parameters to be estimated)

AD = n Check admissibility of the solution after n iterations (n = 0, 1, 2,...,), default = 10

AD = OFF Set admissibility check off. See Section 1.11.4 and Chapter 11

If TM seconds are exceeded, the iterations are stopped and the current "solution" is written onto a file called DUMP unless another filename is specified on the OU line (see below). The "solution" LY, LX, BE, GA, PH, PS, TE and TD is written in format (6D13.6), and is preceded by a line with this format and the name of the matrix. A matrix saved in this way can be read by LISREL with a MA line; see Section 2.12. For example,

MA LY FI=DUMP

This termination of the program will also occur if the program iterates for more than IT iterations or if numerical instabilities are encountered.

In addition to the above parameters, one can specify on the OU line that certain parts of the results should be saved in a file. To do this, set

MN = filename

where MN is the matrix to be saved. MN may be LY, LX, BE, GA, PH, PS, TE, TD, MA, SI, RM, or EC. The first eight matrices refer to the LISREL solution. The last four matrices are as follows

MA is the matrix analyzed, i.e., after selection and reordering of variables

SI is the fitted (moment, covariance or correlation) matrix Σ (SI for SIgma)

RM is the regression matrix of latent variables on observed variables, i.e., the matrix that can be requested by the logical parameter FS

EC is the estimated asymptotic covariance matrix of the LISREL estimators

For example, to save Λ_y and $\mathbf{B}$ in the file LYBE, the matrix analyzed in the file MATRIX, and the asymptotic covariance matrix of the estimators in the file ACOVMATR, put

OU... LY=LYBE BE=LYBE MA=MATRIX EC=ACOVMATR.

These matrices are then written in format (6D13.6) preceded by a line with the format and the name of the saved matrix.

A special parameter in LISREL 7 is the logical parameter SO having to do with the scales for latent variables. The program will check that a scale has been defined for each latent variable as described in Sections 1.2.1 and 1.12. If a scale has not been defined for a latent variable, the program will stop unless the SO parameter appears on the OU line. The SO parameter is needed for very special models where scales for latent variables are defined in a different way; see Example 6.1 in Chapter 6.

All parameters on the OU line may be omitted but a line with the two letters OU must be included in the input file. This is always the last line for each problem.

2.16   Order of LISREL Control Lines

The order of the LISREL control lines is arbitrary except for the following conditions:

- Except for title lines, a DA line must always come first

- The OU line must always be last

- LK, LE, FR, FI, EQ, PA, VA, ST and MA lines must always come after the MO line

- The MO line is optional only if no LISREL model is analyzed. If the MO line is missing only the matrix to be analyzed will be given. Otherwise, the MO line must be given

2.17   Stacked Problems

After all the data for one problem or one group have been read, the program will automatically read the data for the next problem (if NG = 1) or the next group (if NG > 1) unless an end-of-file is encountered. Any number of problems and groups of data may be stacked together and analyzed in one run.

2.18   Input File for Hypothetical Model

The input file for the hypothetical model used to produce the results given in Chapter 1 is

```
HYPOTHETICAL MODEL ESTIMATED BY ML
DA NI=11 NO=100
CM SY FI=EX1.COV
MO NY=4 NX=7 NE=2 NK=3 BE=FU
FR LY 2 1 LY 4 2 LX 2 1 LX 3 1 LX 3 2 LX 5 2 LX 7 3 BE 2 1 BE 1 2
FI GA 1 3 GA 2 2
VA 1 LY 1 1 LY 3 2 LX 1 1 LX 4 2 LX 6 3
OU SE TV MI RS EF MR SS SC
```

In some ways this is a rather typical input file; in other ways it is atypical. Since the model is hypothetical, no labels for variables are used. The input file makes use of many default values.

The first line is the title line. The next line is the DA line which specifies only the number of variables (11) and the number of cases (100). Since MA is default, the program assumes that a covariance matrix is to be analyzed. The next line reads the covariance matrix from the file EX1.COV. The covariance matrix is given in Section 1.13.

The matrix is read by a format given in the first line in EX1.COV, and since each row of the covariance matrix begins on a new line, the parameter SY on the CM line is necessary.

The MO line specifies the number of y-, x-, η-, and ξ-variables in the model and that $\mathbf{B}$ is full and fixed as opposed to $\mathbf{B} = \mathbf{0}$ as it would be by default. All other parameter matrices have the default specifications given in Table 1.3. The FR line specifies the free parameters in $\mathbf{\Lambda}_y$, $\mathbf{\Lambda}_x$ and $\mathbf{B}$ to be estimated. The FI line specifies the fixed zeros in $\mathbf{\Gamma}$. The VA line assigns the value 1 to one element in each column of $\mathbf{\Lambda}_y$ and $\mathbf{\Lambda}_x$ to fix the scales for η- and ξ-variables. The matrices $\mathbf{\Phi}$, $\mathbf{\Psi}$, $\mathbf{\Theta}_\epsilon$, and $\mathbf{\Theta}_\delta$ remain at their default specification: $\mathbf{\Phi}$ and $\mathbf{\Psi}$ being symmetric with all elements free and $\mathbf{\Theta}_\epsilon$ and $\mathbf{\Theta}_\delta$ being diagonal.

The OU line specifies most of the output that can be obtained. Since ME is default on the OU line, the ML method will be used.

Chapter 3

MEASUREMENT MODELS AND CONFIRMATORY FACTOR ANALYSIS

3.1   The LISREL Submodel 1

In this chapter we consider various types of models all fitting the framework of Submodel 1 as defined in Chapter 1. The variables involved in this submodel are

Observed or measured variables: $\mathbf{x}' = (x_1, x_2, ..., x_q)$
Latent variables: $\boldsymbol{\xi}' = (\xi_1, \xi_2, ..., \xi_n)$
Error variables: $\boldsymbol{\delta}' = (\delta_1, \delta_2, ..., \delta_q)$

The model is

$$\mathbf{x} = \boldsymbol{\Lambda}_x \boldsymbol{\xi} + \boldsymbol{\delta}, \tag{3.1}$$

with the assumptions that ξ's and δ's are random variables with zero means and that the δ's are uncorrelated with the ξ's. Equation (3.1) represents the regression of $\mathbf{x}$ on $\boldsymbol{\xi}$ so that the element λ_{ij} of $\boldsymbol{\Lambda}_x$ is the partial regression coefficient of ξ_j in the regression of x_i on $\xi_1, \xi_2, ...,$ ξ_n. As stated in Chapter 1, we assume for convenience that all observed variables are measured in deviations from their means.

The assumptions imply that the covariance matrix of $\mathbf{x}$ is

$$\boldsymbol{\Sigma} = \boldsymbol{\Lambda}_x \boldsymbol{\Phi} \boldsymbol{\Lambda}_x' + \boldsymbol{\Theta}_\delta, \tag{3.2}$$

where $\boldsymbol{\Phi}$ and $\boldsymbol{\Theta}_\delta$ are the covariance matrices of $\boldsymbol{\xi}$ and $\boldsymbol{\delta}$ respectively.

Since no confusion will arise, we shall often in this chapter write $\boldsymbol{\Lambda}$ instead of $\boldsymbol{\Lambda}_x$ and λ_{ij} instead of $\lambda_{ij}^{(x)}$. Also, we shall write $\boldsymbol{\Theta}$ instead of $\boldsymbol{\Theta}_\delta$ and θ_{ij} instead of $\theta_{ij}^{(\delta)}$.

3.1.1   Identification

As defined in (3.1) and (3.2), the model is not identified. Let $\mathbf{T}$ be an arbitrary non-singular matrix of order n x n and let

$$\xi^* = \mathbf{T}\xi \qquad \Lambda^* = \Lambda\mathbf{T}^{-1} \qquad \Phi^* = \mathbf{T}\Phi\mathbf{T}'$$

Then we have identically

$$\Lambda^*\xi^* \equiv \Lambda\xi \qquad \Lambda^*\Phi^*\Lambda^{*'} \equiv \Lambda\Phi\Lambda'$$

This shows that at least n^2 independent conditions must be imposed on Λ and/or Φ to make these identified. Such conditions are necessary for identification but they are not sufficient, for it can happen that Θ is not identified even after these conditions are imposed. For an example of this, see Bollen and Jöreskog (1985).

Various rigorous necessary and sufficient conditions for identification have been given by Howe (1955), Jöreskog (1969, see also correction note, 1979), Dunn (1973), Jennrich (1978), Algina (1980), and Bekker (1986). Unfortunately, most of these conditions are so complicated that they are almost impossible to verify in practice. For an example of how the identification problem may be resolved using the LISREL program itself, see Section 6.6.

3.1.2   Standardization

The standardized solution for this submodel is one in which the ξ-variables are standardized, i.e., Φ is a correlation matrix. Requesting a standardized solution by SS on the OU line is not really meaningful, since one can obtain this solution directly by putting PH=ST on the MO line. This standardizes the latent variables but not the observed variables. A completely standardized solution, i.e., one in which both observed and latent variables are standardized, can be obtained by putting MA=KM on the DA line *and* PH=ST on the MO line. See also Sections 1.18 and 1.20.

3.2   The Congeneric Measurement Model

Broadly speaking, there are two basic problems that are important in the social and behavioral sciences. The first problem is concerned with the measurement properties - validities and reliabilities - of the measurement instruments used. The second problem concerns the causal relationships among the variables used and their relative explanatory power. In this chapter we shall consider problems of the first kind and illustrate how LISREL can be applied in the study of the measurement properties of variables. Problems concerning the causal relationships among variables will be considered in the next chapter.

Most theories and models in the social and behavioral sciences are formulated in terms of theoretical or hypothetical concepts or constructs, or latent variables, which are not directly measurable or observable. However, often a number of indicators or symptoms of these variables can be used to measure the unobserved variables, more or less well. The purpose of a measurement model is to describe how well the observed indicators serve as a measurement instrument for the construct or latent variables. The key concepts here are that of measurement and of reliability and validity. Measurement models often suggest ways in which the observed measurements can be improved.

Measurement models are important in the social and behavioral sciences when one tries to measure such abstractions as people's behavior, attitudes, feelings and motivations. Most measures employed for such purposes contain sizable measurement errors and the measurement models allow us to take these measurement errors into account.

3.2.1 One Set of Congeneric Measures

The most common type of measurement model is the congeneric measurement model; see Jöreskog (1971). A path diagram of the congeneric measurement model is shown in Figure 3.1.

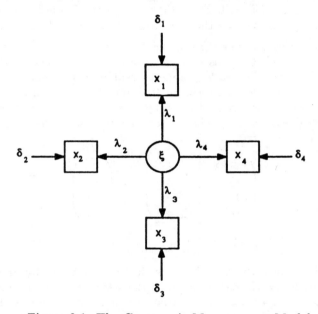

Figure 3.1: The Congeneric Measurement Model

The observed variables are denoted x_1, x_2, x_3, and x_4 and the latent variable is denoted ξ. The measurement errors in x_1, x_2, x_3 and x_4 are denoted δ_1, δ_2, δ_3 and δ_4, respectively. The arrows do not represent direct causal influences in the usual sense, rather in the sense that *if the latent variable were observed* it would produce values of the observed variables x_1, x_2, x_3, and x_4. The coefficients λ_1, λ_2, λ_3, and λ_4 associated with the arrows emanating from ξ represent regression coefficients in the relationships between each of the observed measures x_1, x_2, x_3, x_4 and ξ. Corresponding to the path diagram of Figure 3.1 there are four equations. Following the rules outlined in Chapter 1, the equations corresponding to Figure 3.1 are

$$\left.\begin{aligned} x_1 &= \lambda_1\xi + \delta_1 \\ x_2 &= \lambda_2\xi + \delta_2 \\ x_3 &= \lambda_3\xi + \delta_3 \\ x_4 &= \lambda_4\xi + \delta_4 \end{aligned}\right\} \tag{3.3}$$

The variables x_1, x_2, x_3, x_4, ξ, δ_1, δ_2, δ_3 and δ_4 are regarded as random variables defined in some population. To begin with we shall consider the case when the x-variables are measured on an interval scale. The case of ordinal variables is considered in Chapter 7.

It is assumed that the δ's are uncorrelated with ξ and that the δ's are mutually uncorrelated among themselves and have zero means. The quantities λ_1, λ_2, λ_3 and λ_4 are fixed parameters in the population. The λ's are scale parameters. The equations (3.3) represent relationships that hold between the values of the random variables for a randomly selected person or unit from the population. The interpretation of model (3.3) may be one or both of the following:

- The variable ξ is the theoretical variable we wish to measure and the x-variables are fallible measures that we have chosen to measure ξ. The δ's are random measurement errors in the x-variables.

- The x-variables are correlated because they have a single unobserved common factor ξ. If this is eliminated from the x's there remain only pure random errors.

Using another terminology, we say that the *partial correlation* between any pair of variables x_i and x_j, given ξ, is zero. It is in this sense we say that ξ accounts for the intercorrelations among the x's. Since the latent variable ξ is unobservable, it does not have any definite scale. Both the origin and the unit of measurement in ξ are undefined, and may be assigned arbitrary values. It is common practice to assign such values that ξ has mean zero and unit variance in the population and for the moment we shall follow this practice. The equations corresponding to Figure 3.1 are written in matrix form as

$$
\begin{pmatrix} x_1 \\ x_2 \\ x_3 \\ x_4 \end{pmatrix} = \begin{pmatrix} \lambda_1 \\ \lambda_2 \\ \lambda_3 \\ \lambda_4 \end{pmatrix} \xi + \begin{pmatrix} \delta_1 \\ \delta_2 \\ \delta_3 \\ \delta_4 \end{pmatrix} \tag{3.4}
$$

or

$$
\mathbf{x} = \boldsymbol{\lambda}\xi + \boldsymbol{\delta} \ .
$$

The model (3.4) is not directly verifiable empirically since there are more unobserved variables than observed. However, the equations, with the assumptions about uncorrelatedness and scale that we have made, imply that the covariance matrix of the observed variables is of the form

$$
\boldsymbol{\Sigma} = \boldsymbol{\lambda}\boldsymbol{\lambda}' + \boldsymbol{\Theta} = \begin{pmatrix} \lambda_1^2 + \theta_{11} & & & \\ \lambda_2\lambda_1 & \lambda_2^2 + \theta_{22} & & \\ \lambda_3\lambda_1 & \lambda_3\lambda_2 & \lambda_3^2 + \theta_{33} & \\ \lambda_4\lambda_1 & \lambda_4\lambda_2 & \lambda_4\lambda_3 & \lambda_4^2 + \theta_{44} \end{pmatrix} \tag{3.5}
$$

and this is testable empirically on the basis of a random sample of observations on the observed variables. In (3.5), θ_{ii} is the variance of δ_i, i = 1, 2 ,3 ,4 and $\boldsymbol{\Theta}$ is a diagonal matrix with diagonal elements θ_{11}, θ_{22}, θ_{33} and θ_{44}.

Equation (3.5) expresses the 10 independent elements of $\boldsymbol{\Sigma}$ as *non-linear* functions of the 8 parameters. The identification problem is the question of whether or not the parameters can be solved in terms of the σ's. For λ_1, we find

$$
\lambda_1^2 = \frac{\sigma_{21}\sigma_{31}}{\sigma_{32}} = \frac{\sigma_{21}\sigma_{41}}{\sigma_{42}} = \frac{\sigma_{31}\sigma_{41}}{\sigma_{43}} \ ,
$$

which shows that if the model holds and λ_1 is real, these ratios must be equal and non-negative. Then λ_1 is identified except for its sign. If we assume it is positive, then λ_1 is identified. Similarly, for λ_2 we find

$$
\lambda_2^2 = \frac{\sigma_{32}\sigma_{42}}{\sigma_{43}}.
$$

If the right-hand side is non-negative, λ_2 is identified because once the sign of λ_1 has been fixed, the sign of λ_2 is determined from the sign of σ_{21}, say. By similar arguments one can demonstrate that λ_3 and λ_4 are identified. The error variances θ_{ii} are then identified by

$$\theta_{ii} = \sigma_{ii} - \lambda_i^2 \ , \ i = 1, 2, 3, 4.$$

This demonstration shows that the vector $\boldsymbol{\lambda}$ is identified except for its sign and the matrix Θ is identified. If we assume that λ_1 (or any of the λ's) is positive, all parameters are identified. Then the whole model is identified and has 2 degrees of freedom.

The model defined by (3.4) is called the *congeneric measurement* model (Jöreskog, 1971). Measures $x_1, x_2, ..., x_q$ are said to be *congeneric* if their true values $\tau_1, \tau_2, ..., \tau_q$ are such that every pair of τ_i and τ_j have unit correlation. The true values in model (3.4) are $\tau_i = \lambda_i \xi = x_i - \delta_i$, $i = 1, 2, 3, 4$ and obviously these are all exactly linearly related and hence have unit correlation. The true variance in x_i is λ_i^2 and the reliability of x_i is

$$\rho_{ii} = \frac{\lambda_i^2}{\sigma_{ii}} = \frac{\lambda_i^2}{\lambda_i^2 + \theta_{ii}} = 1 - \frac{\theta_{ii}}{\lambda_i^2 + \theta_{ii}} \tag{3.6}$$

Using the terms measurement error for δ_i and reliability for ρ_{ii}, as we have done, may not be quite correct. The error δ_i is usually considered to be the sum of two uncorrelated random components s_i and e_i, where s_i is a specific factor (specific to x_i) and e_i is the true measurement error. However, unless one makes a carefully designed study with several replicate measures x_i with the same s_i, one cannot distinguish between these two components and separately estimate their variances. A consequence of this is that ρ_{ii} in (3.6) is a lower bound for the true reliability. See also Examples 6.1 and 6.2 in Chapter 6.

Parallel and tau-equivalent measures in the sense of Lord and Novick (1968) are special cases of congeneric measures. Parallel measures have equal true score variances and equal error variances, i.e.,

$$\lambda_1^2 = \ldots = \lambda_4^2 \ , \ \theta_{11} = \ldots = \theta_{44}$$

Tau-equivalent measures have equal true score variances, but possibly different error variances.

Parallel and tau-equivalent measures are directly comparable, i.e., they represent measurements on the same scale. For test scores composed of binary items this can hold only if they have the same number of items and are administered under the same time limits. Congeneric measures need not satisfy such strong restrictions. They need not even be measures consisting of items but can consist of ratings, for example, or even measurements produced by different measuring instruments.

Example 3.1: Analysis of Reader Reliability in Essay Scoring

In an experiment to establish methods of obtaining reader reliability in essay scoring, 126 examinees were given a three-part English Composition examination. Each part required the examinee to write an essay, and for each examinee, scores were obtained on the following four things: (1) the original part-1 essay, (2) a handwritten copy of the original part-1 essay, (3) a carbon copy of the handwritten copy in (2), and (4) the original part-2 essay. Scores were assigned by a group of readers using procedures designed to counterbalance certain experimental conditions. The investigator would like to know whether, on the basis of this sample of size 126, the four scores can be used interchangeably or whether scores on the copies (2) and (3) are less reliable than the originals (1) and (4).

The covariance matrix of the four measurements is given in Table 3.1. Part of this data was previously used by Votaw (1948). We will consider three analyses, namely the hypotheses that the measurements are (1) parallel, (2) tau-equivalent, and (3) congeneric, respectively. All analyses use the ML fit function. The results are summarized in Table 3.2. It is seen that the hypotheses (1) and (2) are untenable, but the hypothesis (3) has a good fit. The results under the hypothesis (3) are given in Table 3.3. Inspecting the different λ's, it is evident that these are different even if one takes their respective standard errors of estimate into account. Comparing the reliabilities in the last column, it is seen that these are high for scores (1) and (4) and low for scores (2) and (3). Thus, it seems that scores obtained from originals are more reliable than scores based on copies.

Table 3.1: Essay Scoring Data: Covariance Matrix

	x_1	x_2	x_3	x_4
ORIGPRT1	25.0704			
WRITCOPY	12.4363	28.2021		
CARBCOPY	11.7257	9.2281	22.7390	
ORIGPRT2	20.7510	11.9732	12.0692	21.8707

Table 3.2: Essay Scoring Data: Summary of Analyses

Hypothesis	d.f.	χ^2	P
Parallel	8	109.12	0.000
Tau-Equivalent	5	40.42	0.000
Congeneric	2	2.28	0.320

Table 3.3: Essay Scoring Data: Results for Congeneric Model

i	$\hat{\lambda}_i$	s.e $(\hat{\lambda}_i)$	$\hat{\rho}_{ii}$
1	4.57	0.36	0.83
2	2.68	0.45	0.25
3	2.65	0.40	0.31
4	4.54	0.33	0.94

The LISREL Input for the congeneric model

```
Analysis of Reader Reliability in Essay Scoring
DA  NI=4  NO=126
LA
ORIGPRT1  WRITCOPY  CARBCOPY  ORIGPRT2
```

```
CM
25.0704
12.4363      28.2021
11.7257       9.2281      22.7390
20.7510      11.9732      12.0692      21.8707
MO  NX=4  NK=1  LX=FR  PH=ST
LK
ESAYABIL
OU SE ND=2
```

The DA line specifies that there are four input variables and that the sample is based on 126 observations. Since MA is default on the DA line, the covariance matrix will be analyzed. The covariance matrix is read in free format. Note that a format line is not necessary when reading in free format. The MO line specifies that the model has four x-variables and one ξ-variable and that the ξ-variable is standardized (PH=ST). The specification LX=FR on the MO line is necessary since otherwise the λ's would be treated as fixed parameters. The OU line specifies that the only output requested, in addition to the standard output, is standard errors (SE). ND=2 specifies that we want only 2 decimals in the output.

The three columns of Table 3.3 can be read off directly from the output for the ML solution. The reliabilities in column 3 appear where the output says "squared multiple correlations for x-variables."

To obtain the input for the hypothesis of tau-equivalence, one needs only insert the line

```
EQ LX(1) - LX(4)
```

before the OU line. This specifies that the elements of λ should be equal. The hypothesis of parallel measurements is specified by adding one more EQ line:

```
EQ LX(1) - LX(4)
```

Table 3.4 shows parameter estimates for the congeneric measurement model obtained with different methods of estimation. Standard errors and goodness-of-fit measures are also shown in some cases. In this case, when the model fits data well, there are only small differences between methods.

3.2.2 Several Sets of Congeneric Measures

The previous model generalizes immediately to several sets of congeneric measures. If there are n sets of such measures, with m_1, m_2, ..., m_n in each set, respectively, we write

$$\mathbf{x}' = (\mathbf{x}_1', \ \mathbf{x}_2', \ \ldots, \ \mathbf{x}_n'),$$

where $\mathbf{x}_g$, g = 1, 2, ..., n, is the vector of observed variables for the g:th set. Associated with the vector $\mathbf{x}_g$ there is a true score ξ_g and vectors λ_g and δ_g defined as in Section 3.2 so that

$$\mathbf{x}_g = \lambda_g \xi_g + \delta_g \tag{3.7}$$

As before we may assume, without loss of generality, that ξ_g is scaled to zero mean and unit variance. If the different latent variables ξ_1, ξ_2, ..., ξ_n are all mutually uncorrelated, then each set of measures can be analyzed separately as in the previous section. However, in most

Table 3.4: Parameter Estimates for Congeneric Measurement Model under Different Estimation Methods

Parameter	IV	TSLS	ULS	GLS	ML
λ_1	4.49	4.59	4.50	4.58(0.36)	4.57(0.36)
λ_2	2.82	2.66	2.82	2.68(0.45)	2.68(0.45)
λ_3	2.80	2.69	2.75	2.66(0.40)	2.65(0.40)
λ_4	4.46	4.58	4.48	4.53(0.33)	4.54(0.33)
θ_1	4.95	4.04	4.79	4.11(1.27)	4.16(1.21)
θ_2	20.27	21.15	20.26	20.37(2.66)	21.04(2.71)
θ_3	14.90	15.50	15.17	15.17(2.01)	15.71(2.04)
θ_4	1.98	0.90	1.79	1.31(1.14)	1.30(1.09)
χ^2			2.31	2.33	2.28
GFI			0.998	0.991	0.991
AGFI			0.992	0.953	0.956
RMR			0.592	0.733	0.691

cases these latent variables correlate with each other and an overall analysis of the entire set of measures must be made. Let

$$q = m_1 + m_2 + \ldots + m_n \ ,$$

be the total number of measurements. Then $\mathbf{x}$ is of order q. Let $\boldsymbol{\delta}$ be the corresponding vector of error scores. Furthermore, let

$$\boldsymbol{\xi}' = (\xi_1, \xi_2, \ldots \xi_n)$$

and let $\boldsymbol{\Lambda}$ be the matrix of order q x n, partitioned as

$$\boldsymbol{\Lambda} = \begin{pmatrix} \lambda_1 & 0 & \cdots & 0 \\ 0 & \lambda_2 & \cdots & 0 \\ \cdot & \cdot & \cdots & \cdot \\ \cdot & \cdot & \cdots & \cdot \\ 0 & 0 & \cdots & \lambda_n \end{pmatrix}$$

Then $\mathbf{x}$ is represented as

$$\mathbf{x} = \boldsymbol{\Lambda}\boldsymbol{\xi} + \boldsymbol{\delta} \ . \tag{3.8}$$

Let $\boldsymbol{\Phi}$ be the correlation matrix of $\boldsymbol{\xi}$. Then the covariance matrix $\boldsymbol{\Sigma}$ of $\mathbf{x}$ is

$$\boldsymbol{\Sigma} = \boldsymbol{\Lambda}\boldsymbol{\Phi}\boldsymbol{\Lambda}' + \boldsymbol{\Theta} \ ,$$

where $\boldsymbol{\Theta}$ is a diagonal matrix of order q containing the error variances.

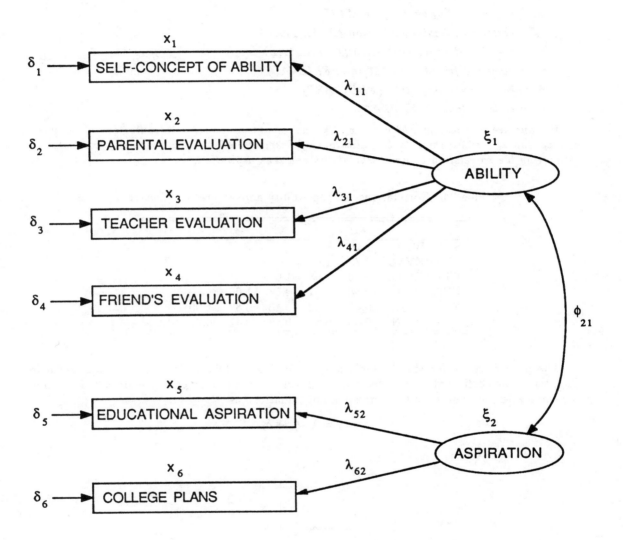

Figure 3.2: Path Diagram for Ability and Aspiration

Example 3.2: Ability and Aspiration

Calsyn and Kenny (1977) presented the correlation matrix in Table 3.5 based on 556 white eighth-grade students. The measures are

x_1 = *self-concept of ability (S-C ABIL)*

x_2 = *perceived parental evaluation (PPAREVAL)*

x_3 = *perceived teacher evaluation (PTEAEVAL)*

x_4 = *perceived friend's evaluation (PFRIEVAL)*

x_5 = *educational aspiration (EDUC ASP)*

x_6 = *college plans (COL PLAN)*

We analyze a model in which x_1, x_2, x_3 and x_4 are assumed to be indicators of "ability" and x_5 and x_6 are assumed to be indicators of "aspiration." We are primarily interested in estimating the correlation between true ability and true aspiration.

Table 3.5: Correlations Among Ability and Aspiration Measures

	x_1	x_2	x_3	x_4	x_5	x_6
S-C ABIL	1.00					
PPAREVAL	0.73	1.00				
PTEAEVAL	0.70	0.68	1.00			
PFRIEVAL	0.58	0.61	0.57	1.00		
EDUC ASP	0.46	0.43	0.40	0.37	1.00	
COL PLAN	0.56	0.52	0.48	0.41	0.72	1.00

The path diagram for this example is given in Figure 3.2. Following the rules given in Chapter 1, the coefficients associated with each arrow are those given in Figure 3.2. Following the same rules, we can write the corresponding equations as

$$x_1 = \lambda_{11}\xi_1 + \delta_1$$
$$x_2 = \lambda_{21}\xi_1 + \delta_2$$
$$x_3 = \lambda_{31}\xi_1 + \delta_3$$
$$x_4 = \lambda_{41}\xi_1 + \delta_4$$
$$x_5 = \lambda_{52}\xi_2 + \delta_5$$
$$x_6 = \lambda_{62}\xi_2 + \delta_6$$

Note that the second subscript of λ is equal to the subscript of the ξ-variable which λ is multiplied with and the first subscript is equal to the subscript of the left-hand variable.

These equations can be written in matrix form as

$$
\begin{pmatrix} x_1 \\ x_2 \\ x_3 \\ x_4 \\ x_5 \\ x_6 \end{pmatrix}
=
\begin{pmatrix}
\lambda_{11} & 0 \\
\lambda_{21} & 0 \\
\lambda_{31} & 0 \\
\lambda_{41} & 0 \\
0 & \lambda_{52} \\
0 & \lambda_{62}
\end{pmatrix}
\begin{pmatrix} \xi_1 \\ \xi_2 \end{pmatrix}
+
\begin{pmatrix} \delta_1 \\ \delta_2 \\ \delta_3 \\ \delta_4 \\ \delta_5 \\ \delta_6 \end{pmatrix}
$$

or

$$x = \Lambda\xi + \delta .$$

Note that the subscripts on λ correspond to the row and column of Λ where the coefficient appears.

This model can be easily formulated with SIMPLIS input; see Jöreskog and Sörbom (1987). To obtain the LISREL output, include a line with LISREL OPTIONS. This approach will give a solution in which the two latent variables ABILITY and ASPIRATION are in the metric of the reference variables S-C ABIL and EDUC ASP, respectively. The solution in which the two latent variables are standardized can only be obtained as a by-product. With LISREL one can obtain either one of these solutions directly.

The model includes only the three parameter matrices Λ, Φ and Θ, where Λ is a 6 x 2 matrix, Φ is a 2 x 2 correlation matrix and Θ is a 6 x 6 diagonal matrix with error variances in the diagonal. Consider first the solution in which the latent variables are in the metric of the reference variables. This is obtained by fixing a one in each column of Λ. The LISREL input is as follows:

```
ABILITY AND ASPIRATION
DA NI=6 NO=556 MA=KM
LA
*
'S-C ABIL' PPAREVAL PTEAEVAL PFRIEVAL 'EDUC ASP' 'COL PLAN'
KM SY
(6F4.2)
 100
  73 100
  70  68 100
  58  61  57 100
  46  43  40  37 100
  56  52  48  41  72 100
MO NX=6 NK=2
LK
ABILITY ASPIRATN
FR LX(2,1) LX(3,1) LX(4,1) LX(6,2)
VA 1  LX(1,1) LX(5,2)
OU SE TV RS MR FS
```

The specification MA=KM on the DA line is not really necessary. Since no standard deviations are entered, the program takes them to be ones. Therefore, if MA=KM is omitted, the program computes the covariance matrix from the input correlation matrix and the unit standard deviations and the result is identical to the input matrix.

The data for this example consists of labels for the x-variables and a correlation matrix. The labels are read in free format. The format line, i.e., the line containing an * in column 1, is not really necessary but is optional for compatibility with LISREL 6. The * signifies that labels will be read in free format, with blanks as separators. The labels which contain blanks are enclosed between single quotes.

The SY parameter on the KM line signifies that the lower half of the correlation matrix will be read with each row beginning on a new line, i.e., one must press the "RETURN" key after each row of the correlation matrix. The correlations are read according to a fixed format. The format must begin with a left parenthesis and end with a right parenthesis. Blanks anywhere within the format are ignored. Blanks may also appear before the left parenthesis. For example, the format can also be written

(6 F4 . 2)

All the parameter matrices Λ, Φ, and Θ are default on the MO line, which means that, at this stage, Λ is a full matrix of fixed zeros, Φ is a symmetric matrix with free elements, and Θ is a diagonal matrix with free diagonal elements. After the MO line the only thing that one needs to do is to specify which elements of Λ are to be estimated and which elements are to be fixed at 1. The free elements of Λ are given by the FR line and the fixed ones are given by the VA line.

The labels ABILITY and ASPIRATN are assigned to ξ_1 and ξ_2, respectively. As will be seen this makes the output much more readable. That labels for ξ-variables are to be read is signaled by an LK line followed by a format line which is optional if labels are read in free format as in this case.

Next consider the case when the two latent variables are standardized. The LISREL input for this case is as follows:

```
ABILITY AND ASPIRATION
DA NI=6 NO=556
LA
'S-C ABIL' PPAREVAL PTEAEVAL PFRIEVAL 'EDUC ASP' 'COL PLAN'
KM SY
(6F4.2)
100
  73 100
  70  68 100
  58  61  57 100
  46  43  40  37 100
  56  52  48  41  72 100
MO NX=6 NK=2 PH=ST
LK
ABILITY ASPIRATN
FR LX(1,1) LX(2,1) LX(3,1) LX(4,1) LX(5,2) LX(6,2)
OU SE TV RS MR FS
```

This input differs from the previous in three ways: PH = ST has been added on the MO line, LX(1,1) and LX(5,2) have been added on the FR line, and the VA line has been deleted. PH = ST fixes the scales for the latent variables such that Φ becomes a correlation matrix, i.e., the two latent variables become standardized. The parameters λ_{11} and λ_{51} will now be estimated instead of being fixed at 1. Note that the number of free parameters in the model remain the same.

The estimated Λ and Φ for the two solutions are shown in Table 3.6. These solutions should be regarded as being the same. They only differ in the sense that the unit of measurement in ξ_1 and ξ_2 is different.

When the scales for the latent variables are fixed by PH=ST, the solution is not unique, for each column of Λ may be multiplied by -1. For this reason, it is better to fix the scales by assigning a fixed 1 in each column of Λ, at least if good reference variables are known.

Table 3.6: The Same Solution in Two Different Scalings of the Latent Variables

	Reference Variables Solution			Standardized Solution	
$\Lambda=$	$\begin{pmatrix} 1 & 0 \\ .984 & 0 \\ .933 & 0 \\ .805 & 0 \\ 0 & 1 \\ 0 & 1.198 \end{pmatrix}$		$\Lambda=$	$\begin{pmatrix} .863 & 0 \\ .849 & 0 \\ .805 & 0 \\ .695 & 0 \\ 0 & .775 \\ 0 & .929 \end{pmatrix}$	
$\Phi=$	$\begin{pmatrix} .745 & \\ .446 & .601 \end{pmatrix}$		$\Phi=$	$\begin{pmatrix} 1 & \\ .666 & 1 \end{pmatrix}$	

We shall now describe most parts of the printed output and explain what these mean in general and how they are interpreted in this example.

The program lists all input lines in the output. This list is shown on the next page.

```
DA NI=6 NO=556
LA
*
'S-C ABIL' PPAREVAL PTEAEVAL PFRIEVAL 'EDUC ASP' 'COL PLAN'
KM SY
(6F4.2)
MO NX=6 NK=2 PH=ST
LK
ABILITY ASPIRATN
FR LX(1,1) LX(2,1) LX(3,1) LX(4,1) LX(5,2) LX(6,2)
OU SE TV RS MR FS
```

The advantage of giving this information in the printout is that it is always documented which input was used to produce the output. If something is wrong, one can see in the output what was wrong in the input. Syntax errors and other errors in the input will result in error messages being printed within the above list.

The standard output always includes the matrix to be analyzed and the parameter specifications. The matrix to be analyzed in this example comes out as

```
     COVARIANCE MATRIX TO BE ANALYZED
              S-C ABIL   PPAREVAL   PTEAEVAL   PFRIEVAL   EDUC ASP   COL PLAN
S-C ABIL        1.000
PPAREVAL         .730      1.000
PTEAEVAL         .700       .680      1.000
PFRIEVAL         .580       .610       .570      1.000
EDUC ASP         .460       .430       .400       .370      1.000
COL PLAN         .560       .520       .480       .410       .720      1.000
```

The tables of parameter specifications consist of integer matrices corresponding to the parameter matrices. In each matrix an element is an integer equal to the index of the corresponding parameter in the sequence of independent parameters. Elements corresponding to fixed parameters are zero and elements constrained to be equal have the same index value. Recall that LISREL orders the parameter matrices in the order Λ_y, Λ_x, $\mathbf{B}$, $\mathbf{\Gamma}$, $\mathbf{\Phi}$, $\mathbf{\Psi}$, Θ_ϵ, Θ_δ and the elements row-wise within matrices. In this example, only Λ_x, $\mathbf{\Phi}$ and Θ_δ are involved. The parameter specifications for the example looks as follows.

```
PARAMETER SPECIFICATIONS
   LAMBDA X
            ABILITY    ASPIRATN
S-C ABIL       1           0
PPAREVAL       2           0
PTEAEVAL       3           0
PFRIEVAL       4           0
EDUC ASP       0           5
COL PLAN       0           6
   PHI
            ABILITY    ASPIRATN
ABILITY        0
ASPIRATN       7           0
   THETA DELTA
      S-C ABIL    PPAREVAL    PTEAEVAL    PFRIEVAL    EDUC ASP    COL PLAN
         8           9          10          11          12          13
```

Since no particular method of analysis is requested on the OU line, the program will compute initial estimates by the two-stage least-squares (TSLS) method and the final solution by the maximum likelihood (ML) method. The initial estimates come out as follows:

```
INITIAL ESTIMATES (TSLS)
   LAMBDA X
            ABILITY    ASPIRATN
S-C ABIL      .866        .000
PPAREVAL      .847        .000
PTEAEVAL      .801        .000
PFRIEVAL      .702        .000
EDUC ASP      .000        .780
COL PLAN      .000        .923
   PHI
            ABILITY    ASPIRATN
ABILITY     1.000
ASPIRATN     .664      1.000
   THETA DELTA
      S-C ABIL    PPAREVAL    PTEAEVAL    PFRIEVAL    EDUC ASP    COL PLAN
        .250        .282        .359        .508        .392        .148
```

A comparison of these estimates with those of the final ML solution given on the next page reveals that they are very accurate. No difference in $\mathbf{\Lambda}$ is larger than 0.02.

In addition to the usual parameter estimates of $\mathbf{\Lambda}$, $\mathbf{\Phi}$ and $\mathbf{\Theta}$, the program gives squared multiple correlations for each observed variable separately and coefficients of determination for all the observed variables jointly. These coefficients were defined in Chapter 1.

```
LISREL ESTIMATES (MAXIMUM LIKELIHOOD)
    LAMBDA X
             ABILITY    ASPIRATN
S-C ABIL        .863        .000
PPAREVAL        .849        .000
PTEAEVAL        .805        .000
PFRIEVAL        .695        .000
EDUC ASP        .000        .775
COL PLAN        .000        .929
    PHI
             ABILITY    ASPIRATN
ABILITY       1.000
ASPIRATN       .666       1.000
    THETA DELTA
      S-C ABIL   PPAREVAL   PTEAEVAL   PFRIEVAL   EDUC ASP   COL PLAN
         .255       .279       .352       .517       .399       .137
    SQUARED MULTIPLE CORRELATIONS FOR X - VARIABLES
      S-C ABIL   PPAREVAL   PTEAEVAL   PFRIEVAL   EDUC ASP   COL PLAN
         .745       .721       .648       .483       .601       .863
    TOTAL COEFFICIENT OF DETERMINATION FOR X - VARIABLES IS    .981

    CHI-SQUARE WITH   8 DEGREES OF FREEDOM =      9.26 (P = .321)
                 GOODNESS OF FIT INDEX = .994
        ADJUSTED GOODNESS OF FIT INDEX = .985
            ROOT MEAN SQUARE RESIDUAL =       .012
```

The squared multiple correlation (SMC) for x_i is the relative amount of variance in x_i which is accounted for by the two ξ-variables jointly. The total coefficient of determination is a measure of how well the x-variables jointly serve as measurement instruments for the two ξ-variables. In this case the total coefficient of determinations is remarkably high, 0.98, indicating that the measurement model is very good. As stated in section 3.2, each δ_i in the model is the sum of two uncorrelated components, one systematic component specific to x_i and one representing pure random measurement error. The SMC is a lower bound for the reliability of the x-variable. Thus each reliability is at least as large as the SMC indicates. Of the four measures of ξ_1 (ability), x_1 (self-concept of ability) is the most reliable and of the two indicators of ξ_2 (aspiration), x_6 (college plans) is the most reliable.

The last lines of the reproduced output above give the four measures of overall fit of the whole model. For the example, all four measures of fit indicate that the model fits the data very well.

Standard errors and t-values for all the estimated parameters of the model are shown on the next page. The standard error is a measure of the precision of the parameter estimate. The t-value for a parameter is defined as the parameter estimate divided by its standard error. This can be used to examine whether the true parameter is zero. Parameters whose t-values are larger than two in magnitude are normally judged to be different from zero.

```
STANDARD ERRORS
    LAMBDA X
              ABILITY    ASPIRATN
S-C ABIL        .035        .000
PPAREVAL        .035        .000
PTEAEVAL        .036        .000
PFRIEVAL        .039        .000
EDUC ASP        .000        .040
COL PLAN        .000        .039
      PHI
              ABILITY    ASPIRATN
ABILITY         .000
ASPIRATN        .031        .000
    THETA DELTA
        S-C ABIL   PPAREVAL   PTEAEVAL   PFRIEVAL   EDUC ASP   COL PLAN
          .023       .024       .027       .035       .038       .044
T-VALUES
    LAMBDA X
              ABILITY    ASPIRATN
S-C ABIL      24.561        .000
PPAREVAL      23.958        .000
PTEAEVAL      22.115        .000
PFRIEVAL      17.996        .000
EDUC ASP        .000      19.206
COL PLAN        .000      23.571
      PHI
              ABILITY    ASPIRATN
ABILITY         .000
ASPIRATN      21.528        .000
    THETA DELTA
        S-C ABIL   PPAREVAL   PTEAEVAL   PFRIEVAL   EDUC ASP   COL PLAN
         10.908     11.549     13.070     14.877     10.453      3.151
```

Here it is seen that all *t*-values are large so that all parameters are highly significant. The correlation between true ability and true aspiration is estimated as 0.67 with a standard error of 0.03. It should be emphasized that this is not a correlation between any linear combinations of observed variables. It is the estimated correlation between two latent unobservable variables. A comparison with the observed correlations shows that the estimated correlation between ability and aspiration is higher than the correlations between any one of the observed ability measures and any one of the observed aspiration measures. These correlations underestimate the true correlation.

We now return to the detailed examination of the fit of the model. For this purpose, LISREL provides estimates of fitted residuals and standardized residuals. For our example, the fitted residuals look like this:

```
    FITTED RESIDUALS
            S-C ABIL   PPAREVAL   PTEAEVAL   PFRIEVAL   EDUC ASP   COL PLAN
S-C ABIL       .000
PPAREVAL      -.003       .000
PTEAEVAL       .005      -.004       .000
PFRIEVAL      -.020       .019       .010       .000
EDUC ASP       .014      -.009      -.016       .011       .000
COL PLAN       .026      -.006      -.018      -.020       .000       .000
```

In general, a fitted residual is the difference between the observed moment s_{ij} and the fitted moment $\hat{\sigma}_{ij}$ (moment = correlation, covariance, or moment about the zero). The size of these residuals must always be judged relative to the size of the elements of **S**. This may be easy when **S** is a correlation matrix but is more difficult when **S** is a covariance matrix or a moment matrix, especially if the size of the covariances or moments vary considerably within the matrix.

When there are many observed variables, the matrix of fitted residuals is large and will be printed in sections. It is seldom useful to inspect the matrix of fitted residuals. Therefore, this will be printed only if requested by the RS parameter on the OU line. In the standard output, an effective summary of the fitted residuals will be given. This summary consists of the largest, smallest and median residual and a stemleaf plot of all residuals. For our example, these summary statistics look like this:

SUMMARY STATISTICS FOR FITTED RESIDUALS

```
SMALLEST FITTED RESIDUAL =      -.020
  MEDIAN FITTED RESIDUAL =       .000
 LARGEST FITTED RESIDUAL =       .026
```

```
STEMLEAF PLOT
-2|00
-1|86
-0|96430000000
 0|5
 1|0149
 2|6
```

The fitted residuals depend on the metric of the observed variables and are therefore difficult to use in the assessment of fit. One way to make them independent of the metric of the observed variables is to divide them by an estimate of their asymptotic standard deviation. This gives what we call STANDARDIZED RESIDUALS:

```
    STANDARDIZED RESIDUALS
            S-C ABIL   PPAREVAL   PTEAEVAL   PFRIEVAL   EDUC ASP   COL PLAN
S-C ABIL       .000
PPAREVAL      -.611       .000
PTEAEVAL       .735      -.497       .000
PFRIEVAL     -1.912      1.694       .719       .000
EDUC ASP      1.012      -.573      -.865       .456       .000
COL PLAN      2.085      -.430     -1.127      -.949       .000       .000
```

Each standardized residual is approximately a standard normal variable. These standardized residuals are correlated from cell to cell but are nevertheless useful in judging the fit of the model and in detecting lack of fit. If the standardized residual in cell (i,j) is larger than 2.58 in magnitude this is an indication that the model does not account for s_{ij} sufficiently well.

The standardized residuals are given in matrix form only if requested by the RS parameter on the OU line; otherwise they are presented in summary form. For the example they look like this.

```
SUMMARY STATISTICS FOR STANDARDIZED RESIDUALS

SMALLEST STANDARDIZED RESIDUAL =    -1.912
  MEDIAN STANDARDIZED RESIDUAL =      .000
 LARGEST STANDARDIZED RESIDUAL =     2.085


STEMLEAF PLOT
-1|91
-0|9966540000000
 0|577
 1|07
 2|1
```

In this case there are no significant standardized residuals. If there were, these would be listed under the stemleaf plot together with the labels for the pair of variables involved.

One may request various covariances to be printed by specifying MR on the OU line. The covariances between $(\mathbf{y}, \eta)$, $(\mathbf{y}, \xi)$, $(\mathbf{x}, \eta)$, and $(\mathbf{x}, \xi)$ may be obtained. In our example, only the covariance matrix $(\mathbf{x}, \xi)$ is relevant. This is given below.

```
COVARIANCES
   X - KSI
           S-C ABIL    PPAREVAL    PTEAEVAL    PFRIEVAL    EDUC ASP    COL PLAN
ABILITY       .863        .849        .805        .695        .516        .619
ASPIRATN      .575        .566        .536        .463        .775        .929
```

In this case, since both $\mathbf{x}$ and ξ are standardized, these are correlations. In factor analysis terminology, this is called the *factor structure* as distinguished from the *factor pattern* in $\hat{\mathbf{\Lambda}}$. In general, the factor pattern is $\hat{\mathbf{\Lambda}}$ and the factor structure is $\hat{\mathbf{\Lambda}}\hat{\mathbf{\Phi}}$.

It should be pointed out that the elements of the factor pattern, i.e., the elements of $\hat{\mathbf{\Lambda}}$ are not in general correlations even if both $\mathbf{x}$ and ξ are standardized. The elements of $\hat{\mathbf{\Lambda}}$ are regression coefficients and, as such, they can exceed the absolute value one even though both $\mathbf{x}$ and ξ are standardized. The elements of the factor structure, i.e., the covariances between $\mathbf{x}$ and ξ, on the other hand, will of course be correlations if both $\mathbf{x}$ and ξ are standardized.

The estimated joint covariance matrix of $\mathbf{x}$ and ξ is (cf. Section 1.17)

$$\begin{pmatrix} \hat{\mathbf{\Lambda}}\hat{\mathbf{\Phi}}\hat{\mathbf{\Lambda}}' + \hat{\mathbf{\Theta}} & \\ \hat{\mathbf{\Phi}}\hat{\mathbf{\Lambda}}' & \hat{\mathbf{\Phi}} \end{pmatrix}$$

The upper left part of this matrix is the estimate $\hat{\mathbf{\Sigma}}$ of $\mathbf{\Sigma}$ in (3.2) after the model has been fitted. This is not printed in the output but may be saved in a file by putting SI = filename on the OU line; see Section 2.15.

For the type of models considered in this chapter, the ML method produces estimates such that
$$diag(\hat{\Sigma}) = diag(\mathbf{S}) \, ,$$
which makes $\hat{\Sigma}$ a correlation matrix if $\mathbf{S}$ is a correlation matrix. However, this does not hold for all models estimated by ML and it does not hold at all for GLS estimates.

The last part of the printed output for this example is the factor scores regressions given by the program as

```
FACTOR SCORES REGRESSIONS
            S-C ABIL   PPAREVAL   PTEAEVAL   PFRIEVAL   EDUC ASP   COL PLAN
ABILITY        .341       .307       .230       .135       .024       .085
ASPIRATN       .043       .038       .029       .017       .205       .717
```

These coefficients represent the estimated bivariate regression of ξ_1 and ξ_2 on all the observed variables and have been computed by the formula (see Lawley & Maxwell, 1971, p. 109).
$$\mathbf{A} = \hat{\Phi}\hat{\Lambda}'\hat{\Sigma}^{-1} \, .$$

The matrix $\mathbf{A}$ may be saved in a file and used to compute estimated factor scores $\hat{\xi}_\alpha$ for any person with observed scores $\mathbf{x}_\alpha$, say, by the formula
$$\hat{\xi}_\alpha = \mathbf{A}\mathbf{x}_\alpha \, .$$

When the LISREL model involves both ξ- and η-variables the factor scores regression will be computed by regressing all the ξ- and η-variables on all the observed variables.

Example 3.3: Estimating the Disattenuated Correlation

Two measures x_1 and x_2 are 15-item vocabulary tests administered under liberal time limits. Two other measures x_3 and x_4 are highly speeded 75-item vocabulary tests. The covariance matrix from Lord (1957) based on $N = 649$ examinees, is given in Table 3.7.

We estimate the disattenuated correlation between the two latent variables that the two pairs of measures represent and test whether this is one. Also, we test whether the two pairs of measures are parallel.

Table 3.7: Covariance Matrix for Four Vocabulary Measures

	x_1	x_2	x_3	x_4
x_1	86.3979			
x_2	57.7751	86.2632		
x_3	56.8651	59.3177	97.2850	
x_4	58.8986	59.6683	73.8201	97.8192

We set up the following measurement model
$$\begin{pmatrix} x_1 \\ x_2 \\ x_3 \\ x_4 \end{pmatrix} = \begin{pmatrix} \lambda_1 & 0 \\ \lambda_2 & 0 \\ 0 & \lambda_3 \\ 0 & \lambda_4 \end{pmatrix} \begin{pmatrix} \xi_1 \\ \xi_2 \end{pmatrix} + \begin{pmatrix} \delta_1 \\ \delta_2 \\ \delta_3 \\ \delta_4 \end{pmatrix}$$

with covariance matrix

$$
\Sigma = \begin{pmatrix} \lambda_1 & 0 \\ \lambda_2 & 0 \\ 0 & \lambda_3 \\ 0 & \lambda_4 \end{pmatrix} \begin{pmatrix} 1 & \phi \\ \phi & 1 \end{pmatrix} \begin{pmatrix} \lambda_1 & \lambda_2 & 0 & 0 \\ 0 & 0 & \lambda_3 & \lambda_4 \end{pmatrix} + \begin{pmatrix} \theta_1 & 0 & 0 & 0 \\ 0 & \theta_2 & 0 & 0 \\ 0 & 0 & \theta_3 & 0 \\ 0 & 0 & 0 & \theta_4 \end{pmatrix}
$$

$$
= \begin{pmatrix} \lambda_1^2 + \theta_1 & & & \\ \lambda_1\lambda_2 & \lambda_2^2 + \theta_2 & & \\ \lambda_1\lambda_3\phi & \lambda_2\lambda_3\phi & \lambda_3^2 + \theta_3 & \\ \lambda_1\lambda_4\phi & \lambda_2\lambda_4\phi & \lambda_3\lambda_4 & \lambda_2^2 + \theta_4 \end{pmatrix}
$$

This is an example of a *non-linear covariance structure* in which the ten variances and covariances of the observed variables are non-linear functions of nine parameters. Each of these nine parameters is identified in terms of the σ's, except possibly for the signs in some of them, as can easily be verified. For example, $\lambda_1^2 = (\sigma_{21}\sigma_{31}/\sigma_{32})$, $\phi^2 = (\sigma_{31}\sigma_{42}/\sigma_{21}\sigma_{43})$, $\theta_1 = \sigma_{11} - \lambda_1^2$, etc.

In this model, x_1 and x_2 are congeneric measures of ξ_1, and x_3 and x_4 are congeneric measures of ξ_2. The disattenuated correlation ϕ is the correlation between ξ_1 and ξ_2. To analyze the data, one can set up the four hypotheses:

$$
\begin{aligned}
H_1 &: \quad \lambda_1 = \lambda_2, \ \lambda_3 = \lambda_4, \ \theta_1 = \theta_2, \ \theta_3 = \theta_4, \ \phi = 1 \\
H_2 &: \quad \lambda_1 = \lambda_2, \ \lambda_3 = \lambda_4, \ \theta_1 = \theta_2, \ \theta_3 = \theta_4 \\
H_3 &: \quad \phi = 1 \\
H_4 &: \quad \lambda_1, \ \lambda_2, \ \lambda_3, \ \lambda_4, \ \theta_1, \ \theta_2, \ \theta_3, \ \theta_4, \text{ and } \phi \text{ unconstrained.}
\end{aligned}
$$

and estimate the model under each of these. Under hypotheses H_1, H_2 and H_3, the model involves *equality constraints*, imposed on the parameters of the base model H_4. All four models can be estimated in one run using stacked input. The input file is as follows: the models are estimated in the order H_4, H_3, H_2 and H_1. The covariance matrix of the four variables is in the file EX33.COV. This is rewound after each problem. Note that AD must be set off in hypotheses 1 and 3 because Φ is specified to be singular (not positive definite) in these cases.

```
ESTIMATING THE DISATTENUATED CORRELATION      HYPOTHESIS 4
DA NI=4 NO=649
CM FI=EX33.COV RE
MO NX=4 NK=2 PH=FI
FR LX 1 1 LX 2 1 LX 3 2 LX 4 2
FR PH 2 1
VA 1 PH 1 1 PH 2 2
OU SE
ESTIMATING THE DISATTENUATED CORRELATION      HYPOTHESIS 3
DA NI=4 NO=649
CM FI=EX33.COV RE
MO NX=4 NK=2 PH=FI
FR LX 1 1 LX 2 1 LX 3 2 LX 4 2
VA 1 PH 1 1 PH 2 1 PH 2 2
OU SE AD=OFF
```

```
ESTIMATING THE DISATTENUATED CORRELATION     HYPOTHESIS 2
DA NI=4 NO=649
CM FI=EX33.COV RE
MO NX=4 NK=2 PH=FI
FR LX 1 1 LX 2 1 LX 3 2 LX 4 2
FR PH 2 1
VA 1 PH 1 1 PH 2 2
EQ LX 1 1 LX 2 1
EQ TD 1 TD 2
EQ LX 3 2 LX 4 2
EQ TD 3 TD 4
OU SE
ESTIMATING THE DISATTENUATED CORRELATION     HYPOTHESIS 1
DA NI=4 NO=649
CM FI=EX33.COV
MO NX=4 NK=2 PH=FI
FR LX 1 1 LX 2 1 LX 3 2 LX 4 2
VA 1 PH 1 1 PH 2 1 PH 2 2
EQ LX 1 1 LX 2 1
EQ TD 1 TD 2
EQ LX 3 2 LX 4 2
EQ TD 3 TD 4
OU SE AD=OFF
```

The results are shown in Table 3.8. Each hypothesis is tested against the general alternative that Σ is unconstrained. To consider various hypotheses that can be tested, the four χ^2 values of Table 3.8 are recorded in a 2 x 2 table as in Table 3.9. Test of H_1 against H_2 gives $\chi^2 = 35.40$ with 1 degree of freedom. An alternative test is H_3 against H_4, which gives $\chi^2 = 35.51$ with 1 degree of freedom. Thus, regardless of whether we treat the two pairs of measures as parallel or congeneric, the hypothesis $\phi = 1$ is rejected. There is strong evidence that the unspeeded and speeded measures do not measure the same trait. The hypothesis that the two pairs of measures are parallel can also be tested by means of Table 3.9. This gives $\chi^2 = 1.12$ or $\chi^2 = 1.23$ with 4 degrees of freedom, depending on whether we assume $\phi = 1$ or $\phi \neq 1$. Thus we cannot reject the hypothesis that the two pairs of measures are parallel. It appears that H_2 is the most reasonable of the four hypotheses. The maximum likelihood estimate of ϕ under H_2 is $\hat{\phi} = 0.899$ with a standard error of 0.019. An approximate 95% confidence interval for ϕ is $0.86 < \phi < 0.94$. The substantive matter is discussed further in Jöreskog (1974).

Table 3.8: Four Vocabulary Measures: Summary of Analyses

Hypothesis	No.par.	χ^2	d.f.	P
H_1	4	37.33	6	0.00
H_2	5	1.93	5	0.86
H_3	8	36.21	2	0.00
H_4	9	0.70	1	0.40

Table 3.9: Four Vocabulary Measures: Test of Hypotheses

	Parallel	Congeneric	
$\phi = 1$	$\chi_6^2 = 37.33$	$\chi_2^2 = 36.21$	$\chi_4^2 = 1.12$
$\phi \neq 1$	$\chi_5^2 = 1.93$	$\chi_1^2 = 0.70$	$\chi_4^2 = 1.23$
	$\chi_1^2 = 35.40$	$\chi_1^2 = 35.51$	

The subscripts on χ^2 denote degrees of freedom

3.3   Confirmatory Factor Analysis

It is important to distinguish between exploratory and confirmatory analysis. In an exploratory analysis, one wants to explore the empirical data to discover and detect characteristic features and interesting relationships without imposing any definite model on the data. An exploratory analysis may be structure generating, model generating and hypothesis generating. In confirmatory analysis, on the other hand, one builds a model assumed to describe, explain or account for the empirical data in terms of relatively few parameters. The model is based on *a priori* information about the data structure in the form of a specified theory or hypothesis, a given classificatory design for items or subtests according to objective features of content and format, known experimental conditions, or knowledge from previous studies based on extensive data.

Exploratory factor analysis is a technique often used to detect and assess latent sources of variation and covariation in observed measurements. It is widely recognized that exploratory factor analysis can be quite useful in the early stages of experimentation or test development. Thurstone's (1938) primary mental abilities, French's (1951) factors in aptitude and achievement tests and Guilford's (1956) structure of intelligence are good examples of this. The results of an exploratory analysis may have heuristic and suggestive value and may generate hypotheses which are capable of more objective testing by other multivariate methods. As more knowledge is gained about the nature of social and psychological measurements, however, exploratory factor analysis may not be a useful tool and may even become a hindrance.

Most studies are to some extent both exploratory and confirmatory since they involve some variables of known and other variables of unknown composition. The former should be chosen with great care in order that as much information as possible about the latter may be extracted. It is highly desirable that a hypothesis which has been suggested by mainly exploratory procedures should subsequently be confirmed, or disproved, by obtaining new data and subjecting these to more rigorous statistical techniques. Although LISREL is most useful in confirmatory studies, it can also be used to do exploratory analysis by means of a sequence of confirmatory analyses. It must be emphasized, however, that one must have at least a tentative theory or hypothesis to start out with.

The basic idea of factor analysis is the following. For a given set of response variables x_1, ..., x_q one wants to find a set of underlying latent factors ξ_1, ..., ξ_n, fewer in number than the observed variables. These latent factors are supposed to account for the intercorrelations of the response variables in the sense that when the factors are partialed out from the observed variables, there should no longer remain any correlations between these. This leads to the model, see Jöreskog (1979),

$$\mathbf{x} = \Lambda\boldsymbol{\xi} + \boldsymbol{\delta} \qquad (3.9)$$

where $E(\boldsymbol{\xi}) = 0$ and $E(\boldsymbol{\delta}) = 0$, $\boldsymbol{\delta}$ being uncorrelated with $\boldsymbol{\xi}$. Let $\boldsymbol{\Phi} = E(\boldsymbol{\xi}\boldsymbol{\xi}')$ which may be taken as a correlation matrix and $\boldsymbol{\Theta} = E(\boldsymbol{\delta}\boldsymbol{\delta}')$ which is diagonal. Then the covariance matrix $\boldsymbol{\Sigma}$ of $\mathbf{x}$ becomes

$$\boldsymbol{\Sigma} = \Lambda\boldsymbol{\Phi}\Lambda' + \boldsymbol{\Theta} \ . \qquad (3.10)$$

If $(q - n)^2 < q + n$, this relationship can be tested statistically, unlike (3.9) which involves hypothetical variables and cannot be verified directly. When $n > 1$ there is an indeterminacy in (3.10) arising from the fact that a nonsingular linear transformation of $\boldsymbol{\xi}$ changes Λ and in general also $\boldsymbol{\Phi}$ but leaves $\boldsymbol{\Sigma}$ unchanged. The usual way to deal with this indeterminacy in exploratory factor analysis (see, e.g., Lawley and Maxwell, 1971, or Jöreskog, 1967) is to choose $\boldsymbol{\Phi} = \mathbf{I}$ and $\Lambda'\boldsymbol{\Theta}\Lambda$ or $\Lambda'\Lambda$ to be diagonal and to estimate the parameters in Λ and $\boldsymbol{\Theta}$ subject to these conditions. This leads to an arbitrary set of factors which may then be subjected to a rotation or a linear transformation to another set of factors which can be given a more meaningful interpretation. The rotation is usually guided by Thurstone's (1947) principle of simple structure which states that in each column of Λ there should only be a relatively small number of large loadings and a relatively large number of small loadings. Efficient computational procedures for estimating the unrotated factor loadings by ULS, GLS or ML have been described by Jöreskog (1977), and a computer program EFAP by Jöreskog and Sörbom (1980a) is available for this. Analytical procedures for rotation to simple structure are described by Harman (1967).

In a confirmatory factor analysis, the investigator has such knowledge about the factorial nature of the variables that he/she is able to specify at least n^2 independent conditions on Λ and $\boldsymbol{\Phi}$. The most common way of doing this, assuming that $\boldsymbol{\Phi}$ is an unconstrained correlation matrix, is to set at least $n - 1$ zeros in each column of Λ. This is a necessary condition but it is not sufficient; see Section 3.1. When there are many variables it usually suffices that the zeros are distributed over the rows of Λ in such a way that Λ has full column rank. We shall illustrate confirmatory factor analysis by means of a detailed example. In particular, this example illustrates the assessment of model fit and the use of the model modification index.

Example 3.4: Nine Psychological Variables - A Confirmatory Factor Analysis

Holzinger and Swineford (1939) collected data on twenty-six psychological tests administered to 145 seventh- and eighth-grade children in the Grant-White school in Chicago. Nine of these tests were selected and for this example it was hypothesized that these measure three common factors: visual perception (P), verbal ability (V) and speed (S) such that the first three variables measure P, the next three measures V, and the last three measures S. The nine selected variables and their intercorrelations are given in Table 3.10. A path diagram is shown in Figure 3.3.

We want to examine the fit of the model implied by the stated hypothesis. If the model does not fit the data well, we want to suggest an alternative model that fits the data better.

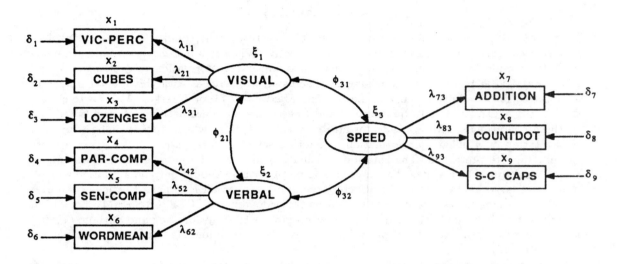

Figure 3.3: Confirmatory Factor Analysis Model for Nine Psychological Variables

Table 3.10: Correlation Matrix for Nine Psychological Variables

VIS-PERC	1.000								
CUBES	0.318	1.000							
LOZENGES	0.436	0.419	1.000						
PAR-COMP	0.335	0.234	0.323	1.000					
SEN-COMP	0.304	0.157	0.283	0.722	1.000				
WORDMEAN	0.326	0.195	0.350	0.714	0.685	1.000			
ADDITION	0.116	0.057	0.056	0.203	0.246	0.170	1.000		
COUNTDOT	0.314	0.145	0.229	0.095	0.181	0.113	0.585	1.000	
S-C-CAPS	0.489	0.239	0.361	0.309	0.345	0.280	0.408	0.512	1.000

The problem can easily be formulated with SIMPLIS input; see Jöreskog and Sörbom (1986). The LISREL input for this analysis is as follows

```
NINE PSYCHOLOGICAL VARIABLES - A CONFIRMATORY FACTOR ANALYSIS
DA NI=9 NO=145 MA=KM
LA
VIS-PERC CUBES LOZENGES PAR-COMP SEN-COMP WORDMEAN ADDITION
COUNTDOT S-C-CAPS
KM FI=EX34.COR
MO NX=9 NK=3 PH=ST
LK
VISUAL VERBAL SPEED
PA LX
3(1 0 0) 3(0 1 0) 3(0 0 1)
PL LX(9,1)
OU SE TV MI
```

The first 9 lines are similar to Example 3.2. Both labels and correlations are read in free format without format lines. The most interesting part of the input is in the lines following labels for the latent variables. Rather than listing all free elements of Λ on an FR line, as we did in the previous example, we enter a pattern matrix of zeros and ones. This is convenient in this case as the first three rows of the pattern matrix are all equal to 1 0 0, the next three rows are all equal to 0 1 0, etc. One line contains the whole pattern matrix of order 9 × 3. The next line requests the program to plot the fitting function (ML in this case) against the parameter λ_{91}. This plot will be discussed later. The OU line requests modification indices (MI) among other things.

The ML solution produced by this input is given below. This looks reasonable except for the fact that χ^2 is rather large. We must therefore examine the fit in more detail.

LISREL ESTIMATES (MAXIMUM LIKELIHOOD)

LAMBDA X

	VISUAL	VERBAL	SPEED
VIS-PERC	.672	.000	.000
CUBES	.513	.000	.000
LOZENGES	.684	.000	.000
PAR-COMP	.000	.867	.000
SEN-COMP	.000	.830	.000
WORDMEAN	.000	.826	.000
ADDITION	.000	.000	.660
COUNTDOT	.000	.000	.801
S-C-CAPS	.000	.000	.677

PHI

	VISUAL	VERBAL	SPEED
VISUAL	1.000		
VERBAL	.543	1.000	
SPEED	.509	.318	1.000

THETA DELTA

VIS-PERC	CUBES	LOZENGES	PAR-COMP	SEN-COMP	WORDMEAN
.548	.737	.532	.248	.311	.318

```
THETA DELTA
    ADDITION    COUNTDOT    S-C-CAPS
      .564        .359        .542
SQUARED MULTIPLE CORRELATIONS FOR X - VARIABLES
    VIS-PERC    CUBES      LOZENGES    PAR-COMP    SEN-COMP    WORDMEAN
      .452       .263        .468        .752        .689        .682
SQUARED MULTIPLE CORRELATIONS FOR X - VARIABLES
    ADDITION    COUNTDOT    S-C-CAPS
      .436        .641        .458
TOTAL COEFFICIENT OF DETERMINATION FOR X - VARIABLES IS     .982

   CHI-SQUARE WITH  24 DEGREES OF FREEDOM IS      52.63 (P =  .001)
             GOODNESS OF FIT INDEX IS     .928
          ADJUSTED GOODNESS OF FIT INDEX IS  .866
          ROOT MEAN SQUARE RESIDUAL IS       .076
```

The summary statistics for standardized residuals are shown below:

```
SUMMARY STATISTICS FOR STANDARDIZED RESIDUALS

SMALLEST STANDARDIZED RESIDUAL =    -3.117
  MEDIAN STANDARDIZED RESIDUAL =      .000
 LARGEST STANDARDIZED RESIDUAL =     5.007


STEMLEAF PLOT
-3|10
-2|910
-1|984311
-0|8766411000000000000
 0|44459
 1|0028
 2|1239
 3|
 4|7
 5|0


LARGEST NEGATIVE STANDARDIZED RESIDUALS
RESIDUAL FOR ADDITION AND LOZENGES =   -3.117
RESIDUAL FOR COUNTDOT AND PAR-COMP =   -3.013
RESIDUAL FOR S-C-CAPS AND COUNTDOT =   -2.886


LARGEST POSITIVE STANDARDIZED RESIDUALS
RESIDUAL FOR COUNTDOT AND ADDITION =    5.007
RESIDUAL FOR S-C-CAPS AND VIS-PERC =    4.650
RESIDUAL FOR S-C-CAPS AND SEN-COMP =    2.904
```

There are 6 large standardized residuals. These do not give a clear-cut suggestion of what is wrong with the model. Note, however, that the variable S-C-CAPS is involved in 3 of the 6 largest standardized residuals.

How should the model be modified to fit the data better? The table of modification indices gives a straightforward answer.

```
MODIFICATION INDICES AND ESTIMATED CHANGE
    MODIFICATION INDICES FOR LAMBDA X
              VISUAL      VERBAL       SPEED
VIS-PERC       .000        .268        3.918
CUBES          .000        .665         .968
LOZENGES       .000        .032        1.346
PAR-COMP       .003        .000         .694
SEN-COMP       .342        .000        2.059
WORDMEAN       .277        .000         .303
ADDITION     10.502        .178         .000
COUNTDOT      2.738      10.078         .000
S-C-CAPS     24.736      10.040         .000
    ESTIMATED CHANGE FOR LAMBDA X
              VISUAL      VERBAL       SPEED
VIS-PERC       .000        .067         .251
CUBES          .000       -.094        -.116
LOZENGES       .000        .023        -.149
PAR-COMP       .005        .000        -.056
SEN-COMP      -.052        .000         .098
WORDMEAN       .047        .000        -.038
ADDITION      -.367        .035         .000
COUNTDOT      -.204       -.278         .000
S-C-CAPS       .565        .265         .000
```

```
NO NON-ZERO MODIFICATION INDICES FOR PHI
NO NON-ZERO MODIFICATION INDICES FOR THETA DELTA
```

```
        MAXIMUM MODIFICATION INDEX IS   24.74 FOR ELEMENT ( 9, 1) OF LAMBDA X
```

The largest modification index is 24.74 and occurs for λ_{91}. This is highly significant. Recall that the modification index is approximately a χ^2 with one degree of freedom. This modification index suggests directly that λ_{91} should be set free and predicts that, if this is done, the overall χ^2 will decrease by approximately 24.74 and that λ_{91} will be approximately 0.57.

The plot in Figure 3.4 gives more precise results. The minimum is located approximately at $\lambda_{91} = 0.46$ and $\chi^2 = 28.87$. The points in this plot represent the concentrated fit function (in this case χ^2); i.e., for each value of λ_{91}, the fit function is minimized with respect to all the free parameters of the model. In this case, when λ_{91} is fixed at zero in the original model and the modification index suggests that λ_{91} will move to 0.565, the scale for the abscissa is chosen so that 0.565 is in the middle and 0.000 is at the left end. The range of the abscissa is divided into 11 equidistant intervals so that 11 points are plotted, 5 on each side of the midpoint. The amount of computation involved in producing the plot is almost equivalent to running 11 LISREL problems with the same data and model. Therefore, this kind of plot is not feasible for large problems unless LISREL is executed on a fast computer.

If the model is true, the sample size large and the asymptotic theory valid, the plotted curve should be quadratic around the minimum.

The input for the modified model is as follows:

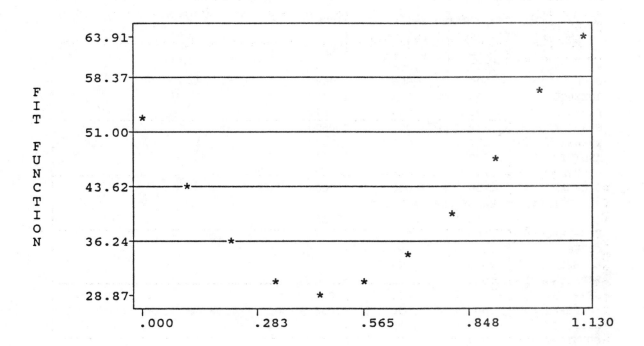

Figure 3.4: Parameter Plot for Nine Psychological Variables: LX(9,1) Fixed

```
NINE PSYCHOLOGICAL VARIABLES - A CONFIRMATORY FACTOR ANALYSIS    SECOND RUN
DA NI=9 NO=145 MA=KM
LA
VIS-PERC CUBES LOZENGES PAR-COMP SEN-COMP WORDMEAN ADDITION
COUNTDOT S-C-CAPS
KM FI=EX34.COR
MO NX=9 NK=3 PH=ST
LK
VISUAL VERBAL SPEED
PA LX
3(1 0 0) 3(0 1 0) 3(0 0 1)
FR LX(9,1)
PL LX(9,1)
OU SE TV MI
```

All we have done is to add the line

```
FR LX(9,1)
```

The overall goodness-of-fit measure for the modified model is $\chi^2 = 28.86$ with 23 degrees of freedom. The difference between the previous χ^2 and this one is $52.63 - 28.86 = 23.77$ which is reasonably close to the value 24.74 predicted by the modification index. The reason for the discrepancy is that the fit function is not quite quadratic in a region of the parameter space around the first solution. The modification index is based on a quadratic approximation of the fit function.

Free parameters may also be plotted as shown in the second run. The parameter plot from the second run is shown in Figure 3.5.

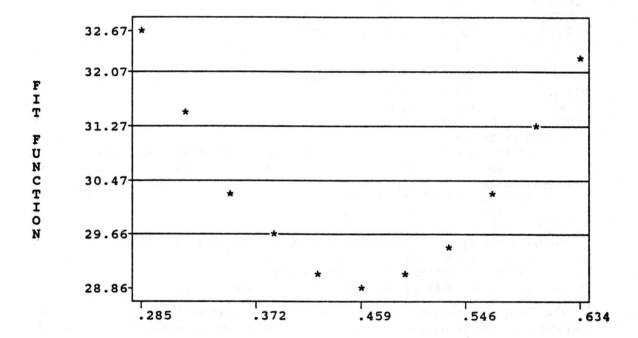

Figure 3.5: Parameter Plot for Nine Psychological Variables: LX(9,1) Free

In this case the minimum value is known and so is the standard error. Therefore the abscissa is chosen as $\hat{\lambda}_{91} \pm 1.96 \text{SE}(\hat{\lambda}_{91})$. The range of the ordinate should be approximately 3.84, the 5% significance level of χ^2 with one degree of freedom. If everything is correct the curve should be symmetric around the minimum. Deviations from this symmetry indicate either that the model is misspecified or the asymptotic normality of parameter estimates does not hold. The latter may be due to small sample size.

```
LISREL ESTIMATES (MAXIMUM LIKELIHOOD)
    LAMBDA X
              VISUAL     VERBAL      SPEED
VIS-PERC      .708       .000        .000
CUBES         .483       .000        .000
LOZENGES      .649       .000        .000
PAR-COMP      .000       .868        .000
SEN-COMP      .000       .830        .000
WORDMEAN      .000       .825        .000
ADDITION      .000       .000        .675
COUNTDOT      .000       .000        .867
S-C-CAPS      .459       .000        .412
    PHI
              VISUAL     VERBAL      SPEED
VISUAL        1.000
VERBAL        .558       1.000
SPEED         .392       .219        1.000
    THETA DELTA
         VIS-PERC    CUBES      LOZENGES    PAR-COMP    SEN-COMP    WORDMEAN
           .498       .767        .578        .247        .311        .319
    THETA DELTA
         ADDITION    COUNTDOT   S-C-CAPS
           .545       .248        .471

    CHI-SQUARE WITH  23 DEGREES OF FREEDOM =     28.86 (P =   .185)
                   GOODNESS OF FIT INDEX = .958
           ADJUSTED GOODNESS OF FIT INDEX = .917
                  ROOT MEAN SQUARE RESIDUAL =        .045
```

The substantive interpretation of the results of these analyses may be as follows. The first factor is "visual perception" as represented by the first three variables containing spatial problems with geometrical configurations. The third factor is a "speed" factor supposed to measure the ability to perform very simple tasks quickly and accurately. However, unlike the two measures "Addition" and "Counting dots" which are purely numerical, variable nine, "Straight-curved capitals" requires the ability to distinguish between capital letters which contain curved parts (like P) from those which contain only straight lines (like L) and to do this quickly and accurately. It is therefore conceivable that "Straight-curved capitals" contains a component which is correlated with "visual perception" as represented in this data and also that it contains a component of "speed". So the variable "Straight-curved capitals" is a composite measure unlike all the other measures in this example, which are all pure measures.

Chapter 4

CAUSAL MODELS FOR DIRECTLY OBSERVED VARIABLES

4.1 The LISREL Submodel 2

In this chapter we shall consider various types of models which all fit within the LISREL Submodel 2. These models involve the variables

$$
\begin{aligned}
\text{Jointly dependent variables:} \quad \mathbf{y'} &= (y_1, y_2, \ldots, y_p) \\
\text{Explanatory variables:} \quad \mathbf{x'} &= (x_1, x_2, \ldots, x_q) \\
\text{Error variables:} \quad \boldsymbol{\zeta'} &= (\zeta_1, \zeta_2, \ldots, \zeta_p)
\end{aligned}
$$

In this submodel there are no latent variables but there are two kinds of directly observed or measured variables: y's and x's. The y's are to be explained by the model; i.e., variation and covariation among the y-variables is to be accounted for by the x-variables. The x-variables may be random variables or a set of fixed values.

The general form of this submodel is

$$ \mathbf{y} = \boldsymbol{\alpha} + \mathbf{By} + \boldsymbol{\Gamma}\mathbf{x} + \boldsymbol{\zeta} \tag{4.1} $$

with the assumptions that

(i) $(\mathbf{I} - \mathbf{B})$ is nonsingular

(ii) $E(\boldsymbol{\zeta}) = 0$, where E is the expected value operator

(iii) $\boldsymbol{\zeta}$ is uncorrelated with $\mathbf{x}$

If a covariance or correlation matrix is analyzed, $\boldsymbol{\alpha}$ in (4.1) may be omitted. See Chapter 10 on how to use $\boldsymbol{\alpha}$ as a real parameter vector.

The $\boldsymbol{\zeta}$-variables are random *disturbance terms*, sometimes called *errors in equations*. They represent an aggregate of all known and unknown influences of the y's which are uncorrelated with the x's.

105

The parameter matrices involved in this model are

$$\mathbf{B}, \mathbf{\Gamma}, \text{and } \mathbf{\Psi} = Cov(\zeta) \, .$$

In this submodel, the matrix $\mathbf{\Phi} = \mathrm{Cov}(\mathbf{x})$ is assumed to be an unconstrained free covariance matrix. If $\mathbf{x}$ is fixed, $\mathbf{\Phi}$ is to be interpreted as the usual matrix of mean sums of squares and cross products formed from the set of fixed values of $\mathbf{x}$. The matrix $\mathbf{\Phi}$ is automatically handled by the program. The estimate of $\mathbf{\Phi}$, under all estimation methods, is taken to be equal to $\mathbf{S}_{xx}$, the observed covariance matrix of $\mathbf{x}$.

Equation (4.1) is called the *structural equation* which should be distinguished from the *reduced form equation*

$$\mathbf{y} = \mathbf{A}\alpha + \mathbf{A}\mathbf{\Gamma}\mathbf{x} + \mathbf{A}\zeta \tag{4.2}$$

where $\mathbf{A} = (\mathbf{I} - \mathbf{B})^{-1}$. Equation (4.2) is obtained from (4.1) by solving for $\mathbf{y}$.

The reduced form equation (4.2) is the regression of $\mathbf{y}$ on $\mathbf{x}$, in contrast to the structural equation (4.1), where each equation is not necessarily a regression equation because the random disturbance term ζ_i in the i:th equation is not necessarily uncorrelated with all the y-variables appearing on the right in that equation.

The covariance matrix $\mathbf{\Sigma}$ [(p + q) × (p + q)] of $(\mathbf{y}', \mathbf{x}')$ is (cf. (1.4))

$$\mathbf{\Sigma} = Cov \left(\begin{array}{c} \mathbf{y} \\ \mathbf{x} \end{array} \right) = \left(\begin{array}{cc} \mathbf{A}\mathbf{\Gamma}\mathbf{\Phi}\mathbf{\Gamma}'\mathbf{A}' + \mathbf{A}\mathbf{\Psi}\mathbf{A}' & \\ \mathbf{\Phi}\mathbf{\Gamma}'\mathbf{A}' & \mathbf{\Phi} \end{array} \right) \tag{4.3}$$

A special case of Submodel 2 is when $\mathbf{B} = \mathbf{0}$, which is the default value for $\mathbf{B}$ in LISREL. Then (4.1) and (4.2) are identical and each equation in (4.1) represents a real regression equation. Such models will be considered in Section 4.2.

Another special case of Submodel 2 is when $\mathbf{B}$ is *sub-diagonal* (or when the y-variables can be ordered so that $\mathbf{B}$ becomes sub-diagonal) and $\mathbf{\Psi}$ is diagonal. Then (4.1) is a *recursive system*. In methodological terms the application of such models is usually called path analysis. This will be considered in section 4.3.

If the equations in (4.1) cannot be ordered such that $\mathbf{B}$ becomes subdiagonal, the system is said to be *non-recursive*. Such models are common in econometrics where they are usually called *interdependent systems* or *simultaneous equations*. Examples of such models will be given in Section 4.4.

Figures 4.1 - 4.4 illustrate general forms of regression models, recursive models and non-recursive models.

4.2   Regression Models

4.2.1   A Single Regression Equation

A regression equation

$$y = \alpha + \gamma_1 x_1 + \gamma_2 x_2 + \ldots + \gamma_q x_q + \zeta \tag{4.4}$$

is an equation in which the random error term ζ is uncorrelated with the explanatory variables x_1, x_2, ..., x_q. If the x-variables are fixed, it is assumed that the distribution of ζ does not depend on the values of x_1, x_2, ..., x_q.

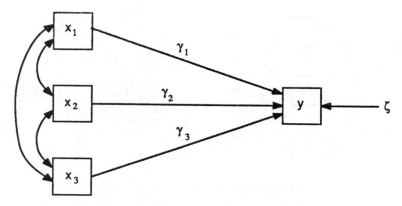

Figure 4.1: A Single Regression Equation

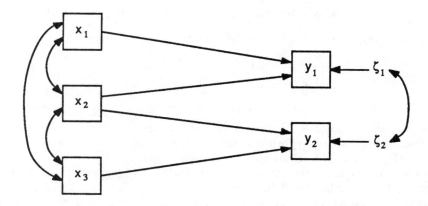

Figure 4.2: Bivariate Regression

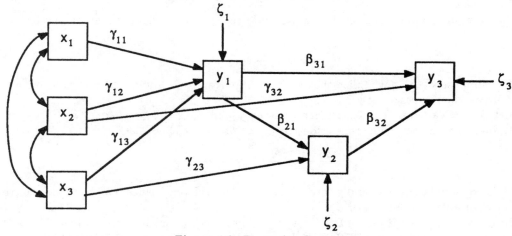

Figure 4.3: Recursive System

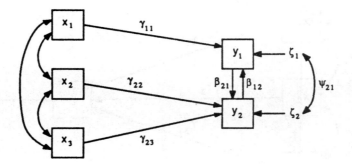

Figure 4.4: Non-recursive System

If we write (4.4) for the i:th case (observation, individual, sample unit) as

$$y_i = \alpha + \gamma_1 x_{i1} + \gamma_2 x_{i2} + \ldots + \gamma_q x_{iq} + \zeta_i \; ,$$

the assumptions of regression analysis can be stated as

$$E(\zeta_i \mid \mathbf{X}) = 0$$

$$E(\zeta_i \zeta_j \mid \mathbf{X}) = \psi \text{ if } i = j \text{ and } = 0 \text{ if } i \neq j$$

$$rank(\mathbf{X}) = q < N$$

where $\mathbf{X}$ is the matrix of order $N \times q$ formed from the observed values $x_{im}, i = 1, 2, \ldots, N, m = 1, 2, \ldots, q$. For formal tests of hypotheses, an additional assumption is usually made, namely that ζ_i is normally distributed. E denotes conditional expectation.

The error term ζ is an aggregate of all variables influencing y but not included in the relationship. The uncorrelatedness between ζ and the x-variables is a crucial assumption. Studies should be planned and designed so that this assumption is met. Failure to observe this may lead to considerable bias in estimated γ-coefficients. This is sometimes called *omitted variables bias.*

Suppose, for example, that both x_1 and x_2 influence y so that the true regression relationship is

$$y = \gamma_1 x_1 + \gamma_2 x_2 + \zeta \; .$$

But suppose we do not realize that x_2 is an important determinant of y so that we set out to estimate the regression of y on x_1.

Let $\phi_{11} = \text{Var}(x_1)$. The covariance between y and x_1 is $\gamma_1 \phi_{11} + \gamma_2 \phi_{21}$, where ϕ_{21} is the covariance of x_1 and x_2. The regression coefficient of y on x_1 becomes

$$\frac{\gamma_1 \phi_{11} + \gamma_2 \phi_{21}}{\phi_{11}} = \gamma_1 + \frac{\gamma_2 \phi_{21}}{\phi_{11}} \; ,$$

which is not equal to γ_1 if x_1 and x_2 are correlated. The difference (bias) can be made arbitrarily large by suitable choice of γ_2 or ϕ_{21}.

Regression analysis is one of the most widely used techniques in the social as well as other sciences; see, e.g., Johnston (1972), Goldberger (1964), and Draper and Smith (1967).

As an example of how to use LISREL to estimate a single regression equation consider the following example from Goldberger (1964), p.187.

Example 4.1: Regression of GNP

Goldberger (1964, p.187) presented the following data (Table 4.1) on y = gross national product in billions of dollars, x_1 = labor inputs in millions of man-years, x_2 = real capital in billions of dollars, and x_3 = the time in years measured from 1928. The data consist of 23 annual observations for the United States during 1929-1941 and 1946-1955.

Table 4.1: Data for Regression of GNP

Year	x_1	x_2	x_3	y
1929	47	54	1	142
1930	43	59	2	127
1931	39	57	3	118
1932	34	48	4	98
1933	34	36	5	94
1934	36	24	6	102
1935	38	19	7	116
1936	41	18	8	128
1937	42	22	9	140
1938	37	24	10	131
1939	40	23	11	143
1940	42	27	12	157
1941	47	36	13	182
1946	51	9	18	209
1947	53	25	19	214
1948	53	39	20	225
1949	50	51	21	221
1950	52	62	22	243
1951	54	75	23	257
1952	54	94	24	265
1953	55	108	25	276
1954	52	118	26	271
1955	54	124	27	291

One way to estimate a regression equation is to use PRELIS or any other program to compute the covariance matrix first and then use this in SIMPLIS to estimate the regression. One advantage with PRELIS is that one can take missing values and other data problems into account when computing the covariance matrix.

Using LISREL, one can estimate the regression directly from raw data. The LISREL input file is

```
DA NI=4
LA
GNP LABOR CAPITAL TIME
RA FI=EX41.DAT
MO NY=1 NX=3
OU SE TV
```

The output file reveals that the TSLS-solution and the ML-solution produced by LISREL are identical. In fact all methods in LISREL will produce the same solution, namely the classical ordinary least-squares (OLS) solution. This is a consequence of the fact that, as a LISREL model, a single regression equation is a just-identified model which fits the data perfectly in the sense fit is measured in LISREL. To examine the model fit in another sense, one should inspect the estimated error terms ζ_i for each case to see if there are indications of outliers or other forms of non-normality. This cannot be done with LISREL, however.

To determine the significance of each explanatory variable, one examines the estimated regression coefficients in relation to their standard errors or one simply looks at the t-values. A formal test of the significance of the whole regression equation, i.e., a test of the hypothesis that all γ's are zero, can be obtained by computing

$$F = \frac{R^2/q}{(1 - R^2)/(N - q - 1)} \tag{4.5}$$

where R^2 is the squared multiple correlation listed in the output file, N is the total sample size and q is the number of genuine x-variables. F is used as an F-statistic with q and N - q - 1 degrees of freedom. For our example, $R^2 = 0.997$ and $F = 2104.8$ with 3 and 19 degrees of freedom. All regression coefficients are highly significant.

The regression model (4.4) is scale-invariant in the following sense. If y is replaced by $y^* = c_0 y$ and x_i replaced by $x_i^* = c_i x_i, i = 1, 2, ..., q$, where the c's are arbitrary non-zero constants, the analysis of these scaled variables will yield regression coefficients

$$\hat{\gamma}_i^* = (c_0/c_i)\hat{\gamma}_i.$$

The standard error will change similarly but the t-values are invariant under such scalings of the variables.

To estimate the constant intercept term α in (4.4), one can either add AL=FR on the MO line as in Chapter 10 or one can analyze the augmented moment matrix instead of the covariance matrix. In the latter case add MA=AM (Augmented Moment Matrix) on the DA line and change NX=3 to NX=4 on the MO line. The program will then automatically add the variable CONST as the last variable and estimate the coefficient α as the last γ (γ_4 in this case). The variable CONST is a "variable" on which every case has the value 1.

4.2.2 Stepwise Regression

Regression analysis is often used as a part of a model building process, in which one wants to determine an equation for y such that only the most significant determinants of $x_1, x_2, ..., x_q$ are included. This is often done by some form of stepwise procedure; see Draper and Smith

(1967). There is no unique statistical procedure for doing this, however, and personal judgment is necessary.

One way to do stepwise regression with LISREL is to start with an equation in which all γ's are zero and add successively the one particular x-variable which improves fit maximally. The fit can be measured by χ^2 and the improvement in fit by the modification index (MI). If a correlation matrix is analyzed and the GLS fit function is used, the MI's will be exact χ^2-differences. Although it is often a good idea to run each step separately and inspect the results after each step, the procedure can be made fully automatic using the automatic model modification option (AM). Each MI is then used as a χ^2 with one degree of freedom and variables are added to the regression equation until the largest MI is no longer significant. The significance level in percent is specified by the SL parameter. The default value for SL is 1.

Example 4.2: Stepwise Regression

Dixon (1981) gives the following covariance matrix (Table 4.2) for the Werner Blood Chemistry Data based on N = 180.

The variables are

$y = Cholesterol$ $x_1 = Age$ $x_2 = Height$ $x_3 = Weight$
$x_4 = Birthpill$ $x_5 = Albumin$ $x_6 = Calcium$ $x_7 = Uric\ Acid$

Table 4.2: Covariance Matrix for Werner Blood Chemistry Data

	y	x_1	x_2	x_3	x_4	x_5	x_6	x_7
CHOLEST	1857.015							
AGE	154.514	97.978						
HEIGHT	1.220	2.192	6.161					
WEIGHT	128.106	51.804	24.093	420.242				
BIRTHPIL	1.965	0.279	0.204	0.823	0.251			
ALBUMIN	0.882	-0.280	-0.005	-1.725	-0.042	0.129		
CALCIUM	5.149	-0.040	0.168	0.627	-0.015	0.077	0.224	
URICACID	13.130	2.314	0.349	6.977	0.009	0.012	0.088	1.257

The LISREL input for this example is

```
Stepwise Regression for Werner Blood Chemistry Data
Using GLS on Correlation Matrix
DA NI=8 NO=180 MA=KM
LA
CHOLEST AGE HEIGHT WEIGHT BIRTHPIL ALBUMIN CALCIUM
URICACID
CM FI=EX42.COV
MO NY=1 NX=7 GA=FI
OU ME=GLS TV SE MI AM
```

The results are shown in Table 4.3.

Table 4.3: Stepwise Regression for Werner Blood Chemistry Data

Step	Parameter to free	MI	χ^2	d.f.	P-value
0	γ_1	30.82	55.89	7	0.000
1	γ_6	15.34	25.07	6	0.000
2	γ_7	5.95	9.73	5	0.083

4.2.3   Analysis of Variance and Covariance

Suppose there are G groups and we want to compare their means on a response variable y. This is usually done by one-way ANOVA. In LISREL this can be done by forming dummy variables $d_1, d_2, \ldots, d_{G-1}$ and regressing y on these dummy variables. These dummy variables represent group memberships such that $d_{ig} = 1$ if case i belongs to group g and $d_{ig} = 0$ otherwise. The raw data is of the form

Case	y	d_1	d_2	$\cdots$	d_G
1	y_1	d_{11}	d_{12}	$\cdots$	d_{1G}
2	y_2	d_{21}	d_{22}	$\cdots$	d_{2G}
$\vdots$	$\vdots$	$\vdots$	$\vdots$		$\vdots$
N	y_N	d_{N1}	d_{N2}	$\cdots$	d_{NG}

It is not necessary that the number of cases per group is the same.

The hypothesis that all group means are equal is the same as the hypothesis that $\gamma_1 = \gamma_2 = \ldots = \gamma_{G-1} = 0$. A formal F statistic can be computed as

$$F = \frac{R^2/(G-1)}{(1-R^2)/(N-G)} \tag{4.6}$$

where R^2 is the squared multiple correlation in the regression of y on $d_1, d_2, ..., d_{G-1}$. Each γ_i measures the mean difference $\mu_i - \mu_G$, the significance of which can be tested by the corresponding t-value used as a t-statistic.

Analysis of covariance (ANCOVA) can be done in a similar way. First, regress the response variable y on the covariates $x_1, x_2, \ldots, x_q$ yielding squared multiple correlation R^2_{yx}. Second, regress y on $x_1, x_2, \ldots, x_q$ and $d_1, d_2, \ldots, d_{G-1}$ yielding squared multiple correlation R^2_{yxd}. Then

$$F = \frac{R^2_{yxd} - R^2_{yx}/(G-1)}{(1-R^2_{yxd})/(N-G-1)} \tag{4.7}$$

can be used as an F statistic with $(G-1)$ and $(N-G-1)$ degrees of freedom for testing the hypothesis that the group means, adjusted for mean differences in the covariates, are zero.

Both the ANOVA and the ANCOVA considered above assume that the within-group variances of y are equal. In addition, ANCOVA assumes that the regressions of y on $x_1, x_2, \ldots, x_q$ are the same for each group. These are in fact assumptions which can be tested using multiple groups in LISREL; see Chapter 10.

Table 4.4: Fictitious Data for ANOVA and ANCOVA

	Aptitude Test Score (x)	Biology Achievement Score (y)
	29	15
	49	19
	48	21
	35	27
Treatment 1	53	35
	47	39
	46	23
	74	38
	72	33
	67	50
	22	20
	24	34
	49	28
	46	35
Treatment 2	52	42
	43	44
	64	46
	61	47
	55	40
	54	54
	33	14
	45	20
	35	30
	39	32
Treatment 3	36	34
	48	42
	63	40
	57	38
	56	54
	78	56

The following example adapted from Huitema (1980) illustrates both ANOVA and AN-COVA.

Example 4.3: ANOVA and ANCOVA

Two investigators are interested in academic achievement. Investigator A is primarily concerned with the effects of three different types of study objectives on student achievement in freshman biology. The three types of objectives are:

- *General - Students are told to know and understand everything in the text.*

- *Specific - Students are provided with a clear specification of the terms and concepts they are expected to master and of the testing format.*

- *Specific with study time allocations - The amount of time that should be spent on each topic is provided in addition to specific objectives that describe the type of behavior expected on examinations.*

The dependent variable is the biology achievement test.

Investigator B is interested in predicting student achievement using a recently developed aptitude test. This investigator is not particularly concerned with differences in the mean level of achievement resulting from the use of different types of study objective, but rather with making a general statement of the predictive efficiency of the test across a population of freshmen biology students of whom one-third have been exposed to general study objectives, one-third to specific behavioral objectives, and one-third to specific behavioral objectives with study time allocations. More specifically, he wants to know (1) whether the regression of achievement scores on aptitude scores is statistically significant and (2) the regression equation.

A population of freshmen students scheduled to enroll in biology is defined, and 30 students are randomly selected. Investigator B obtains aptitude test scores (X) for all students before investigator A randomly assigns 10 students to each of the three treatments. Treatments are administered, and scores on the dependent variable are obtained for all students.

The data are shown in Table 4.4.

Investigator B examines the results of his colleague's ANOVA and suggests that a more powerful technique, one that controls for aptitude differences among subjects, might reveal significant treatment effects; ANCOVA is one such technique.

In a problem like this, in which several runs will be necessary, it is a good idea to make up a data file containing all the variables that one will need. In this case, the data file will be as shown on the next page. The last column of the data matrix is not used in this example, but it could be useful in other problems.

```
15 29 1 0 0
19 49 1 0 0
21 48 1 0 0
27 35 1 0 0
35 53 1 0 0
39 47 1 0 0
23 46 1 0 0
38 74 1 0 0
33 72 1 0 0
50 67 1 0 0
20 22 0 1 0
34 24 0 1 0
28 49 0 1 0
35 46 0 1 0
42 52 0 1 0
44 43 0 1 0
46 64 0 1 0
47 61 0 1 0
40 55 0 1 0
54 54 0 1 0
14 33 0 0 1
20 45 0 0 1
30 35 0 0 1
32 39 0 0 1
34 36 0 0 1
42 48 0 0 1
40 63 0 0 1
38 57 0 0 1
54 56 0 0 1
56 78 0 0 1
```

For the ANOVA part of the problem, we run the regression of y on d_1 and d_2. The input file for this is

```
ANOVA
DA NI=5
LA
Y X D1 D2 D3
RA FI=EX43.RAW
SE
1 3 4 /
MO NY=1 NX=2
OU SE TV
```

The squared multiple correlation, R^2, is 0.106. The hypothesis that the three group means are equal (equivalent to the hypothesis that γ_1 and γ_2 are both zero) is tested via the F statistic (4.6) with 2 and 27 degrees of freedom. F becomes

$$F = \frac{0.106/2}{(1 - 0.106)/27} = 1.60$$

This is not significant so no differences in group means on the response variable y are detected.

For the ANCOVA, we first run the regression of y on x using the input file

```
ANCOVA Part 1
DA NI=5
LA;Y X D1 D2 D3
RA FI=EX43.RAW
SE
1 2 /
MO NY=1 NX=1
OU SE TV
```

This yields an $R^2 = 0.396$. We then run the regression of y on x, d_1, and d_2 using the following input file:

```
ANCOVA Part 2
DA NI=5
LA;Y X D1 D2 D3
RA FI=EX43.RAW
SE
1 2 3 4/
MO NY=1 NX=3
OU SE TV
```

This gives an $R^2 = 0.575$.

The F statistic (4.7) with 2 and 26 degrees of freedom for testing the equality of adjusted means is

$$\frac{(0.575 - 0.396)/2}{(1 - 0.575)/26} = 5.47$$

which is significant at the 5% level. Thus there is some evidence that the group means of the Biology Achievement Score are different when they are adjusted for difference in the Aptitude Test Score. By controlling for x we get a more powerful test for testing group differences on y than we get by using y alone.

4.2.4   Bivariate Regression

The following example illustrates the case of two dependent variables y_1 and y_2 and three explanatory variables x_1, x_2, and x_3.

Example 4.4: Bivariate Regression

Finn (1974) presents the data given in Table 4.5. These data represent the scores of fifteen freshmen at a large midwestern university on five educational measures. The five measures are

- *y_1 = grade average for required courses taken*

- *y_2 = grade average for elective courses taken*

- *x_1 = high-school general knowledge test, taken previous year*

- *x_2 = IQ score from previous year*

- x_3 = *educational motivation score from previous year*

We examine the predictive value of x_1, x_2 and x_3 in predicting the grade averages y_1 and y_2.

Table 4.5: Scores for Fifteen College Freshmen on Five Educational Measures

Case	y_1	y_2	x_1	x_2	x_3
1	.8	2.0	72	114	17.3
2	2.2	2.2	78	117	17.6
3	1.6	2.0	84	117	15.0
4	2.6	3.7	95	120	18.0
5	2.7	3.2	88	117	18.7
6	2.1	3.2	83	123	17.9
7	3.1	3.7	92	118	17.3
8	3.0	3.1	86	114	18.1
9	3.2	2.6	88	114	16.0
10	2.6	3.2	80	115	16.4
11	2.7	2.8	87	114	17.6
12	3.0	2.4	94	112	19.5
13	1.6	1.4	73	115	12.7
14	.9	1.0	80	111	17.0
15	1.9	1.2	83	112	16.1

Taking the variables as measured from their means and omitting the intercept terms, the bivariate regression of y_1 and y_2 on x_1, x_2 and x_3 may be written

$$y_1 = \gamma_{11}x_1 + \gamma_{12}x_2 + \gamma_{13}x_3 + \zeta_1$$

$$y_2 = \gamma_{21}x_1 + \gamma_{22}x_2 + \gamma_{23}x_3 + \zeta_2$$

or in matrix form

$$\mathbf{y} = \mathbf{\Gamma x} + \zeta \,,$$

where $\mathbf{\Gamma}$ is the regression matrix of order 2 x 3. This is a LISREL model of the form (4.1) with $\mathbf{B}$ zero, $\mathbf{\Gamma}$ a full free matrix, and $\mathbf{\Psi}$ a symmetric free matrix. A path diagram of this model is shown in Figure 4.5.

The LISREL input for such a model is extremely simple, as shown below.

```
PREDICTION OF GRADE AVERAGES
DA NI=5 NO=15
LA
GRAVEREQ GRAVELEC KNOWLEDG IQPREVYR 'ED MOTIV'
RA FI=EX44.RAW
MO NY=2 NX=3
OU TV SE
```

As in the case of a single regression equation, the initial estimates produced by the program are identical to the maximum likelihood estimates. This is a consequence of the fact that, as

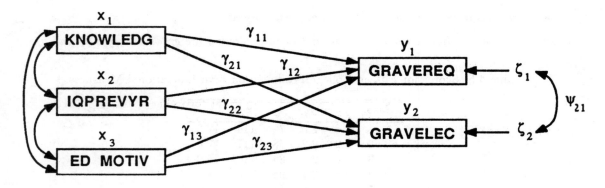

Figure 4.5: Path Diagram for Prediction of Grade Averages

a covariance structure, the model is just identified with zero degrees of freedom and fits the data perfectly; see the three measures of overall fit. The model is only useful to the extent that it gives information about the relative importance of the x-variables as predictors of the two grade averages.

Parameter estimates, standard errors, and *t*-values are given in the output file as

```
LISREL ESTIMATES (MAXIMUM LIKELIHOOD)
        GAMMA
          KNOWLEDG    IQPREVYR   ED MOTIV
GRAVEREQ      .085        .008      -.015
GRAVELEC      .047        .145       .126
        PSI
          GRAVEREQ    GRAVELEC
GRAVEREQ      .257
GRAVELEC      .169        .237
STANDARD ERRORS
        GAMMA
          KNOWLEDG    IQPREVYR   ED MOTIV
GRAVEREQ      .027        .049       .112
GRAVELEC      .026        .047       .107
        PSI
          GRAVEREQ    GRAVELEC
GRAVEREQ      .109
GRAVELEC      .090        .101
T-VALUES
        GAMMA
          KNOWLEDG    IQPREVYR   ED MOTIV
GRAVEREQ     3.168        .169      -.134
GRAVELEC     1.823       3.117      1.170
```

```
     PSI
          GRAVEREQ    GRAVELEC
GRAVEREQ    2.345
GRAVELEC    1.875      2.345
```

The t-values reveal immediately that only x_1 is a significant predictor of y_1 and only x_2 is a significant predictor of y_2. The variable x_3 is not significant for either purpose. It should be noted, however, that the sample size is too small to draw any safe conclusions.

The maximum likelihood estimate of $\boldsymbol{\Psi}$ is

$$\hat{\boldsymbol{\Psi}} = \left(\begin{array}{cc} 0.257 & \\ 0.169 & 0.237 \end{array} \right)$$

This is the partial covariance matrix of y for given x. The partial covariance 0.169 has a t-value of 1.875 and is therefore not significant, despite the fact that the partial correlation between y_1 and y_2

$$r_{y_1 y_2 \cdot x_1 x_2 x_3} = 0.169/(0.257 \times 0.237)^{\frac{1}{2}} = 0.685$$

is quite large. This seemingly contradictory result occurs because the sample size is too small.

4.3   Path Analysis

Path analysis, due to Wright (1934), is a technique to assess the direct causal contribution of one variable to another in a non-experimental condition. The problem, in general, is that of estimating the coefficients of a set of linear structural equations, representing the cause and effect relationships hypothesized by the investigator. The system involves variables of two kinds: independent or cause variables x_1, x_2, ..., x_q and dependent or effect variables y_1, y_2, ..., y_p. The classical technique consists of solving the structural equations for the dependent variables in terms of the independent and the random disturbance terms ζ_1, ζ_2, ..., ζ_p to obtain the reduced form equations, estimating the regression of the dependent variables on the independent variables and then solving for the structural parameters in terms of the regression coefficients. The last step is not always possible. Models of this kind and a variety of estimation techniques have been extensively studied by econometricians; see Theil (1971), by biometricians; see Turner and Stevens (1959) and references therein, and by sociologists; see Blalock (1964) and Duncan (1975). Some of these models involve latent variables; see Duncan (1966), Werts and Linn (1970), and Hauser and Goldberger (1971).

Estimating a path analysis model for directly observed variables with LISREL is straightforward. Rather than estimating each equation separately, LISREL considers the model as a system of equations and estimates all the structural coefficients directly. The reduced form is obtained as a by-product.

Example 4.5: Ambition and Attainment

Kerchoff (1974, p. 46) reports the correlations between a number of variables for 767 twelfth-grade males. Some of these correlations are given in Table 4.6. The variables, in the order in which they appear in the table, are

- $x_1 =$ *intelligence*

- $x_2 =$ *number of siblings*

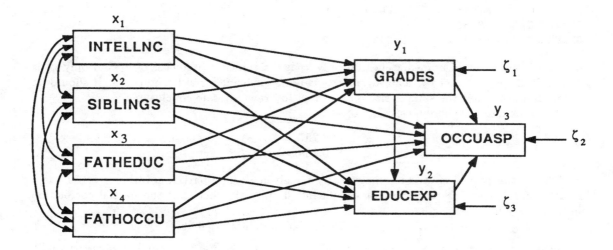

Figure 4.6: Path Diagram for Recursive Model of Ambition and Attainment

- x_3 = *father's education*
- x_4 = *father's occupation*
- y_1 = *grades*
- y_2 = *educational expectation*
- y_3 = *occupational aspiration*

Kenny (1979, pp.47-73) reanalyzed these data according to the recursive system shown in Figure 4.6. This is a rather typical model for sociological attainment studies. We shall use these data and this model to illustrate the simplicity of the LISREL *input and also to explain some new sections of the printout: total effects.*

Table 4.6: Correlations for Background, Ambition and Attainment Variables

	x_1	x_2	x_3	x_4	y_1	y_2	y_3
INTELLNC	1.000						
SIBLINGS	-.100	1.000					
FATHEDUC	.277	-.152	1.000				
FATHOCCU	.250	-.108	.611	1.000			
GRADES	.572	-.105	.294	.248	1.000		
EDUCEXP	.489	-.213	.446	.410	.597	1.000	
OCCUASP	.335	-.153	.303	.331	.478	.651	1.000

The model is a *complete recursive system* with *exogenous variables* x_1, x_2, x_3, and x_4, and *jointly dependent variables* y_1, y_2, and y_3. To avoid cluttering the figure we have omitted all the coefficients in Figure 4.6. The structural equations are

$$y_1 = \gamma_{11}x_1 + \gamma_{12}x_2 + \gamma_{13}x_3 + \gamma_{14}x_4 + \zeta_1$$
$$y_2 = \beta_{21}y_1 + \gamma_{21}x_1 + \gamma_{22}x_2 + \gamma_{23}x_3 + \gamma_{24}x_4 + \zeta_2$$
$$y_3 = \beta_{31}y_1 + \beta_{32}y_2 + \gamma_{31}x_1 + \gamma_{32}x_2 + \gamma_{33}x_3 + \gamma_{34}x_4 + \zeta_3$$

or in matrix form as (4.1) with $\mathbf{B}$ sub-diagonal, $\mathbf{\Gamma}$ full and free, and $\mathbf{\Psi}$ diagonal.

The model specification is extremely simple, as shown in the following input file.

```
Ambition and Attainment
DA NI=7 NO=767 MA=KM
LA
INTELLNC SIBLINGS FATHEDUC FATHOCCU GRADES EDUCEXP OCCUASP
KM FI=EX45.COR
SE
5 6 7 1 2 3 4
MO NY=3 NX=4 BE=SD PS=DI
OU SE TV EF
```

When there are no *a priori* fixed elements among the β's or γ's, the model is just identified and fits the data perfectly. The initial estimates are identical to the maximum likelihood estimates. The ML estimates and the *t*-values are

```
LISREL ESTIMATES (MAXIMUM LIKELIHOOD)
        BETA
             GRADES    EDUCEXP    OCCUASP
   GRADES      .000       .000       .000
  EDUCEXP      .405       .000       .000
  OCCUASP      .158       .550       .000
        GAMMA
             INTELLNC  SIBLINGS   FATHEDUC   FATHOCCU
   GRADES      .526      -.030       .119       .041
  EDUCEXP      .160      -.112       .173       .152
  OCCUASP     -.039      -.019      -.041       .100
T-VALUES
        BETA
             GRADES    EDUCEXP    OCCUASP
   GRADES      .000       .000       .000
  EDUCEXP    12.554       .000       .000
  OCCUASP     4.291     14.616       .000
        GAMMA
             INTELLNC  SIBLINGS   FATHEDUC   FATHOCCU
   GRADES    17.161     -1.011      3.164      1.093
  EDUCEXP     4.986     -4.232      5.123      4.587
  OCCUASP    -1.162      -.679     -1.161      2.858
```

It is obvious from the model in Figure 4.6 that there are both direct and indirect effects of the the x-variables on y_2 and y_3. For example, the direct effect of x_1 on y_2 is $\gamma_{21} = 0.160$ and the indirect effect of x_1 on y_2 via y_1 is $\gamma_{11}\beta_{21} = 0.526 \times 0.405 = 0.213$. The sum of the direct effect and all indirect effects is called total effects. These total effects are given by LISREL if one writes EF on the OU line. The total effects and indirect effects and their standard errors are

```
TOTAL AND INDIRECT EFFECTS
        TOTAL EFFECTS OF X ON Y
             INTELLNC    SIBLINGS    FATHEDUC    FATHOCCU
   GRADES       .526       -.030        .119        .041
  EDUCEXP       .373       -.124        .221        .168
  OCCUASP       .249       -.092        .099        .198
        STANDARD ERRORS FOR TOTAL EFFECTS OF X ON Y
             INTELLNC    SIBLINGS    FATHEDUC    FATHOCCU
   GRADES       .031        .030        .038        .037
  EDUCEXP       .030        .029        .037        .036
  OCCUASP       .034        .033        .042        .041
        INDIRECT EFFECTS OF X ON Y
             INTELLNC    SIBLINGS    FATHEDUC    FATHOCCU
   GRADES       .000        .000        .000        .000
  EDUCEXP       .213       -.012        .048        .016
  OCCUASP       .288       -.073        .140        .099
        STANDARD ERRORS FOR INDIRECT EFFECTS OF X ON Y
             INTELLNC    SIBLINGS    FATHEDUC    FATHOCCU
   GRADES       .000        .000        .000        .000
  EDUCEXP       .021        .012        .016        .015
  OCCUASP       .027        .019        .025        .024
        TOTAL EFFECTS OF Y ON Y
              GRADES     EDUCEXP     OCCUASP
   GRADES       .000        .000        .000
  EDUCEXP       .405        .000        .000
  OCCUASP       .381        .550        .000
   LARGEST EIGENVALUE OF B*B' (STABILITY INDEX) IS      .349
        STANDARD ERRORS FOR TOTAL EFFECTS OF Y ON Y
              GRADES     EDUCEXP     OCCUASP
   GRADES       .000        .000        .000
  EDUCEXP       .032        .000        .000
  OCCUASP       .038        .038        .000
        INDIRECT EFFECTS OF Y ON Y
              GRADES     EDUCEXP     OCCUASP
   GRADES       .000        .000        .000
  EDUCEXP       .000        .000        .000
  OCCUASP       .223        .000        .000
        STANDARD ERRORS FOR INDIRECT EFFECTS OF Y ON Y
              GRADES     EDUCEXP     OCCUASP
   GRADES       .000        .000        .000
  EDUCEXP       .000        .000        .000
  OCCUASP       .023        .000        .000
```

It is seen that the total effect of x_1 on y_2 is 0.373. This is the sum of the direct effect of 0.160 and the indirect effect 0.213 computed above.

The t-values for the solution of Example 4.5 reveal that the effects γ_{12}, γ_{14}, γ_{31}, γ_{32} and γ_{33} may not be significant. A formal test of the hypothesis that these five γ's are zero should be based on an independent sample. This can be obtained by running the model again, inserting a line

```
FIX GA(1,2) GA(1,4) GA(3,1)-GA(3,3)
```

after the MO line. However, this test should be made on an independent sample.

4.4   Econometric Models

Unlike the previous example, where the system of equations was recursive, *econometric models* are usually *non-recursive* or so called *interdependent systems*; see Goldberger (1964) or Theil (1971). Data for econometric models are usually in the form of *time series* and the models are usually *dynamic* in the sense that elements of time play important roles in the model. Another characteristic of econometric models is that they often contain definitional equations or *identities*. These are exact relationships without disturbance terms and with no unknown parameters to be estimated.

It should be understood that although the identities are not subject to estimation, they must nevertheless be specified in the input file in order to define which variables are *independent (exogenous)* and which are *jointly dependent (endogenous)*. If the identities are omitted, the program will estimate the behavioral equations by ordinary least squares (OLS), yielding inconsistent (biased) estimates.

Example 4.6: Klein's Model I of US Economy

Klein's (1950) Model I is a classical econometric model which has been used extensively as a benchmark problem for studying econometric methods. It is a eight-equation system based on annual data for the United States in the period between the two World Wars. It is dynamic in the sense that elements of time play important roles in the model.

Following Goldberger's (1964, pp.303-325) formulation of the model, it will be illustrated how LISREL *can be used to estimate econometric models of this kind. In particular, the example illustrates how one can handle identities. The three behavioral equations of Klein's Model I are*

$$
\begin{aligned}
C_t &= a_1 P_t + a_2 P_{t-1} + a_3 W_t + \xi_1 \\
I_t &= b_1 P_t + b_2 P_{t-1} + b_3 K_{t-1} + \zeta_2 \\
W_t^* &= c_1 E_t + c_2 E_{t-1} + c_3 A_t + \zeta_3
\end{aligned}
$$

In addition to these stochastic equations the model includes five identities:

$$
\begin{aligned}
P_t &= Y_t - W_t \\
Y_t &= C_t + I_t + G_t - T_t \\
K_t &= K_{t-1} + I_t \\
W_t &= W_t^* + W_t^{**} \\
E_t &= Y_t + T_t - W_t^{**}
\end{aligned}
$$

The endogenous variables are

$$
\begin{aligned}
C_t &= \text{Aggregate Consumption}(y_1) \\
I_t &= \text{Net Investment}(y_2) \\
W_t^* &= \text{Private Wage Bill}(y_3) \\
P_t &= \text{Total Profits}(y_4) \\
Y_t &= \text{Total Income}(y_5) \\
K_t &= \text{End-of-Year Capital Stock}(y_6) \\
W_t &= \text{Total Wage Bill}(y_7) \\
E_t &= \text{Total Production of Private Industry}(y_8)
\end{aligned}
$$

The predetermined variables are the exogenous variables

$$
\begin{aligned}
W_t^{**} &= \text{Government Wage Bill}(x_1) \\
T_t &= \text{Taxes}(x_2) \\
G_t &= \text{Government Non-Wage Expenditures}(x_3) \\
A_t &= \text{Time in Years From } 1931(x_4)
\end{aligned}
$$

and the lagged endogenous variables $P_{t-1}(x_5)$, $K_{t-1}(x_6)$ *and* $E_{t-1}(x_7)$. *All variables except* A_t *are in billions of 1934 dollars. Annual time series data for 1921-1941 are given in Table 4.7, which has been computed from Theil's (1971) Table 9.1.*

Rules for identification of a model of this type have been given by econometricians; see Goldberger (1964, pp.313-318). A necessary condition for identification of each equation is that the number of x-variables excluded from the equation is at least as great as one less the number of y-variables included in the equation. This is the so-called *order condition*. In other words, for every y-variable on the right side of an equation there must be one x-variable excluded from that equation. For example, in the consumption function there are 3 y-variables included (C_t, P_t and W_t) and 6 x-variables excluded (W_t^{**}, T_t, G_t, A_t, K_{k-1} and E_{t-1}) so that the condition is fulfilled. Similarly, it can be verified that the condition is met also for the other two equations.

There is also a sufficient condition for identification, the so-called *rank condition*, but this is often difficult to verify in practice.

The model can be formulated as a **LISREL** model of the form (4.1) with p = 8 and q = 7 and with **B**, $\mathbf{\Gamma}$, and $\mathbf{\Psi}$ as

$$
\mathbf{B} = \begin{pmatrix}
0 & 0 & 0 & a_1 & 0 & 0 & a_3 & 0 \\
0 & 0 & 0 & b_1 & 0 & 0 & 0 & 0 \\
0 & 0 & 0 & 0 & 0 & 0 & 0 & c_1 \\
0 & 0 & 0 & 0 & 1 & 0 & -1 & 0 \\
1 & 1 & 0 & 0 & 0 & 0 & 0 & 0 \\
0 & 1 & 0 & 0 & 0 & 0 & 0 & 0 \\
0 & 0 & 1 & 0 & 0 & 0 & 0 & 0 \\
0 & 0 & 0 & 0 & 1 & 0 & 0 & 0
\end{pmatrix}
$$

Table 4.7: Time Series Data for Klein's Model I

t	C_t	P_{t-1}	W_t^*	I_t	K_{t-1}	E_{t-1}	W_t^{**}
1921	41.9	12.7	25.5	-0.2	182.8	44.9	2.7
1922	45.0	12.4	29.3	1.9	182.6	45.6	2.9
1923	49.2	16.9	34.1	5.2	184.5	50.1	2.9
1924	50.6	18.4	33.9	3.0	189.7	57.2	3.1
1925	52.6	19.4	35.4	5.1	192.7	57.1	3.2
1926	55.1	20.1	37.4	5.6	197.8	61.0	3.3
1927	56.2	19.6	37.9	4.2	203.4	64.0	3.6
1928	57.3	19.8	39.2	3.0	207.6	64.4	3.7
1929	57.8	21.1	41.3	5.1	210.6	64.5	4.0
1930	55.0	21.7	37.9	1.0	215.7	67.0	4.2
1931	50.9	15.6	34.5	-3.4	216.7	61.2	4.8
1932	45.6	11.4	29.0	-6.2	213.3	53.4	5.3
1933	46.5	7.0	28.5	-5.1	207.1	44.3	5.6
1934	48.7	11.2	30.6	-3.0	202.0	45.1	6.0
1935	51.3	12.3	33.2	-1.3	199.0	49.7	6.1
1936	57.7	14.0	36.8	2.1	197.7	54.4	7.4
1937	58.7	17.6	41.0	2.0	199.8	62.7	6.7
1938	57.5	17.3	38.2	-1.9	201.8	65.0	7.7
1939	61.6	15.3	41.6	1.3	199.9	60.9	7.8
1940	65.0	19.0	45.0	3.3	201.2	69.5	8.0
1941	69.7	21.1	53.3	4.9	204.5	75.7	8.5

t	T_t	A_t	P_t	K_t	E_t	W_t	Y_t	G_t
1921	7.7	-10.0	12.4	182.6	45.6	28.2	40.6	6.6
1922	3.9	-9.0	16.9	184.5	50.1	32.2	49.1	6.1
1923	4.7	-8.0	18.4	189.7	57.2	37.0	55.4	5.7
1924	3.8	-7.0	19.4	192.7	57.1	37.0	56.4	6.6
1925	5.5	-6.0	20.1	197.8	61.0	38.6	58.7	6.5
1926	7.0	-5.0	19.6	203.4	64.0	40.7	60.3	6.6
1927	6.7	-4.0	19.8	207.6	64.4	41.5	61.3	7.6
1928	4.2	-3.0	21.1	210.6	64.5	42.9	64.0	7.9
1929	4.0	-2.0	21.7	215.7	67.0	45.3	67.0	8.1
1930	7.7	-1.0	15.6	216.7	61.2	42.1	57.7	9.4
1931	7.5	0.0	11.4	213.3	53.4	39.3	50.7	10.7
1932	8.3	1.0	7.0	207.1	44.3	34.3	41.3	10.2
1933	5.4	2.0	11.2	202.0	45.1	34.1	45.3	9.3
1934	6.8	3.0	12.3	199.0	49.7	36.6	48.9	10.0
1935	7.2	4.0	14.0	197.7	54.4	39.3	53.3	10.5
1936	8.3	5.0	17.6	199.8	62.7	44.2	61.8	10.3
1937	6.7	6.0	17.3	201.8	65.0	47.7	65.0	11.0
1938	7.4	7.0	15.3	199.9	60.9	45.9	61.2	13.0
1939	8.9	8.0	19.0	201.2	69.5	49.4	68.4	14.4
1940	9.6	9.0	21.1	204.5	75.7	53.0	74.1	15.4
1941	11.6	10.0	23.5	209.4	88.4	61.8	85.3	22.3

$$\boldsymbol{\Gamma} = \begin{pmatrix} 0 & 0 & 0 & 0 & a_2 & 0 & 0 \\ 0 & 0 & 0 & 0 & b_2 & b_3 & 0 \\ 0 & 0 & 0 & c_3 & 0 & 0 & c_2 \\ 0 & 0 & 0 & 0 & 0 & 0 & 0 \\ 0 & -1 & 1 & 0 & 0 & 0 & 0 \\ 0 & 0 & 0 & 0 & 0 & 1 & 0 \\ 1 & 0 & 0 & 0 & 0 & 0 & 0 \\ -1 & 1 & 0 & 0 & 0 & 0 & 0 \end{pmatrix}$$

$$\boldsymbol{\Psi} = \begin{pmatrix} \psi_{11} \\ \psi_{21} & \psi_{22} \\ \psi_{31} & \psi_{32} & \psi_{33} \\ 0 & 0 & 0 & 0 \\ 0 & 0 & 0 & 0 & 0 \\ 0 & 0 & 0 & 0 & 0 & 0 \\ 0 & 0 & 0 & 0 & 0 & 0 & 0 \\ 0 & 0 & 0 & 0 & 0 & 0 & 0 & 0 \end{pmatrix}$$

Note that, as a consequence of the identities in the model, the last five rows of $\mathbf{B}$, $\boldsymbol{\Gamma}$ and $\boldsymbol{\Psi}$ do not contain any parameters to be estimated. Another consequence of the identities is that both $\boldsymbol{\Sigma}$ and $\mathbf{S}$ will be singular matrices if one uses all the 15 variables in the model. This makes it impossible to use the ML method or GLS method since they require either $\boldsymbol{\Sigma}$ or $\mathbf{S}$ to be positive definite. However, five of the y-variables are of course redundant. By eliminating them, ML estimation is in fact possible as will be demonstrated. First, however, consider IV and ULS estimates.

The labels and the raw data with their formats are stored in the file EX46.DAT. The input for a ULS run is as follows:

```
KLEIN'S MODEL I ESTIMATED BY IV AND ULS
DA NI=15 NO=21
LA FI=EX46.DAT
RA FI=EX46.DAT
SE
1 4 3 10 14 11 13 12 7 8 15 9 2 5 6
MO NY=8 NX=7 BE=FU GA=FI PS=FI
FR BE(1,4) BE(1,7) BE(2,4) BE(3,8)
FR GA(1,5) GA(2,5) GA(2,6) GA(3,4) GA(3,7)
FR PS(1,1)-PS(3,3)
VA 1 BE(4,5) BE(5,1) BE(5,2) BE(6,2) BE(7,3) BE(8,5) GA(5,3) GA(6,6) C
GA(7,1) GA(8,2)
VA -1 BE(4,7) GA(5,2) GA(8,1)
OU ME=UL AD=OFF
```

The variables in Table 4.7 are not in the same order as in the model. The selection line puts them in the order $y_1, y_2, \ldots y_8, x_1, x_2, \ldots x_7$. The only parameter matrices needed are $\mathbf{B}$, $\boldsymbol{\Gamma}$ and $\boldsymbol{\Psi}$. $\mathbf{B}$ is declared full on the MO line and is fixed by default. $\boldsymbol{\Gamma}$ is declared fixed on the MO line and is full by default. $\boldsymbol{\Psi}$ is declared fixed on the MO line and is symmetric by default. After the MO line the only thing that needs to be done is to define the free elements and the values of the non-zero fixed elements in $\mathbf{B}$ and $\boldsymbol{\Gamma}$. This is done by the FR and VA lines.

Table 4.8: Parameter Estimates for Klein's Model I

Parameter	IV	TSLS	ULS	MLR	ML
a_1	0.04	0.02	0.04	-0.04	-0.23
a_2	0.19	0.22	0.21	0.29	0.38
a_3	0.82	0.81	0.81	0.79	0.80
b_1	0.04	0.15	0.05	-0.45	-0.80
b_2	0.69	0.62	0.68	0.98	1.05
b_3	-0.17	-0.16	-0.17	-0.17	-0.15
c_1	0.39	0.44	0.39	0.31	0.23
c_2	0.20	0.15	0.20	0.25	0.28
c_3	0.14	0.13	0.15	0.19	0.23

The results of the ULS run give two different sets of estimates for the structural parameters: IV and ULS estimates. The estimates are given in Table 4.8.

The ULS estimates are not identical to any known estimates. Consider what ULS is doing. ULS minimizes the sum of squares of all the elements of the matrix

$$\mathbf{S} - \mathbf{\Sigma} = \begin{pmatrix} \mathbf{S}_{yy} & \mathbf{S}_{yx} \\ \mathbf{S}_{xy} & \mathbf{S}_{xx} \end{pmatrix} - \begin{pmatrix} \mathbf{\Sigma}_{yy} & \mathbf{\Sigma}_{yx} \\ \mathbf{\Sigma}_{xy} & \mathbf{\Sigma}_{xx} \end{pmatrix}$$

For simplicity, assume that there are no identities in the model. Then

$$\begin{aligned} \mathbf{\Sigma}_{yy} &= \mathbf{\Pi}\mathbf{\Phi}\mathbf{\Pi}' + \mathbf{\Psi}^* \\ \mathbf{\Sigma}_{yx} &= \mathbf{\Pi}\mathbf{\Phi} \\ \mathbf{\Sigma}_{xx} &= \mathbf{\Phi} \end{aligned}$$

where

$$\begin{aligned} \mathbf{\Pi} &= (\mathbf{I} - \mathbf{B})^{-1}\mathbf{\Gamma} \\ \mathbf{\Psi}^* &= (\mathbf{I} - \mathbf{B})^{-1}\mathbf{\Psi}(\mathbf{I} - \mathbf{B}')^{-1} \end{aligned}$$

are the reduced form regression matrix and the reduced form residual covariance matrix implied by the model. Since both $\mathbf{\Phi}$ and $\mathbf{\Psi}$ are unconstrained, the sums of squares of $\mathbf{S}_{yy} - \mathbf{\Sigma}_{yy}$ and $\mathbf{S}_{xx} - \mathbf{\Sigma}_{xx}$ can be made zero, regardless of the values of the parameters in $\mathbf{B}$ and $\mathbf{\Gamma}$, by choosing $\mathbf{\Phi} = \mathbf{S}_{xx}$ and $\mathbf{\Psi} = (\mathbf{I} - \mathbf{B})\mathbf{S}_{yy}(\mathbf{I} - \mathbf{B}') - \mathbf{\Gamma}\mathbf{S}_{xx}\mathbf{\Gamma}'$. It follows that the ULS estimates of $\mathbf{B}$ and $\mathbf{\Gamma}$ are those which minimize the sum of squares of

$$\mathbf{S}_{yx} - (\mathbf{I} - \mathbf{B})^{-1}\mathbf{\Gamma}\mathbf{S}_{xx}$$

Other alternative estimates could be obtained by minimizing the sum of squares of

$$\mathbf{S}_{yx}\mathbf{S}_{xx}^{-1} - (\mathbf{I} - \mathbf{B})^{-1}\mathbf{\Gamma}$$

or the sum of squares of

$$(\mathbf{I} - \mathbf{B})\mathbf{S}_{yx} - \mathbf{\Gamma}\mathbf{S}_{xx}$$

The latter has a simple closed form solution.

Next consider how to obtain *ridge estimates*. All one needs to do is to delete the parameter ME=UL on the OU line. The program will then attempt to do ML. However, the covariance matrix is singular so ML is not possible. The program will then automatically invoke the Ridge Option with Ridge Constant 0.001; see Section 1.11.6. This gives the estimates shown in Table 4.8.

The estimation of Klein's Model I by the ML method will be considered next. As already noted, the covariance matrices Σ and S as well as the data matrix in Table 4.7 are singular because of the five identities in the model. The rank of these matrices is not 15 but 10. It is possible to solve the identities for the redundant variables P_t, Y_t, K_t, W_t and E_t in terms of the other 10 variables and substitute these solutions into the behavioral equations. This results in a system with 3 y-variables and 7 x-variables and with coefficients which are linear combinations of the structural parameters. While it is possible to estimate the model in this form also (see Jöreskog, 1973), this approach, which is rather complicated, is unnecessary since LISREL will estimate the model directly if one treats all the y-variables as η-variables of which only the first 3 are observed. Thus the LISREL specification

$$\mathbf{y}' = (C_t,\ I_t,\ W_t^*)$$
$$\boldsymbol{\eta}' = (C_t,\ I_t,\ W_t^*,\ P_t,\ Y_t,\ K_t,\ W_t,\ E_t)$$
$$\mathbf{x}' \equiv \boldsymbol{\xi}' = (W,\ T_t,\ G_t,\ A_t,\ P_{t-1},\ K_{k-1},\ E_{t-1})$$

The $\boldsymbol{\Lambda}_y$-matrix is

$$\boldsymbol{\Lambda}_y = \begin{pmatrix} 1 & 0 & 0 & 0 & 0 & 0 & 0 & 0 \\ 0 & 1 & 0 & 0 & 0 & 0 & 0 & 0 \\ 0 & 0 & 1 & 0 & 0 & 0 & 0 & 0 \end{pmatrix}$$

This is the matrix form called IZ in Table 1.3. The matrices $\mathbf{B}$, $\boldsymbol{\Gamma}$ and $\boldsymbol{\Psi}$ are the same as before. The input for the ML solution is as follows

```
KLEIN'S MODEL I ESTIMATED BY TSLS AND ML
DA NI=15 NO=21
LA FI=EX46.DAT
RA FI=EX46.DAT
SE
1 4 3 7 8 15 9 2 5 6 /
MO NY=3 NE=8 NX=7 FI LY=IZ BE=FU GA=FI PS=FI TE=ZE
FR BE(1,4) BE(1,7) BE(2,4) BE(3,8)
FR GA(1,5) GA(2,5) GA(2,6) GA(3,4) GA(3,7)
FR PS(1,1)-PS(3,3)
VA 1 BE(4,5) BE(5,1) BE(5,2) BE(6,2) BE(7,3) BE(8,5) GA(5,3) GA(6,6) C
GA(7,1) GA(8,2)
VA -1 BE(4,7) GA(5,2) GA(8,1)
ST 5 PS(1,1) PS(2,2) PS(3,3)
OU NS AD=OFF IT=80
```

The input data is the same as before. However, in this case NY = 3 and NX = 7 so only 10 variables are selected (note that the data on P_t, Y_t, K_t, W_t and E_t are not used). The MO line specifies NE = 8. Since only NK is default on the MO line one must use FI to specify FIxed-x and LY = IZ and TE = ZE to specify that $\mathbf{y}' = (\eta_1, \eta_2, \eta_3)$. Otherwise, the MO, FR and VA lines are the same as in the previous run. One further complication arises. Since there are more η-variables than y-variables the assumption for the starting value algorithm is not fulfilled (see Section 1.12). One must provide such starting values that Σ becomes positive definite at the starting point. This is simply done by putting something positive in the first three diagonal elements of Ψ, as shown by the ST line in the above input. It is also recommended to write the parameter NS on the OU line to tell the program to use the steepest descent method to improve the starting point before the real minimization of the fit function begins.

This run gives TSLS and ML estimates of the structural parameters. These are given in the columns 3 and 6 of Table 4.8. It is seen that ML and ridge estimates are considerably different from the IV, TSLS, and ULS estimates which are more close to each other.

The ML estimates for econometric models of the form considered in this section are sometimes called FIML (Full Information Maximum Likelihood) estimates or FILGRV (Full Information Least Generalized Residual Variance) estimates. It has been shown that these estimates minimize the generalized variance of the reduced form residuals, i.e., the determinant of the reduced form residual covariance matrix (see Jöreskog, 1973). Hence the ML estimates can be justified without the assumption of normality. The user should be warned not to rely heavily on the standard errors and/or the χ^2-measure of fit, since they depend on both the assumption of normality and a large sample. Also, because autocorrelation is often present in time series data, the assumption of independent observations is questionable.

Chapter 5

STRUCTURAL EQUATION MODELS FOR LATENT VARIABLES

5.1 The Full LISREL Model

In Chapter 3 we considered the LISREL Submodel 1, specifically designed to study the measurement properties of observed variables. In Chapter 4 we considered the LISREL Submodel 2, specifically designed to estimate "causal" relationships among directly observed "causal" and "caused" variables. The full LISREL model to be considered in this chapter combines features of both of these submodels.

As outlined in Chapter 1, the full LISREL model consists of a structural equation system among latent variables η's and ξ's (cf. 4.1):

$$\eta = \mathbf{B}\eta + \mathbf{\Gamma}\xi + \zeta , \tag{5.1}$$

and measurement models for observed y's and x's (c.f. 3.1):

$$\mathbf{y} = \mathbf{\Lambda}_y \eta + \epsilon , \tag{5.2}$$

$$\mathbf{x} = \mathbf{\Lambda}_x \xi + \delta , \tag{5.3}$$

where we have omitted the constant intercept terms and assumed that all variables, observed as well as latent, are measured in deviations from their means.

The full LISREL model, thus, involves the following variables:

Observed Variables:	$\mathbf{y}' = (y_1, y_2, \ldots, y_p)$	
	$\mathbf{x}' = (x_1, y_2, \ldots, x_q)$	
Latent Variables:	$\eta' = (\eta_1, \eta_2, \ldots, \eta_m)$	
	$\xi' = (\xi_1, \xi_2, \ldots, \xi_n)$	
Error Variables:	$\epsilon' = (\epsilon_1, \epsilon_2, \ldots, \epsilon_p)$	
	$\delta' = (\delta_1, \delta_2, \ldots, \delta_q)$	
	$\zeta' = (\zeta_1, \zeta_2, \ldots, \zeta_m)$	

131

In the usual terminology, ϵ's and δ's are *errors in variables* or measurement errors and ζ's are *errors in equations* or structural disturbance terms.

In addition to the four matrices Λ_y, Λ_x, $\mathbf{B}$, and $\boldsymbol{\Gamma}$, the model involves the four covariance matrices $\boldsymbol{\Phi}$, $\boldsymbol{\Psi}$, $\boldsymbol{\Theta}_\epsilon$, and $\boldsymbol{\Theta}_\delta$, the covariance matrices of $\boldsymbol{\xi}$, $\boldsymbol{\zeta}$, $\boldsymbol{\epsilon}$, and $\boldsymbol{\delta}$, respectively.

5.2   Measurement Errors in Regression Models

Consider the regression of y on x:

$$y = \gamma_{y.x} x + z \;, \tag{5.4}$$

and suppose x is measured with error, so that

$$x = \xi + \delta \;, \tag{5.5}$$

where δ is the measurement error and ξ is the true value. Suppose we are interested in the relationship between y and ξ:

$$y = \gamma \xi + \zeta \;. \tag{5.6}$$

The γ in (5.6) is not the same as $\gamma_{y.x}$ in (5.4). We say that $\gamma_{y.x}$ in (5.4) is a *regression parameter* and γ in (5.6) is a *structural parameter*. The true mechanism that generates the observed variables is shown in Figure 5.1.

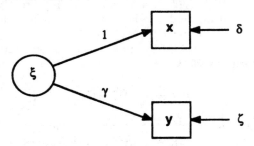

Figure 5.1: Path Diagram for Observed y and x and True ξ

Assuming that ξ, ζ, and δ are mutually uncorrelated, the covariance matrix $\boldsymbol{\Sigma}$ of (y,x) is

$$\boldsymbol{\Sigma} = \begin{pmatrix} \gamma^2 \phi + \psi & \\ \gamma\phi & \phi + \theta \end{pmatrix}$$

where $\phi = \mathrm{Var}(\xi)$, $\psi = \mathrm{Var}(\zeta)$, and $\theta = \mathrm{Var}(\delta)$. The regression coefficient $\gamma_{y.x}$ in (5.4) is

$$\gamma_{y.x} = \frac{Cov(y,x)}{Var(x)} = \frac{\gamma\phi}{\phi + \theta} = \gamma\frac{\phi}{\phi + \theta} = \gamma\rho_{xx} \tag{5.7}$$

where ρ_{xx} is the reliability of x. It is seen in (5.7) that the regression parameter $\gamma_{y.x}$ is not equal to the structural parameter γ but is smaller than γ if $\theta > 0$. If one estimates γ by the sample regression coefficient of y on x, one obtains an estimate which is biased downwards. This bias does not decrease as the sample size increases, i.e., $\hat{\gamma}_{y.x}$ is *not a consistent estimate* of γ.

Equation (5.7) suggests one way to *disattenuate* $\hat{\gamma}_{y.x}$ if the reliability ρ_{xx} of x is known, namely to use the estimate

$$\hat{\gamma} = \hat{\gamma}_{y.x}/\rho_{xx} . \tag{5.8}$$

In this context we refer to $\hat{\gamma}_{y.x}$ as the *attenuated* coefficient and $\hat{\gamma}$ as the *disattenuated* coefficient.

In practice, ρ_{xx} is not known but has to be estimated from data. If r_{xx} is a consistent estimate of ρ_{xx},

$$\hat{\gamma} = \hat{\gamma}_{y.x}/r_{xx} \tag{5.9}$$

can be used to estimate γ. This reduces the bias in $\hat{\gamma}_{y.x}$ at the expense of an increased sampling variance.

Example 5.1: Verbal Ability in Grades 4 and 5

Härnqvist (1962) provided data on a 40-item similarities test for 262 boys who were tested first in grade 4 (x) and then in grade 5 (y). The covariance matrix is

$$\mathbf{S} = \begin{array}{cc} \text{y} & \text{x} \\ \left(\begin{array}{cc} 46.886 & \\ 45.889 & 59.890 \end{array} \right) \end{array} .$$

The reliability of the test is estimated at $r_{xx} = 0.896$. The regression estimate (5.7) is

$$\hat{\gamma}_{y.x} = \frac{45.889}{59.890} = 0.766 .$$

Corrected for attenuation, this becomes

$$\hat{\gamma} = \frac{0.766}{0.896} = 0.855 .$$

A better way to estimate γ is to split the test into two random 20-item tests and use these in the model to estimate γ directly using the LISREL model shown in Figure 5.2.

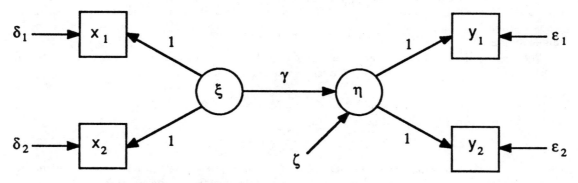

Figure 5.2: Path Diagram for Verbal Ability in Grades 4 and 5

Let x_1 and x_2 be random split-halfs 20-item tests in grade 4 and let y_1 and y_2 be the same measures in grade 5. The covariance matrix is

$$\mathbf{S} = \begin{pmatrix} \begin{array}{cccc} \text{y}_1 & \text{y}_2 & \text{x}_1 & \text{x}_2 \\ 12.522 & & & \\ 10.405 & 13.554 & & \\ 11.723 & 11.494 & 16.684 & \\ 10.988 & 11.684 & 13.560 & 16.086 \end{array} \end{pmatrix}.$$

The two split-halfs are treated as parallel measures; see Section 3.2.

The LISREL input is

```
Verbal Ability in Grades 4 and 5
DA NI=4 NO=262
CM FI=EX51.COV
MO NY=2 NX=2 NE=1 NK=1
VA 1 LY(1) LY(2) LX(1) LX(2)
EQ TD(1) TD(2)
EQ TE(1) TE(2)
OU SE
```

The ML estimate of γ obtained by LISREL is

$$\hat{\gamma}_{ML} = 0.846(0.032).$$

Assuming that this contains no bias, we can summarize the relative advantages and disadvantages of the three estimates as in Table 5.1. The ordinary regression estimate $\hat{\gamma}_{y.x}$ has the

Table 5.1: Bias, Variance and MSE of Three Estimates of γ

Estimate	Bias	Variance	MSE
$\hat{\gamma}_{y.x}$	-0.080	0.000747	0.007147
$\hat{\gamma}$	0.009	0.001010	0.001091
$\hat{\gamma}_{ML}$	0.000	0.001034	0.001034

largest bias and the smallest variance. The ML estimate from LISREL has no bias but a larger variance. Because the reliability of x, 0.896, is quite large and because the corrected estimate $\hat{\gamma}$ has a small bias, the MSE of this estimate is comparable to the MSE of the ML estimator in this example.

The issue considered above can be extended to the case of multiple regression with several explanatory variables $x_1, x_2, \ldots, x_n$. Consider the relationship

$$y = \gamma_1 \xi_1 + \gamma_2 \xi_2 + \ldots + \gamma_n \xi_n + \zeta.$$

The estimator of γ corresponding to (5.9) is

$$\hat{\gamma} = (\mathbf{S}_{xx} - \hat{\mathbf{\Theta}}_\delta)^{-1} \mathbf{s}_{y.x} \tag{5.10}$$

where $\mathbf{S}_{xx}$ is the sample covariance matrix of the x's, $\hat{\mathbf{\Theta}}_\delta$ is a diagonal matrix of estimated error variances in the x's, and $\mathbf{s}_{y.x}$ is a vector of sample covariances between y and the x's.

Formula (5.10) does not work well in practice because $\mathbf{S}_{xx} - \hat{\mathbf{\Theta}}_\delta$ is often not positive definite. A better approach is to read $\hat{\mathbf{\Theta}}_\delta$ into LISREL as fixed quantities and let LISREL estimate γ from the information provided in the covariance matrix and $\hat{\mathbf{\Theta}}_\delta$. This is illustrated in the next example.

Table 5.2: Covariance Matrix for Example 5.2A

	y	x_1	x_2	x_3	x_4
ROLBEHAV	0.0209				
KNOWLEDG	0.0177	0.0520			
VALORIEN	0.0245	0.0280	0.1212		
ROLSATIS	0.0046	0.0044	-0.0063	0.0901	
TRAINING	0.0187	0.0192	0.0353	-0.0066	0.0946

Example 5.2A: Role Behavior of Farm Managers, Part A

Warren, White and Fuller (1974) report on a study wherein a random sample of 98 managers of farmer cooperatives operating in Iowa was selected with the objective of studying managerial behavior.

The role behavior of a manager in farmer cooperatives, as measured by his Role Performance, was assumed to be linearly related to the four variables:

- x_1: *Knowledge of economic phases of management directed toward profit-making in a business and product knowledge*

- x_2: *Value Orientation: tendency to rationally evaluate means to an economic end*

- x_3: *Role Satisfaction: gratification obtained by the manager from performing the managerial role*

- x_4: *Past Training: amount of formal education*

To measure Knowledge, sets of questions were formulated by specialists in the relevant fields of economics and fertilizers and chemicals. The measure of rational Value Orientation to economic ends was a set of 30 items administrated to respondents by questionnaire on which the respondents were asked to indicate the strength of their agreement or disagreement. The respondents indicated the strength of satisfaction or dissatisfaction for each of 11 statements covering four areas of satisfaction: (1) managerial role itself, (2) the position, (3) rewards and (4) performance of complementary role players. The amount of past training was the total number of years of formal schooling divided by six.

Role Performance was measured with a set of 24 questions covering the five functions of planning, organizing, controlling, coordinating and directing. The recorded verbal responses of managers on how they performed given tasks were scored by judges on a scale of 1 to 99 on the basis of performance leading to successful management. Responses to each question were randomly presented to judges and the raw scores were transformed by obtaining the "Z" value for areas of 0.01 to 0.99 from a cumulative normal distribution (a raw score of 40 received transformed score of -0.253). For each question, the mean of transformed scores of judges was calculated.

The covariance matrix of the five variables is given in Table 5.2.

The ordinary least squares (OLS) regression estimates are, with standard errors below,

$$\hat{\gamma}' = \quad (0.230 \quad 0.120 \quad 0.056 \quad 0.110)$$
$$0.053 \quad 0.036 \quad 0.037 \quad 0.039$$

Now suppose the reliabilities of the x-variables are

$$0.60, 0.64, 0.81, 1.00$$

and suppose we take these numbers to be known values. We can then re-estimate γ to reduce or eliminate the effects of measurement errors by using a LISREL model of the form

$$\mathbf{x} = \boldsymbol{\xi} + \boldsymbol{\delta}$$

$$y = \gamma'\boldsymbol{\xi} + \zeta \, ,$$

i.e., we take $\Lambda_y(1\text{x}1) = 1$, $\Lambda_x(4\text{x}4) = \mathbf{I}$, $\mathbf{B}(1\text{x}1) = 0$, $\Gamma(1\text{x}4) = \gamma'$, $\Phi = \text{Cov}(\boldsymbol{\xi})$, unconstrained, $\Psi(1\text{x}1) = \text{Var}(\zeta)$, $\Theta_\epsilon(1\text{x}1) = 0$ and $\Theta_\delta = $ diagonal with fixed values 0.0208, 0.0436, 0.0171, 0.0000. These values are obtained by taking 1 minus the reliabilities above times the observed variance.

The LISREL input is

```
Role Behavior of Farm Managers, Part A
DA   NI=4   NO=98
CM   FI=EX52A.COV
LA
ROLBEHAV  KNOWLEDG  VALORIEN  ROLSATIS  TRAINING
MO   NY=1   NE=1   NX=4   NK=4   LY=ID   LX=ID   TE=ZE   TD=FI
MA   TD
0.0208   0.0436   0.0171   0
MA   PH
0.0312
0.0280   0.0776
0.0044  -0.0063   0.0730
0.0192   0.0353  -0.0066   0.0946
OU   SE   AD=OFF
```

The specification AD = OFF on the OU line is necessary because of the fixed zero in TD(4), i.e., because it is assumed that x_4 has no measurement error.

This results in the following estimates of γ and standard errors

$$\hat{\gamma}' = \begin{array}{cccc} (0.380 & 0.152 & 0.059 & 0.068). \\ 0.127 & 0.079 & 0.050 & 0.044 \end{array}$$

Some of these estimates and standard errors differ considerably from the OLS estimates.

The problem with this analysis is that the error variances in Θ_δ must be known *a priori*. These error variances cannot be estimated from the information provided in the covariance matrix if there is only one measure x for each ξ. However, for each ξ for which there are two or more indicators, one can estimate the measurement errors as well as the structural parameters directly from the data. This is illustrated in the following continuation of the previous example.

Table 5.3: Covariance Matrix for Example 5.2B

		y_1	y_2	x_{11}	x_{12}	x_{21}	x_{22}	x_{31}	x_{32}	x_4
y_1	(12)	.0271								
y_2	(12)	.0172	.0222							
x_{11}	(13)	.0219	.0193	.0876						
x_{12}	(13)	.0164	.0130	.0317	.0568					
x_{21}	(15)	.0284	.0294	.0383	.0151	.1826				
x_{22}	(15)	.0217	.0185	.0356	.0230	.0774	.1473			
x_{31}	(5)	.0083	.0011	-.0001	.0055	-.0087	-.0069	.1137		
x_{32}	(6)	.0074	.0015	.0035	.0089	-.0007	-.0088	.0722	.1024	
x_4		.0180	.0194	.0203	.0182	.0563	.0142	-.0056	-.0077	.0946

Example 5.2B: Role Behavior of Farm Managers, Part B

To estimate the effect of measurement error in the observed variables, Rock et. al. (1977) split each of the measures y, x_1, x_2 and x_3 randomly into two parallel halves. The full covariance matrix of all the split-halves is given in Table 5.3 (the number of items in each split-half is given in parentheses).

This can be used to estimate the true regression equation

$$\eta = \gamma_1\xi_1 + \gamma_2\xi_2 + \gamma_3\xi_3 + \gamma_4\xi_4 + \zeta \qquad (5.11)$$

using the following measurement models

$$\begin{pmatrix} y_1 \\ y_2 \end{pmatrix} = \begin{pmatrix} 1 \\ 1 \end{pmatrix} \eta + \begin{pmatrix} \epsilon_1 \\ \epsilon_2 \end{pmatrix} \qquad (5.12)$$

$$\begin{pmatrix} x_{11} \\ x_{12} \\ x_{21} \\ x_{22} \\ x_{31} \\ x_{32} \\ x_4 \end{pmatrix} = \begin{pmatrix} 1 & 0 & 0 & 0 \\ 1 & 0 & 0 & 0 \\ 0 & 1 & 0 & 0 \\ 0 & 1 & 0 & 0 \\ 0 & 0 & 1 & 0 \\ 0 & 0 & 1.2 & 0 \\ 0 & 0 & 0 & 1 \end{pmatrix} \begin{pmatrix} \xi_1 \\ \xi_2 \\ \xi_3 \\ \xi_4 \end{pmatrix} + \begin{pmatrix} \delta_{11} \\ \delta_{12} \\ \delta_{21} \\ \delta_{22} \\ \delta_{31} \\ \delta_{32} \\ 0 \end{pmatrix} \qquad (5.13)$$

The value 1.2 in the last equation reflects the fact that x_{32} has six items whereas x_{31} has only five.

The latent variables are

- η = role behavior

- ξ_1 = knowledge

- ξ_2 = value orientation

- ξ_3 = role satisfaction

- ξ_4 = past training

The observed variables are

- y_1 = a split-half measure of role behavior

- y_2 = a split-half measure of role behavior

- x_{11}= a split-half measure of knowledge

- x_{12}= a split-half measure of knowledge

- x_{21}= a split-half measure of value orientation

- x_{22}= a split-half measure of value orientation

- x_{31}= a split-half measure of role satisfaction

- x_{32}= a split-half measure of role satisfaction

- $x_4 = \xi_4$= a measure of past training

The input file is

```
Role Behavior of Farm Managers, Part B
DA NI=9 NO=98
CM FI=EX52B.COV
LA
Y1 Y2 X11 X12 X21 X22 X31 X32 X4
MO NY=2 NE=1 NX=7 NK=4
FI TD 7
VA 1 LY 1 LY 2 LX 1 1 LX 2 1 LX 3 2 LX 4 2 LX 5 3 LX 7 4
VA 1.2 LX 6 3
OU SE AD=OFF
```

The fit of the model is $\chi^2 = 26.97$ with 22 degrees of freedom, which represents a rather good fit. The ML estimates of the γ's and their standard errors (below) are

$$\hat{\gamma}' = \begin{array}{cccc} (0.350 & 0.168 & 0.045 & 0.071). \\ 0.133 & 0.079 & 0.054 & 0.045 \end{array}$$

Comparing these with the ordinary least squares (OLS) estimates, previously given, for the regression of y on x_1, x_2, x_3 and x_4, it is seen that there is considerable bias in the OLS estimates although their standard errors are smaller.

Estimates of the true and error score variances for each observed measure are also obtained. These can be used to compute the reliabilities of the composite measures. The reliability estimates are

y	x_1	x_2	x_3
0.82	0.60	0.64	0.81

The model defined by (5.11) - (5.13) can be generalized directly to the case when there are several jointly dependent variables η. The only differences will be that λ and γ will be replaced by matrices Λ_y and Γ, respectively, and ψ by a full symmetric positive definite matrix Ψ.

5.3 Measurement Errors in Path Analysis

Path analysis models for directly observed variables were considered in Section 4.3 of Chapter 4. Problems with measurement errors in the observed variables can be dealt with in much the same way as in Section 5.2. If the reliability or error variance in a variable y or x is known, the error variance can be used as a fixed quantity in Θ_ϵ or Θ_δ and the structural parameters in $\mathbf{B}$ and Γ estimated directly with LISREL. For each latent variable of η and/or ξ, for which there are two or more observed indicators, the measurement errors can be estimated from the data. Sometimes it is possible to estimate the measurement error in an observed variable even though only a single measure is available. This is illustrated in the following example. The example also illustrates how one can use the modification index to determine whether a parameter is identified.

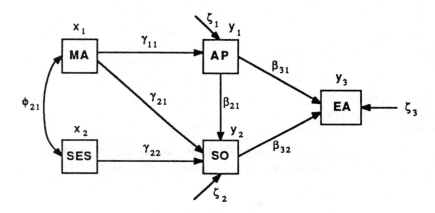

Figure 5.3: Path Diagram for Educational Attainment Model

Example 5.3: Educational Attainment

Wiley (1973) used a subset of variables from Sewell, Haller, and Ohlendorf (1970) to estimate the following structural equation model:

$$y_1 = \gamma_{11}x_1 + \zeta_1$$
$$y_2 = \beta_{21}y_1 + \gamma_{21}x_1 + \gamma_{22}x_2 + \zeta_2$$
$$y_3 = \beta_{31}y_1 + \beta_{32}y_2 + \zeta_3$$

The variables and their intercorrelations ($N \approx 3500$) are given in Table 5.4. The model is shown in Figure 5.3.

The model in Figure 5.3 is a Submodel 2. Following Example 4.5 in Section 4.3, it is straightforward to set up the LISREL input file. Such an input file might be

Table 5.4: Correlation Matrix for Variables in Educational Attainment Model

	x_1	x_2	y_1	y_2	y_3
Mental ability (MA)	1.000				
Socioeconomic status (SES)	.288	1.000			
Academic performance (AP)	.589	.194	1.000		
Significant others' influence (SO)	.438	.359	.473	1.000	
Educational aspiration (EA)	.418	.380	.459	.611	1.000

```
Educational Attainment Problem A
DA NI=5 NO=3500 MA=KM
LA
MA SES AP SO EA
KM FI=EX53.COR
SE
3 4 5 1 2
MO NY=3 NX=2 BE=SD PS=DI
FI GA(1,2) GA(3,1) GA(3,2)
OU SE TV MI
```

The output file reveals very large modification indices for β_{23} and γ_{32}, and it may be tempting to set these free. However, suppose there is measurement error in the SO-variable and we write

$$SO = y_2 = \eta_2 + \epsilon_2 \ ,$$

where η_2 is "true SO" and ϵ_2 is the measurement error. The path diagram for this model is given in Figure 5.4. Is $\theta_{22}^{(\epsilon)}$, the variance of ϵ_2, an identified parameter? As there is only a single

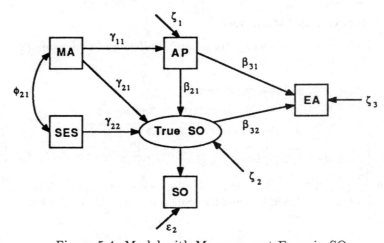

Figure 5.4: Model with Measurement Error in SO

observed indicator of true SO one would normally assume that $\theta_{22}^{(\epsilon)}$ is not identified. However, because of the overidentifying constraints in the model in this case, it is in fact possible to identify $\theta_{22}^{(\epsilon)}$. In principle, this statement should be proved algebraically, but here we shall demonstrate how the program can be used to determine whether $\theta_{22}^{(\epsilon)}$ is identified or not. The LISREL specification of the model is

$$\begin{aligned} x_1 &= MA \equiv \xi_1 & \delta_1 &= 0 \\ x_2 &= SES \equiv \xi_2 & \delta_2 &= 0 \\ y_1 &= AP \equiv \eta_1 & \epsilon_1 &= 0 \\ y_2 &= SO \equiv \eta_2 & \epsilon_2 &= 0 \\ y_3 &= EA \equiv \eta_3 & \epsilon_3 &= 0 \,, \end{aligned}$$

i.e., $\Lambda_y = I$, $\Lambda_x = I$, $\Theta_\epsilon = 0$ $\Theta_\delta = 0$

$$\mathbf{B} = \begin{pmatrix} 0 & 0 & 0 \\ \beta_{21} & 0 & 0 \\ \beta_{31} & \beta_{32} & 0 \end{pmatrix} \quad \Gamma = \begin{pmatrix} \gamma_{11} & 0 \\ \gamma_{21} & \gamma_{22} \\ 0 & 0 \end{pmatrix} \quad \Psi = diag(\psi_{11}, \psi_{22}, \psi_{33}) \,.$$

Formally this model is identical to the previous one. The difference is that it is now formulated as a full LISREL model rather than as a Submodel 2.

The specification $\Lambda_x = I$, $\Theta_\delta = 0$ is done by the FI parameter. This will also set $\hat{\Phi} = S_{xx}$ the correlation matrix of the x-variables. The trick is to specify Θ_ϵ to be a diagonal matrix fixed at zero rather than specifying that Θ_ϵ is a zero matrix. In this way, modification indices will be obtained for the diagonal elements of Θ_ϵ. Technically, the difference is as follows. When TE=ZE, Θ_ϵ is not stored in the computer memory so that no modification indices can be computed. When TE=FI, space is allocated for the diagonal elements of Θ_ϵ, so that modification indices can be computed for these elements.

The LISREL input file is

```
Educational Attainment Problem B
DA NI=5 NO=3500 MA=KM
LA
MA SES AP SO EA
KM FI=EX53.COR
SE
3 4 5 1 2
MO NY=3 NX=2 FI NE=3 BE=SD PS=DI LY=ID TE=FI
FI GA(1,2) GA(3,1) GA(3,2)
OU SE TV MI AD=OFF ND=2
```

AD=OFF on the OU line is essential because Θ_ϵ is a fixed zero matrix by intention.

The resulting output file shows a χ^2 of overall fit equal to 193.53 with 3 degrees of freedom and the following modification indices:

```
    BETA
             AP        SO        EA
AP          .00      3.47     33.92
SO          .00       .00    176.97
EA          .00       .00       .00
```

```
      GAMMA
                  MA          SES
AP               .00          3.47
SO               .00           .00
EA             42.75        163.52
      THETA EPS
                  AP           SO           EA
                19.96       176.97          .00
```

The modification index for $\theta_{22}^{(\epsilon)}$ is 176.97. This means that $\theta_{22}^{(\epsilon)}$ will be identified if it is set free. The modification index for β_{23} is identical. This means that these two models are equivalent; see Chapter 8. However, the model with β_{23} free does not make sense.

To run the model with $\theta_{22}^{(\epsilon)}$ free, all that needs to be done is to add the line

FR TE(2)

The resulting solution has $\chi^2 = 7.14$ with 2 degrees of freedom. Thus, adding the single parameter $\theta_{22}^{(\epsilon)}$, gives a reduction in χ^2 of 186.39 which is close to the value predicted by the modification index. The estimated value of $\theta_{22}^{(\epsilon)}$ is 0.40 with a standard error of 0.02. Thus, if the model is correct, the reliability of SO is only 60%. This example demonstrates that one possible source of misspecification in the model of Figure 5.3 may be that there is measurement error in the SO-variable.

5.4   MIMIC Models

The simplest form of a MIMIC model involves a single unobserved latent variable "caused" by several observed x-variables and indicated by several observed y-variables. The term MIMIC stands for Multiple Indicators and Multiple Causes. The model equations are

$$\mathbf{y} = \lambda\eta + \epsilon\,, \tag{5.14}$$

$$\eta = \gamma'\mathbf{x} + \zeta\,, \tag{5.15}$$

where $\mathbf{y}' = (y_1, y_2, \ldots, y_p)$ are indicators of the latent variable η, and $\mathbf{x}' = (x_1, x_2, \ldots, x_q)$ are the "causes" of η. From the LISREL point of view one can regard (5.14) as the measurement model for η and (5.15) as the structural equation for η. The ϵ's and ζ are assumed to be mutually uncorrelated. Equation (5.14) says that the y's are congeneric measures of η and (5.15) says that η is linear in the x's plus a random disturbance term.

This type of model was introduced by Hauser and Goldberger (1971) and discussed by Goldberger (1972). Jöreskog and Goldberger (1975) pointed out that the model can be viewed as a multivariate regression model with two specific constraints:

- the regression matrix must have rank 1

- the residual covariance matrix must satisfy the congeneric measurement model

This can be seen by substituting (5.15) into (5.14) yielding

$$
\begin{aligned}
\mathbf{y} &= \lambda\gamma'\mathbf{x} + \lambda\zeta + \epsilon\,, \\
&= \Pi\mathbf{x} + \mathbf{z}\,,
\end{aligned}
$$

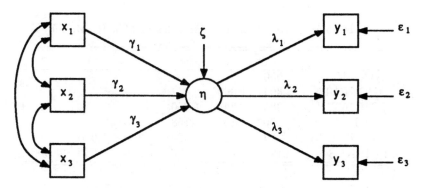

Figure 5.5: Path Diagram for MIMIC Model

which shows that $\mathbf{\Pi} = \boldsymbol{\lambda}\boldsymbol{\gamma}'$ and $\mathrm{Cov}(\mathbf{z}) = \boldsymbol{\lambda}\boldsymbol{\lambda}'\psi + \boldsymbol{\Theta}_\epsilon$, where $\psi = \mathrm{Var}(\zeta)$ and $\boldsymbol{\Theta}_\epsilon$ is the diagonal covariance matrix of ϵ. Jöreskog and Goldberger (1975) showed how to obtain maximum likelihood estimates of parameters, large sample standard errors and tests of the two kinds of constraints involved.

This simple MIMIC model has been generalized in various ways, see e.g. Robinson (1974). Numerous applications have been given in the literature by Chamberlain (1977), Robins and West (1977), Van de Ven and Van der Gaag (1982), Frey and Weck-Hanneman (1984), Smith and Patterson (1984), Bye, Gallichio, and Dykacz (1985), among others.

To estimate a MIMIC model with LISREL is straightforward. Equations (5.14) and (5.15) correspond to (5.2) and (5.1), respectively. Equation (5.3) in this case says simply that $\mathbf{x} \equiv \boldsymbol{\xi}$, i.e., $\mathbf{\Lambda}_x = \mathbf{I}$ and $\boldsymbol{\Theta}_\delta = \mathbf{0}$. The latter specification is handled by the FI parameter which also implies that $\boldsymbol{\Phi} = \mathrm{Cov}(\boldsymbol{\xi})$ will be estimated by $\mathbf{S}_{xx}$, the sample covariance matrix of $\mathbf{x}$.

Example 5.4: Social Status and Social Participation

Hodge and Treiman (1968) studied the relationship between social status and social participation. For a sample of 530 women, they report data on $x_1 =$ income, $x_2 =$ occupation, $x_3 =$ education, $y_1 =$ church attendance, $y_2 =$ memberships, $y_3 =$ friends seen. All variables are expressed in standardized form. The y's are viewed as independent indicators of a latent variable $\eta =$ social participation which is caused by the x's. Thus,

$$\eta = \gamma_1 x_1 + \gamma_2 x_2 + \gamma_3 x_3 + \zeta ,$$

$$y_1 = \lambda_1 \eta + \epsilon_1, \ y_2 = \lambda_2 \eta + \epsilon_2, \ y_3 = \lambda_3 \eta + \epsilon_3 .$$

From a substantive viewpoint, it may be helpful to view the x's as determining

$$\xi = \gamma_1 x_1 + \gamma_2 x_2 + \gamma_3 x_3 = social \ status ,$$

which in turn determines

$$\eta = \xi + \epsilon = social \ participation .$$

A path diagram is given in Figure 5.5. The correlations of the variables are given in Table 5.5.

The LISREL input file is

Table 5.5: Correlations for Variables in MIMIC Model

	x_1	x_2	x_3	y_1	y_2	y_3
INCOME	1.000					
OCCUPATN	.304	1.000				
EDUCATIN	.305	.344	1.000			
CHURCHAT	.100	.156	.158	1.000		
MEMBERSH	.284	.192	.324	.360	1.000	
FRIENDS	.176	.136	.226	.210	.265	1.000

```
Social Status and Participation
DA NI=6 NO=530 MA=KM
LA
INCOME OCCUPATN EDUCATIN CHURCHAT MEMBERSH FRIENDS
KM FI=EX54.COR
SE
4 5 6 1 2 3
MO NY=3 NE=1 NX=3 FI LY=FR
LE
PARTICIP
FI LY(1)
VA 1 LY(1)
OU SE TV
```

The output file gives the following maximum likelihood solution:

```
LISREL ESTIMATES (MAXIMUM LIKELIHOOD)
    LAMBDA Y
          PARTICIP
CHURCHAT    1.000
MEMBERSH    1.579
FRIENDS      .862
    GAMMA
            INCOME   OCCUPATN   EDUCATIN
PARTICIP     .108       .045       .155
    PSI
          PARTICIP
PARTICIP     .161
    THETA EPS
        CHURCHAT   MEMBERSH   FRIENDS
          .783       .459       .839
```

```
     SQUARED MULTIPLE CORRELATIONS FOR Y - VARIABLES
        CHURCHAT    MEMBERSH    FRIENDS
          .217        .541        .161
     TOTAL COEFFICIENT OF DETERMINATION FOR Y - VARIABLES IS    .621
     SQUARED MULTIPLE CORRELATIONS FOR STRUCTURAL EQUATIONS
        PARTICIP
          .258


     CHI-SQUARE WITH    6 DEGREES OF FREEDOM =     12.50 (P =   .052)
                GOODNESS OF FIT INDEX = .992
         ADJUSTED GOODNESS OF FIT INDEX = .974
                ROOT MEAN SQUARE RESIDUAL =        .026
```

Although the overall fit of the model is not too bad, most of the relationships in the model are poorly determined as revealed by the low squared multiple correlation. The *t*-values reveal that OCCUPATION may not be a significant determinant of social participation although INCOME and EDUCATION are.

5.5 Path Analysis with Latent Variables

Path analysis with directly observed variables was discussed in Section 4.3. It is also possible to consider path analysis for latent variables. In its most general form there is a structural equation system of the form (5.1) for a set of latent variables η's and ξ's. In most applications, the system is recursive but models with non-recursive systems have also been proposed. A recursive system based on longitudinal data is considered in Example 6.4 in Chapter 6. Here we consider first a non-recursive system for latent variables and then an example illustrating how one can examine various alternative models in a sequential way.

Example 5.5: Peer Influences on Ambition

Sociologists have often called attention to the way in which one's peers – e.g., best friends – influence one's decisions – e.g., choice of occupation. They have recognized that the relation must be reciprocal – if my best friend influences my choice, I must influence his. Duncan, Haller and Portes (1968) present a simultaneous equation model of peer influences on occupational choice, using a sample of Michigan high-school students paired with their best friends. The authors interpret educational and occupational choice as two indicators of a single latent variable "ambition", and specify the choices. This model with simultaneity and errors of measurement is displayed in Figure 5.6.
    Let

- x_1 = respondent's parental aspiration (REPARASP)

- x_2 = respondent's intelligence (REINTGCE)

- x_3 = respondent's socioeconomic status (RESOCIEC)

- x_4 = best friend's socioeconomic status (BFSOCIEC)

- x_5 = best friend's intelligence (BFINTGCE)

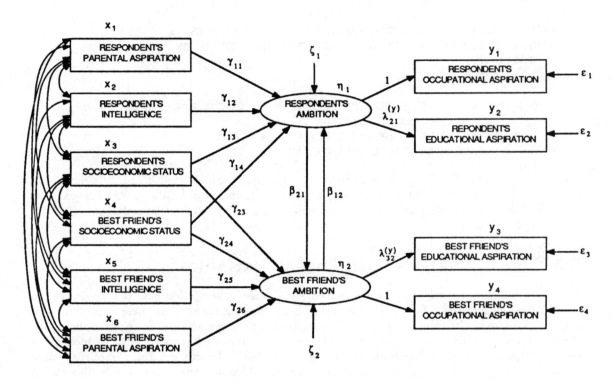

Figure 5.6: Path Diagram for Peer Influences on Ambition

- x_6 = best friend's parental aspiration (BFPARASP)

- y_1 = respondent's occupational aspiration (REOCCASP)

- y_2 = respondent's educational aspiration (REEDASP)

- y_3 = best friend's educational aspiration (BFEDASP)

- y_4 = best friend's occupational aspiration (BFOCCASP)

- η_1 = respondent's ambition (REAMBITN)

- η_2 = best friend's ambition (BFAMBITN)

In terms of the full LISREL model, we take $\xi_i \equiv x_i$, i.e., in equation (5.3) we take $\Lambda_x(6 \times 6) = I$ and $\Theta_\delta = 0$. This is specified by the FI parameter.

Writing $\lambda_2 = \lambda_{21}^{(y)}$, $\lambda_3 = \lambda_{32}^{(y)}$, $\beta_1 = \beta_{12}$, $\beta_2 = \beta_{21}$, $\gamma_1 = \gamma_{11}$, $\gamma_2 = \gamma_{12}$, $\gamma_3 = \gamma_{13}$, $\gamma_4 = \gamma_{14}$, $\gamma_5 = \gamma_{23}$, $\gamma_6 = \gamma_{24}$, $\gamma_7 = \gamma_{25}$, $\gamma_8 = \gamma_{26}$, the structural equations (5.1) are

$$\begin{pmatrix} \eta_1 \\ \eta_2 \end{pmatrix} = \begin{pmatrix} 0 & \beta_1 \\ \beta_2 & 0 \end{pmatrix} \begin{pmatrix} \eta_1 \\ \eta_2 \end{pmatrix} + \begin{pmatrix} \gamma_1 & \gamma_2 & \gamma_3 & \gamma_4 & 0 & 0 \\ 0 & 0 & \gamma_5 & \gamma_6 & \gamma_7 & \gamma_8 \end{pmatrix} \begin{pmatrix} \xi_1 \\ \xi_2 \\ \xi_3 \\ \xi_4 \\ \xi_5 \\ \xi_6 \end{pmatrix} + \begin{pmatrix} \zeta_1 \\ \zeta_2 \end{pmatrix}$$

and the equations (5.2) relating the η's to the y's are

$$\begin{pmatrix} y_1 \\ y_2 \\ y_3 \\ y_4 \end{pmatrix} = \begin{pmatrix} 1 & 0 \\ \lambda_2 & 0 \\ 0 & \lambda_3 \\ 0 & 1 \end{pmatrix} \begin{pmatrix} \eta_1 \\ \eta_2 \end{pmatrix} + \begin{pmatrix} \epsilon_1 \\ \epsilon_2 \\ \epsilon_3 \\ \epsilon_4 \end{pmatrix}$$

In $\mathbf{\Lambda}_y$ we have fixed the scales for η_1 and η_2 to be the same as in y_1 and y_4, respectively. Since y_1 and y_4 are on the same scale, this implies that η_1 and η_2 are also on the same scale, which is necessary to make meaningful comparisons between the respondent and the best friend. Since $\mathbf{\xi} \equiv \mathbf{x}$ and there are no constraints on $\mathbf{\Phi}$, $\mathbf{\Phi} = \mathbf{\Sigma}_{xx}$, which is estimated as $\mathbf{S}_{xx}$. The matrix $\mathbf{\Psi}(2 \times 2)$ is

$$\mathbf{\Psi} = \begin{pmatrix} \psi_{11} & \\ \psi_{21} & \psi_{22} \end{pmatrix}$$

with $\psi_{ii} = \mathrm{Var}(\zeta_i)$, $i = 1, 2$ and $\psi_{21} = \mathrm{Cov}(\zeta_1, \zeta_2)$ and the matrix $\mathbf{\Theta}_\epsilon$ is diagonal with diagonal elements $\theta_{ii}^{(\epsilon)} = \mathrm{Var}(\epsilon_i)$. Since $\mathbf{\xi} \equiv \mathbf{x}$, the structural equations are equivalent to

$$\mathbf{\eta} = \mathbf{B}\mathbf{\eta} + \mathbf{\Gamma}\mathbf{x} + \mathbf{\zeta}$$

with reduced form

$$\mathbf{\eta} = (\mathbf{I} - \mathbf{B})^{-1}\mathbf{\Gamma}\mathbf{x} + (\mathbf{I} - \mathbf{B})^{-1}\mathbf{\zeta} . \tag{5.16}$$

Furthermore, we have

$$\mathbf{y} = \mathbf{\Lambda}_y\mathbf{\eta} + \mathbf{\epsilon} = \mathbf{\Lambda}_y(\mathbf{I} - \mathbf{B})^{-1}\mathbf{\Gamma}\mathbf{x} + \mathbf{\Lambda}_y(\mathbf{I} - \mathbf{B})^{-1}\mathbf{\zeta} + \mathbf{\epsilon} = \mathbf{P}\mathbf{x} + \mathbf{z} , \tag{5.17}$$

where

$$\mathbf{P} = \mathbf{\Sigma}_{yx}\mathbf{\Sigma}_{xx}^{-1} = \mathbf{\Lambda}_y(\mathbf{I} - \mathbf{B})^{-1}\mathbf{\Gamma} = \mathbf{\Lambda}_y\mathbf{\Pi} \text{ say}$$

and

$$\mathbf{z} = \mathbf{\Lambda}_y(\mathbf{I} - \mathbf{B})^{-1}\mathbf{\zeta} + \mathbf{\epsilon} .$$

5.5.1 Identification

Since $\mathbf{\Psi}$ is unconstrained, it follows from (5.16) that for any given $\mathbf{B}$ and $\mathbf{\Gamma}$, there is a one-to-one correspondence between $\mathbf{\Psi}$ and the covariance matrix of $\mathbf{\eta}$, $\mathbf{\Omega}$ say, where

$$\mathbf{\Omega} = \begin{pmatrix} \omega_{11} & \\ \omega_{21} & \omega_{22} \end{pmatrix}$$

From the first part of (5.17) we have

$$\Sigma_{yy} = \Lambda_y \Omega \Lambda_y{}' + \Theta_\epsilon$$

$$= \begin{pmatrix} \omega_{11} + \theta_{11}^{(\epsilon)} & & & \\ \lambda_2 \omega_{11} & \lambda_2^2 \omega_{11} + \theta_{22}^{(\epsilon)} & & \\ \lambda_3 \omega_{21} & \lambda_2 \lambda_3 \omega_{21} & \lambda_3^2 \omega_{22} + \theta_{33}^{(\epsilon)} & \\ \omega_{21} & \lambda_2 \omega_{21} & \lambda_3 \omega_{22} & \omega_{22} + \theta_{44}^{(\epsilon)} \end{pmatrix}$$

Furthermore, we have

$$(\mathbf{I} - \mathbf{B})^{-1} = (1 - \beta_1 \beta_2)^{-1} \begin{pmatrix} 1 & \beta_1 \\ \beta_2 & 1 \end{pmatrix}$$

$$\mathbf{\Pi} = (1 - \beta_1 \beta_2)^{-1} \begin{pmatrix} \gamma_1 & \gamma_2 & \gamma_3 + \beta_1 \gamma_5 & \gamma_4 + \beta_1 \gamma_6 & \beta_1 \gamma_7 & \beta_1 \gamma_8 \\ \beta_2 \gamma_1 & \beta_2 \gamma_2 & \gamma_5 + \beta_2 \gamma_3 & \gamma_6 + \beta_2 \gamma_4 & \gamma_7 & \gamma_8 \end{pmatrix}$$

The first and last rows of $\mathbf{P}$ are identical to the first and second row of $\mathbf{\Pi} = (\mathbf{I} - \mathbf{B})^{-1} \mathbf{\Gamma}$, respectively. The second row of $\mathbf{P}$ is λ_2 times the first row of $\mathbf{\Pi}$ and the third row of $\mathbf{P}$ is λ_3 times the second row of $\mathbf{\Pi}$. Hence it is clear that λ_2 and λ_3 are identified and that

$$\lambda_2 = \frac{p_{2i}}{p_{1i}} \text{ and } \lambda_3 = \frac{p_{3i}}{p_{4i}}, i = 1, 2, \ldots, 6.$$

Since $\mathbf{\Pi}$ consists of two rows of $\mathbf{P}$, $\mathbf{\Pi}$ is identified. From $\mathbf{\Pi}$ it follows that γ_1, γ_2, γ_7, γ_8, β_1 and β_2 are determined as

$$\gamma_1 = \pi_{11}, \; \gamma_2 = \pi_{12}, \; \gamma_7 = \pi_{25}, \; \gamma_8 = \pi_{26}$$

$$\beta_1 = (\pi_{15}/\pi_{25}) = (\pi_{16}/\pi_{26}),$$

$$\beta_2 = (\pi_{21}/\pi_{11}) = (\pi_{22}/\pi_{12}).$$

γ_3, γ_4, γ_5 and γ_6 are then obtained from π_{13}, π_{14}, π_{23} and π_{24}. With λ_2 and λ_3 determined we can now obtain ω_{11}, ω_{21} and ω_{22} from the off-diagonal elements of Σ_{yy}. Finally, the $\theta_{ii}^{(\epsilon)}$, $i = 1, 2, 3, 4$, can be determined from the diagonal elements of Σ_{yy}.

This analysis shows that all parameters are identified. Altogether there are 19 parameters (2 β's, 8 γ's, 3 ω's, 2 λ's, and 4 $\theta^{(\epsilon)}$'s) if $\mathbf{x}$ is fixed. When $\mathbf{x}$ is random there will be an additional 21 parameters in $\mathbf{\Phi} = \Sigma_{xx}$. In both cases the degrees of freedom will be 15.

5.5.2   Analysis

The correlation matrix based on $N = 329$ observations taken from Duncan, Haller and Portes (1968) is given in Table 5.4. Strictly speaking, the covariance matrix should be used in this example, see Section 1.21.

The overall goodness-of-fit measure is $\chi^2 = 26.70$ with 15 degrees of freedom. A test of the hypothesis $\psi_{21} = 0$ gives $\chi^2 = 0.19$ with 1 degree of freedom and a test of $\beta_1 = \beta_2$, given $\psi_{21} = 0$, gives $\chi^2 = 0.01$ with 1 degree of freedom. Hence, it is clear that these hypotheses cannot be rejected. The overall goodness-of-fit of the model with $\psi_{21} = 0$ and $\beta_1 = \beta_2$ is given by $\chi^2 = 26.90$ with 17 degrees of freedom. This has a probability level of 0.06.

The input for this model is as follows:

Table 5.6: Correlations for Background and Aspiration Measures for 329 Respondents and Their Best Friends

Respondent										
REINTGCE	1.0000									
REPARASP	.1839	1.0000								
RESOCIEC	.2220	.0489	1.0000							
REOCCASP	.4105	.2137	.3240	1.0000						
RE EDASP	.4043	.2742	.4047	.6247	1.0000					
Best Friend										
BFINTGCE	.3355	.0782	.2302	.2995	.2863	1.0000				
BFPARASP	.1021	.1147	.0931	.0760	.0702	.2087	1.0000			
BFSOCIEC	.1861	.0186	.2707	.2930	.2407	.2950	-.0438	1.0000		
BFOCCASP	.2598	.0839	.2786	.4216	.3275	.5007	.1988	.3607	1.0000	
BF EDASP	.2903	.1124	.3054	.3269	.3669	.5191	.2784	.4105	.6404	1.0000

```
Peer Influences on Ambition: Model with BE(2,1) = BE(1,2) and PS(2,1) = 0
DA NI=10 NO=329
LA FI=EX55.LAB
KM= FI=EX55.COR
SELECT
4 5 10 9 2 1 3 8 6 7
MO NY=4 NE=2 NX=6 FIXED-X PS=DI BE=FU
LE
REAMBITN BFAMBITN
FR LY(2,1) LY(3,2) BE(1,2)
FI GA(5) - GA(8)
VA 1 LY(1) LY(8)
EQ BE(1,2) BE(2,1)
OU SE TV EF SS
```

The labels and the correlations are read from the files EX56.LAB and EX56.COR, respectively. The variables in the correlation matrix are in the order x_2, x_1, x_3, y_1, y_2, x_5, x_6, x_4, y_4 and y_3. The SE line is necessary to order the variables to correspond to the model. The MO line specifies FIXED-X which takes care of NK=6, LX=ID, TD=ZE and PH=$\mathbf{S}_{xx}$. The other parameter matrices are default except PS=DI and BE=FU. The FR line specifies the free elements in LY, and the FI line specifies the four fixed zeros in GA. Note that these four zeros are consecutive elements in GA and we specify these by their linear index. The VA line sets the scale for the two η's. Finally, the EQ line specifies that the two β's are equal.

The TSLS estimates and the maximum likelihood estimates with their standard errors are given in Table 5.7. The standardized solution in which η_1 and η_2 are scaled to unit variance is also given in Table 5.7. It is seen in Table 5.7 that the corresponding parameters for the respondent and his best friend are very close. There are good reasons to suggest that the whole model should be completely symmetric between the respondent and his best friend so that not only $\beta_1 = \beta_2$ but also $\lambda_2 = \lambda_3$, $\gamma_1 = \gamma_8$, $\gamma_2 = \gamma_7$, $\gamma_3 = \gamma_6$, $\gamma_4 = \gamma_5$, $\psi_{11} = \psi_{22}$, $\theta_{11}^{(\epsilon)} = \theta_{44}^{(\epsilon)}$, and $\theta_{22}^{(\epsilon)} = \theta_{33}^{(\epsilon)}$. The overall χ^2 for this model is 30.76 with 25 degrees of freedom. This has a probability level of 0.20. Thus, this model is more parsimonious and has a better fit than the other models. The input for this model is the same as the previous but with the following lines added before the OU line:

```
EQ LY(2,1) LY(3,2)
EQ GA(1,1) GA(2,6)
EQ GA(1,2) GA(2,5)
EQ GA(1,3) GA(2,4)
EQ GA(1,4) GA(2,3)
EQ PS(1)   PS(2)
EQ TE(1)   TE(4)
EQ TE(2)   TE(3)
```

Table 5.7: Estimates for the Model in Figure 5.6 with $\psi_{21} = 0$ and $\beta_1 = \beta_2$

Parameter	TSLS Estimates	Unscaled Solution (ML)	Standardized Solution (ML)
λ_1	1.000	1.000	0.767
λ_2	1.122	1.061 (0.089)	0.813
λ_3	1.120	1.074 (0.081)	0.828
λ_4	1.000	1.000	0.771
β_1	0.210	0.180 (0.039)	0.181
β_2	0.210	0.180 (0.039)	0.179
γ_1	0.156	0.164 (0.039)	0.214
γ_2	0.242	0.254 (0.042)	0.331
γ_3	0.208	0.221 (0.042)	0.288
γ_4	0.072	0.077 (0.041)	0.101
γ_5	0.058	0.068 (0.039)	0.089
γ_6	0.208	0.218 (0.039)	0.283
γ_7	0.314	0.331 (0.041)	0.429
γ_8	0.150	0.152 (0.036)	0.197
ψ_{11}	0.266	0.281 (0.046)	0.478
ψ_{22}	0.220	0.229 (0.039)	0.385
$\theta_{11}^{(\epsilon)}$	0.443	0.412 (0.051)	0.412
$\theta_{22}^{(\epsilon)}$	0.299	0.338 (0.052)	0.338
$\theta_{33}^{(\epsilon)}$	0.283	0.313 (0.046)	0.313
$\theta_{44}^{(\epsilon)}$	0.428	0.404 (0.046)	0.404

A final comment on this example concerns the total effects and the test of stability of non-recursive models. The total and indirect effects of η on η are given on the next page.

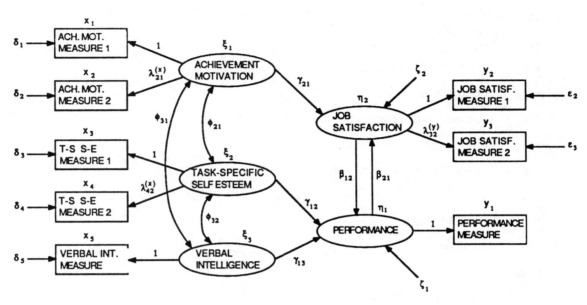

Figure 5.7: Bagozzi's Model for Performance and Satisfaction

```
TOTAL AND INDIRECT EFFECTS
      TOTAL EFFECTS OF ETA ON  ETA
           REAMBITN    BFAMBITN
REAMBITN     .034        .186
BFAMBITN     .186        .034
      LARGEST EIGENVALUE OF B*B' (STABILITY INDEX) IS    .032
      STANDARD ERRORS FOR TOTAL EFFECTS OF ETA ON  ETA
           REAMBITN    BFAMBITN
REAMBITN     .015        .043
BFAMBITN     .043        .015
      INDIRECT EFFECTS OF ETA ON  ETA
           REAMBITN    BFAMBITN
REAMBITN     .034        .006
BFAMBITN     .006        .034
      STANDARD ERRORS FOR INDIRECT EFFECTS OF ETA ON  ETA
           REAMBITN    BFAMBITN
REAMBITN     .015        .004
BFAMBITN     .004        .015
```

Example 5.6: Performance and Satisfaction

Bagozzi (1980c) formulated a structural equation model to study the relationship between performance and satisfaction in an industrial sales force. His model was designed specifically to answer such questions as: "Is the link between performance and job satisfaction myth or reality? Does performance influence satisfaction, or does satisfaction influence performance?" (Bagozzi, 1980, p.65). Figure 5.7 is a path diagram for the final model adopted by Bagozzi.

The variables are:

- y_1 = performance measure
- y_2 = job satisfaction measure 1
- y_3 = job satisfaction measure 2
- x_1 = achievement motivation measure 1
- x_2 = achievement motivation measure 2
- x_3 = task-specific self-esteem measure 1
- x_4 = task-specific self-esteem measure 2
- x_5 = verbal intelligence
- η_1 = performance
- η_2 = job satisfaction
- ξ_1 = achievement motivation
- ξ_2 = task-specific self-esteem
- ξ_3 = verbal intelligence

Detailed information about the observed variables are given in Bagozzi's article. Table 5.8 gives the means, standard deviations, and product moment correlations of the observed variables based on sample of $N = 122$.

Table 5.8: Means, Standard Deviations and Correlations for the Observed Variables in Bagozzi's Model

Variable	y_1	y_2	y_3	x_1	x_2	x_3	x_4	x_5
PERFORMM	1.000							
JBSATIS1	.418	1.000						
JBSATIS2	.394	.627	1.000					
ACHMOT1	.129	.202	.266	1.000				
ACHMOT2	.189	.284	.208	.365	1.000			
T-S S-E1	.544	.281	.324	.201	.161	1.000		
T-S S-E2	.507	.225	.314	.172	.174	.546	1.000	
VERBINTM	-.357	-.156	-.038	-.199	-.277	-.294	-.174	1.000
Mean	720.86	15.54	18.46	14.90	14.35	19.57	24.16	21.36
St. Dev.	2.09	3.43	2.81	1.95	2.06	2.16	2.06	3.65

Our reanalysis of these data differs slightly from Bagozzi's in two respects.

1. We scale the performance measure y_1 so that it is measured in hundreds of dollars rather than in dollars. Otherwise no scaling of the variables is used, and the analysis is based on the covariance matrix rather than the correlation matrix used by Bagozzi. When constraints are imposed on Θ_ϵ or Θ_δ, the normal theory standard errors in LISREL are valid only when the covariance matrix is analyzed.

2. Although no replicate measure is available for ξ_3 (verbal intelligence), it is argued that x_5 (the verbal intelligence test) is a fallible measure. We therefore assume that the reliability of x_5 is 0.85. It is argued that an arbitrary value of 0.85 is a better assumption than an equally arbitrary value of 1.00. The assumed value of the reliability will affect parameter estimates as well as standard errors. Technically, the specification of the reliability 0.85 of x_5 in LISREL is done by assigning the fixed value 0.15 times the variance of x_5 to the element $\theta_{55}^{(\epsilon)}$. Thus, this is held fixed at $0.15 \times 3.65^2 = 1.998$.

The correlations between y_1 and y_2 and between y_1 and y_3 are 0.418 and 0.394, respectively, which are both very significant. Once a correlation between η_1 and η_2 has been established, four rival hypotheses may be considered to account for it, namely: η_1 and η_2 are correlated because

- H_1: they have ξ_1, ξ_2, and ξ_3 as common causes (spurious correlation)

- H_{2a}: η_2 influences η_1

- H_{2b}: η_1 influences η_2

- H_3: η_1 and η_2 influence each other reciprocally

H_1 is equivalent to the hypothesis that the partial correlation between η_1 and η_2 after elimination of ξ_1, ξ_2, and ξ_3 is zero. To examine this hypothesis we set up a LISREL model with $\mathbf{B} = 0$, $\mathbf{\Gamma}(2 \times 3) = $ full and free, and $\mathbf{\Psi}(2 \times 2) = $ symmetric and free. The partial covariance between η_1 and η_2 is estimated as $\hat{\psi}_{21} = 1.063$ with a standard error of $\hat{\psi}_{21} = 0.477$, so H_1 is rejected. The partial correlation between η_1 and η_2 for given ξ_1, ξ_2, and ξ_3 is estimated as $\hat{\psi}_{21}/(\hat{\psi}_{11}\hat{\psi}_{22})$ $= 0.356$. The estimated regressions of η_1 and η_2 on ξ_1, ξ_2, and ξ_3 are, with standard errors in parentheses,

$$\eta_1 = -0.139(0.242)\xi_1 + 0.846(0.165)\xi_2 - 0.112(0.062)\xi_3 + \zeta_1 \quad R^2 = 0.529$$

and

$$\eta_2 = 1.010(0.462)\xi_1 + 0.631(0.238)\xi_2 + 0.159(0.107)\xi_3 + \zeta_2 \quad R^2 = 0.385.$$

In the first equation, only the effect of ξ_2 is significant. In the second equation the effects of ξ_1 and ξ_2 are significant. The variable ξ_3 is not significant in either of the two equations. Thus, when measurement error is introduced into x_5, ξ_3 apparently is not a significant determinant of either η_1 or η_2. However, ξ_3 should not be excluded from the analysis because ξ_3 correlates significantly with both ξ_1 and ξ_2 and therefore has significant indirect effects on η_1 and η_2 via ξ_1 and ξ_2. Because $\hat{\psi}_{21}$ is significant, we proceed with the analysis of H_{2a} and H_{2b}.

In the H_{2a} and H_{2b} models, ζ_1 and ζ_2 are uncorrelated. The correlation between η_1 and η_2 is accounted for by a direct causal relationship between η_1 and η_2. In the H_{2a} model we estimate the two relations

$$\eta_1 = 0.246(0.103)\eta_2 - 0.387(0.290)\xi_1 + 0.691(0.168)\xi_2 - 0.151(0.065)\xi_3 + \zeta_1 \quad R^2 = 0.589$$

$$\eta_2 = 1.010(0.462)\xi_1 + 0.631(0.238)\xi_2 + 0.159(0.107)\xi_3 + \zeta_2 \quad R^2 = 0.385$$

In this model, η_2, ξ_2, and ξ_3 have significant effects on η_1 and ξ_2 has a significant effect on η_2. In the H_{2b} model we estimate the two relations

$$\eta_1 = -0.139(0.242)\xi_1 + 0.846(0.165)\xi_2 - 0.112(0.062)\xi_3 + \zeta_1 \quad R^2 = 0.529$$

$$\eta_2 = 0.516(0.209)\eta_1 + 1.082(0.462)\xi_1 + 0.195(0.312)\xi_2 + 0.217(0.106)\xi_3 + \zeta_2 \quad R^2 = 0.463$$

In this model only ξ_2 has a significant effect on η_1 and η_1, ξ_1, and ξ_3 have significant effects on η_2.

The H_1, H_{2a} and H_{2b} models fit the observed covariance matrix equally well. These models are in fact equivalent in the sense of Chapter 8. The overall $\chi^2 = 10.31$ with 12 degrees of freedom, representing a very good fit. From statistical fit criteria alone we cannot distinguish between the three models. Perhaps one would have a slight preference for the H_{2b} model because the sum of the two R^2's is somewhat higher than it is for the H_{2a} model. Because η_2 has a significant effect on η_1 in the H_{2b} model, we cannot settle the question of their causal relationship by a choice between H_{2a} and H_{2b} based solely on statistical grounds. This question can be settled only by substantive arguments. However, we can set up a model in which η_1 and η_2 affect each other reciprocally and investigate the fit of this model. This approach corresponds to H_3.

To make a model with reciprocal causation identified, one must exclude one of the three variables ξ_1, ξ_2, and ξ_3 from each equation. It seems best to exclude that variable which in the previous analysis had the least significant effect. Thus we exclude ξ_1 from the equation for η_1 because ξ_1 is least significant in the H_{2a} model and we exclude ξ_2 from the equation for η_2 because ξ_2 is least significant in the H_{2b} model.

The following structural equations are estimated in the H_3 model:

$$\eta_1 = -0.136(0.151)\eta_2 + 0.931(0.220)\xi_2 - 0.090(0.062)\xi_3 + \zeta_1 \quad R^2 = 0.444$$

$$\eta_2 = 0.748(0.220)\eta_1 + 1.113(0.452)\xi_1 + 0.243(0.109)\xi_3 + \zeta_2 \quad R^2 = 0.447$$

This model has an overall χ^2 of 10.31, the same value as for the previous models, but has one parameter less. The probability level of this χ^2 is 0.668.

In the first equation the effect of η_2 on η_1 is not significant, indicating the causal relationship between η_1 and η_2 is indeed one way rather than reciprocal. Also, in the first equation, the effect of ξ_3 is not significant. In the second equation all included variables are significant. If we clean up the model by eliminating the direct paths which are insignificant, we obtain a model estimated as follows:

$$\eta_1 = 0.923(0.140)\xi_2 + \zeta_1 \quad R^2 = 0.533$$

$$\eta_2 = 0.594(0.140)\eta_1 + 1.228(0.477)\xi_1 + 0.213(0.107)\xi_3 + \zeta_2 \quad R^2 = 0.478$$

This model has a χ^2 of 14.19 with 15 degrees of freedom which still represents a very good fit. The sum of the two R^2's, 1.011, is now higher than for all previous models. The effect of ξ_3 on η_2 is barely significant but this effect is likely to be larger in a larger sample.

Our analysis confirms Bagozzi's results with one modification. Bagozzi formulated his model on the basis of previous research and substantive arguments. His model included the hypothesis

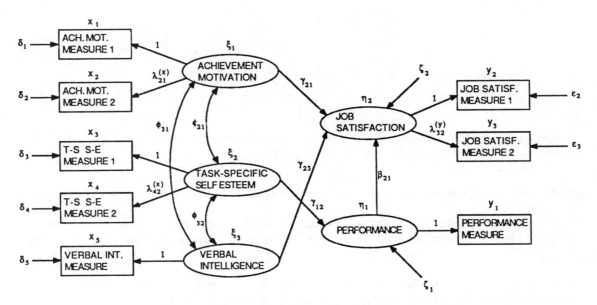

Figure 5.8: Modified Model for Performance and Satisfaction

that verbal intelligence (ξ_3) should have a positive effect on performance (η_1), but he found that this effect was negative and not significant. Our analysis is not based on a given hypothesis, but rather on an exploratory analysis of the data in a stepwise manner. It confirms Bagozzi's finding that the effect of ξ_3 on η_1 is negative and non-significant, but shows instead that verbal intelligence (ξ_3) has a slightly significant positive effect on satisfaction (η_2). The difference in the results is due to our inclusion of 15% measurement error in the verbal intelligence measure, x_5. The effect of this measurement error in general can be seen in Table 5.9, where we compare the results obtained with and without measurement error in the model. The effects of measurement error in x_5 are rather small.

Table 5.9: Performance and Satisfaction: Final H_3 Model with and without Measurement Error in x_5

Parameter	Without measurement error	With measurement error
γ_{12}	0.923 (0.144)	0.923 (0.144)
β_{21}	0.583 (0.139)	0.594 (0.140)
γ_{21}	1.179 (0.464)	1.228 (0.477)
γ_{23}	0.175 (0.095)	0.213 (0.107)

A path diagram for the final model is shown in Figure 5.8.
The model specification for this model is

$$LY = \begin{pmatrix} 1 & 0 \\ 0 & 1 \\ 0 & x \end{pmatrix} \qquad TE = diag \begin{pmatrix} 0 \\ x \\ x \end{pmatrix}$$

$$
LX = \begin{pmatrix} 1 & 0 & 0 \\ x & 0 & 0 \\ 0 & 1 & 0 \\ 0 & x & 0 \\ 0 & 0 & 1 \end{pmatrix} \quad TD = diag \begin{pmatrix} x \\ x \\ x \\ x \\ 1.998 \end{pmatrix}
$$

$$
BE = \begin{pmatrix} 0 & 0 \\ x & 0 \end{pmatrix} \quad GA = \begin{pmatrix} 0 & x & 0 \\ x & 0 & x \end{pmatrix} \quad PS = diag \begin{pmatrix} x \\ x \end{pmatrix}
$$

where x means a free parameter to be estimated and all other values are fixed. As before, the fixed ones in Λ_y and Λ_x set the scales for η's and ξ's.

The LISREL input file is

```
Modified Model for Performance and Satisfaction
References
Bagozzi, R.P. Performance and satisfaction in an industrial sales force: An
examination of their antecedents and simultaneity. Journal of Marketing, 1980,
44, 65-77.

Joreskog, K.G. and Sorbom, D. Recent developments in structural equation
modeling. Journal of Marketing Research, 1982, 19, 404-416.

Da ni=8 no=122
La
(8A8)
performmjbsatis1jbsatis2 achmot1 achmot2t-s s-e1t-s s-e2verbintm
km file=ex56.dat
sd file=ex56.dat

mo ny=3 nx=5 ne=2 nk=3 be=fu ps=di
le
perform jobsatis
lk
achmot 't-s s-e' 'verb int'
fr ly 3 2 lx 2 1 lx 4 2 be 2 1
fi te 1 td 5 ga 1 1 ga 2 2 ga 1 3
va 1 ly 1 1 ly 2 2 lx 1 1 lx 3 2 lx 5 3;va 1.998 td 5

ou se tv rs ef mi ss ad=off
```

This input file illustrates the following features:

- Upper case or lower case characters may be used freely on all lines

- Several title lines are allowed, as long as they do not begin with DA

- Blank lines are allowed between title lines as well as between control lines

- Labels are enclosed between single quotes if they contain blank spaces

Chapter 6

THE LISREL SUBMODEL 3

6.1 The LISREL Submodel 3

The full LISREL model was defined in Chapter 1 and illustrated by examples in Chapter 5. It consists of the three matrix equations (1.1), (1.2), and (1.3). In Submodel 1 considered in Chapter 3, only equation (1.3) is operational; the other two equations are not involved. In Submodel 2 considered in Chapter 4, we have $\mathbf{y} \equiv \boldsymbol{\eta}$ and $\mathbf{x} \equiv \boldsymbol{\xi}$ so that only equation (1.1) is operational. There is still another submodel in LISREL. This is called Submodel 3 and is defined by (1.1) and (1.2). There are no x-variables in this submodel, so that equation (1.3) is not involved.

The variables involved in this submodel are

Observed variables:	$\mathbf{y}'= (y_1, y_2, \ldots, y_p)$
Latent variables:	$\boldsymbol{\eta}'= (\eta_1, y_2, \ldots, \eta_m)$
	$\boldsymbol{\xi}'= (\xi_1, \xi_2, \ldots, \xi_n)$
Error variables:	$\boldsymbol{\epsilon}'= (\epsilon_1, \epsilon_2, \ldots, \epsilon_p)$
	$\boldsymbol{\zeta}'= (\zeta_1, \zeta_2, \ldots, \zeta_m)$

It may seem strange that there are ξ-variables but no x-variables; yet formally this is possible. Several examples of such a models will be given in this chapter.

The Submodel 3A is defined by the two equations:

$$\mathbf{y} = \boldsymbol{\Lambda}_y \boldsymbol{\eta} + \boldsymbol{\epsilon} \tag{6.1}$$

$$\boldsymbol{\eta} = \mathbf{B}\boldsymbol{\eta} + \boldsymbol{\Gamma}\boldsymbol{\xi} + \boldsymbol{\zeta} \tag{6.2}$$

By solving (6.2) for $\boldsymbol{\eta}$ and substituting into (6.1), we get the single defining equation

$$\mathbf{y} = \boldsymbol{\Lambda}_y (\mathbf{I} - \mathbf{B})^{-1}(\boldsymbol{\Gamma}\boldsymbol{\xi} + \boldsymbol{\zeta}) + \boldsymbol{\epsilon} \tag{6.3}$$

A special case of this is when $\mathbf{B}= 0$ (default). Then

$$\mathbf{y} = \boldsymbol{\Lambda}_y (\boldsymbol{\Gamma}\boldsymbol{\xi} + \boldsymbol{\zeta}) + \boldsymbol{\epsilon}, \tag{6.4}$$

with covariance matrix

$$\boldsymbol{\Sigma} = \boldsymbol{\Lambda}_y (\boldsymbol{\Gamma}\boldsymbol{\Phi}\boldsymbol{\Gamma}' + \boldsymbol{\Psi})\boldsymbol{\Lambda}_y' + \boldsymbol{\Theta}_\epsilon \tag{6.5}$$

This is Jöreskog's (1970, 1973, 1974) ACOVS model.

Another special case of (6.3) is when there are no ξ-variables. This is what we call Submodel 3B. Then (6.2) and (6.3) reduce to

$$\eta = \mathbf{B}\eta + \zeta \tag{6.6}$$

$$\mathbf{y} = \Lambda_y(\mathbf{I} - \mathbf{B})^{-1}\zeta + \epsilon \tag{6.7}$$

This particular submodel is then defined by (6.1) and (6.6). There are only four parameter matrices in this submodel, namely $\Lambda_y, \mathbf{B}, \Psi$, and Θ_ϵ. Under this model, the covariance matrix of $\mathbf{y}$ is

$$\Sigma = \Lambda_y(\mathbf{I} - \mathbf{B})^{-1}\Psi(\mathbf{I} - \mathbf{B}')^{-1}\Lambda_y' + \Theta_\epsilon \tag{6.8}$$

Consider the following seemingly paradoxical statement:

The full LISREL *model is a special case of a submodel of itself.*

The submodel referred to in this statement is the Submodel 3B defined by (6.1) and (6.6). The paradox disappears when one realizes that it is indeed the Submodel 3B which is more general than the full LISREL model.

To see this, we write (1.1), (1.2), and (1.3) in the form

$$\begin{pmatrix} \mathbf{y} \\ \mathbf{x} \end{pmatrix} = \begin{pmatrix} \Lambda_y & 0 \\ 0 & \Lambda_x \end{pmatrix} \begin{pmatrix} \eta \\ \xi \end{pmatrix} + \begin{pmatrix} \epsilon \\ \delta \end{pmatrix} \tag{6.9}$$

$$\begin{pmatrix} \eta \\ \xi \end{pmatrix} = \begin{pmatrix} \mathbf{B} & \Gamma \\ 0 & 0 \end{pmatrix} \begin{pmatrix} \eta \\ \xi \end{pmatrix} + \begin{pmatrix} \zeta \\ \xi \end{pmatrix} \tag{6.10}$$

Equations (6.9) and (6.10) are in the form of (6.1) and (6.6), respectively. The lower part of (6.10) is just a tautology which says that $\xi \equiv \xi$.

The conclusion is

Every LISREL *model can be written as a* LISREL *model with only y- and η-variables.*

What is the advantage of using this submodel rather than the full LISREL model? Some people may prefer it because it has fewer parameter matrices, although each one is larger. However, the important reason is that one can handle models in which a δ correlates with an ϵ. This is not possible in the full LISREL model. Examples of models with such correlated error terms will be given in the Section 6.5.

Important Note: Since Submodel 3A has ξ-variables but no x-variables, our method of computing TSLS and IV estimates will not work. Obviously, there are no reference variables for the ξ's. Starting values must be provided by the user. The NS parameter on the OU line tells the program to use these starting values instead of TSLS and IV estimates.

6.2   A Model for Tests that Differ Only in Length

Kristof (1971) formulated a model for tests that differ only in length. This model assumes that there is a length parameter λ_i associated with observed test score y_i in such a way that the true score variance is proportional to λ_i^4 and that the error variance is proportional to λ_i^2. It can be shown that the covariance structure for this model is of the form

$$\Sigma = \mathbf{D}_\lambda(\lambda\lambda' + \psi\mathbf{I})\mathbf{D}_\lambda ,$$

where $\mathbf{D}_\lambda = \mathrm{diag}(\lambda_1, \lambda_2, \ldots, \lambda_p)$ and $\boldsymbol{\lambda}' = (\lambda_1, \lambda_2, \ldots, \lambda_p)$. This is of the form (6.5) with $\boldsymbol{\Lambda}_y = \mathbf{D}_\lambda$, $\boldsymbol{\Gamma} = \boldsymbol{\lambda}$, $\boldsymbol{\Phi} = 1$, $\boldsymbol{\Psi} = \psi\mathbf{I}$, and $\boldsymbol{\Theta}_\epsilon = \mathbf{0}$. The model specifies equality constraints between the diagonal elements of $\boldsymbol{\Lambda}_y$ and the elements of the column vector $\boldsymbol{\Gamma}$ and also the equality of all the diagonal elements of $\boldsymbol{\Psi}$. The model has p + 1 parameters and is less restrictive than the parallel model but more restrictive than the congeneric model. A summary of various test theory models and their number of parameters is given in Table 6.1. In this table, $\mathbf{j}$ denotes a column vector with all elements equal to one.

Table 6.1: Various Test Theory Models

Model	Covariance Structure	No. of Parameters
Parallel	$\boldsymbol{\Sigma} = \lambda^2 \mathbf{jj}' + \theta\mathbf{I}$	2
Tau-equivalent	$\boldsymbol{\Sigma} = \lambda^2 \mathbf{jj}' + \boldsymbol{\Theta}$	$p + 1$
Variable-length	$\boldsymbol{\Sigma} = \mathbf{D}_\lambda(\boldsymbol{\lambda\lambda}' + \psi\mathbf{I})\mathbf{D}_\lambda$	$p + 1$
Congeneric	$\boldsymbol{\Sigma} = \boldsymbol{\lambda\lambda}' + \boldsymbol{\Theta}$	$2p$

Example 6.1: Three Subtests of SAT

Kristof (1971) gave the following covariance matrix:

$$\mathbf{S} = \begin{pmatrix} 54.85 & & \\ 60.21 & 99.24 & \\ 48.42 & 67.00 & 63.81 \end{pmatrix}.$$

This is based on candidates (N = 900) who took the January, 1969, administration of the Scholastic Aptitude Test (SAT). The first test, Verbal Omnibus, was administered in 30 minutes, and the second test, Reading Comprehension, in 45 minutes. These two tests contained 40 and 50 items, respectively. The third test is an additional section of the SAT not normally administered.

To examine whether the three tests can be considered as differing only in length, we set up the following input file:

```
Kristof's Model Estimated for Three Subtests of SAT
DA NI=3 NO=900
CM
54.85 60.21 99.24 48.42 67.00 63.81
MO NY=3 NE=3 NK=1 LY=DI,FR PH=ST PS=DI TE=ZE
EQ LY 1 GA 1
EQ LY 2 GA 2
EQ LY 3 GA 3
EQ PS 1 - PS 3
ST 2 ALL
OU SE TV RS MI SO NS
```

There are some important differences between this example and all previous examples:

- The scales for the three η's are defined by the particular constraints imposed in the model. *They are not defined in the usual way by fixing elements of Λ_y.* The SO parameter on the OU line tells the program *not* to check that scales have been defined in the usual way.

- As already stated in Section 6.1, starting values must be specified and the NS parameter must be set on the OU line.

The following ML estimates are obtained:

$$\hat{\lambda}_1 = 2.58, \; \hat{\lambda}_2 = 3.03, \; \hat{\lambda}_3 = 2.69, \; \hat{\psi}_1 = 1.60$$

The χ^2 goodness-of-fit measure is 4.91 with 2 degrees of freedom. The P-value is 0.086 and the output file shows that no standardized residuals and modification indices are significant. Hence it seems that this model fits the data reasonably well.

6.3   Second-Order Factor Analysis

Equation (6.1) is in the form of a factor analysis model for **y** with first-order factors η and measurement errors ϵ; cf. (3.1). Now suppose that the variables η in turn can be accounted for by a set of factors ξ, so-called second-order factors, so that

$$\eta = \Gamma\xi + \zeta \,, \tag{6.11}$$

where Γ is a matrix of second-order factor loadings and ζ is a vector of unique variables for η. Combining (6.1) and (6.11) gives (6.4) with covariance matrix (6.5). A path diagram for second-order factor analysis is shown in Figure 6.1.

Example 6.2: Second-Order Factor Analysis

To illustrate the model, we use data on some cognitive ability tests. The standard deviations and correlations of two forms of each of five tests are given in Table 6.2. The sample size is N = 267.

We shall examine the hypothesis that the two forms of each test are tau-equivalent, except for the two word fluency tests "Things Round" and "Things Blue" which are only assumed to be congeneric. The five true scores are postulated to depend on two factors, the first, "Speed of Closure," being measured by the first three tests and the second, "Vocabulary," being measured by the last two tests.

The model specification is

$$\Lambda_y = \begin{pmatrix} 1 & 0 & 0 & 0 & 0 \\ 1 & 0 & 0 & 0 & 0 \\ 0 & 1 & 0 & 0 & 0 \\ 0 & 1 & 0 & 0 & 0 \\ 0 & 0 & 1 & 0 & 0 \\ 0 & 0 & 1 & 0 & 0 \\ 0 & 0 & 0 & 1 & 0 \\ 0 & 0 & 0 & x & 0 \\ 0 & 0 & 0 & 0 & 1 \\ 0 & 0 & 0 & 0 & 1 \end{pmatrix} \quad \Gamma = \begin{pmatrix} x & 0 \\ x & 0 \\ x & 0 \\ 0 & x \\ 0 & x \end{pmatrix} \quad \Phi = \begin{pmatrix} 1 & \\ x & 1 \end{pmatrix} \quad \Psi = \text{diagonal} \; \Theta_\epsilon = \text{diagonal.}$$

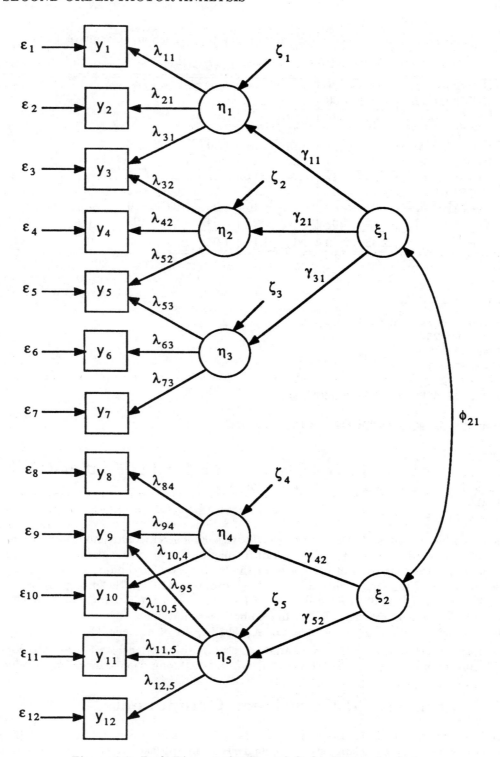

Figure 6.1: Path Diagram for Second-Order Factor Analysis

Table 6.2: Correlations and Standard Deviations for Some Cognitive Tests

	Correlations									
GESCOM - A	1.00									
GESCOM - B	.74	1.00								
CONWOR - A	.33	.42	1.00							
CONWOR - B	.34	.39	.65	1.00						
HIDPAT - A	.26	.21	.15	.18	1.00					
HIDPAT - B	.23	.24	.22	.21	.77	1.00				
THIROUND	.15	.12	.14	.11	.17	.20	1.00			
THIBLUE	.14	.14	.14	.15	.06	.09	.42	1.00		
VOCABU - A	-.04	-.03	.09	.16	.06	.09	.19	.21	1.00	
VOCABU - B	.02	.02	.10	.23	.04	.07	.09	.21	.72	1.00
Stand. Dev.	2.42	2.80	3.40	3.19	1.94	1.79	5,63	3.10	3.05	2.25

The LISREL input file is

```
Second Order Factor Analysis
DA NI=10 NO=267
LA FI=EX62.DAT
KM FI=EX62.DAT
SD FI=EX62.DAT
MO NY=10 NE=5 NK=2 GA=FI PH=ST PS=DI
LE
GESCOM CONWOR HIDPAT THINGS VOCABU
LK
SPEEDCLO VOCABUL
VA 1 LY 1 1 LY 2 1 LY 3 2 LY 4 2 LY 5 3 LY 6 3 LY 7 4 LY 9 5 LY 10 5
FR LY 8 4 GA 1 1 GA 2 1 GA 3 1 GA 4 2 GA 5 2
ST 1 ALL
OU SE TV SS NS
```

The goodness-of-fit statistic is $\chi^2 = 53.06$ with 33 degrees of freedom, which does not represent a particularly good fit. The lack of fit may be due to either the assumption of tau-equivalence for the four pairs of test forms or the hypothesized second-order structure. When the assumption of tau-equivalence is relaxed, χ^2 drops to 41.69 with 29 degrees of freedom. The difference in χ^2, 11.37, with 4 degrees of freedom, has a probability level of 0.025. This suggests that the lack of fit is probably due to both assumptions.

By computing the diagonal elements of $\hat{\Lambda}_y \hat{\Gamma} \hat{\Phi} \hat{\Gamma}' \hat{\Lambda}_y'$, $\hat{\Lambda}_y \hat{\Psi} \hat{\Lambda}_y'$, and $\hat{\Theta}_\epsilon$ and relating these to the total variance in $\hat{\Sigma}$, one gets a variance decomposition of each test form into common, specific and error components respectively. These variance components are given in Table 6.3.

6.4   Variance and Covariance Components

Several authors (Bock, 1960; Bock and Bargmann, 1966; and Wiley, Schmidt, and Bramble, 1973) have considered covariance structure analysis as an approach to study differences in test

Table 6.3: Variance Components for Cognitive Tests

	Error	Specific	Common
GESCOM - A	0.193	0.428	0.379
GESCOM - B	0.338	0.351	0.311
CONWOR - A	0.386	0.279	0.335
CONWOR - B	0.313	0.313	0.374
HIDPAT - A	0.291	0.587	0.122
HIDPAT - B	0.163	0.694	0.144
THIROUND	0.682	0.145	0.172
THIBLUE	0.445	0.254	0.301
VOCABU - A	0.468	0.465	0.067
VOCABU - B	0.044	0.835	0.121

performance when the tests have been constructed by assigning items or subtests according to objective features of content or format to subclasses of a factorial or hierarchical classification.

Bock (1960) suggested that the scores of N subjects on a set of tests classified in a 2^q factorial design may be viewed as data from an $N \times 2^q$ experimental design, where the subjects represent a random mode of classification and the tests represent n fixed modes of classification. Bock pointed out that conventional mixed-model analysis of variance gives useful information about the psychometric properties of the tests. In particular, the presence of non-zero variance components for the random mode of classification and for the interaction of the random and fixed modes of classification provides information about the number of dimensions in which the tests are able to discriminate among subjects. The relative size of these components measures the power of the tests to discriminate among subjects along the respective dimensions.

The following example was given in an unpublished paper by Browne (1970).

Example 6.3: The Rod and Frame Test

The Rod and Frame (RF) test is used as a measure of field dependence. A subject is seated in a darkened room on a chair which may be tilted to the left or to the right. In front of him is a luminous rod located in a luminous square frame. The chair, frame and rod are tilted to pre-specified positions. By operating push buttons connected to an electric motor, the subject is to move the rod to the vertical position. The score on the trial is the angle of the rod from the vertical. This can assume positive and negative values. Each subject undergoes 12 trials. The last two columns of the design matrix $\mathbf{A}$ below give initial positions of the frame and chair for each trial.

$$\mathbf{A}' = \begin{pmatrix} 1 & 1 & 1 & 1 & 1 & 1 & 1 & 1 & 1 & 1 & 1 & 1 \\ 1 & -1 & 1 & -1 & -1 & 1 & -1 & 1 & 1 & -1 & 1 & -1 \\ 1 & -1 & 1 & -1 & 1 & -1 & 1 & -1 & 0 & 0 & 0 & 0 \end{pmatrix}$$

A value of +1 denotes that the position of the frame or chair was at +28° from the vertical, a value of -1 denotes that the angle was -28° and a value of 0 denotes that the initial position was vertical (Browne, 1970).

The covariance matrix between trials of the RF test obtained from a sample of 107 eighteen-year-old males is given in Table 6.4.

We want to estimate the variance components associated with general bias, frame effect, chair effect and error.

Table 6.4: Inter-Trial Covariance Matrix for the Rod and Frame Test

1	2	3	4	5	6	7	8	9	10	11	12
51.6											
-27.7	72.1										
38.9	-41.1	69.9									
-36.4	40.7	-39.1	75.8								
13.8	-5.2	17.9	1.9	84.8							
-13.6	10.9	9.5	17.8	-37.4	91.1						
21.5	-9.4	8.5	-13.1	59.7	-54.4	79.9					
-12.8	-17.2	-3.1	22.0	-43.3	52.7	-49.9	87.2				
11.0	-8.9	19.2	-11.2	-12.6	21.9	-10.6	17.5	27.6			
-4.5	10.2	-7.6	12.7	20.4	-11.5	16.5	-14.8	-8.8	19.9		
9.2	-.3	18.9	-13.6	-3.9	19.0	-8.3	13.1	17.7	-2.8	27.3	
-3.7	7.5	-4.5	12.8	19.9	-8.8	15.5	-8.6	-5.4	13.3	-1.0	16.0

Let a, b and c be uncorrelated random components associated with general bias, frame effect and chair effect, respectively, and let e denote an error component uncorrelated with a, b and c and uncorrelated over trials. Let

$$\mathbf{u}_\nu' = (a_\nu, b_\nu, c_\nu)$$

be the values of a, b and c for subject ν. Then the scores on the twelve trials for subject ν is

$$\mathbf{x}_\nu = \mathbf{A}\mathbf{u}_\nu + \mathbf{e}_\nu$$

with covariance matrix

$$\boldsymbol{\Sigma} = \mathbf{A}\boldsymbol{\Phi}\mathbf{A}' + \sigma_e^2 \mathbf{I} , \tag{6.12}$$

where

$$\boldsymbol{\Phi} = diag(\sigma_a^2, \sigma_b^2, \sigma_c^2) .$$

Equation (6.12) shows that all the 78 variances and covariances in $\boldsymbol{\Sigma}$ are *linear* functions of the four parameters σ_a^2, σ_b^2, σ_c^2 and σ_e^2. To see this explicitly, consider the covariance matrix generated by trials 1, 2, 5 and 9:

$$\boldsymbol{\Sigma} = \begin{pmatrix} \sigma_a^2 + \sigma_b^2 + \sigma_c^2 + \sigma_e^2 & & & \\ \sigma_a^2 - \sigma_b^2 - \sigma_c^2 & \sigma_a^2 + \sigma_b^2 + \sigma_c^2 + \sigma_e^2 & & \\ \sigma_a^2 - \sigma_b^2 + \sigma_c^2 & \sigma_a^2 + \sigma_b^2 - \sigma_c^2 & \sigma_a^2 + \sigma_b^2 + \sigma_c^2 + \sigma_e^2 & \\ \sigma_a^2 + \sigma_b^2 & \sigma_a^2 - \sigma_b^2 & \sigma_a^2 - \sigma_b^2 & \sigma_a^2 + \sigma_b^2 + \sigma_e^2 \end{pmatrix}$$

This is an example of *a linear covariance structure*. If this structure holds, the four parameters can be solved in terms of the elements of $\boldsymbol{\Sigma}$. For example, $\sigma_a^2 = \frac{1}{2}(\sigma_{41} + \sigma_{42})$, $\sigma_b^2 = \frac{1}{2}(\sigma_{41} + \sigma_{42} - \sigma_{21} - \sigma_{31})$, $\sigma_c^2 = \sigma_{31} - \sigma_{42}$, etc. There are many ways in which the four parameters can be solved in terms of the σ's. If the ten equations are consistent, however, all solutions are identical. In this case the parameters are *overidentified*.

Consider the covariance structure generated by the first four rows of $\mathbf{A}$:

$$\boldsymbol{\Sigma} = \begin{pmatrix} \sigma_a^2 + \sigma_b^2 + \sigma_c^2 + \sigma_e^2 & & & \\ \sigma_a^2 - \sigma_b^2 - \sigma_c^2 & \sigma_a^2 + \sigma_b^2 + \sigma_c^2 + \sigma_e^2 & & \\ \sigma_a^2 + \sigma_b^2 + \sigma_c^2 & \sigma_a^2 - \sigma_b^2 - \sigma_c^2 & \sigma_a^2 + \sigma_b^2 + \sigma_c^2 + \sigma_e^2 & \\ \sigma_a^2 - \sigma_b^2 - \sigma_c^2 & \sigma_a^2 + \sigma_b^2 + \sigma_c^2 & \sigma_a^2 - \sigma_b^2 - \sigma_c^2 & \sigma_a^2 + \sigma_b^2 + \sigma_c^2 + \sigma_e^2 \end{pmatrix}$$

In this case we can solve for $\sigma_a^2 = \frac{1}{2}(\sigma_{21} + \sigma_{31})$, say, but it is impossible to solve for σ_b^2 and σ_c^2 separately. Only the sum $\sigma_b^2 + \sigma_c^2$ is identified. This is an example of a *non-identified model* in which some parameters are identified and others are not. The reason for this is that the matrix $\mathbf{A}$ has rank 2 and not rank 3 as in the previous case. The example will be continued later.

In general, if $\mathbf{A}$ is of order $q \times n$ and of rank k, one may choose k independent linear functions, each one linearly dependent on the rows of $\mathbf{A}$, and estimate the covariance matrix of these functions. It is customary to choose linear combinations that are mutually uncorrelated but this is not necessary. Let $\mathbf{L}$ be the matrix of coefficients of the chosen linear functions and let $\mathbf{K}$ be any matrix such that $\mathbf{A} = \mathbf{KL}$. For example, $\mathbf{K}$ may be obtained from

$$\mathbf{K} = \mathbf{A}(\mathbf{L'L})^{-1}\mathbf{L'}$$

The model may then be reparameterized to full rank by defining $\mathbf{u^*} = \mathbf{Lu}$. We then have $\mathbf{x} = \mathbf{Au} + \mathbf{e} = \mathbf{KLu} + \mathbf{e} = \mathbf{Ku^*} + \mathbf{e}$.

The covariance matrix of $\mathbf{x}$ is represented as

$$\boldsymbol{\Sigma} = \mathbf{K}\boldsymbol{\Phi^*}\mathbf{K'} + \boldsymbol{\Psi}$$

where $\boldsymbol{\Phi^*}$, the covariance matrix of $\mathbf{u^*}$ is not necessarily diagonal and $\boldsymbol{\Psi}$ is the diagonal covariance matrix of $\mathbf{e}$. The latter may be taken to be homogeneous, if desired.

The above model assumes that all measurements are on the same scale. Wiley, Schmidt, and Bramble (1973) suggested the study of a general class of components of covariance models which would allow different variables to be on different scales. The covariance matrix $\boldsymbol{\Sigma}$ will then be of the form

$$\boldsymbol{\Sigma} = \boldsymbol{\Delta}\mathbf{A}\boldsymbol{\Phi}\mathbf{A'}\boldsymbol{\Delta} + \boldsymbol{\Theta} \qquad (6.13)$$

or

$$\boldsymbol{\Sigma} = \boldsymbol{\Delta}(\mathbf{A}\boldsymbol{\Phi}\mathbf{A'} + \boldsymbol{\Psi})\boldsymbol{\Delta} \qquad (6.14)$$

The matrix $\mathbf{A}(p \times k)$ is assumed to be known and gives the coefficients of the linear functions connecting the manifest and latent variables; $\boldsymbol{\Delta}$ is a $p \times p$ diagonal matrix of unknown scale factors, $\boldsymbol{\Phi}$ is the $k \times k$ symmetric and positive definite covariance matrix of the latent variables, and $\boldsymbol{\Psi}$ and $\boldsymbol{\Theta}$ are $p \times p$ diagonal matrices of error variances.

The model (6.13) can be estimated as a LISREL Submodel 3A with $\mathbf{B} = 0$ (default). The LISREL parameterization is $\boldsymbol{\Lambda}_y = \boldsymbol{\Delta}$, $\boldsymbol{\Gamma} = \mathbf{A}$, $\boldsymbol{\Phi} = \boldsymbol{\Phi}$, $\boldsymbol{\Psi} = \boldsymbol{\Psi}$ and $\boldsymbol{\Theta}_\epsilon = \boldsymbol{\Theta}$.

Within this class of models, eight different special cases are of interest. These are generated by the combination of the following set of conditions:

$$\text{on } \boldsymbol{\Delta}: \quad \left.\begin{array}{l} \boldsymbol{\Delta} = \mathbf{I} \\ \boldsymbol{\Delta} \neq \mathbf{I} \end{array}\right\}$$

$$\text{on } \boldsymbol{\Phi}: \quad \left.\begin{array}{l} \boldsymbol{\Phi} \text{ is diagonal} \\ \boldsymbol{\Phi} \text{ is not diagonal} \end{array}\right\}$$

$$\text{on } \boldsymbol{\Psi} \text{or } \boldsymbol{\Theta} : \quad \left. \begin{array}{l} \boldsymbol{\Psi} \text{ or } \boldsymbol{\Theta} = \gamma \mathbf{I} \\ \boldsymbol{\Psi} \text{ or } \boldsymbol{\Theta} \text{ general diagonal} \end{array} \right\}$$

The classical formulation of the mixed model and its generalizations assume that $\boldsymbol{\Delta} = \mathbf{I}$. This is appropriate if the observed variables are in the same metric as, for example, when the observed variables represent physical measurements, time to criterion measures, reaction times or items similarly scaled such as semantic differential responses. However, if the observed variables are measured in different metrics then the classical model would not fit. In such cases the inclusion of $\boldsymbol{\Delta}$ in the model as a general diagonal matrix of scaling factors would provide a useful alternative specification. It should be pointed out that the elements of $\boldsymbol{\Delta}$ do not have to be related to the variances of the variables.

The classical components of variance model assume that $\boldsymbol{\Phi}$ is diagonal. However, there are usually no substantive reasons for assuming this.

The two conditions on $\boldsymbol{\Psi}$ or $\boldsymbol{\Theta}$ correspond to homogenous and heterogeneous error variances. If the variables are in the same metric and if the measurement situation is sufficiently similar from variable to variable then it would seem reasonable to hypothesize that the variances of the errors of measurement ought to be homogeneous, i.e., in (6.13) we take $\boldsymbol{\Delta} = \mathbf{I}$ and $\boldsymbol{\Theta} = \sigma^2 \mathbf{I}$.

If, on the other hand, the scale of measurement is the same but the measurement situation from variable to variable is different enough to generate different kinds of error structures, then the variances of the errors of measurement might differ systematically from variable to variable. For this situation it would seem best to take $\boldsymbol{\Delta} = \mathbf{I}$ but leave $\boldsymbol{\Theta}$ free in (6.13). If the manifest variables were in different metrics then clearly the error variances in the observed metric will most likely be heterogeneous. One useful hypothesis to test in this context would be that the standard deviations of the errors of measurement are proportional to the rescaling factors. This would correspond to taking $\boldsymbol{\Psi} = \sigma^2 \mathbf{I}$ in (6.14). When both $\boldsymbol{\Delta}$ and $\boldsymbol{\Psi}$ are free, (6.13) and (6.14) are equivalent.

Returning to the example, estimation of the variance components according to model (6.12) gives

$$\sigma_a^2 = 3.52 \quad \sigma_b^2 = 14.23 \quad \sigma_c^2 = 27.45 \quad \sigma_e^2 = 22.56$$

However, examination of the fit of the model to the data reveals that the fit is very poor: $\chi^2 = 464.3$ with 74 degrees of freedom. We shall therefore seek an alternative model which better accounts for the data. This is obtained by structuring the error component e.

There are six distinct experimental conditions among the twelve trials, each one repeated twice. Let τ_i, i = 1, 2, ..., 6 be random components associated with these experimental conditions. Then

$$x_{i\alpha} = \tau_i + e_{i\alpha}$$

where $\alpha = 1, 2$ indexes the two replications. This simply means that one should allow the error variances to be different for different experimental conditions but still equal within replications of the same condition. An analysis according to this model gives $\chi^2 = 311.2$ with 69 degrees of freedom. The reduction in χ^2 clearly indicates that the error variances depend on the experimental condition.

The LISREL input file for this analysis is

```
The Rod and Frame Test
DA  NI = 12  NO = 107
CM  FI = EX63.COV
MO  NX = 12  NK = 3  LX = FI  PH = DI
MA  LX
1   1   1
1  -1  -1
1   1   1
1  -1  -1
1  -1   1
1   1  -1
1  -1   1
1   1  -1
1   1   0
1  -1   0
1   1   0
1  -1   0
EQ  TD(1)  TD(3)
EQ  TD(2)  TD(4)
EQ  TD(5)  TD(7)
EQ  TD(6)  TD(8)
EQ  TD(9)  TD(11)
EQ  TD(10) TD(12)
OU  SE  TV
```

The ML estimates of the variance components are now, with standard errors below the estimates,

$$\sigma_a^2 = 4.08 \quad \sigma_b^2 = 11.27 \quad \sigma_c^2 = 26.19$$
$$(0.74) \qquad\quad (1.73) \qquad\quad (4.13)$$

$$\sigma_{e_1}^2 = 22.03 \quad \sigma_{e_2}^2 = 37.63 \quad \sigma_{e_3}^2 = 28.57 \quad \sigma_{e_4}^2 = 40.50 \quad \sigma_{e_5}^2 = 11.63 \quad \sigma_{e_6}^2 = 5.07$$
$$(2.69) \qquad\quad (4.20) \qquad\quad (3.29) \qquad\quad (4.63) \qquad\quad (1.41) \qquad\quad (.66)$$

The results indicate that most of the variance in the trials is associated with the chair effect. The variance due to the frame effect is less than half of this and the variance due to general bias is still smaller. The error variances are generally quite large, except for the two experimental conditions in which the chair is already vertical.

Since the fit of the model is still not satisfactory one could allow the variance components to be correlated. However, an analysis with Φ free reveals that none of the covariances in Φ is significant.

6.5   Two-Wave Models

LISREL may be useful in analyzing data from longitudinal studies in psychology, education and sociology. In the sociological literature there have been a number of articles concerned with the specification of models incorporating causation and measurement errors, and analysis of data from panel studies; see Bohrnstedt (1969), Heise (1969, 1970), and Duncan (1969, 1972). Jöreskog and Sörbom (1976, 1977, 1985), Jöreskog (1979), Jagodzinski and Kühnel (1988), among others, discuss statistical models and methods for analysis of longitudinal data.

The characteristic feature of a longitudinal research design is that the same measurements are obtained from the same people at two or more occasions. The purpose of a longitudinal or panel study is to assess the changes that occur between the occasions and to attribute these changes to certain background characteristics and events existing or occurring before the first occasion and/or to various treatments and developments that occur after the first occasion.

Suppose that two variables are used on two occasions, i.e., in a two-wave longitudinal design. Assume that the two variables measure the same latent variable η on two different occasions, i.e., y_1 and y_2 measure η_1 on the first occasion and y_3 and y_4 measure η_2 on the second occasion. The equations defining the measurement relations are

$$\left.\begin{array}{l} y_1 = \eta_1 + \epsilon_1 \\ y_2 = \lambda_1 \eta_1 + \epsilon_2 \\ y_3 = \eta_2 + \epsilon_3 \\ y_4 = \lambda_2 \eta_2 + \epsilon_4 \end{array}\right\}$$

The main interest is in the stability of η over time. This can be studied by means of the structural relationship

$$\eta_2 = \beta \eta_1 + \zeta \ .$$

In particular, one is interested in whether β is close to one and ζ is small.

Let $\boldsymbol{\Omega}$ be the covariance matrix of (η_1, η_2) and let $\boldsymbol{\Theta}$ be the covariance matrix of $(\epsilon_1, \epsilon_2, \epsilon_3, \epsilon_4)$. If all the ϵ's are uncorrelated so that $\boldsymbol{\Theta}$ is diagonal, the covariance matrix of (y_1, y_2, y_3, y_4) is

$$\boldsymbol{\Sigma} = \begin{pmatrix} \omega_{11} + \theta_{11} & & & \\ \lambda_1 \omega_{11} & \lambda_1^2 \omega_{11} + \theta_{22} & & \\ \omega_{21} & \lambda_1 \omega_{21} & \omega_{22} + \theta_{33} & \\ \lambda \omega_{21} & \lambda_1 \lambda_2 \omega_{21} & \lambda_2 \omega_{22} & \lambda_2^2 \omega_{22} + \theta_{44} \end{pmatrix}$$

The matrix $\boldsymbol{\Sigma}$ has 10 variances and covariances which are functions of 9 parameters. It is readily verified that all 9 parameters are identified so the model has one degree of freedom.

Often when the same variables are used repeatedly, there is a tendency for the corresponding errors (the ϵ's) to correlate over time because of memory or other retest effects. Hence there is a need to generalize the above model to allow for correlations between ϵ_1 and ϵ_3 and also between ϵ_2 and ϵ_4. This means that there will be two non-zero covariances θ_{31} and θ_{42} in $\boldsymbol{\Theta}$. The covariance matrix of the observed variables will now be

$$\boldsymbol{\Sigma} = \begin{pmatrix} \omega_{11} + \theta_{11} & & & \\ \lambda_1 \omega_{11} & \lambda_1^2 \omega_{11} + \theta_{22} & & \\ \omega_{21} + \theta_{31} & \lambda_1 \omega_{21} & \omega_{22} + \theta_{33} & \\ \lambda_2 \omega_{21} & \lambda_1 \lambda_2 \omega_{21} + \theta_{42} & \lambda_2 \omega_{22} & \lambda_2^2 \omega_{22} + \theta_{44} \end{pmatrix}$$

This $\boldsymbol{\Sigma}$ has its 10 independent elements expressed in terms of 11 parameters. Hence it is clear that the model is not identified. In fact, none of the 11 parameters is identified without further conditions imposed. The loadings λ_1 and λ_2 may be multiplied by a constant and the ω's divided by the same constant. This does not change σ_{21}, σ_{32}, σ_{41} and σ_{43}. The change in the other σ's may be compensated by adjusting the θ's additively. Hence to make the model identified one must fix one λ or one ω at a non-zero value or one θ at some arbitrary value. However, the *correlation* between η_1 and η_2 is identified without any restrictions, since

$$\text{Corr}(\eta_1, \eta_2) = (\omega_{21}^2/\omega_{11}\omega_{22})^{\frac{1}{2}} = [(\sigma_{32}\sigma_{41})/(\sigma_{21}\sigma_{43})]^{\frac{1}{2}} \ .$$

The model may therefore be used to estimate this correlation coefficient and to test whether this is one. The maximum likelihood estimate of the correlation coefficient is $[(s_{32}s_{41})/(s_{21}s_{43})]^{\frac{1}{2}}$. To make further use of the model it is necessary to make some assumption about the nature of the variables. For example, if it can be assumed that the two variables on each occasion are tau-equivalent, we can set both λ_1 and λ_2 equal to one. Then the model can be estimated and tested with one degree of freedom. If $\lambda_1 = \lambda_2$ the model is just identified.

While the above model is not identified as it stands it becomes so as soon as there is information about one or more background variables affecting η_1 or η_2 or both.

Example 6.4: Stability of Alienation

Wheaton et al. (1977) reports on a study concerned with the stability over time of attitudes such as alienation and the relation to background variables such as education and occupation. Data on attitude scales were collected from 932 persons in two rural regions in Illinois at three points in time: 1966, 1967 and 1971. The variables used for the present example are the Anomia subscale and the Powerlessness subscale, taken to be indicators of Alienation. This example uses data from 1967 and 1971 only. The background variables are the respondent's education (years of schooling completed) and Duncan's Socioeconomic Index (SEI). These are taken to be indicators of the respondent's socioeconomic status (SES). The sample covariance matrix of the six observed variables is given in Table 6.5.

Table 6.5: Covariance Matrix for Variables in the Stability of Alienation Example

	y_1	y_2	y_3	y_4	x_1	x_2
ANOMIA67	11.834					
POWERL67	6.947	9.364				
ANOMIA71	6.819	5.091	12.532			
POWERL71	4.783	5.028	7.495	9.986		
EDUCATIN	-3.839	-3.889	-3.841	-3.625	9.610	
SOCIOIND*	-2.190	-1.883	-2.175	-1.878	3.552	4.503

* The variable SOCIOIND has been scaled down by a factor 10.

Four models will be considered as given in Figures 6.2 – 6.5. In these path diagrams we have abandoned our tradition to label the coefficients with two subscripts according to the rules given in Chapter 1. In Figures 6.2-6.5 we have simply labeled the coefficients with one index instead.

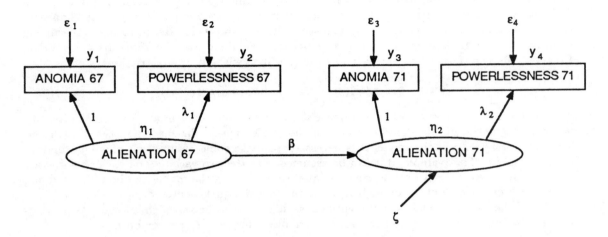

Figure 6.2: Path Diagrams for Models of Stability and Alienation: Model A

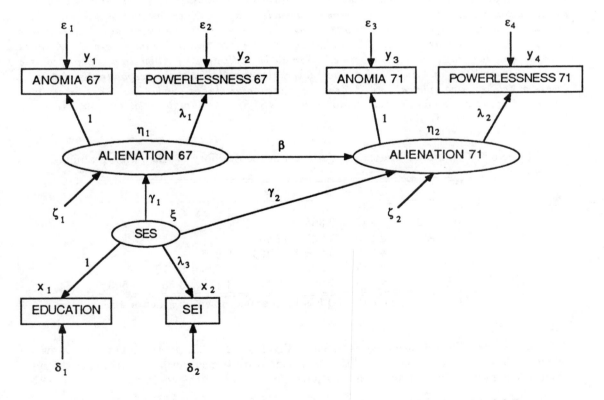

Figure 6.3: Path Diagrams for Models of Stability and Alienation: Model B

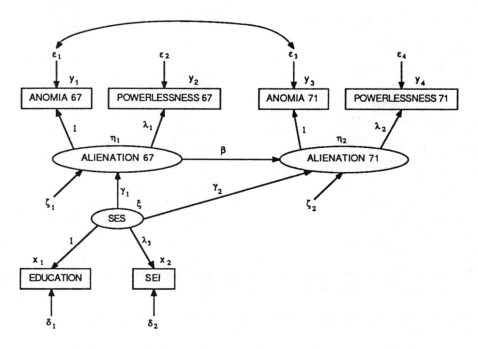

Figure 6.4: Path Diagrams for Models of Stability and Alienation: Model C

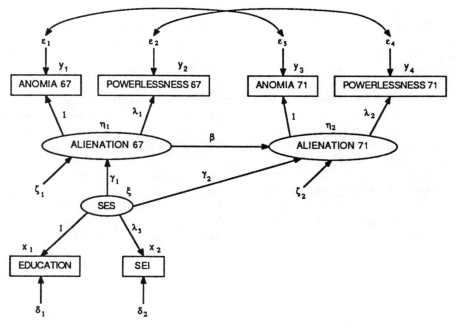

Figure 6.5: Path Diagrams for Models of Stability and Alienation: Model D

The variables in the models are

- y_1 = Anomia 67

- y_2 = Powerlessness 67

- y_3 = Anomia 71

- y_4 = Powerlessness 71

- x_1 = Education

- x_2 = SEI

- ξ = SES

- η_1 = Alienation 67

- η_2 = Alienation 71

In the first model we use only the y's and η's and the model (6.14) with all ϵ's uncorrelated. This is a Submodel 3A with $\mathbf{B} = \mathbf{0}$. The input file is

```
Stability of Alienation, Model A (uncorrelated error terms)
DA NI=4 NO=932
LA
ANOMIA67 POWER67 ANOMIA71 POWER71 EDUCATIN SOCIOIND
CM FI=EX64.COV
MO NY=4 NE=2 BE=SD PS=DI TE=SY
LE
ALIEN67 ALIEN71
FR LY(2,1) LY(4,2)
VA 1 LY(1,1) LY(3,2)
OU SE TV MI ND=2
```

The file EX64.COV contains a covariance matrix for 6 variables but only four of them are used in Model A. No SE line is necessary, however, because the four variables in the model are the *first four* variables in the file. The specification TE = SY on the MO line does the same thing as if TE is default. The only difference is that when TE = SY, the entire lower half of Θ_ϵ is stored in the computer. The off-diagonal elements of Θ_ϵ are still fixed zeroes but, with TE = SY, any such element can be declared free. Also, by this specification, one can get modification indices for the off-diagonal elements of Θ_ϵ and this is important in this example.

The results are summarized in Table 6.6, column 2. The overall χ^2 is 61.11 with 1 degree of freedom. The model suffers from two kinds of specification errors: there is bias in β due to omitted variables and the error terms are correlated for the same variables. The modification indices for Θ_ϵ are

	ANOMIA67	POWER67	ANOMIA71	POWER71
ANOMIA67	.00			
POWER67	.00	.00		
ANOMIA71	59.15	59.14	.00	
POWER71	59.15	59.14	.00	.00

indicating that ϵ_1, ϵ_2 and ϵ_3, ϵ_4 should be correlated between sets but not within sets. However, as the model has only one degree of freedom, only one parameter can be relaxed. The modification indices show that any one of the four correlations can be relaxed yielding a model with perfect fit. This is an example of a case when the modification indices reveal several equivalent models in the sense defined in Chapter 8.

To deal with the omitted variables bias, one must include the education measures in the model. Consider first the model in Figure 6.3 (Model B).

This model is specified as

$$\begin{pmatrix} y_1 \\ y_2 \\ y_3 \\ y_4 \end{pmatrix} = \begin{pmatrix} 1 & 0 \\ \lambda_1 & 0 \\ 0 & 1 \\ 0 & \lambda_2 \end{pmatrix} \begin{pmatrix} \eta_1 \\ \eta_2 \end{pmatrix} + \begin{pmatrix} \epsilon_1 \\ \epsilon_2 \\ \epsilon_3 \\ \epsilon_4 \end{pmatrix} \tag{6.15}$$

$$\begin{pmatrix} x_1 \\ x_2 \end{pmatrix} = \begin{pmatrix} 1 \\ \lambda_3 \end{pmatrix} \begin{pmatrix} \delta_1 \\ \delta_2 \end{pmatrix} \tag{6.16}$$

$$\begin{pmatrix} \eta_1 \\ \eta_2 \end{pmatrix} = \begin{pmatrix} 0 & 0 \\ \beta & 0 \end{pmatrix} \begin{pmatrix} \eta_1 \\ \eta_2 \end{pmatrix} + \begin{pmatrix} \gamma_1 \\ \gamma_2 \end{pmatrix} \xi + \begin{pmatrix} \zeta_1 \\ \zeta_2 \end{pmatrix} \tag{6.17}$$

It is assumed that ζ_1 and ζ_2 are uncorrelated. The scales for η_1, η_2, and ξ have been chosen to be the same as for y_1, y_3, and x_1, respectively. In Model B all four ϵ-terms are uncorrelated whereas in Model C, ϵ_1 and ϵ_3 are correlated and in Model D also ϵ_2 and ϵ_4 are correlated.

Consider first the identification of Model B. Let $\phi = \text{Var}(\xi)$. We have six observed variables with 21 variances and covariances. Model B has 15 parameters (3 λ's, 1 β, 2 γ's, 1 ϕ, 2 ψ's and 6 θ's) so that, if all these are identified, the model will have 6 degrees of freedom. The structural equations are

$$\begin{aligned} \eta_1 &= \gamma_1 \xi + \zeta_1 \\ \eta_2 &= \beta\eta_1 + \gamma_2 \xi + \zeta_2 \end{aligned}$$

with reduced form

$$\begin{aligned} \eta_1 &= \gamma_1 \xi + \zeta_1 \\ \eta_2 &= (\gamma_2 + \beta\gamma_1)\xi + (\zeta_2 + \beta\zeta_1) = \pi\xi + \nu, \text{ say,} \end{aligned}$$

we have

$$\begin{aligned} Cov(y_1, x_1) &= Cov(\eta_1, x_1) = \gamma_1\phi & (6.18) \\ Cov(y_2, x_1) &= \lambda_1 Cov(\eta_1, x_1) = \lambda_1\gamma_1\phi & (6.19) \\ Cov(y_3, x_1) &= Cov(\eta_2, x_1) = \pi\phi & (6.20) \\ Cov(y_4, x_1) &= \lambda_2 Cov(\eta_2, x_1) = \lambda_2\pi\phi & (6.21) \end{aligned}$$

If we use x_2 instead of x_1 in these equations, all four right sides will be multiplied by λ_3. Hence, λ_3 is overdetermined since

$$\lambda_3 = Cov(y_i, x_2)/Cov(y_i, x_1) \quad i = 1, 2, 3, 4 \ .$$

With λ_3 determined, ϕ is determined by

$$Cov(x_1, x_2) = \lambda_3\phi \ .$$

With ϕ determined, equations (6.18) - (6.21) determine γ_1, λ_1, π and λ_2, respectively. Furthermore,

$$Cov(y_1, y_2) = \lambda_1 Var(\eta_1) = \lambda_1(\gamma_1^2\phi + \psi_{11})$$

which determines ψ_{11}, and

$$Cov(y_3, y_4) = \lambda_2 Var(\eta_2) = \lambda_2[\pi^2\phi + Var(\nu)]$$

which determines

$$Var(\nu) = \psi_{22} + \beta^2\psi_{11} \ .$$

For given λ_1, λ_2, γ_1, π, ϕ and ψ_{11} the four equations

$$
\begin{align}
Cov(y_1, y_3) &= \gamma_1\pi\phi + \beta\psi_{11} \ , & (6.22)\\
Cov(y_1, y_4) &= \lambda_2(\gamma_1\pi\phi + \beta\psi_{11}) \ , & (6.23)\\
Cov(y_2, y_3) &= \lambda_1(\gamma_1\pi\phi + \beta\psi_{11}) \ , & (6.24)\\
Cov(y_2, y_4) &= \lambda_1\lambda_2(\gamma_1\pi\phi + \beta\psi_{11}) \ , & (6.25)
\end{align}
$$

show that β is overdetermined. Then, with β determined, $\gamma_2 = \pi - \beta\gamma_1$ and ψ_{22} are obtained. The error variances $\theta_{ii}^{(\epsilon)}$ are determined from $Var(y_i)$, $i = 1,2,3,4$ and $\theta_{ii}^{(\delta)}$ from $Var(x_i)$, $i = 1,2$. Hence it is clear that Model B is identified and has six independent restrictions on Σ.

In Model D there are two more parameters, namely $\theta_{31}^{(\epsilon)}$ and $\theta_{42}^{(\epsilon)}$. These are added to the right sides of (6.22) and (6.25). However, since (6.23) or (6.24) can be used to determine β it is clear that $\theta_{31}^{(\epsilon)}$ is determined by (6.22) and $\theta_{42}^{(\epsilon)}$ is determined by (6.25). Hence Model D is also identified and has four degrees of freedom. The input for Model B is

```
Stability of Alienation, Model B (Uncorrelated Errors)
DA NI=6 NO=932
LA
ANOMIA67 POWERL67 ANOMIA71 POWERL71 EDUCATIN SOCIOIND
CM FI=EX64.COV
MO NY=4 NX=2 NE=2 NK=1 BE=SD PS=DI TE=SY
LE
ALIEN67 ALIEN71
LK
SES
FR LY(2,1) LY(4,2) LX(2,1)
VA 1 LY(1,1) LY(3,2) LX(1,1)
OU SE TV MI ND=2
```

The model includes all eight parameter matrices but only two need to be declared on the MO line: $\mathbf{B}$ is subdiagonal and $\boldsymbol{\Psi}$ is diagonal. As before, in order to see the modification indices for the off-diagonal elements of Θ_ϵ we also include the specification TE=SY. The free parameters λ_1, λ_2 and λ_3 in $\boldsymbol{\Lambda}_y$ and $\boldsymbol{\Lambda}_x$ must be declared free by a FR line. One element in each column of $\boldsymbol{\Lambda}_y$ and $\boldsymbol{\Lambda}_x$ is assigned the value one to fix the scales for η_1, η_2 and ξ. Note that neither ξ nor η_1 or η_2 are standardized in this example.

The value of χ^2 for this model is 71.47 with 6 degrees of freedom. This is not considered an acceptable fit. As in Model A, the modification indices for $\theta_{31}^{(\epsilon)}$ and $\theta_{42}^{(\epsilon)}$ are large:

```
       MODIFICATION INDICES FOR THETA EPS
              ANOMIA67    POWER67    ANOMIA71   POWER71
ANOMIA67         .00
POWER67          .00        .00
ANOMIA71       63.71      49.75        .00
POWER71        49.83      37.26        .00        .00
```

As in many other longitudinal studies, where the same measures are repeated over time, there is a tendency for the measurement errors in these measures to correlate over time due to memory or other retest effects. This suggests that the most likely improvement of the model is obtained by freeing the elements $\theta_{31}^{(\epsilon)}$ and $\theta_{42}^{(\epsilon)}$ of Θ_ϵ. The largest modification index is 63.71 for element $\theta_{31}^{(\epsilon)}$ of Θ_ϵ, predicting a drop in χ^2 of about 63.71 if $\theta_{31}^{(\epsilon)}$ is relaxed. This can be verified by running the model again adding TE(3,1) on the FR line. This is Model C. The χ^2 for this modified model is 6.33 with 5 degrees of freedom. The drop in χ^2 from Model B to Model C is 65.14 with one degree of freedom, which is about what the modification index predicted. Model C fits quite well. For Model C, the largest modification index, 1.59, now occurs for the element $\theta_{42}^{(\epsilon)}$ but this is not significant. By running Model D as well, one can verify that the estimate of $\theta_{42}^{(\epsilon)}$ is not significant. Thus, in this example, it seems that there is strong autocorrelation in the measurement error of ANOMIA only. The memory or retest effect in POWERLESSNESS seems to be much weaker. The results for Models B, C, and D are given in Table 6.6.

For this example (Model C), it may be instructive to examine the sections of the output called TOTAL AND INDIRECT EFFECTS and COVARIANCES. These are displayed below.

The total effect of SES on Alienation 71 is almost equal to the direct effect of SES on Alienation 67, although the direct effect of SES on Alienation 71 is much smaller. The effects of SES on Alienation are negative, indicating that Alienation decreases when SES increases. Also shown in the section of TOTAL EFFECTS are the total effects of SES on the observed y-measures and also the total effects of η_1 and η_2 on these observed measures. Although, according to the model, SES does not have a direct effect on any observed y, there are negative indirect effects via η_1 and η_2. Similarly, although η_1 does not have a direct effect on y_3 and y_4, η_1 affects y_3 and y_4 indirectly via η_2.

```
TOTAL AND INDIRECT EFFECTS
          TOTAL EFFECTS OF KSI ON  ETA
              SES
ALIEN67      -.55
ALIEN71      -.55
```

Table 6.6: Maximum Likelihood Estimates for the Models in Figures 6.2-6.5

Parameter	Model A	Model B	Model C	Model D
λ_1	.85(.04)	.89(.04)	1.03(.05)	.98(.06)
λ_2	.82(.04)	.85(.04)	.97(.05)	.92(.06)
λ_3		.53(.04)	.52(.04)	.52(.04)
β	.79(.04)	.70(.05)	.62(.05)	.61(.05)
γ_1		-.61(.06)	-.55(.05)	-.58(.06)
γ_2		-.17(.05)	-.21(.05)	-.23(.05)
ϕ		6.67(.64)	6.88(.66)	6.80(.65)
ψ_{11}	8.20(.62)	5.31(.47)	4.71(.43)	4.85(.47)
ψ_{22}	4.09(.43)	3.74(.39)	3.87(.34)	4.09(.40)
$\theta_{11}^{(\epsilon)}$	3.63(.37)	4.02(.34)	5.07(.37)	4.74(.45)
$\theta_{22}^{(\epsilon)}$	3.48(.29)	3.19(.27)	2.21(.32)	2.57(.40)
$\theta_{33}^{(\epsilon)}$	3.34(.40)	3.70(.37)	4.81(.40)	4.40(.52)
$\theta_{44}^{(\epsilon)}$	3.88(.30)	3.62(.29)	2.68(.33)	3.07(.43)
$\theta_{31}^{(\epsilon)}$			1.89(.24)	1.62(.31)
$\theta_{42}^{(\epsilon)}$				.34(.26)
$\theta_{11}^{(\delta)}$		2.95(.50)	2.73(.52)	2.81(.51)
$\theta_{22}^{(\delta)}$		2.61(.18)	2.67(.18)	2.65(.18)
χ^2	61.11	71.47	6.33	4.73
d.f.	1	6	5	4

Standard Errors in Parentheses

```
            INDIRECT EFFECTS OF KSI ON   ETA
                    SES
ALIEN67             .00
ALIEN71            -.34
            TOTAL EFFECTS OF ETA ON   ETA
                 ALIEN67     ALIEN71
ALIEN67             .00         .00
ALIEN71             .62         .00
            TOTAL EFFECTS OF ETA ON   Y
                 ALIEN67     ALIEN71
ANOMIA67           1.00         .00
POWER67            1.03         .00
ANOMIA71            .62        1.00
POWER71             .60         .97
            INDIRECT EFFECTS OF ETA ON   Y
                 ALIEN67     ALIEN71
ANOMIA67            .00         .00
POWER67             .00         .00
ANOMIA71            .62         .00
POWER71             .60         .00
```

```
        TOTAL EFFECTS OF KSI ON   Y
                    SES
ANOMIA67          -.55
POWER67           -.56
ANOMIA71          -.55
POWER71           -.53
```

```
COVARIANCES
        Y - ETA
                ANOMIA67      POWER67      ANOMIA71      POWER71
ALIEN67           6.78         6.96          4.99          4.84
ALIEN71           4.99         5.12          7.75          7.52
        Y - KSI
                ANOMIA67      POWER67      ANOMIA71      POWER71
SES              -3.78        -3.88         -3.79         -3.68
        X - ETA
                EDUCATIN      SOCIOIND
ALIEN67          -3.78        -1.95
ALIEN71          -3.79        -1.96
        X - KSI
                EDUCATIN      SOCIOIND
SES               6.88         3.55
```

Example 6.5: Change in Verbal and Quantitative Ability between Grades 7 and 9

For the second illustration we use some longitudinal data from a large growth study conducted at the Educational Testing Service (Anderson and Maier, 1963; Hilton, 1969). In this study, a nationwide sample of fifth graders was tested in 1961 and then again in 1963, 1965, and 1967 as seventh, ninth, and eleventh graders, respectively. The test scores include the verbal (SCATV) and quantitative (SCATQ) parts of the SCAT (Scholastic Aptitude Test) and achievement tests in mathematics (MATH), science (SCI), social studies (SS), reading (READ), listening (LIST), and writing (WRIT). The examinees for whom complete data were available for all the grades 5, 7, 9 and 11, were divided into four groups according to sex and whether or not they participated in an academic curriculum in Grade 12. The four groups and their sample sizes are as follows:

- *Boys academic (BA):   N = 373*

- *Boys nonacademic (BNA): N = 249*

- *Girls academic (GA):   N = 383*

- *Girls nonacademic (GNA) N = 387*

Scores on each test have been scaled so that the unit of measurement is approximately the same at all occasions.

In this example we use the six tests MATH, SCI, SS, READ, SCATV, and SCATQ in Grades 7 and 9 only and only for the group GA. Earlier studies (Jöreskog, 1970c) suggest that these tests measure two oblique factors that may reasonably be interpreted as a verbal (V) and a quantitative (Q) factor. We set up the model in Figure 6.6, which represents a model for the

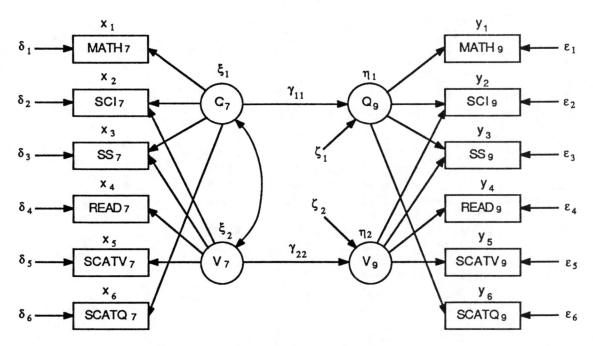

Figure 6.6: Verbal and Quantitative Ability in Grades 7 - 9

measurement of change in verbal and quantitative ability between Grades 7 and 9. Since there are no background variables in this model, we may for estimation purposes treat the pretests as the independent variables. Hence we use the notation x for these. Note that the model includes the following features:

1. On each occasion the factor pattern is postulated to be restricted in the following way: MATH and SCATQ are pure measures of Q. READ and SCATV are pure measures of V. SCI and SS are composite measures of V and Q. This implies that there are four zero loadings in both Λ_x and Λ_y. To fix the scales for V and Q we assume that they are measured in the same units as SCATV and SCATQ, respectively. This means that there is a fixed 1 in each column of Λ_x and Λ_y and SCATV and SCATQ are reference variables.

2. It is postulated that Q_7 affects Q_9 only and not V_9, and similarly for V_7. This means that there are two zero coefficients in Γ. Furthermore, we postulate that the residuals ζ_1 and ζ_2 are uncorrelated, which means that, whatever remains in Q_9 and V_9 after Q_7 and V_7 are accounted for is uncorrelated with everything else.

3. The errors or unique factors in δ and ϵ are assumed to be uncorrelated both within and between occasions.

The input file for this model is

```
Verbal and Quantitative Ability In Grades 7 and 9.
Model: GA = DI and PS = DI
DA NI=12 NO=383
LA
MATH7 SCI7 SS7 READ7 SCATV7 SCATQ7 MATH9 SCI9 SS9 READ9 SCATV9 SCATQ9
KM FI=EX65.DAT
SD FI=EX65.DAT
SE
7 8 9 10 11 12 1 2 3 4 5 6
MO NX=6 NY=6 NK=2 NE=2 PS=DI
LE
Q9 V9
LK
Q7 V7
FI GA 1 2 GA 2 1
FR LY 1 1 LY 2 1 LY 2 2 LY 3 1 LY 3 2 LY 4 2
FR LX 1 1 LX 2 1 LX 2 2 LX 3 1 LX 3 2 LX 4 2
VA 1 LX 5 2 LX 6 1
VA 1 LY 5 2 LY 6 1
OU ND=2 SE TV MI RS
```

The maximum likelihood estimates are given in Table 6.7. The rather low loadings of SCI and SS on Q at both occasions may seem a little surprising. However, an inspection of the items in tests SCI and SS reveals that these are mostly verbal problems concerned with logical reasoning in contrast to the items in SCATQ, which are mostly numerical items measuring the ability to work with numbers. The small residual variance 1.85 of ζ_2 means that V_9 can be predicted almost perfectly from V_7. This is not quite so for Q_7 since here we have a residual variance of 18.49. However, this may be due to the more rapid increase in variance of Q from Grade 7 to 9, which is manifested in the increase in variances, which is 143.55 - 103.87 = 39.68 for Q and 117.15 - 115.40 = 1.75 for V.

There is a reason not to look at each number in Table 6.7 too seriously, and this is the poor overall fit of the model as evidenced by the χ^2-value of 217.68 with 47 *df*. We shall therefore investigate the reason for this poor fit and demonstrate that LISREL may be used not only to assess or measure the goodness-of-fit of a model but also to detect the parts of the model where the fit is poor. Taking the more fundamental assumptions of linearity and multinormality for granted, lack of fit of the model in Figure 6.6 may be due to the fact that one or more of the postulates 1, 2, or 3 is not reasonable. We shall therefore investigate each of these separately.

To investigate (1), we set up a factor analysis model of the pre- and post-tests separately, assuming the postulated two-factor structure. This gives $\chi^2 = 17.64$ for the pretests and $\chi^2 = 2.62$ for the post-tests, both with 10 degrees of freedom. Although the fit is not quite acceptable in Grade 7, we take the postulated factor structure to hold for both the pre- and post-tests. So we must continue to look for lack of fit due to postulate (2) or (3).

Postulate 2 is concerned with the interrelationships between the four factors Q_7, V_7, Q_9, and V_9. The most general assumption is that these four factors are freely intercorrelated, and this is equivalent to a LISREL model with all four coefficients in Γ free and with Ψ free as a full symmetric matrix. Hence, it is clear that the assumption made in (2) is the intersection of the two hypotheses "Γ is diagonal" and "Ψ is diagonal." It is therefore useful to test each of the four possible hypotheses. The results of these analyses may be presented in a 2 x 2 table as in

Table 6.7: Maximum Likelihood Estimates for the Model in Figure 6.6

$$\hat{\boldsymbol{\Lambda}}_x = \begin{pmatrix} .97 & 0. \\ .20 & .52 \\ .25 & .84 \\ 0. & 1.21 \\ 0. & 1. \\ 1. & 0. \end{pmatrix} \qquad \hat{\boldsymbol{\Theta}}_\delta = \begin{pmatrix} 32.25 \\ 30.14 \\ 43.63 \\ 46.19 \\ 19.69 \\ 50.40 \end{pmatrix}$$

$$\hat{\boldsymbol{\Lambda}}_y = \begin{pmatrix} .89 & 0. \\ .24 & .64 \\ .36 & .69 \\ 0. & .95 \\ 0. & 1. \\ 1. & 0. \end{pmatrix} \qquad \hat{\boldsymbol{\Theta}}_\epsilon = \begin{pmatrix} 23.07 \\ 43.20 \\ 52.46 \\ 42.15 \\ 19.95 \\ 67.71 \end{pmatrix}$$

$$\hat{\boldsymbol{\Gamma}} = \begin{pmatrix} 1.10 & 0. \\ 0. & 1.00 \end{pmatrix}$$

$$\hat{\boldsymbol{\Phi}} = \begin{pmatrix} 103.87 & 92.58 \\ 92.58 & 115.40 \end{pmatrix}$$

$$\hat{\boldsymbol{\Psi}} = \begin{pmatrix} 18.50 & 0. \\ 0. & 1.85 \end{pmatrix}$$

$$\hat{\boldsymbol{\Omega}} = \begin{pmatrix} 143.55 & 101.54 \\ 101.54 & 117.15 \end{pmatrix}$$

$$\chi^2 = 217.68 \text{ with } df = 47$$

Table 6.8. The row marginals of the table represent χ^2-values with one degree of freedom for testing the hypothesis that $\boldsymbol{\Psi}$ is diagonal. It is seen that this hypothesis may be rejected. The column marginals represent χ^2-values with 2 df for testing the hypothesis that $\boldsymbol{\Gamma}$ is diagonal. This hypothesis seems quite reasonable. From these analyses it is clear that "$\boldsymbol{\Gamma}$ diagonal and $\boldsymbol{\Psi}$ free" is the most reasonable assumption to retain. The overall fit of this model is $\chi^2 = 196.2$ with 46 df. Since this is still too large, we must continue to investigate Postulate 3.

The assumption in Postulate 3 is that the unique factors in δ and ϵ are uncorrelated both within and between sets. That they are uncorrelated within sets should not be questioned, since we have already found that the postulated factor-analysis model holds for both pre- and post-test. That they are uncorrelated between sets, however, is more questionable because of specific factors in each test. This means that the unique factors for corresponding tests should be allowed to correlate. To account for such correlations, Jöreskog (1970c) introduced so-called *test-specific factors*; that is, factors that do not contribute to correlations between tests within occasions but between the *same* tests at different occasions. In this case, when there are only two occasions, it is not possible to define (identify) test-specific factors; we can merely introduce correlations between unique factors for corresponding pre- and post-tests.

All these analyses are in fact unnecessary as the output file from the initial model (Figure 6.6) suggests immediately that the largest source of misspecification in the model is likely to be

Table 6.8: Test of Assumptions (2) for the Model in Figure 6.6

	Ψ diagonal	Ψ free	
Γ diagonal	$\chi^2_{47} = 217.7$	$\chi^2_{46} = 196.2$	$\chi^2_1 = 21.5$
Γ free	$\chi^2_{45} = 216.7$	$\chi^2_{44} = 193.6$	$\chi^2_1 = 23.1$
	$\chi^2_2 = 1.0$	$\chi^2_2 = 2.6$	

The subscripts on χ^2 denote degrees of freedom

the autocorrelation, i.e. the correlation between error terms for the same variables over time. This can be seen from the standardized residuals:

```
         STANDARDIZED RESIDUALS
            MATH9      SCI9       SS9      READ9     SCATV9     SCATQ9
MATH9        .00
SCI9         .74       .04
SS9         1.19      3.65       .05
READ9       3.15      1.02       .33       .00
SCATV9      2.14      -.77     -1.44      1.04       .00
SCATQ9       .34     -1.37     -1.63      1.95      -.26        .00
MATH7       -.13      -.16       .12      1.35       .82      -1.34
SCI7       -1.25      4.97      1.65     -2.11     -1.34      -2.65
SS7         -.81      3.27      2.61      -.02     -3.73      -3.28
READ7       1.21     -2.32       .42      2.75     -3.16      -1.55
SCATV7      -.81     -4.10     -2.91     -2.95      7.35      -2.17
SCATQ7      -.25     -2.71     -2.06      -.61     -2.26       5.62
         STANDARDIZED RESIDUALS
            MATH7      SCI7       SS7      READ7     SCATV7     SCATQ7
MATH7        .00
SCI7        1.00       .00
SS7          .51      3.12       .00
READ7       2.92      -.10      -.13       .00
SCATV7       .69     -2.45      -.96      1.66       .00
SCATQ7      -.68      -.41       .29      -.32     -2.03        .00
```

The model in Figure 6.6 is therefore modified as in Figure 6.7. This revised model can also be estimated with LISREL. In order to accommodate the correlated error terms we must write the model as a Submodel 3B with parameter matrices Λ_y, $\mathbf{B}$, Ψ, and Θ_ϵ. The input file is

```
Verbal and Quantitative Ability In Grades 7 and 9.
Model: BE Diagonal and Autocorrelated Errors
DA NI=12 NO=383
LA
MATH7 SCI7 SS7 READ7 SCATV7 SCATQ7 MATH9 SCI9 SS9 READ9 SCATV9 SCATQ9
KM FI=EX65.DAT
SD FI=EX65.DAT
MO NY=12 NE=4 BE=FU TE=SY
LE
Q7 V7 Q9 V9
FR LY 1 1 LY 2 1 LY 2 2 LY 3 1 LY 3 2 LY 4 2
FR LY 7 3 LY 8 3 LY 8 4 LY 9 3 LY 9 4 LY 10 4
VA 1 LY 5 2 LY 6 1
VA 1 LY 11 4 LY 12 3
FR BE 3 1 BE 4 2
FI PS 3 1 PS 3 2 PS 4 1 PS 4 2
FR TE 7 1 TE 8 2 TE 9 3 TE 10 4 TE 11 5 TE 12 6
OU SE TV RS
```

The analysis of the revised model gives results shown in Tables 6.9 and 6.10. All estimated parameters are significantly different from zero.

The test of overall goodness of fit gives $\chi^2 = 65.61$ with 40 df. This represents a reasonably good fit of the model to the data. An approximate test of the hypothesis that the unique factors are uncorrelated between occasions is obtained as $\chi^2 = 196.2 - 65.6 = 130.6$ with 6 df so that it is clear that this hypothesis is quite unreasonable. The variances, covariances, and correlations of the unique factors are given in Table 6.10. A comparison of the covariances with their standard errors reveals that all covariances except possibly the one between ϵ_1 and ϵ_7 are significantly non-zero.

6.6 Simplex Models

A simplex model is a type of covariance structure which often occurs in longitudinal studies when the same variable is measured repeatedly on the same people over several occasions. The simplex model is equivalent to the covariance structure generated by a first-order non-stationary autoregressive process. Guttman (1954) used the term simplex also for variables which are not ordered through time but by other criteria. One of his examples concerns tests of verbal ability ordered according to increasing complexity. The typical feature of a simplex correlation structure is that the entries in the correlation matrix decrease as one moves away from the main diagonal.

Jöreskog (1970b) formulated various simplex models in terms of the well-known Wiener and Markov stochastic processes. A distinction was made between a perfect simplex and a quasi-simplex. A *perfect simplex* is reasonable only if the measurement errors in the variables are negligible. A *quasi-simplex*, on the other hand, allows for sizable errors of measurement.

Consider p fallible variables $y_1, y_2, \ldots, y_p$. The unit of measurement in the true variables η_i may be chosen to be the same as in the observed variables y_i. The equations defining the model are then

$$y_i = \eta_i + \epsilon_i, \quad i = 1, 2, \ldots, p,$$

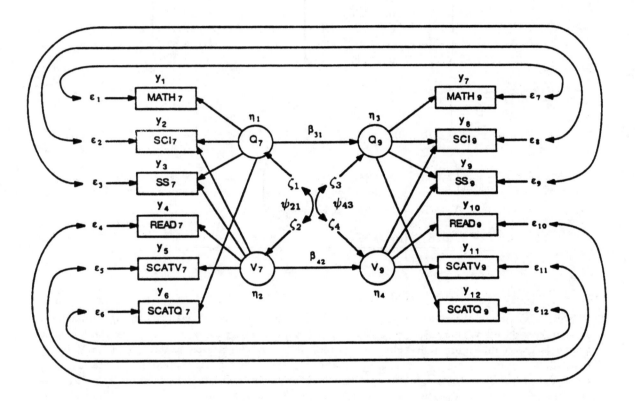

Figure 6.7: Verbal and Quantitative Ability in Grades 7 - 9. Model with Autocorrelated Errors

Table 6.9: Maximum Likelihood Estimates for the Model in Figure 6.7

$$
\hat{\mathbf{\Lambda}}_y = \begin{pmatrix}
1.01 & 0. & 0. & 0. \\
.13 & .60 & 0. & 0. \\
.12 & .98 & 0. & 0. \\
0. & 1.24 & 0. & 0. \\
0. & 1. & 0. & 0. \\
1. & 0. & 0. & 0. \\
0. & 0. & .93 & 0. \\
0. & 0. & .13 & .77 \\
0. & 0. & .25 & .82 \\
0. & 0. & 0. & .98 \\
0. & 0. & 0. & 1. \\
0. & 0. & 1. & 0.
\end{pmatrix}
\qquad
\hat{\mathbf{\Theta}}_\epsilon = \begin{pmatrix}
27.75 \\
29.59 \\
40.28 \\
44.21 \\
24.37 \\
54.24 \\
17.66 \\
41.14 \\
50.90 \\
40.34 \\
24.84 \\
74.52
\end{pmatrix}
$$

$$
\hat{\mathbf{B}} = \begin{pmatrix}
0. & 0. & 0. & 0. \\
0. & 0. & 0. & 0. \\
1.06 & 0. & 0. & 0. \\
0. & 0.98 & 0. & 0.
\end{pmatrix}
$$

$$
\hat{\mathbf{\Psi}} = \begin{pmatrix}
100.57 & & & \\
90.53 & 110.45 & & \\
0. & 0. & 22.63 & \\
0. & 0. & 8.42 & 6.94
\end{pmatrix}
$$

$\chi^2 = 65.61$ with $df = 40$

$$
\eta_i = \beta_i \eta_{i-1} + \zeta_i, \quad i = 2,3,\ \ldots, p\,,
$$

where the ϵ_i are uncorrelated among themselves and uncorrelated with all the η_i and where ζ_i is uncorrelated with η_{i-1}, $i = 2, 3, \ldots, p$. A path diagram of the simplex model with $p = 4$ is given in Figure 6.8. The parameters of the model are $\omega_1 = \text{Var}(\eta_1)$, $\psi_i = \text{Var}(\zeta_i)$, $i = 2, 3, \ldots, p, \theta_i = Var(\epsilon_i)$, $i = 1, 2, \ldots, p$ and $\beta_2, \beta_3, \ldots, \beta_p$. Let $\omega_i = \text{Var}(\eta_i) = \beta_i^2 \omega_{i-1} + \psi_i$, $i = 2, 3, \ldots, p$. Then there is a one-to-one correspondence between the parameters $\beta_2, \beta_3, \ldots,$ $\beta_p, \omega_1, \psi_2, \psi_3, \ldots, \psi_p$ and the parameters $\beta_2, \beta_3, \ldots, \beta_p, \omega_1, \omega_2, \ldots, \omega_p$. The ω's are not parameters in the LISREL model, so in LISREL the first set of parameters must be used. However, for identification purposes it is more convenient to use the second set of parameters. In terms of the ω's, for $p = 4$ measurement occasions, the covariance matrix of $y_1, y_2, \ldots, y_p$ has the form

$$
\mathbf{\Sigma} = \begin{pmatrix}
\omega_1 + \theta_1 & & & \\
\beta_2 \omega_1 & \omega_2 + \theta_2 & & \\
\beta_2 \beta_3 \omega_1 & \beta_3 \omega_2 & \omega_3 + \theta_3 & \\
\beta_2 \beta_3 \beta_4 \omega_1 & \beta_3 \beta_4 \omega_2 & \beta_4 \omega_3 & \omega_4 + \theta_4
\end{pmatrix} \tag{6.26}
$$

It is seen from (6.26) that, although the product $\beta_2 \omega_1 = \sigma_{21}$ is identified, β_2 and ω_1 are not separately identified. The product $\beta_2 \omega_1$ is involved in the off-diagonal elements in the first column (and row) only. One can multiply β_2 by a non-zero constant and divide ω_1 by the same

Table 6.10: Variances, Covariances, and Correlations for the Unique Factors in Table 6.9

i	$\text{Var}(\epsilon_i)$	$\text{Var}(\epsilon_{i+6})$	$\text{Cov}(\epsilon_i \epsilon_{i+6})$	$\text{Corr}(\epsilon_i \epsilon_{i+6})$
1	27.75(3.78)	17.66(3.88)	-3.47(2.78)	-.157
2	29.59(2.37)	41.14(3.38)	9.60(2.10)	.275
3	40.28(3.60)	50.90(4.21)	6.16(2.82)	.136
4	44.21(4.25)	40.34(3.59)	7.52(2.89)	.178
5	24.37(2.47)	24.84(2.60)	12.04(2.05)	.489
6	54.24(4.87)	74.52(6.73)	22.83(4.40)	.359

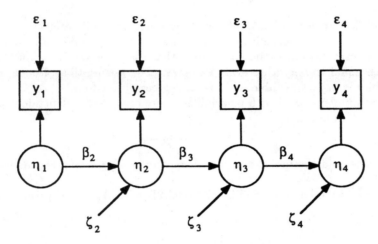

Figure 6.8: A Simplex Model

constant without changing the product. The change induced by ω_1 in σ_{11} can be absorbed in θ_1 in such a way that σ_{11} remains unchanged. Hence $\theta_1 = \text{Var}(\epsilon_1)$ is not identified. For η_2 and η_3 we have

$$\omega_2 = \frac{\sigma_{32}\sigma_{21}}{\sigma_{31}},$$
$$\omega_3 = \frac{\sigma_{43}\sigma_{32}}{\sigma_{42}},$$

so that ω_2 and ω_3, and hence also θ_2 and θ_3, are identified. With ω_2 and ω_3 identified, β_3 and β_4 are identified by σ_{32} and σ_{43}. The middle coefficient β_3 is overidentified since

$$\beta_3\omega_2 = \frac{\sigma_{31}\sigma_{42}}{\sigma_{41}} = \sigma_{32}.$$

Since both ω_4 and θ_4 are involved in σ_{44} only, these are not identified. Only their sum σ_{44} is.

This analysis of the identification problem shows that for the "inner" variables y_2 and y_3, the parameters ω_2, ω_3, θ_2, θ_3, and β_3 are identified, whereas there is an indeterminacy associated with each of the "outer" variables y_1 and y_4. To eliminate these indeterminacies one condition must be imposed on the parameters ω_1, θ_1 and β_2, and another on the parameters ω_4 and θ_4. In terms of the original LISREL parameters, β_2, $\psi_1 = \omega_1$, ψ_2, ψ_4, θ_1, and θ_4 are not identified whereas β_3, β_4, ψ_3, θ_2, and θ_3 are identified. One indeterminacy is associated with β_2, ψ_1, ψ_2 and θ_1 and another indeterminacy is associated with ψ_4 and θ_4. The parameters β_2, ψ_1, ψ_2, and θ_1 are only determined by the three equations

$$\begin{aligned}
\sigma_{11} &= \psi_1 + \theta_1 \\
\sigma_{21} &= \beta_2\psi_1 \\
\omega_2 &= \beta_2^2\psi_1 + \psi_2 \,,
\end{aligned}$$

where ω_2 is identified. The parameters ψ_4 and θ_4 are only determined by the single equation

$$\sigma_{44} = \beta_4^2\omega_3 + \psi_4 + \theta_4$$

where ω_3 is identified. The most natural way of eliminating the indeterminacies is to set $\theta_1 = \theta_2$ and $\theta_4 = \theta_3$, which makes sense if the y-variables are on the same scale. It is not necessary to assume that all error variances are equal, only that the error variances for the first and last variable are each equal to one other error variance. The assumption of equal error variances across all variables is in fact testable with $p - 3$ degrees of freedom.

In the general simplex model with p variables, there are $3p - 3$ independent parameters and the degrees of freedom are

$$\frac{1}{2}p(p + 1) - 3p + 3 \,.$$

If $p = 3$, this is zero and the model is a tautology. For testing a simplex model, p must be at least 4.

The *quasi-simplex* model is a LISREL submodel 3B with $\Lambda_y = \mathbf{I}$, Θ_ϵ diagonal, Ψ diagonal, and

$$\mathbf{B} = \begin{pmatrix} 0 & 0 & 0 & 0 \\ \beta_2 & 0 & 0 & 0 \\ 0 & \beta_3 & 0 & 0 \\ 0 & 0 & \beta_4 & 0 \end{pmatrix} \,.$$

This specification automatically defines ζ_1 as η_1 so that $\psi_1 = \omega_1$.

The *perfect simplex* is obtained by setting $\Theta_\epsilon = \mathbf{0}$ (TE=ZE). This is testable when $p \geq 3$. The perfect simplex implies that the *partial correlation* $\rho_{ik \cdot j} = 0$, whenever $i < j < k$. Higher-order partial correlations, with two or more intermediate variables held constant, also vanish.

Example 6.6: A Simplex Model for Academic Performance

Humphreys (1968) presented the correlation matrix shown in Table 6.11. The variables include eight semesters of grade-point averages, y_1, y_2, ..., y_8, high school rank y_0 and a composite score on the American College Testing test y_0' for approximately 1600 undergraduate students at the University of Illinois.

Strictly speaking, the covariance matrix should be used rather than the correlation matrix in this example, see Section 1.21.

We shall first use the variables y_1, y_2, ..., y_8 and illustrate what happens when one runs a model which is not identified. We have made three runs with the same data and model. In Run 1 we specified the model *as if* all the parameters were identified. The input for this run is as follows:

Table 6.11: Correlations among Grade Point Averages, High School Rank and Aptitude Test

	y_0	y_0'	y_1	y_2	y_3	y_4	y_5	y_6	y_7	y_8
y_0	1.000									
y_0'	.393	1.000								
y_1	.387	.375	1.000							
y_2	.341	.298	.556	1.000						
y_3	.278	.237	.456	.490	1.000					
y_4	.270	.255	.439	.445	.562	1.000				
y_5	.240	.238	.415	.418	.496	.512	1.000			
y_6	.256	.252	.399	.383	.456	.469	.551	1.000		
y_7	.240	.219	.387	.364	.445	.442	.500	.544	1.000	
y_8	.222	.173	.342	.339	.354	.416	.453	.482	.541	1.000

```
Simplex Model for Academic Performance   Run 1
DA NI=10 NO=1600
LA
(10A3)
 YOYO' Y1 Y2 Y3 Y4 Y5 Y6 Y7 Y8
KM FI=EX66.COR
SE
3 4 5 6 7 8 9 10/
MO NY=8 NE=8 LY=ID BE=FU PS=DI
FR BE(2,1) BE(3,2) BE(4,3) BE(5,4) BE(6,5) BE(7,6) BE(8,7)
OU SE SS AD=OFF
```

In Run 2 we imposed the condition that $\theta_1 = \theta_2$ to eliminate the first indeterminacy and in Run 3 we imposed the condition $\theta_8 = \theta_7$, in addition, to eliminate the second indeterminacy also. The results are shown in Table 6.12. Run 1 gave the message that the parameter TE(1) may not be identified. TE(1) is θ_1, the last of the four parameters involved in the first indeterminacy. In Run 2 the corresponding message was that the parameter TE(8) may not be identified. TE(8) equals θ_8, the last parameter involved in the second indeterminacy. In Run 3 no such message was given indicating that the model is identified. All three solutions in Table 6.12 have the same $\chi^2 = 23.91$ and it is seen that all parameters which are identified come out with the same parameter estimate in all three runs. Only the non-identified parameters vary over the three solutions. The values given for the non-identified parameters are of course arbitrary to some extent. However, these values are such that the following three quantities are invariant over all solutions:

$$\hat{\psi}_1 + \hat{\theta}_1$$
$$\hat{\beta}_2 \hat{\psi}_1$$
$$\hat{\psi}_8 + \hat{\theta}_8$$

These computer runs illustrate that LISREL behaves reasonably for models which are non-identified and that the program correctly identifies the last parameter involved in an indeterminacy as a non-identified parameter.

Table 6.12: Results for Simplex Model

Parameter number	Parameter	Parameter "Estimates"		
		Run 1	Run 2	Run 3
1	β_2	0.52	0.98	0.98
2	β_3	0.84	0.84	0.84
3	β_4	0.96	0.96	0.96
4	β_5	0.91	0.91	0.91
5	β_6	0.93	0.93	0.93
6	β_7	0.94	0.94	0.94
7	β_8	0.89	0.89	0.89
8	ψ_1	1.06	0.57	0.57
9	ψ_2	0.28	0.03	0.03
10	ψ_3	0.17	0.17	0.17
11	ψ_4	0.03	0.03	0.03
12	ψ_5	0.12	0.12	0.12
13	ψ_6	0.07	0.07	0.07
14	ψ_7	0.10	0.10	0.10
15	ψ_8	0.61	0.61	0.13
16	θ_1	-0.06	0.43	0.43
17	θ_2	0.43	0.43	0.43
18	θ_3	0.43	0.43	0.43
19	θ_4	0.44	0.44	0.44
20	θ_5	0.42	0.42	0.42
21	θ_6	0.42	0.42	0.42
22	θ_7	0.39	0.39	0.39
23	θ_8	-0.09	-0.09	0.39
	$\psi_1 + \theta_1$	1.00	1.00	1.00
	$\beta_2\psi_1$	0.56	0.56	0.56
	$\psi_8 + \theta_8$	0.52	0.52	0.52

The parameter SS on the OU line gives the standardized solution, i.e., the correlation matrix of $\boldsymbol{\eta}$. The intercorrelations among $\eta_2, \eta_3, \ldots, \eta_7$ are the same for all three solutions in Table 6.12. These are given in Table 6.13. Here every correlation ρ_{ij} with $\mid i - j \mid > 1$ is the product of the correlations just below the diagonal. For example, $\rho(\eta_5, \eta_2) = 0.838 \times 0.969 \times 0.892 = 0.724$. These correlations form a perfect simplex. The reliabilities of the semester grades $y_2, y_3, \ldots, y_7$ can be obtained directly from the solution in which the η's are standardized. The reliabilities are

y_2	y_3	y_4	y_5	y_6	y_7
0.569	0.574	0.563	0.584	0.581	0.608

A test of the hypothesis that all reliabilities are equal gives $\chi^2 = 2.17$ with 5 degrees of freedom, so that this hypothesis is not rejected by the data despite the large sample size.

Without identification conditions imposed, as in Run 1, the correlations $\rho(\eta_1, \eta_j)$, $j \neq 1$ and $\rho(\eta_i, \eta_8)$, $i \neq 8$ and the reliabilities of y_1 and y_8 are not identified. However, in view of the above test of equality of reliabilities it seems reasonable to assume that all reliabilities or

Table 6.13: Intercorrelations of a Perfect Simplex

	η_2	η_3	η_4	η_5	η_6	η_7
η_2	1.000					
η_3	0.838	1.000				
η_4	0.812	0.969	1.000			
η_5	0.724	0.865	0.892	1.000		
η_6	0.677	0.809	0.834	0.935	1.000	
η_7	0.619	0.739	0.763	0.855	0.914	1.000

equivalently all error variances in the standardized solution are equal for y_1 through y_8. This assumption makes it possible to estimate the intercorrelations among all the η's.

Assuming that y_0 and y_0' are indicators of pre-college academic achievement η_0 which is assumed to influence the true academic achievement in the first semester η_1, one can estimate again the quasi-Markov simplex and show how this use of y_0 and y_0' helps identify the parameters of the model. The only parameters which are now not identified are ψ_8 and θ_8. This gives a χ^2 = 36.92 with 28 degrees of freedom. If we assume that the reliabilities of all the semester grades are equal, all parameters are identified and the goodness of fit becomes 45.22 with 34 degrees of freedom. The difference 8.30 with 6 degrees of freedom provides another test of equality of the reliabilities. Given that all error variances are equal, a test of the hypothesis that

$$\beta_1 = \beta_2 = \beta_3 = ... = \beta_8$$

gives $\chi^2 = 6.48$ with 7 degrees of freedom so that this hypothesis cannot be rejected. The input file for the last run is

```
Simplex Model for Academic Performance  Last Model
DA NI=10 NO=1600
LA
(10A3)
 Y0Y0' Y1 Y2 Y3 Y4 Y5 Y6 Y7 Y8
KM FI=EX66.COR SY
MO NY=10 NE=9 BE=FU PS=DI
FR LY 2 1 BE 2 1 BE 3 2 BE 4 3 BE 5 4 BE 6 5 BE 7 6 BE 8 7 BE 9 8
VA 1 LY 1 1 LY 3 2 LY 4 3 LY 5 4 LY 6 5 LY 7 6 LY 8 7 LY 9 8 LY 10 9
EQ TE 3 - TE 10
EQ BE 2 1 BE 3 2 BE 4 3 BE 5 4 BE 6 5 BE 7 6 BE 8 7 BE 9 8
ST .5 ALL
OU SE SS NS
```

Further analysis shows that the variances $\psi_1, \psi_2, \ldots, \psi_8$ of the random disturbance terms are not equal, so the whole autoregressive process is not completely stationary.

Chapter 7

ANALYSIS OF ORDINAL AND OTHER NON-NORMAL VARIABLES

7.1 Consequences of Non-Normality

In the previous chapters we have assumed that the observed variables to be analyzed by the LISREL computer program are quantitative variables in the sense that they represent measurements which are, at least approximately, on an interval scale. If such variables are approximately normally distributed, in addition, the use of ML and GLS estimates and their associated standard errors and χ^2 goodness-of-fit measure may be justified. If the distribution of the observed variables are moderately non-normal, skewed or peaked, the ML and GLS methods may still be used to fit the model to the data and, if interpreted with caution, standard errors and χ^2 values together with other fit statistics can still be used to assess the fit of the model. However, especially χ^2 is sensitive to departures from normality.

The presentation in Chapter 1 formulated the model and the problem of estimation in terms of the joint distribution of the *observed variables*. Another way to discuss the problem of non-normality in these variables is to focus on the joint distribution of the latent and error variables which *generate* the observed variables.

For example, consider LISREL Submodel 1. The x-variables are then generated by ξ- and δ-variables which are assumed to be independent. If ξ and δ have multivariate normal distributions, it follows that $\mathbf{x}$ is multivariate normal. However, if either ξ or δ are non-normal, then $\mathbf{x}$ will be non-normal. In general, each x-variable is a mixture of ξ-variables and a δ-variable.

Recent theoretical studies (e.g., Anderson and Amemiya, 1985; Browne, 1987; Shapiro, 1987) have shown that the normal asymptotic theory for ML and GLS estimators is still valid under more general distributions for ξ and δ than the normal. For example, Browne (1987) shows that ξ may be a set of fixed values or have a non-normal distribution as long as δ is normal. Sufficient conditions for valid normal theory application are given by Anderson and Amemiya (1985) for some ξ's being fixed, some ξ's being random with finite second moments and δ's being independent with finite second moments.

On the other hand, other studies focusing on elliptical distributions (e.g., Harlow, 1985, and Laake, 1987) suggest that standard errors of ML and GLS estimates may be systematically under- or overestimated if the distributions have heavier or lighter tails than the normal distribution.

In this chapter we distinguish between two cases of non-normality:

(a) Some or all of the observed variables are ordinal or discrete

(b) The observed variables are continuous (i.e., on interval scales) and non-normal

Case (a) is by far the most common situation in practice. In this case, it is a widespread misuse of LISREL methodology

- to use arbitrary scale scores such as 1, 2, 3, ... for categories, pretending that these scores have interval scale properties

- to compute a covariance matrix or a product-moment (Pearson) correlation matrix for such scores

- to analyze such covariance or correlation matrices with the ML method

This can lead to greatly distorted parameter estimates and incorrect χ^2 goodness-of-fit measures and standard errors. Instead, the matrix of polychoric correlations should be analyzed with the WLS method with a correct weight matrix. This is discussed in Section 7.2. The special case when all variables are dichotomous is discussed in Section 7.3.

In case (b), if the observed variables are continuous and *highly* non-normal, it may be best to use an ordinary sample covariance matrix and analyze this with WLS, using a correct weight matrix. This requires a large sample so that the asymptotic covariance matrix of the sample variances and covariances can be estimated accurately. A poorly estimated asymptotic covariance matrix, such as estimated from a small sample, can do more harm than good, when used with WLS. If the sample size is not sufficiently large to produce an accurate estimate of the asymptotic covariance matrix, it is probably better to use ML or GLS. The use of WLS with sample covariance matrices is discussed in Section 7.4. Section 7.5 shows how to analyze a matrix of product moment (Pearson) correlations with WLS to estimate a *correlation structure*.

7.2   Analysis of Ordinal Variables

In many cases, especially when data are collected through questionnaires, the variables are ordinal, i.e., responses are classified into different ordered categories.

An ordinal variable z (z may be either a y- or an x-variable in LISREL sense) may be regarded as a crude measurement of an underlying unobserved or unobservable continuous variable z^*. For example, a four-point ordinal scale may be conceived as

- If $z^* \leq \alpha_1$, z is scored 1

- If $\alpha_1 < z^* \leq \alpha_2$, z is scored 2

- If $\alpha_2 < z^* \leq \alpha_3$, z is scored 3

- If $\alpha_3 < z^*$, z is scored 4

where $\alpha_1 < \alpha_2 < \alpha_3$ are threshold values for z^*. It is often assumed that z^* has a standard normal distribution, in which case the thresholds can be estimated from the inverse of the normal distribution function.

Suppose z_1 and z_2 are two ordinal variables with underlying continuous variables z_1^* and z_2^*, respectively. Assuming that z_1^* and z_2^* have a bivariate normal distribution, their correlation is called *the polychoric correlation coefficient*. A special case of this is *the tetrachoric correlation coefficient* when both z_1 and z_2 are dichotomous. Now, suppose further that z_3 is a continuous variable measured on an interval scale. The correlation between z_1^* and z_3 is called *the polyserial correlation coefficient* assuming that z_1^* and z_3 have a bivariate normal distribution. A special case of this is the *biserial correlation* when z_1 is dichotomous.

An ordinal variable z does not have a metric scale. To use such a variable in a linear relationship we use the corresponding underlying variable z^* instead. The polychoric and polyserial correlations are not correlations computed from actual scores but are rather theoretical correlations of the underlying z^* variables. These correlations are estimated from the observed pairwise contingency tables of the ordinal variables. See Jöreskog and Sörbom (1986) and references therein for the theory on which the polychoric and polyserial correlations are based.

When the observed variables in LISREL are all ordinal or are of mixed scale types (ordinal and interval), the use of ordinary product moment correlations based on raw scores is not recommended. Instead it is suggested that estimates of polychoric and polyserial correlations be computed and that the matrix of such correlations be analyzed by the WLS method.

The weight matrix required for such an analysis is the inverse of the estimated asymptotic covariance matrix **W** of the polychoric and polyserial correlations. The asymptotic covariance matrix as well as the matrix of polychoric and polyserial correlations are obtained by PRELIS.

The steps involved in this analysis will be described in the following two examples. These examples involve only ordinal variables and only polychoric correlations. For other examples involving also continuous and/or censored variables and other types of correlations, see the PRELIS User's Guide (Jöreskog and Sörbom, 1986).

Example 7.1: Attitudes of Morality and Equality

Swedish school children in Grade 9 were asked questions about their attitudes regarding social issues in family, school, and society. Among the questions asked were the following eight items (in free translation from Swedish, Hasselrot and Lernberg, 1980):

*   For me questions about ...*

1. *human rights*
2. *equal conditions for all people*
3. *racial problems*
4. *equal value of all people*
5. *euthanasia*
6. *crime and punishment*
7. *conscientious objectors*
8. *guilt and bad conscience*

... are:

*   unimportant   not important   important   very important*

For the present example we use a subsample of 200 cases. Responses to the eight questions were scored 1, 2, 3, and 4, where 4 = very important. The data matrix consists of 200 rows and 8 columns, and is stored in the file EX71.RAW. The PRELIS input file is

```
ATTITUDES OF MORALITY AND EQUALITY
DA NI=8
LA
HUMRGHTS EQUALCON RACEPROB EQUALVAL EUTHANAS CRIMEPUN CONSCOBJ GUILT
RA FI=EX71.RAW
OR ALL
OU MA=PM SM=EX71.PML SA=EX71.ACP PA
```

The OU line requests that the matrix of polychoric correlations be saved in the file EX71.PML and that the asymptotic covariance matrix be saved in the file EX71.ACP.

The matrix of polychoric correlations as printed by PRELIS is

ESTIMATED CORRELATION MATRIX

	HUMRGHTS	EQUALCON	RACEPROB	EQUALVAL	EUTHANAS	CRIMEPUN
HUMRGHTS	1.000					
EQUALCON	.423	1.000				
RACEPROB	.219	.202	1.000			
EQUALVAL	.367	.631	.283	1.000		
EUTHANAS	.439	.703	.312	.692	1.000	
CRIMEPUN	.210	.232	.275	.423	.218	1.000
CONSCOBJ	.185	.291	.304	.340	.224	.312
GUILT	.102	.311	.234	.314	.337	.204

ESTIMATED CORRELATION MATRIX

	CONSCOBJ	GUILT
CONSCOBJ	1.000	
GUILT	.202	1.000

The first part of the asymptotic covariance matrix as given in the PRELIS output file looks like:

ASYMPTOTIC COVARIANCE MATRIX OF ESTIMATED CORRELATIONS

	R(2,1)	R(3,1)	R(3,2)	R(4,1)	R(4,2)	R(4,3)
R(2,1)	.00610					
R(3,1)	.00011	.00776				
R(3,2)	.00011	.00006	.00716			
R(4,1)	.00019	.00010	.00002	.00638		
R(4,2)	.00023	.00001	.00012	.00021	.00315	
R(4,3)	.00003	.00008	.00008	.00013	.00016	.00640
R(5,1)	.00023	.00011	.00003	.00020	.00010	.00004
R(5,2)	.00022	.00001	.00011	.00008	.00026	.00005
R(5,3)	.00004	.00009	.00010	.00004	.00007	.00013
R(5,4)	.00008	.00002	.00004	.00020	.00027	.00016
R(6,1)	.00010	.00006	.00001	.00010	.00002	.00001

The polychoric correlations are saved in the file EX71.PML which will be read by LISREL.

The asymptotic covariance matrix saved in the file EX71.ACP is not equal to the matrix given in the PRELIS output file, but is equal to N times this matrix, as required by LISREL, where N is the sample size. The file EX71.ACP is not meant to be printed but is only supposed to be read by LISREL. The first part of this file looks like this:

```
.122087D+01   .212944D-01   .155224D+01   .212244D-01   .121896D-01   .143271D+01
.385111D-01   .196011D-01   .483477D-02   .127678D+01   .452811D-01   .279864D-02
.238811D-01   .411283D-01   .629524D+00   .639631D-02   .162831D-01   .169912D-01
.258421D-01   .317738D-01   .128021D+01   .451902D-01   .223750D-01   .618344D-02
.408478D-01   .190719D-01   .785462D-02   .119829D+01   .439276D-01   .290477D-02
.228146D-01   .150894D-01   .527725D-01   .104412D-01   .442987D-01   .505023D+00
.832846D-02   .180195D-01   .190576D-01   .789013D-02   .131586D-01   .256843D-01
.320429D-01   .327086D-01   .131104D+01   .166502D-01   .300922D-02   .831413D-02
```

There are $(1/2)8 \times 7 = 28$ correlations in the polychoric correlation matrix. Hence, there should be $(1/2)28 \times 29 = 406$ elements in the asymptotic covariance matrix. These are stored as 67 lines with 6 elements each plus one line with 4 elements. The list above contains only the first 8 lines of the file.

The LISREL model to be estimated is a two-factor confirmatory factor analysis model, in which the variables HUMRGHTS, EQUALCON, EQUALVAL, and EUTHANAS are assumed to measure EQUALITY, and RACEPROB, CRIMEPUN, CONSCOBJ, and GUILT are assumed to measure MORALITY.

The LISREL input file is

```
ATTITUDES OF MORALITY AND EQUALITY
DA NI=8 NO=200 MA=PM
LA
HUMRGHTS EQUALCON RACEPROB EQUALVAL EUTHANAS CRIMEPUN CONSCOBJ GUILT
PM FI=EX71.PML
AC FI=EX71.ACP
MO NX=8 NK=2 PH=ST
FR LX 1 1 LX 2 1 LX 4 1 LX 5 1 LX 3 2 LX 6 2 LX 7 2 LX 8 2
OU SE TV
```

The MA = PM on the DA line is essential. Otherwise, the program will think that a covariance matrix will be analyzed and, as a consequence, the program will think that the file EX71.ACP contains 666 elements instead of 406, as there are 666 asymptotic variances and covariances of the 36 variances and covariances in a covariance matrix for 8 variables.

The PM line tells the program to read the matrix of polychoric correlations and the AC line tells the program to read the asymptotic covariance matrix.

The AC line implies that the WLS method will be used as default method instead of the ML method. So it is not necessary to put ME = WLS on the OU line.

The results are shown in the last column of Table 7.1. For comparison, the results obtained by normal theory GLS and the results from using the product moment correlations based on normal scores are also given in Table 7.1. In this table, MA = KM means "matrix analyzed = matrix of product moment correlations based on normal scores" and MA = PM means "matrix analyzed = matrix of polychoric correlations." Of these results, only WLS with MA = PM are asymptotically correct. WLS with MA = KM is incorrect because the product-moment correlations based on normal scores are biased (inconsistent); see Jöreskog and Sörbom (1986,

Table 7.1: Results Using Different Types of Correlations and Different Estimation Methods

Parameter	Normal Theory GLS		Non-Normal Theory WLS	
	MA=KM	MA=PM	MA=KM	MA=PM
LX(1,1)	.430(.074)	.506(.070)	.431(.049)	.498(.053)
LX(2,1)	.733(.066)	.790(.062)	.763(.029)	.795(.046)
LX(3,2)	.470(.087)	.534(.082)	.429(.056)	.499(.065)
LX(4,1)	.769(.066)	.814(.061)	.804(.029)	.816(.047)
LX(5,1)	.801(.065)	.878(.059)	.876(.030)	.853(.048)
LX(6,2)	.450(.086)	.479(.081)	.456(.059)	.530(.066)
LX(7,2)	.469(.086)	.494(.081)	.485(.057)	.514(.064)
LX(8,2)	.439(.087)	.488(.082)	.496(.062)	.481(.064)
PH(2,1)	.690(.083)	.703(.070)	.708(.060)	.708(.070)
χ^2	20.06	37.15	37.27	11.11
GFI	.975	.953	.983	.992
AGFI	.952	.912	.969	.985
RMR	.042	.057	.050	.044

Standard Errors in Parentheses

Table 2). The standard errors of the GLS estimates are wrong because they are based on the wrong formula.

Example 7.2: A Panel Model for Political Efficacy

Aish and Jöreskog (1989) analyze data on political attitudes. Their data consist of 16 ordinal variables measured on the same people at two occasions. Six of the 16 variables were considered to be indicators of Political Efficacy and System Responsiveness. The attitude questions corresponding to these six variables are

- *People like me have no say in what the government does (NOSAYPO)*
- *Voting is the only way that people like me can have any say about how the government runs things (VOTONLW)*
- *Sometimes politics and government seem so complicated that a person like me cannot really understand what is going on (POLCOMP)*
- *I don't think that public officials care much about what people like me think (PODCARE)*
- *Generally speaking, those we elect to Parliament lose touch with the people pretty quickly (ELECTLT)*
- *Parties are only interested in people's votes but not in their opinions (PARTVOT)*

Responses to these questions were scored

- *1 = agree strongly*
- *2 = agree*
- *3 = disagree*
- *4 = disagree strongly*

Table 7.2: Variables in the Model and in the Dataset

	Time 1	Time 2
NOSAYPO	9	25
VOTONLW	10	26
POLCOMP	11	27
PODCARE	12	28
ELECTLT	13	29
PARTVOT	14	30

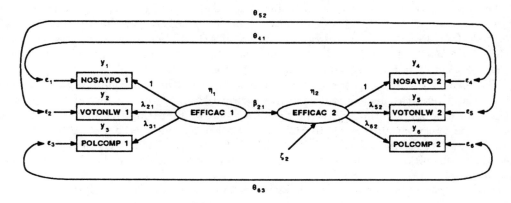

Figure 7.1: Panel Model for Political Efficacy

- $8 = don't\ know$
- $9 = no\ answer$

The raw data consist of 32 variables, 16 variables at two occasions. In the data file, the variables are packed with one variable per column and no blanks between variables. Table 7.2 shows which variables in the data file correspond to the variables in the model.

We will not repeat the whole analysis of Aish and Jöreskog here. Rather, we will only consider a part of their model, namely the part that corresponds to the panel model for efficacy. This is shown in Figure 7.1.

The example illustrates the following steps:

1. How to use a FORTRAN format in PRELIS to select variables and to select a random subsample for exploration

2. How to do a data screening with PRELIS

3. How to obtain the matrix of polychoric correlations and the corresponding asymptotic covariance matrix with PRELIS

4. How to select a subset of variables from the matrices in step 3 and analyze these with LISREL 7 using WLS

For step 1, the PRELIS input file is

```
PRELIS RUN 1: DATA SCREENING OF EFFICACY AND RESPONSIVENESS VARIABLES.
RAW DATA: PANELUSA. VARIABLES: 9 - 14 AND 25 - 30 (6 VARIABLES X 2 OCCASIONS)
DA NI=12
LA FI=PANEL.LAB
RA FI=PANELUSA.RAW FO
(8X,6F1.0,10X,6F1.0/)
OR ALL
OU
```

The first two lines are title lines. Line 3 specifies that there are 12 variables - not 32. Note that the number of cases need not be specified. Also note that no missing value is specified. Line 4 reads the labels from file PANEL.LAB and line 5 reads the raw data from file PANELUSA.RAW. The FO on the RA line means that the format is in the input file and not in the data file. The format follows immediately after the RA line.

The format means: skip the first 8 columns, read the next 6 columns, skip the next 10 columns and read the next 6 columns. The forward slash (/) in the format means: skip the entire next case and continue with the case after that by repeating the format. This is a very easy way to select variables 9 - 14 and 25 - 30 for every odd-numbered case in the sample. The purpose of selecting half the sample is to use this for exploration so that the other half can be used for confirmation. To choose the confirmation sample, just move the slash to the front of the format.

Line 6 in the input file declares all variables to be ordinal. The OU line specifies no output which means that only univariate data screening will be done. The purpose of this data screening is to check the data and verify that everything is correct.

The output file contains two tables. The first table lists all the distinct values that were found in the data. This table looks as follows:

```
TOTAL SAMPLE SIZE =   467
CONVERSION OF ORIGINAL VALUES TO CATEGORIES
                            CATEGORY
VARIABLE        1       2       3       4       5       6
NOSAYPO1      1.00    2.00    3.00    4.00    8.00    9.00
VOTONLW1      1.00    2.00    3.00    4.00    8.00    9.00
POLCOMP1      1.00    2.00    3.00    4.00    8.00    9.00
MPNCARE1      1.00    2.00    3.00    4.00    8.00    9.00
ELECTNT1      1.00    2.00    3.00    4.00    8.00    9.00
PARTVOT1      1.00    2.00    3.00    4.00    8.00    9.00
NOSAYPO2      1.00    2.00    3.00    4.00    8.00    9.00
VOTONLW2      1.00    2.00    3.00    4.00    8.00    9.00
POLCOMP2      1.00    2.00    3.00    4.00    9.00
MPNCARE2      1.00    2.00    3.00    4.00    8.00    9.00
ELECTNT2      1.00    2.00    3.00    4.00    8.00    9.00
PARTVOT2      1.00    2.00    3.00    4.00    8.00    9.00
```

Thus PRELIS found 467 cases in the datafile. This is exactly half the sample. PRELIS also found that each variable had values 1, 2, 3, 4, 8, 9, except POLCOMP2 which had no values 8.

The other table is as follows:

UNIVARIATE FREQUENCY DISTRIBUTIONS FOR ORDINAL VARIABLES

VARIABLE	CATEGORY 1	2	3	4	5	6
NOSAYPO1	35	127	257	37	9	2
VOTONLW1	66	184	192	18	5	2
POLCOMP1	89	261	100	14	1	2
MPNCARE1	45	182	216	17	5	2
ELECTNT1	63	236	147	9	10	2
PARTVOT1	50	210	183	10	9	5
NOSAYPO2	22	138	266	35	4	2
VOTONLW2	54	192	202	13	5	1
POLCOMP2	58	285	110	12	2	
MPNCARE2	34	208	203	13	5	4
ELECTNT2	53	270	125	3	14	2
PARTVOT2	40	227	181	4	14	1

For each variable, this shows the actual frequency of each distinct value in the data file. Thus, on POLCOMP2 there are 58 values 1, 285 values 2, 110 values 3, 12 values 4, and 2 values 9. Each row in this table sums to 467.

The next step is to compute the matrix of polychoric correlations and the corresponding asymptotic covariance matrix. To do this we must first decide how to treat the 8's and 9's. If we treat both of these as missing values, we must either recode all 8 to 9 or vice versa as PRELIS can only have one missing value for each variable.

The input file for this step is

```
PRELIS RUN 2: COMPUTING POLYCHORIC CORRELATION MATRIX
              AND ASYMPTOTIC COVARIANCE MATRIX
DATA: PANELUSA. VARIABLES: 9 - 14 AND 25 - 30 (6 VARIABLES X 2 OCCASIONS)
RECODING ALL 8 TO 9 (9 = MISSING VALUE)
LISTWISE DELETION
DA NI=12 MI=9
LA FI=PANEL.LAB
RA FI=PANELUSA.RAW FO
(8X,6F1.0,10X,6F1.0/)
OR ALL
RE 1-12 OLD=8 NEW=9
OU MA=PM SM=PANELUSA.PML SA=PANELUSA.ACP
```

This is very similar to the previous input file. The differences are

- The missing value is defined as 9 on the DA line

- All 8 are converted to 9 in RE (recode) line

- On the OU line,

  - MA=PM means that polychoric correlations should be computed,
  - SM=PANELUSA.PML means that the matrix of polychoric correlations should be saved in the file PANELUSA.PML, and
  - SA=PANELUSA.ACP means that the asymptotic covariance matrix should be saved in the file PANELUSA.ACP.

For further information on how to set up the PRELIS input file, see PRELIS User's Guide by Jöreskog and Sörbom (1986).

To obtain an asymptotic covariance matrix in PRELIS, listwise deletion must be used. In this case, this means that all cases with 8 or 9 on any of the 12 variables will be discarded. The PRELIS output file will tell how many cases remain in the listwise sample.

```
DISTRIBUTION OF MISSING VALUES
TOTAL SAMPLE SIZE =  467
NUMBER OF MISSING VALUES   0   1   2   3   4   5   6
         NUMBER OF CASES 410  34  12   3   2   3   3
LISTWISE DELETION
TOTAL EFFECTIVE SAMPLE SIZE =   410
```

As shown in the PRELIS output file, the matrix of polychoric correlations are

```
        ESTIMATED CORRELATION MATRIX
             NOSAYPO1   VOTONLW1   POLCOMP1   MPNCARE1   ELECTNT1   PARTVOT1
NOSAYPO1      1.000
VOTONLW1       .542      1.000
POLCOMP1       .392       .362      1.000
MPNCARE1       .604       .374       .441      1.000
ELECTNT1       .446       .340       .405       .609      1.000
PARTVOT1       .539       .351       .417       .705       .713      1.000
NOSAYPO2       .477       .309       .210       .391       .237       .367
VOTONLW2       .341       .511       .308       .351       .298       .388
POLCOMP2       .224       .227       .525       .241       .210       .273
MPNCARE2       .454       .296       .308       .507       .374       .485
ELECTNT2       .275       .210       .300       .323       .368       .466
PARTVOT2       .312       .298       .294       .388       .392       .547
        ESTIMATED CORRELATION MATRIX
             NOSAYPO2   VOTONLW2   POLCOMP2   MPNCARE2   ELECTNT2   PARTVOT2
NOSAYPO2      1.000
VOTONLW2       .482      1.000
POLCOMP2       .345       .312      1.000
MPNCARE2       .605       .514       .406      1.000
ELECTNT2       .443       .534       .298       .630      1.000
PARTVOT2       .450       .524       .288       .687       .774      1.000
```

This matrix is stored in the file PANELUSA.PML (**PML** = **P**olychoric correlation **M**atrix, estimated under **L**istwise deletion) in a more compact form.

The asymptotic covariance matrix stored in the file PANELUSA.ACP (**ACP** = **A**symptotic **C**ovariance matrix for **P**olychoric correlations) is a very large matrix. It has 2211 distinct elements.

These two files will now be used in the following LISREL runs. The input file for the first run is

```
LISREL 7: RUN 1
TWO-WAVE PANEL MODEL FOR POLITICAL EFFICACY
USING DATA: PANEL USA (6 VARIABLES X 2 OCCASIONS)
USING WLS WITH POLYCHORIC CORRELATIONS AND ASYMPTOTIC COVARIANCE MATRIX
OBTAINED IN PRELIS RUN 2
DA NI=12 NO=410 MA=PM
LA FI=PANEL.LAB
PM FI=PANELUSA.PML
AC FI=PANELUSA.ACP
SE
1 2 3 7 8 9 /
MO NY=6 NE=2 BE=SD PS=DI TE=SY
LE
EFFICAC1 EFFICAC2
FR LY 2 1 LY 3 1 LY 5 2 LY 6 2
VA 1 LY 1 1 LY 4 2
OU SE TV MI SS RS
```

This input file is similar to that of Example 7.1 but differs from it in the following ways:

- We select 6 variables out of 12 to be analyzed. The selection takes place in the ACP matrix as well as in the PML matrix.

- The model is a LISREL Submodel 3B, see Chapter 6 (in Example 7.1, the model was a Submodel 1).

- We specify TE=SY rather than TE=DI to obtain modification indices for off-diagonal elements of Θ_ϵ. As argued in Chapter 6, these may be interesting in a longitudinal model.

This first model assumes that the ϵ's are uncorrelated. The χ^2 goodness-of-fit measure is 58.44 with 8 degrees of freedom, indicating rather poor fit. The standardized residuals are

```
          STANDARDIZED RESIDUALS
             NOSAYPO1    VOTONLW1    POLCOMP1    NOSAYPO2    VOTONLW2    POLCOMP2
NOSAYPO1       .000
VOTONLW1      2.555        .000
POLCOMP1      -.905      -1.504        .000
NOSAYPO2     2.386      -2.443      -2.742        .000
VOTONLW2    -1.828       2.174      -1.670       1.377        .000
POLCOMP2    -3.236      -2.361       4.889        .002      -1.587        .000
```

Note that the standardized residuals for cells (4,1), (5,2), and (6,3) are all positive and significant. This indicates that the error terms might be correlated over time for the same variable. This can be seen also in the modification indices for elements of Θ_ϵ and their estimated changes. Note that the estimated change is positive for these three elements.

MODIFICATION INDICES FOR THETA EPS

	NOSAYPO1	VOTONLW1	POLCOMP1	NOSAYPO2	VOTONLW2	POLCOMP2
NOSAYPO1	.000					
VOTONLW1	5.133	.000				
POLCOMP1	.588	2.698	.000			
NOSAYPO2	6.777	4.072	6.719	.000		
VOTONLW2	4.596	9.142	1.727	3.015	.000	
POLCOMP2	6.114	6.257	44.431	.020	2.931	.000

ESTIMATED CHANGE FOR THETA EPS

	NOSAYPO1	VOTONLW1	POLCOMP1	NOSAYPO2	VOTONLW2	POLCOMP2
NOSAYPO1	.000					
VOTONLW1	.180	.000				
POLCOMP1	−.055	−.119	.000			
NOSAYPO2	.178	−.145	−.180	.000		
VOTONLW2	−.156	.207	−.089	.141	.000	
POLCOMP2	−.174	−.174	.384	−.010	−.129	.000

To run the model with autocorrelated error terms requires the following input file:

```
LISREL 7: RUN 2
TWO-WAVE PANEL MODEL FOR POLITICAL EFFICACY
USING DATA: PANEL USA (6 VARIABLES X 2 OCCASIONS)
USING WLS WITH POLYCHORIC CORRELATIONS AND ASYMPTOTIC COVARIANCE MATRIX
OBTAINED IN PRELIS RUN 2
DA NI=12 NO=410 MA=PM
LA FI=PANEL.LAB
PM FI=PANELUSA.PML
AC FI=PANELUSA.ACP
SE
1 2 3 7 8 9 /
MO NY=6 NE=2 BE=SD PS=DI TE=SY
LE
EFFICAC1 EFFICAC2
FR LY 2 1 LY 3 1 LY 5 2 LY 6 2
VA 1 LY 1 1 LY 4 2
FR TE 4 1 TE 5 2 TE 6 3
OU SE TV MI SS RS
```

The resulting solution is entirely satisfactory. It has a χ^2 goodness-of-fit measure of 2.05 with 5 degrees of freedom and no significant standardized residuals or modification indices. The standardized regression coefficient β_{21} is estimated as 0.66. The squared multiple correlation for EFFICAC2 on EFFICAC1 is 0.44.

7.3 Factor Analysis of Dichotomous Variables

To factor analyze a set of dichotomous items to determine whether they can be used to represent an underlying unidimensional scale is a common problem in test theory. There are many methods and programs available for doing this; see Mislevy (1986) and references therein. The following example demonstrates that it can also conveniently and efficiently be done by LISREL.

Example 7.3: Factor Analysis of Dichotomous Variables

Bock and Lieberman (1970) and Christoffersson (1975) published the data in Table 6 in the
PRELIS *User's Guide giving the observed frequencies for the 32 response patterns arising from
five dichotomous items (11 through 15) of Section 6 of the Law School Admissions Test (LSAT).
The sample is a subsample of 1000 from a larger sample of those who took the test.*

First we use the following PRELIS input file to produce the tetrachoric correlations and their
asymptotic variances and covariances:

```
LSAT SECTION 6
DA NI=6 NO=1000; RA FI=LSAT6.DAT
WE 6; OR ALL
OU MA=PM SM=EX73.PML SA=EX73.ACP
```

This produces the following matrix of tetrachoric correlations:

```
      ESTIMATED CORRELATION MATRIX
                VAR 1       VAR 2       VAR 3       VAR 4       VAR 5
      VAR 1     1.000
      VAR 2      .170       1.000
      VAR 3      .228        .189       1.000
      VAR 4      .107        .111        .187       1.000
      VAR 5      .067        .172        .105        .201       1.000
```

and the following asymptotic covariance matrix in the file EX73.ACP:

```
.550285D+01   .109483D-01   .505161D+01   .906021D-03   .251738D-03   .262720D+01
.531451D-02   .694758D-02   .203331D-03   .611807D+01   .600611D-03   .231417D-03
.693954D-03   .731754D-03   .321899D+01   .226451D-03   .175806D-03   .100382D-03
.111134D-02   .121977D-02   .284216D+01   .333677D-02   .432947D-02   .174388D-03
.215123D-02   .194784D-03   .184838D-03   .819351D+01   .808527D-03   .300431D-03
.959327D-03   .356445D-03   .703434D-03   .357838D-03   .188474D-02   .408939D+01
.166248D-03   .902893D-04   .133053D-03   .154732D-03   .178463D-03   .193661D-03
.114775D-02   .293583D-02   .391731D+01   .468106D-03   .295901D-03   .311322D-03
.114217D-02   .126882D-02   .196358D-02   .215242D-02   .541568D-02   .336893D-02
.426110D+01
```

We can now analyze the data with LISREL using the following input file:

```
FACTOR ANALYSIS OF DICHOTOMOUS VARIABLES: LSAT6 DATA
DA NI=5 NO=1000 MA=PM
PM FI=EX73.PML; AC FI=EX73.ACP
MO NX=5 NK=1 LX=FR PH=ST
OU SE TV RS
```

The resulting output file shows the following solution, standard errors, and standardized
residuals, indicating that the five items may well fit a unidimensional scale. The only item
which is a little bit odd is item 5:

```
LISREL ESTIMATES (WEIGHTED LEAST SQUARES)
        LAMBDA X
              KSI 1
    VAR 1      .389
    VAR 2      .397
    VAR 3      .471
    VAR 4      .377
    VAR 5      .342
        PHI
              KSI 1
    KSI 1     1.000
        THETA DELTA
              VAR 1      VAR 2      VAR 3      VAR 4      VAR 5
               .848       .842       .778       .858       .883
        SQUARED MULTIPLE CORRELATIONS FOR X - VARIABLES
              VAR 1      VAR 2      VAR 3      VAR 4      VAR 5
               .152       .158       .222       .142       .117


      CHI-SQUARE WITH   5 DEGREES OF FREEDOM =     4.05 (P = .542)
                  GOODNESS OF FIT INDEX = .998
            ADJUSTED GOODNESS OF FIT INDEX = .995
                ROOT MEAN SQUARE RESIDUAL =       .036


        STANDARDIZED RESIDUALS
              VAR 1      VAR 2      VAR 3      VAR 4      VAR 5
    VAR 1      .000
    VAR 2     2.644       .000
    VAR 3      .859       .035       .000
    VAR 4    -2.053      -.583       .255       .000
    VAR 5    -2.623       .456     -1.289      1.518       .000

STANDARD ERRORS
        LAMBDA X
              KSI 1
    VAR 1      .100
    VAR 2      .082
    VAR 3      .090
    VAR 4      .081
    VAR 5      .086
        THETA DELTA
              VAR 1      VAR 2      VAR 3      VAR 4      VAR 5
               .090       .079       .096       .076       .074
```

Table 7.3: Population Moments for Eight Distributions

	\multicolumn{8}{c}{Distribution}
	1	2	3	4	5	6	7	8
Mean	0.00	5.00	1.00	0.50	3.00	2.50	0.67	3.50
Variance	1.00	10.00	2.00	0.08	1.50	1.87	0.55	2.92
Skewness	0.00	1.26	2.82	0.00	0.00	0.36	0.63	0.00
Kurtosis	0.00	2.40	12.00	-1.20	-0.33	-0.07	-0.95	-1.27

7.4 Analysis of Continuous Non-Normal Variables

When some or all observed variables are continuous, i.e., measured on interval scales, it is best to analyze the covariance matrix $\mathbf{S}$ rather than the correlation matrix $\mathbf{R}$. If the variables are highly non-normal, it is still an open question whether to use ML (or GLS) or WLS with a general weight matrix. The latter approach has been termed *Best Asymptotically Distribution Free Method - ADF* by Browne (1984). Previous Monte Carlo studies have not given a clear-cut answer as to when it is necessary to use WLS rather than ML.

Rather than trying to give a general answer as to which method should be used in which situations, we shall provide a simple tool by which this methodological question can be studied. We shall also demonstrate how WLS is used to analyze a sample covariance matrix $\mathbf{S}$.

There are very many non-normal distributions. Any robustness study will have to consider what type of non-normal distribution one would like to be robust against. Consider the following 8 distributions:

1. Normal with mean 0 and variance 1

2. Chi-square with 5 degrees of freedom

3. Chi-square with 1 degree of freedom

4. Continuous Uniform Distribution

5. Binomial with $p = 0.5$ and $n = 6$

6. Binomial with $p = 0.25$ and $n = 10$

7. A three-point distribution with probabilities $\frac{1}{2}, \frac{1}{3}, \frac{1}{6}$ at 0, 1, and 2, respectively

8. A uniform discrete distribution with probability $\frac{1}{6}$ at $1, 2, \ldots, 6$

Only one of these is normal. The others vary with respect to skewness and kurtosis. Distributions 1, 4, 5, and 8 are symmetrical; 2, 3, 6, and 7 are skewed. The mean, variance, skewness, and kurtosis are shown in Table 7.3.

Now consider the congeneric measurement model with 4 x-variables; see Section 3.1. We write this model as

$$x_i = \lambda_i \xi + \sqrt{\theta_i}\delta_i, i = 1, 2, 3, 4 \qquad (7.1)$$

where ξ and δ_i are independently distributed each having one of these eight distributions.

We can generate a random sample of x-vectors as follows:

1. Choose parameter values λ_i and θ_i

2. Choose a distribution for ξ (1 through 8) and a distribution for each δ_i (1 through 8)

3. Generate random numbers for ξ and δ_1, δ_2, δ_3 and δ_4 and adjust these to zero mean and unit variance, using the population means and variances given in Table 7.3

4. Compute x_1, x_2, x_3, and x_4 from (7.1)

5. Repeat steps 3 and 4 N times, where N is the required sample size

The program GENRAW2 generates raw data according to specifications provided in this way. Each x_i is a mixture of two distributions. For a fixed set of parameter values with four x-variables, there are $8^5 = 32768$ possible combinations of distributions that one can study in this way. The generated data matrix comes from a multivariate population with covariance matrix Σ in (3.5). However, the distribution is not multivariate normal, except in the case when all 5 distributions are specified to be normal.

To see how this works, we generated a random sample in the following way:

1. Parameter values: λ= (0.9, 0.7, 0.5, 0.5), θ= (0.19, 0.51, 0.75, 0.75)

2. Distribution for ξ: 3, Distribution for δ_i: 2 for all variables

3. Sample size: $N = 200$

The resulting raw data matrix is stored in the file EX74.RAW.

Example 7.4: Analysis of Covariance Matrices with WLS

To analyze the raw data in file EX74.RAW with WLS, we first run PRELIS to compute the sample variances and covariances and their asymptotic covariance matrix. This run will also give information about the skewness and kurtosis of each of the four variables. These measures are useful in evaluation of the robustness.

The PRELIS input file is

```
ANALYSIS OF RAW DATA GENERATED BY GENRAW2
DA NI=4
RA FI=EX74.RAW
OU MA=CM SM=EX74.CML SA=EX74.ACC PA
```

The PRELIS output file gives the following summary statistics:

UNIVARIATE SUMMARY STATISTICS FOR CONTINUOUS VARIABLES

VARIABLE	MEAN	ST. DEV.	SKEWNESS	KURTOSIS	MINIMUM	FREQ.	MAXIMUM	FREQ.
VAR 1	.071	.941	1.587	3.433	-1.213	1	4.788	1
VAR 2	.092	.981	.845	.768	-1.517	1	3.929	1
VAR 3	.079	.932	1.033	1.182	-1.537	1	3.313	1
VAR 4	-.001	1.008	1.265	2.639	-1.536	1	4.908	1

These numbers suggest that the variables are consistent with the assumption of population mean zero and variance one, but they are far from being normally distributed. All variables are positively skewed and VAR 1 has an excessive kurtosis.

The sample covariance matrix estimated by PRELIS is

```
ESTIMATED COVARIANCE MATRIX
            VAR 1       VAR 2       VAR 3       VAR 4
VAR 1       .885
VAR 2       .544        .962
VAR 3       .377        .332        .868
VAR 4       .449        .291        .256       1.016
```

and the asymptotic covariance matrix is

```
ASYMPTOTIC COVARIANCE MATRIX OF ESTIMATED VARIANCES AND COVARIANCES
          S(1,1)      S(2,1)      S(2,2)      S(3,1)      S(3,2)      S(3,3)
S(1,1)    .02080
S(2,1)    .01327      .01071
S(2,2)    .00796      .00733      .01252
S(3,1)    .01060      .00760      .00483      .00867
S(3,2)    .00717      .00573      .00396      .00627      .00668
S(3,3)    .00557      .00455      .00309      .00591      .00451      .01171
S(4,1)    .01295      .00911      .00596      .00824      .00561      .00479
S(4,2)    .00904      .00731      .00444      .00581      .00450      .00368
S(4,3)    .00796      .00566      .00376      .00624      .00451      .00374
S(4,4)    .00989      .00737      .00539      .00777      .00578      .00573
ASYMPTOTIC COVARIANCE MATRIX OF ESTIMATED VARIANCES AND COVARIANCES
          S(4,1)      S(4,2)      S(4,3)      S(4,4)
S(4,1)    .01334
S(4,2)    .00946      .00981
S(4,3)    .00909      .00708      .00977
S(4,4)    .01366      .01009      .01169      .02341
```

The sample covariance matrix is saved in the file EX74.CML and the same matrix multiplied by the sample size of 200 is saved in the file EX74.ACC.

The LISREL input file for WLS is

```
ANALYSIS OF COVARIANCE MATRIX WITH WLS
DA NI=4 NO=200
CM FI=EX74.CML
AC FI=EX74.ACC
MO NX=4 NK=1 LX=FR PH=ST
OU SE
```

Parameter estimates and standard errors are shown in the last column of Table 7.4. For comparison, results are also given for all the other estimation methods.

We started out with the intention of generating variables which are highly non-normal in the hope of demonstrating the superiority of WLS over ML. The results of Table 7.4 do not lead to such a conclusion. The model fits very well for all methods and, as far as parameter estimates are concerned, there are very small differences between methods. However, χ^2 and standard errors are larger for WLS than for the other methods. This suggests that χ^2 and standard errors produced by ULS, DWLS, GLS, and ML may be underestimated when the observed variables deviate far from normality. On the other hand, the results in Table 7.4 are quite in line with theoretical results by Browne (1987) and Anderson and Amemiya (1985) which suggest that ML is robust against non-normality when observed variables are generated in this way.

Table 7.4: Parameter Estimates for Hypothetical Model

Parameter	True	IV	TSLS	ULS	DWLS	GLS	ML	WLS
LX(1)	0.90	0.85	0.85	0.84	0.83	0.84(0.07)	0.84(0.07)	0.84(0.09)
LX(2)	0.70	0.63	0.63	0.64	0.65	0.65(0.07)	0.64(0.07)	0.66(0.07)
LX(3)	0.50	0.50	0.50	0.48	0.48	0.46(0.07)	0.46(0.07)	0.45(0.08)
LX(4)	0.50	0.49	0.49	0.51	0.51	0.52(0.07)	0.52(0.07)	0.52(0.10)
TD(1)	0.19	0.17	0.17	0.17	0.19	0.17(0.08)	0.17(0.08)	0.18(0.09)
TD(2)	0.51	0.57	0.56	0.56	0.54	0.53(0.07)	0.55(0.07)	0.52(0.10)
TD(3)	0.75	0.62	0.61	0.64	0.63	0.65(0.07)	0.66(0.07)	0.67(0.09)
TD(4)	0.75	0.77	0.78	0.76	0.76	0.73(0.08)	0.74(0.08)	0.71(0.09)
χ^2	0.00	n.a.	n.a.	2.10	2.12	2.29	2.19	2.52
GFI	1.00	n.a.	n.a.	1.00	1.00	0.99	1.00	0.99
AGFI	1.00	n.a.	n.a.	0.99	1.00	0.97	0.97	0.94
RMR	0.00	n.a.	n.a.	0.02	0.02	0.02	0.02	0.03

n.a. = not available

Standard Errors in Parentheses

This example represents only a single observation from which no safe conclusion can be drawn concerning possible bias in χ^2 and standard errors. A comprehensive Monte Carlo study is needed for this purpose. A recent study by Laake (1987) indicates that standard errors for ML estimates are underestimated if the observed variables have heavier tails than the normal distribution. Laake suggests that bootstrap methods should be used to estimate standard errors for ML estimates under non-normality.

7.5   Estimating a Correlation Structure with WLS

Example 7.5: Estimating and Testing a Correlation Structure

Psychologist A consults Statistician K about her data analysis problem. She does not want to reveal her raw data but says that she has used PRELIS to compute the product-moment (Pearson) correlations for her five variables and that the PRELIS output suggests that the variables are non-normal. Fortunately, she has also computed the asymptotic covariance matrix of the product-moment correlations.

Psychologist A claims that her theory is that the correlations should be of the form

$$\mathbf{P}(\theta) = \begin{pmatrix} 1 & & & & \\ \rho_1 & 1 & & & \\ \rho_2 & \rho_2 & 1 & & \\ \rho_2 & \rho_2 & \rho_3 & 1 & \\ \rho_2 & \rho_2 & \rho_3 & \rho_3 & 1 \end{pmatrix},$$

where $\theta' = (\rho_1, \rho_2, \rho_3)$.

How should the data be analyzed to estimate and test this correlation structure?

The observed correlation matrix is

$$\mathbf{R} = \begin{pmatrix} 1.000 & & & & \\ .526 & 1.000 & & & \\ .402 & .482 & 1.000 & & \\ .391 & .424 & .400 & 1.000 & \\ .417 & .489 & .274 & .442 & 1.000 \end{pmatrix}$$

The asymptotic covariance matrix of product-moment correlations is not of the form (1.21). Hence, ML or GLS should not be used in this case. The only way to get correct χ^2, standard errors, standardized residuals and modification indices is to use WLS with a weight matrix equal to the inverse of the asymptotic covariance matrix of the estimated correlations.

We assume here that the correlation matrix is stored in the file EX75.KML and that the asymptotic covariance matrix is stored in the file EX75.ACK. The LISREL input file is

```
ESTIMATING AND TESTING OF A CORRELATION STRUCTURE
DA NI=5 NO=200 MA=KM
KM FI=EX75.KML
AC FI=EX75.ACK
MO NX=5 NK=5 LX=ID PH=ST TD=ZE
EQ PH 3 1 PH 3 2 PH 4 1 PH 4 2 PH 5 1 PH 5 2
EQ PH 4 3 PH 5 3 PH 5 4
OU SE TV RS MI
```

The MO line specifies $\mathbf{\Lambda}_x = \mathbf{I}$ and $\mathbf{\Theta}_\delta = \mathbf{0}$. By default, $\mathbf{\Phi}$ is unconstrained. The VA line specifies $\mathbf{\Phi}$ to be a correlation matrix. The EQ lines specify the equality constraints in the correlation structure.

The output file gives the following solution, standardized residuals, and modification indices:

```
LISREL ESTIMATES (WEIGHTED LEAST SQUARES)
      PHI
              VAR 1      VAR 2      VAR 3      VAR 4      VAR 5
    VAR 1    1.000
    VAR 2     .603     1.000
    VAR 3     .513      .513     1.000
    VAR 4     .513      .513      .429     1.000
    VAR 5     .513      .513      .429      .429     1.000

        CHI-SQUARE WITH  12 DEGREES OF FREEDOM =    16.31 (P = .177)
                   GOODNESS OF FIT INDEX = .976
          ADJUSTED GOODNESS OF FIT INDEX = .970
                ROOT MEAN SQUARE RESIDUAL =       .072
```

STANDARDIZED RESIDUALS

	VAR 1	VAR 2	VAR 3	VAR 4	VAR 5
VAR 1	.000				
VAR 2	-.824	.000			
VAR 3	-2.254	-.649	.000		
VAR 4	-2.758	-1.109	-.430	.000	
VAR 5	-1.603	-.494	-10.111	.270	.000

MODIFICATION INDICES FOR PHI

	VAR 1	VAR 2	VAR 3	VAR 4	VAR 5
VAR 1	.000				
VAR 2	.000	.000			
VAR 3	2.816	4.759	.000		
VAR 4	1.033	1.302	1.838	.000	
VAR 5	.577	3.236	11.915	4.666	.000

ESTIMATED CHANGE FOR PHI

	VAR 1	VAR 2	VAR 3	VAR 4	VAR 5
VAR 1	.000				
VAR 2	.000	.000			
VAR 3	-.072	.060	.000		
VAR 4	-.066	-.069	.052	.000	
VAR 5	-.035	.041	-.161	.055	.000

The program gives correct results but *incorrect* degrees of freedom. The correct degrees of freedom are 7, the number of correlations (10) minus the number of parameters (3). By putting TD = FR (or TD default) instead of TD = ZE on the MO line, one will obtain identically the same results but with *correct* degrees of freedom. Incorrect degrees of freedom when TD = ZE are obtained because the program always assumes that a covariance structure is estimated, so that the diagonal elements of **S** are always counted in the degrees of freedom. The reason why TD = FR and TD = ZE give the same result, apart from the degrees of freedom, is that in both cases the term (1.47) vanishes, so that both problems minimize the same fit function of the parameters.

Both the standardized residuals and the modification indices show that $\hat{\rho}_{53}$ violates the equality constraint. The negative sign of the standardized residual and of the estimated change of ρ_{53} suggests that ρ_{53} should be smaller than the estimated value 0.43. In fact, the estimated change is -0.16.

When the model is reestimated with ρ_{53} free, the goodness-of-fit χ^2 is 4.40 with 6 degrees of freedom. This represents a very good fit. The estimate of ρ_{53} is 0.27, which is in fact just 0.16 smaller than the previous value.

The analysis suggests that A's "theory" is in agreement with the data except that ρ_{53} is not equal to ρ_{43} and ρ_{54}.

Chapter 8

MISCELLANEOUS TOPICS

8.1 Constraints

LISREL does not directly impose constraints on the covariance matrices $\boldsymbol{\Phi}$, $\boldsymbol{\Psi}$, $\boldsymbol{\Theta}_\epsilon$, and $\boldsymbol{\Theta}_\delta$ so as to make these positive definite. If an estimate of any one of these matrices is not positive definite, *when they are supposed to be so,* this is an indication that the model is wrong.

LISREL checks the positive definiteness of $\boldsymbol{\Phi}$, $\boldsymbol{\Psi}$, $\boldsymbol{\Theta}_\epsilon$, and $\boldsymbol{\Theta}_\delta$ as part of the admissibility test; see Chapter 2. If after AD iterations (default value = 10) one of these matrices is not positive definite, the iterations will stop and the current "solution" will be printed. If one believes strongly that there is an admissible solution for the model and the data analyzed, one should increase the value of AD and rerun the problem with different and better starting values. Our experience suggests, however, that when the "solution" is non-admissible after 10 iterations, and the program is allowed to continue to iterate, it will either converge to a non-admissible solution or not converge at all. As already stated, this is usually the fault of the model rather than the program. However, this problem has also occurred in Monte Carlo studies for occasional odd samples, where it cannot be blamed on the model; see, for example, Anderson and Gerbing (1984), Boomsma (1985) and Example 8.1 that follows.

8.1.1 Constraining Error Variances to be Non-Negative

Suppose we believe in the model and cannot accept a negative estimate of an error variance. If the LISREL estimates are admissible, there is no problem. However, if one or more of the estimates of error variances is negative one must reparameterize the model in a way to prevent this.

Suppose, for example, we are estimating a LISREL Submodel 1 with $\boldsymbol{\Theta}_\delta$ diagonal. This model can be reparameterized as

$$\Lambda_x^* = \begin{pmatrix} \boldsymbol{\Lambda}_x & \mathbf{D}_\delta \end{pmatrix} \quad \boldsymbol{\Phi}^* = \begin{pmatrix} \boldsymbol{\Phi} & \\ 0 & \mathbf{I} \end{pmatrix} \quad \boldsymbol{\Theta}_\delta^* = 0 \tag{8.1}$$

where $\mathbf{D}_\delta$ is a diagonal matrix such as that $\boldsymbol{\Theta}_\delta = \mathbf{D}_\delta^2$. It is easily verified that

$$\Lambda_x^* \boldsymbol{\Phi}^* \Lambda_x^{*\prime} + \boldsymbol{\Theta}_\delta^* = \boldsymbol{\Lambda}_x \boldsymbol{\Phi} \boldsymbol{\Lambda}_x^{\prime} + \mathbf{D}_\delta^2 = \boldsymbol{\Lambda}_x \boldsymbol{\Phi} \boldsymbol{\Lambda}_x^{\prime} + \boldsymbol{\Theta}_\delta$$

Estimates of error variances are obtained as $\hat{\mathbf{D}}_\delta^2$. The elements d_i of $\mathbf{D}_\delta$ may come out positive or negative (or zero) but the error variances are estimated as d_i^2 which cannot be negative.

212   CHAPTER 8. MISCELLANEOUS TOPICS

It should be noted that the reparameterized model has NK > NX so that the IV and TSLS
procedures for generating starting values will not work; see Section 1.12. Starting values must
be provided by the user.

Example 8.1: Gösta's Bad Sample

*In a Monte Carlo study reported by Gösta Hägglund (1982), random samples were generated
from the following population parameters:*

$$\Lambda_x = \begin{pmatrix} 1 & 0 \\ 0 & 1 \\ 0.889 & 0 \\ 0 & 0.857 \\ 0 & 0.714 \\ 0.333 & 0 \end{pmatrix} \quad \Phi = \begin{pmatrix} 0.810 \\ 0.378 & 0.490 \end{pmatrix} \quad \Theta_\delta = diag \begin{pmatrix} 0.19 \\ 0.51 \\ 0.36 \\ 0.64 \\ 0.75 \\ 0.91 \end{pmatrix}$$

The population covariance matrix

$$\Sigma = \Lambda_x \Phi \Lambda_x' + \Theta_\delta$$

formed from these parameter matrices is

$$\Sigma = \begin{pmatrix} 1.000 \\ 0.378 & 1.000 \\ 0.720 & 0.336 & 1.000 \\ 0.324 & 0.420 & 0.288 & 1.000 \\ 0.270 & 0.350 & 0.240 & 0.300 & 1.000 \\ 0.270 & 0.126 & 0.240 & 0.108 & 0.090 & 1.000 \end{pmatrix}$$

This is Jöreskog's (1979b) artificial population with the variables reordered so that the two
reference variables appear first.

LISREL can be used to compute Σ from Λ_x, Φ, and Θ_δ. The following input file will do
the job:

```
Ex8.1a: Computing Population Sigma
DA NI=6 NO=10
CM
1 0 1 2*0 1 3*0 1 4*0 1 5*0 1
MO NX=6 NK=2  PH=FI TD=FI
MA LX
1 0 0 1 .889 0 0 .857 0 .714 .333 0
MA PH
.810 .378 .490
MA TD
.19 .51 .36 .64 .75 .91
OU SI=EX81.SIG
```

The trick is to specify all parameter matrices to be fixed and enter the parameter matrices
by MA lines. There are no parameters to estimate, so LISREL will just compute Σ and save
it in the file EX81.SIG as requested in the OU line. However, LISREL always need some data

to analyze. The matrix to be "analyzed" may be *any* positive definite matrix. Here we use an identity matrix as this is particularly easy to enter. If one prints the file EX81.SIG it looks like this:

```
(6D13.6)        SI
  .100000D+01  .378000D+00  .100000D+01  .720090D+00  .336042D+00  .100016D+01
  .323946D+00  .419930D+00  .287988D+00  .999880D+00  .269892D+00  .349860D+00
  .239934D+00  .299830D+00  .999800D+00  .269730D+00  .125874D+00  .239790D+00
  .107874D+00  .898740D-01  .999820D+00
```

Hägglund (1982) was concerned with unrestricted factor analysis. In this context, this corresponds to the model where all elements in rows 3-6 in Λ_x are unknown parameters. To see that LISREL works correctly, when the population Σ is analyzed, we run the following input file:

```
Ex8.1b: Analyzing Population Sigma
DA NI=6 NO=200
CM FI=EX81.SIG
MO NX=6 NK=2
FR LX(5)-LX(12)
VA 1 LX(1) LX(4)
OU SE
```

The output file reveals that LISREL correctly recovers all the parameters including the zeros in Λ_x. (A program that does not do this for an identified model is not worth keeping as it means that it does not produce consistent estimates.) The output file also shows that all residuals are zero.

The sample size specified on the DA line is of course arbitrary and irrelevant. For reasons which will be obvious in a moment, we chose NO = 200. The output file suggests that the *true* standard error of $\theta_{11}^{(\delta)}$ is 0.166. This suggests that if we were to take repeated random samples of size 200 from the population, the estimated $\hat{\theta}_{11}^{(\delta)}$ in these samples should fall in the interval

$$0.19 \pm 1.96 \times 0.166 = 0.19 \pm 0.33$$

in 95% of cases. This interval is from -0.14 to 0.52. Thus, some of the estimates are likely to be negative. In fact, if the normality approximation holds, we should expect 13% negative estimates. It should therefore not come as a surprise that negative estimates of error variances (Heywood cases) occur in a Monte Carlo study designed like this.

Hägglund generated many random sample covariance matrices of size 200 based on Σ. One of these was (EX81.COV)

```
1.277
0.584 1.125
0.938 0.422 1.149
0.491 0.426 0.400 0.952
0.408 0.457 0.350 0.360 1.062
0.126 0.147 0.224 0.117 0.182 1.012
```

Although this matrix does not "look strange," it is an extremely odd sample. No matter what one does, one almost always ends up with a non-admissible solution. We shall illustrate how LISREL behaves in a case like this.

Suppose we proceed in the usual way to estimate the model with free λ's in rows 3-6. The input file is

```
Ex8.1c: Analyzing Gosta's Bad Sample
DA NI=6 NO=200
CM FI=EX81.COV
MO NX=6 NK=2
FR LX(5)-LX(12)
VA 1 LX(1) LX(4)
OU
```

Since AD is default on the OU line, LISREL stops after 10 iterations (see Section 2.15) with a large negative estimate of TD(1). There is no admissible solution for this data and model. This can be verified by starting at different initial values and allowing the program to iterate further. For example, if one sets AD = OFF and IT = 250, say, LISREL iterates "forever" producing larger and larger negative estimates of TD(1). This can also be verified by fixing TD(1) at zero and plotting the fit function against TD(1). This plot looks like this:

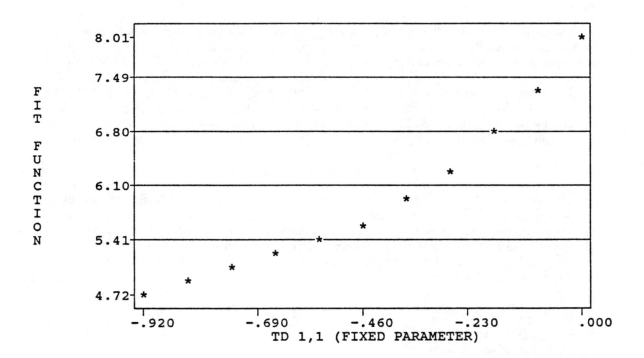

Next let us constrain the error variances to be non-negative using the reparameterized model (8.1). This can be done with the following input file:

```
Ex8.1d: Analyzing Gosta's Bad Sample by Reparameterized Model
DA NI=6 NO=200
CM FI=EX81.COV
MO NX=6 NK=8 LX=FI PH=FI TD=ZE
FR LX 1 3 LX 2 4 LX 3 5 LX 4 6 LX 5 7 LX 6 8
FR LX 3 1 LX 3 2 LX 4 1 LX 4 2 LX 5 1 LX 5 2 LX 6 1 LX 6 2
FR PH 1 1 PH 2 1 PH 2 2
VA 1 LX 1 1 LX 2 2 PH 3 3 PH 4 4 PH 5 5 PH 6 6 PH 7 7 PH 8 8
ST .5 ALL; ST 0 PH 2 1
OU NS AD=OFF
```

Note that starting values for $\mathbf{D}_\delta$ must be given. Otherwise, the matrix $\mathbf{\Sigma}$ computed at initial values is singular which means that the ML fit function cannot be computed. Also, as this is a very problematic case, we have to allow for more iterations than does the default value of IT (in this case 51 iterations). The resulting solution shows that all the error variances are positive except for variable 1 which is zero. Other starting values produce other solutions with other Heywood variables. There is no admissible solution for this data.

It should be emphasized that constraining error variances to be non-negative does not really solve the problem. Zero estimates of error variances are as unacceptable as are negative estimates. The root of the problem is that the model is empirically overparameterized. Instead of estimating *all* the λ's in rows 3-6 of $\mathbf{\Lambda}_x$, one should ask the question: which of these 8 λ's are statistically (and substantively) zero and which are statistically (and substantively) non-zero? One can answer this question by starting with the model in which all 8 λ's are fixed at zero and free one λ at a time using the information provided by the modification index and estimated change. If the non-zero λ's should be positive, one should not free a λ for which the estimated change is negative even if its modification index is large. When the four λ's which are zero in the population are fixed at zero, the following solution is obtained:

```
LISREL ESTIMATES (MAXIMUM LIKELIHOOD)
    LAMBDA X
            KSI 1      KSI 2
    VAR 1    1.000       .000
    VAR 2     .000      1.000
    VAR 3     .820       .000
    VAR 4     .000       .824
    VAR 5     .000       .788
    VAR 6     .142       .000
    PHI
            KSI 1      KSI 2
    KSI 1    1.143
    KSI 2     .569       .546
    THETA DELTA
            VAR 1      VAR 2      VAR 3      VAR 4      VAR 5      VAR 6
             .134       .579       .380       .581       .723       .989
```

This may be compared with the population parameters.

8.1.2 Constraining Covariance Matrices to be Non-Negative Definite

Consider LISREL Submodel 1 with Φ free and suppose we want to constrain Φ to be non-negative definite. We can then specify Φ as

$$\Phi = \mathbf{T}_\phi \mathbf{T}'_\phi \, ,$$

where $\mathbf{T}_\phi$ is a lower-triangular matrix. This can be parameterized as a Submodel 3A with

$$\Lambda_y = \Lambda_x, \ \mathbf{B} = 0, \ \Gamma = \mathbf{T}_\phi, \ \Phi = \mathbf{I}, \ \text{and} \ \Theta_\epsilon = \Theta_\delta \, .$$

The covariance matrix $\hat{\Phi} = \hat{\mathbf{T}}_\phi \hat{\mathbf{T}}'_\phi$ is obtained as the covariance matrix of η in the output.

To constrain Ψ to be non-negative definite in the full model, we can specify this as

$$\begin{aligned}
\eta &= \mathbf{B}\eta + \Gamma\xi + \zeta \\
&= \mathbf{B}\eta + \left(\begin{array}{cc} \Gamma & \mathbf{T}_\psi \end{array} \right) \left(\begin{array}{c} \xi \\ \zeta^* \end{array} \right) ,
\end{aligned}$$

where $\mathbf{T}_\psi$ is a lower triangular matrix such that $\Psi = \mathbf{T}_\psi \mathbf{T}'_\psi$ and $\mathrm{Cov}(\zeta^*) = \mathbf{I}$.

8.1.3 Other Constraints

Rindskopf (1983, 1984) has shown how one can impose almost any constraints on individual parameters in a LISREL model by introducing phantom and imaginary latent variables. These constraints include interval restrictions on λ's, β's and γ's, and on error variances, ordered inequalities on error variances and reliabilities, and constraints to make the covariance matrix of η a correlation matrix. Wothke and Browne (1989) have shown that simple equality constraints can be used to estimate Browne's (1984) multiplicative model for multitrait-multimethod matrices. Hayduk (1987) demonstrates how the model of Kenny and Judd (1984), involving multiplicative interaction terms among latent variables, can be reparameterized in LISREL.

8.2 Tests of Hypotheses

Once the validity of a model has been reasonably well established, various structural hypotheses about the parameters $\theta(t \times 1)$ in this model may be tested. One can test hypotheses of the forms

- that certain θ's have particular values

- that certain θ's are equal

Each of these two types of hypotheses leads to a model with fewer parameters ν, where ν (ux1) is a subset of the parameters in θ, u<t. In conventional statistical terminology, the model with parameters ν is called the *null hypothesis* H_0 and the model with parameters θ is called the *alternative hypothesis* H_1. Let χ_0^2 and χ_1^2 be the χ^2 goodness-of-fit measures for models H_0 and H_1, respectively. The test statistic for testing H_0 against H_1 is then

$$D^2 = \chi_0^2 - \chi_1^2 \qquad (8.2)$$

which is used as χ^2 with d = t - u degrees of freedom. The degrees of freedom can also be computed as the difference between the degrees of freedom associated with χ_0^2 and χ_1^2. To use the test statistic formally, one chooses a significance level α (probability of type 1 error) and rejects H_0 if D^2 exceeds the $(1-\alpha)$-percentile of the χ^2 distribution with d degrees of freedom.

The test statistic D^2 can only be used with GLS, ML and WLS and is valid under the following assumptions:

- with GLS and ML if the observed variables have a multivariate normal distribution and the sample covariance matrix is analyzed; with WLS if the correct weight matrix is used

- if the model H_0 is true

- if the sample size is large

A common type of hypothesis H_0 postulates that a single parameter θ be restricted to a specified value θ_0. The corresponding alternative hypothesis H_1 specifies θ as a free parameter in the same model. In this case there are two alternative test statistics that can be used, both of which are easier to compute in that they require only one LISREL run rather than two as D^2 does. These alternatives are

- run LISREL under H_1 and use the t-value of $\hat{\theta}$ as a standard normal two-sided test statistic

- run LISREL under H_0 and use the modification index for $\theta = 0$ as a χ^2 with one degree of freedom

In very large samples, if H_0 is true, we have approximately

$$t^2 = D^2 = \text{modification index}$$

These three quantities will not be equal in small samples, however, and it can happen, although rarely, that one or two of them is significant when the others are not.

8.2.1 Power

In the general context of (8.2), if H_0 cannot be rejected at a given level of significance α, it does not necessarily mean that H_0 is true, because the power of the test may be low. The *power* of a test is the probability of rejecting H_0 when H_1 is true (one minus the probability of type 2 error). The higher the power, the better the test.

The power of the D^2 test in (8.2) depends on

- what the true model is

- the significance level α; power increases with α

- the degrees of freedom; power decreases with degrees of freedom

- the sample size; power increases with sample size

Satorra and Saris (1985) and Matsueda and Bielby (1986) have shown how the power of the D^2 test can be calculated approximately and have investigated various model conditions which affect power. Although these conditions can be expressed in various ways, essentially they are that the power of the test increases with the strength of the relationships in the model, in the sense of squared multiple correlations R^2.

Under H_1, D^2 is distributed approximately as noncentral χ^2 with noncentrality parameter λ, which depends on the residuals $s_{ij} - \sigma_{ij}$ and derivatives $\partial\sigma_{ij}/\partial\theta_k$ at the minimum of the fit function as well as on $\mathbf{W}$, the weight matrix used (Browne, 1984). As stated by Satorra and Saris (1985), λ can be calculated approximately using LISREL.

The procedure for computing the power of the D^2 test is as follows:

Step 1: Specify the model completely under H_1. The power can only be computed for a completely specified model, i.e., all parameters must be numerically specified and satisfy H_1.

Step 2: Compute the covariance matrix Σ for the model specified in Step 1. Σ is given by equation (1.4) but can be computed using LISREL. To do this, use any input covariance matrix and put SI = filename on the OU line. Σ will then be saved in the file specified by filename.

Step 3: Run LISREL under H_0 using the Σ matrix computed in Step 2 as input covariance matrix. The χ^2 goodness-of-fit measure obtained in this step is the noncentrality parameter λ.

Step 4: Using tables of the noncentral χ^2 distribution with noncentrality parameter λ and degrees of freedom d = t - u (Haynam, Govindarajulu and Leone, 1970), determine the probability of obtaining a value larger than the $(1 - \alpha)$ percentile of the central χ^2 distribution with d degrees of freedom. Rather than using the tables of the non-central chi-square distribution, it may be more convenient to use our program LISPOWER (on the LISREL distribution diskette) to calculate the power. Just type LISPOWER and respond to the questions asked by specifying the significance level α, the degrees of freedom d, and the non-centrality parameter λ.

Example 8.2: Power Calculation

To illustrate tests of hypothesis and power calculation, we use an artificial example. Suppose we have a random sample of 100 cases observed on x_1, x_2, y_1, y_2, y_3 and y_4 with the following sample covariance matrix:

$$\mathbf{S} = \begin{pmatrix} 1.531 & & & & & \\ .579 & .991 & & & & \\ .644 & .502 & 1.449 & & & \\ .262 & .276 & .445 & .718 & & \\ .418 & .286 & .492 & .249 & 1.111 & \\ .464 & .279 & .523 & .276 & .657 & 1.144 \end{pmatrix}$$

We are interested in the model shown in Figure 8.1. In particular, we are interested in whether $\gamma_{21} = 0$: i.e., whether the effect of ξ on η_2 is only indirect via η_1.

To test the hypothesis H_0: $\gamma_{21} = 0$, we first run LISREL under H_1 using the following input file:

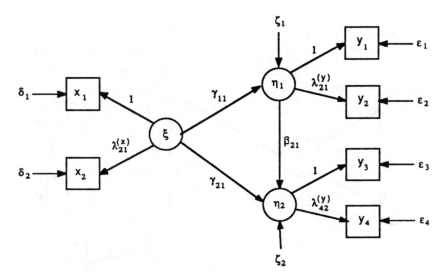

Figure 8.1: Hypothetical Model for Example 8.2

```
EXAMPLE 8.2 Run 1. Using sample covariance matrix and Model H1
DA NI=6 NO=100
CM FI=EX82.COV
MO NY=4 NX=2 NE=2 NK=1 BE=SD PS=DI
FR LY(2,1) LY(4,2) LX(2)
VA 1 LY(1,1) LY(3,2) LX(1)
OU SE TV
```

This run gives a $\chi^2 = 1.97$ with 6 degrees of freedom indicating that model H_1 fits well. The estimate of γ_{21} is 0.391 with a t-value of 1.80. Using this as a test statistic, H_0 cannot be rejected at the 5% level since the t-value does not exceed 1.96, the 97.5 percentile of the standard normal distribution. Next we run LISREL under H_0 to obtain the other two test statistics. Except for the title lines we can use the same input file and just add the line FI GA(2,1) and add MI on the OU line.

This run gives $\chi^2 = 4.52$ with 7 degrees of freedom and the modification index for γ_{21} is 2.695. The D^2 statistic is computed as

$$D^2 = 4.52 - 1.97 = 2.55.$$

Thus both D^2 and the modification index are non-significant at the 5% level since they don't exceed 3.84, the 95th percentile of the χ^2 distribution with 1 degree of freedom.

To calculate the power of the D^2 test we follow the steps outlined in the previous section.

Step 1: We are interested in testing $H_0 : \gamma_{21} = 0$ against the alternative $H_1 : \gamma_{21} = 0.3$, say. However, all the parameters of the H_1 model must be specified numerically. We choose these to be

$$\lambda_{21}^{(x)} = 0.8 \quad \lambda_{21}^{(y)} = 0.7 \quad \lambda_{42}^{(y)} = 0.6$$
$$\beta_{21} = 0.4 \quad \gamma_{11} = 0.5 \quad \gamma_{21} = 0.3$$
$$\phi = 1 \text{ and all error variances} = 0.5$$

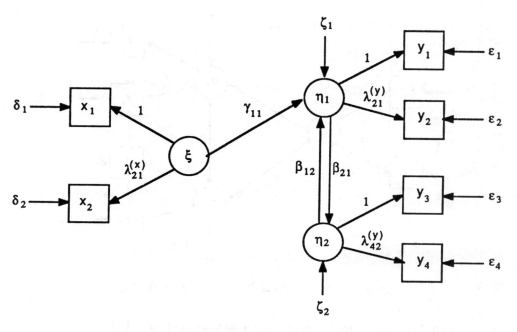

Figure 8.2: Equivalent Model

This means that the parameter matrices in LISREL are

$$\Lambda_y = \begin{pmatrix} 1 & 0 \\ .7 & 0 \\ 0 & 1 \\ 0 & .6 \end{pmatrix} \quad \Theta_\epsilon = diag(.5, .5, .5, .5)$$

$$\Lambda_x = \begin{pmatrix} 1 \\ .8 \end{pmatrix} \quad \Theta_\delta = diag(.5, .5)$$

$$\mathbf{B} = \begin{pmatrix} 0 & 0 \\ .4 & 0 \end{pmatrix} \quad \Gamma = \begin{pmatrix} .5 \\ .3 \end{pmatrix}$$

$$\Phi = (1) \quad \Psi = diag(.5, .5)$$

Step 2: To illustrate how Σ can be computed, we use an input file with an identity matrix as input covariance matrix. One can also use the sample covariance matrix or any other positive definite matrix. The LISREL input file for this step is

```
EXAMPLE 8.2 Run 3. Computing Sigma
DA NI=6 NO=100
CM
1 0 1  2*0 1  3*0 1  4*0 1  5*0 1
MO NY=4 NX=2 NE=2 NK=1 BE=FU,FI GA=FI PH=FI PS=DI,FI TE=FI TD=FI
MA LY
1 0 .7 0 0 1 0 .6
MA LX
1 .8
MA BE
0 0 .4 0
MA GE
.5 .3
MA PH
1
MA PS
.5 .5
MA TE
.5 .5 .5 .5
MA TD
.5 .5
OU SI=EX82.SIG
```

The resulting Σ in file EX82.SIG is

$$
\Sigma = \begin{pmatrix}
1.250 & & & & & \\
.525 & .868 & & & & \\
.450 & .315 & 1.330 & & & \\
.270 & .189 & .498 & .799 & & \\
.500 & .350 & .500 & .300 & 1.500 & \\
.400 & .280 & .400 & .240 & .800 & 1.140
\end{pmatrix}
$$

Step 3: The input file for this step is the same as in run 1 except that the file EX82.SIG is used instead of EX82.COV, i.e. Σ is "analyzed" instead of **S**. This results in $\chi^2 = 3.12$ which is the required noncentrality parameter λ. Note that this value is approximately the same as the modification index for γ_{21}. The power computed by our LISPOWER program for $d = 1$, $\alpha = 0.05$, and $\lambda = 3.12$ is 0.42.

8.3 Equivalent Models

Everyone knows that by merely observing y_1 and y_2, one cannot infer whether y_1 causes y_2 (Figure 8.3, Part A) or y_2 causes y_1 (Figure 8.3, Part B). In fact, all one can do is to determine whether or not y_1 and y_2 are correlated (Figure 8.3, Part C). For causal inference, one must know something more than just the observed values of y_1 and y_2. For example, such additional information may come from

- an experiment in which values of y_1 are controlled or manipulated to produce effects on y_2; then models B and C can be excluded *a priori*

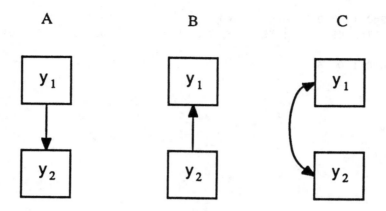

Figure 8.3: Equivalent Models with Two y-Variables

- a longitudinal design in which y_1 is measured or observed before y_2; this excludes model B

- a substantive theory for the mechanism that generate values of y_1 and y_2, such that model B, say, can be excluded

These well-known facts can be extended to more complex situations. If there are three y-variables y_1, y_2, and y_3, many models are possible depending on the causal ordering of the three variables. Figure 8.4, Parts A-C, shows three models in which y_1 is first. There will be three similar models with y_2 first and three more with y_3 first. We may also include the "model" in Figure 8.4, Part D. Hence there are at least ten possible models for three y-variables. With four y-variables there are 24 models just within the class of recursive models. If we allow correlated error terms and/or reciprocal causation, there will be many more.

As demonstrated by Stelzl (1986), all such models are *equivalent* in the sense that they all fit a given dataset equally well. To claim that only one particular model is valid, one must be able to logically exclude all the other equivalent models.

Equivalent models have the same number of independent parameters, the same fitted residuals and the same goodness-of-fit measures (χ^2, GFI, AGFI, and RMR). In the examples just considered all the models are "saturated" in the sense that they fit the data perfectly, i.e., all residuals are zero. However, equivalent models also exist for overidentified models. For instance, in the examples just considered, if we replace all the y-variables by η-variables and add y-variables assumed to be indicators of these η-variables, then all these models are still equivalent, regardless of the structure of the measurement model for the y-variables. These models are equivalent but they do not have a perfect fit. As a second example, consider the models in Figures 8.1 and 8.2. These are equivalent but they are not saturated.

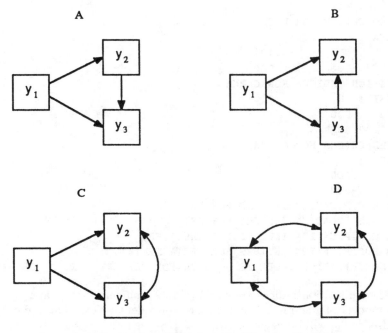

Figure 8.4: Equivalent Models with Three y-Variables

8.3.1 How Can Equivalent Models be Recognized?

Suppose we have an overidentified model which does not fit the data well. We can then examine the modification indices for the fixed parameters. If some of these are equal, this indicates that the corresponding models are equivalent. To illustrate this we use the data in the previous section. In Run 2, the following modification indices are obtained:

```
MODIFICATION INDICES AND ESTIMATED CHANGE
    MODIFICATION INDICES FOR LAMBDA Y
          ETA 1      ETA 2
    VAR 1      .000      2.361
    VAR 2      .000       .020
    VAR 3      .000       .000
    VAR 4      .000       .000
    ESTIMATED CHANGE FOR LAMBDA Y
          ETA 1      ETA 2
    VAR 1      .000     -1.143
    VAR 2      .000      -.079
    VAR 3      .000       .000
    VAR 4      .000       .000
NO NON-ZERO MODIFICATION INDICES FOR LAMBDA X
    MODIFICATION INDICES FOR BETA
          ETA 1      ETA 2
    ETA 1      .000      2.695
    ETA 2      .000       .000
```

```
      ESTIMATED CHANGE FOR BETA
             ETA 1        ETA 2
   ETA 1        .000       -1.194
   ETA 2        .000        .000
      MODIFICATION INDICES FOR GAMMA
             KSI 1
   ETA 1        .000
   ETA 2       2.695
      ESTIMATED CHANGE FOR GAMMA
             KSI 1
   ETA 1        .000
   ETA 2        .533
NO NON-ZERO MODIFICATION INDICES FOR PHI
NO NON-ZERO MODIFICATION INDICES FOR PSI
NO NON-ZERO MODIFICATION INDICES FOR THETA EPS
NO NON-ZERO MODIFICATION INDICES FOR THETA DELTA
   MAXIMUM MODIFICATION INDEX IS     2.70 FOR ELEMENT ( 2, 1) OF GAMMA
```

Two of the modification indices are equal to 2.695, namely for β_{12} and γ_{21}. This indicates that the two models of Figures 8.1 and 8.2 are equivalent. Note that the output also shows that if β_{12} is freed, $\hat{\beta}_{12}$ will be negative, whereas if γ_{21} is freed, $\hat{\gamma}_{21}$ will be positive. If negative values of β_{12} are unreasonable or undesirable, this result can be used to exclude the model in Figure 8.2 in favor of the model in Figure 8.1.

It should be noted that the modification indices for β_{12} and γ_{21} will be equal regardless of what covariance matrix is analyzed. For example, it can be verified that if the population covariance matrix is analyzed instead, the two modification indices will both be 3.262.

Model equivalence is a property of models independently of the data being analyzed. Equivalent models represent *different* (conceptual) parameterizations of the same covariance matrix. For two equivalent models there is usually a one-to-one transformation between the two sets of parameters.

The problem of model equivalence should not be confused with the problem of identification. In the identification problem we have a *given* parameterization of a model and ask whether there are two or more sets of parameter *values* that generate the same covariance matrix.

8.3.2 Specification Searches

The LISREL methodology works best when it is applied to designed studies based on a definite theory and with a clear objective. The initial model of the investigator need not be correct or best for the data but the number of alternative models should be fairly limited. However, LISREL has often been applied to more exploratory situations in which the initial model is set up more or less arbitrarily and then successively modified, perhaps numerous times, so as to improve the parsimony and fit of the model. This process has been termed *specification search* by Leamer (1978), Long (1983), and MacCallum (1986). Search procedures are supposed to detect and correct for *specification errors* (Sörbom, 1975; Saris and Stronkhorst, 1984; Gallini, 1983; Billings and Wroten, 1978; Anderson and Gerbing 1982; Gerbing and Anderson, 1984). Specification errors represent a lack of correspondence between a model studied and the "true" model characterizing the population and variables under study. The goal of the search procedure is to find a model which fits the data well and in which all parameters have real significance and substantive meaning. After such an exploratory search it is important that the final model be cross-validated on a different data set. Procedures and problems for cross-validation have been discussed by Cudeck and Browne (1983) and Kroonenberg and Lewis (1982).

A typical step in the specification search procedure involves the examination and assessment of fit of the current model, in particular, the t-values of estimated parameters and the modification indices for fixed parameters. The modification of the model may involve

- elimination of parameters whose t-values are small

- adding parameters whose modification index is large

Because there may be many equivalent models and many models that fit the data *about* the same, these steps must be used with very careful judgment. LISREL can only discriminate sharply between models that fit the data *very badly* and those that fit the data *fairly well*. One should only add a parameter if its estimated value can be interpreted and justified from a substantive point of view. The table of modification indices also contains values of estimated change, i.e., in what direction and to what extent the parameter will change if it is set free. This can be used to exclude models for which a parameter changes in the wrong direction.

It is best to change only one parameter in each step but it does not have to be the one with the largest modification index. If it makes more sense from a substantive point of view to free a parameter with a smaller modification index this could (should) be done.

Eliminating a parameter on the basis of its t-value may also be dangerous especially in a small sample. Even non-significant parameters may be of practical importance. If the substantive theory suggests that a particular parameter should be included in the model, it is probably better to retain it even though it is not significant, because the sample size may be too small to detect its real significance. This can be examined more closely by hypothesis testing and power calculation; see Section 8.2.

In exploratory situations with many variables and weak or non-existing substantive theory, LISREL is probably not a useful tool. For exploring measurement models (Submodel 1) one should use exploratory factor analysis, and for exploring structural relationships (Submodel 2) one can regress every variable on all other variables, an option which is included in PRELIS.

Chapter 9

MULTI-SAMPLE ANALYSIS

9.1 Analysis Based on Covariance Matrices

In the previous chapters of this book we have shown how LISREL models and LISREL methodology can be used to analyze data from a single sample. LISREL can also be used to analyze data from several samples simultaneously according to LISREL models for each group with some or all parameters constrained to be equal over groups. Examples of such simultaneous analysis have been given by Jöreskog (1971a), McGaw and Jöreskog (1971), Sörbom (1974, 1975, 1978, 1981), Sörbom and Jöreskog (1981), Werts, Linn, and Jöreskog (1976a,1977), Alwin and Jackson (1981), Mare and Mason (1981), and Lomax (1983) among others.

Consider a set of G populations. These may be different nations, states or regions, culturally or socioeconomically different groups, groups of individuals selected on the basis of some known or unknown selection variables, groups receiving different treatments, etc. In fact, they may be any set of mutually exclusive groups of individuals which are clearly defined. It is assumed that a number of variables have been measured on a number of individuals from each population. This approach is particularly useful in comparing a number of treatment and control groups regardless of whether individuals have been assigned to the groups randomly or not.

It is assumed that a LISREL model of the form (1.1), (1.2), and (1.3) holds in each group. The model for group g is defined by the parameter matrices

$$\Lambda_y^{(g)}, \ \Lambda_x^{(g)}, \ \mathbf{B}^{(g)}, \ \Gamma^{(g)}, \ \Phi^{(g)}, \ \Psi^{(g)}, \ \Theta_\epsilon^{(g)}, \ \Theta_\delta^{(g)} \ ,$$

where the superscript (g) refers to the g:th group, $g = 1, 2, ..., G$. Each of these matrices may contain fixed, free and constrained parameters as before. If there are no constraints across groups, each group can be analyzed separately. However, if there are constraints across groups, the data from all groups must be analyzed simultaneously to get fully efficient estimates of the parameters.

Multi-sample LISREL analysis can be used to test whether the covariance or correlation matrices of the observed variables are equal for different groups.

To test the equality of covariance matrices of $\mathbf{x}$, one specifies $\Lambda_x^{(g)} = \mathbf{I}$ and $\Theta_\delta^{(g)} = \mathbf{0}$ for all groups and tests the hypothesis that $\Phi^{(1)} = \Phi^{(2)} = \ldots = \Phi^{(G)}$.

To test the equality of correlation matrices of $\mathbf{x}$, one specifies that $\Theta_\delta^{(g)} = \mathbf{0}$ for all groups and that $\Lambda_x{}^{(g)}$ is a diagonal matrix of standard deviations of $\mathbf{x}$ for the g:th group. The test of equality of correlation matrices is then equivalent to the specification that

$$\Phi^{(1)} = \Phi^{(2)} = \ldots = \Phi^{(G)} \ ,$$

all Φ-matrices having ones in the diagonal. The standard deviations in the diagonal of the Λ_x-matrices are estimated from the data and their estimates are not necessarily equal to the sample standard deviations in each group.

One can also test various forms of less strong equalities. For example, with measurement models of the forms (1.2) and (1.3), if the measurement properties of the observed variables are the same in all groups, one would postulate that

$$\begin{aligned}
\Lambda_y^{(1)} &= \Lambda_y^{(2)} = \ldots = \Lambda_y^{(G)} \ , \\
\Lambda_x^{(1)} &= \Lambda_x^{(2)} = \ldots = \Lambda_x^{(G)} \ ,
\end{aligned}$$

and perhaps also that

$$\begin{aligned}
\Theta_\epsilon^{(1)} &= \Theta_\epsilon^{(2)} = \ldots = \Theta_\epsilon^{(G)} \ , \\
\Theta_\delta^{(1)} &= \Theta_\delta^{(2)} = \ldots = \Theta_\delta^{(G)} \ .
\end{aligned}$$

The possible differences between groups would then be represented by differences in the distributions of the latent variables, i.e., by $\Phi^{(g)}$ and $\Psi^{(g)}$. By postulating

$$\begin{aligned}
\mathbf{B}^{(1)} &= \mathbf{B}^{(2)} = \ldots = \mathbf{B}^{(G)} \ , \\
\mathbf{\Gamma}^{(1)} &= \mathbf{\Gamma}^{(2)} = \ldots = \mathbf{\Gamma}^{(G)} \ ,
\end{aligned}$$

one can test the hypothesis that the structural relations are also invariant over groups.

In general, any degree of invariance can be tested, from the one extreme where all parameters are assumed to be invariant over groups to the other extreme when there are no constraints across groups. For example, if $\Phi^{(g)}$, $g = 1, 2, ..., G$ are matrices of order 3×3, one can specify that $\phi_{31}^{(g)}$, $\phi_{32}^{(g)}$, and $\phi_{33}^{(g)}$ should be equal across groups whereas $\phi_{11}^{(g)}$, $\phi_{21}^{(g)}$, and $\phi_{22}^{(g)}$ are free parameters for each group.

To estimate all the models simultaneously, LISREL minimizes the fit function

$$F = \sum_{g=1}^{G} (N_g/N) F_g(\mathbf{S}^{(g)}, \mathbf{\Sigma}^{(g)}, \mathbf{W}^{(g)}) \ , \tag{9.1}$$

where F_g is any of the fit functions defined in Section 1.11, i.e., ULS, GLS, ML, DWLS and WLS. Here N_g is the sample size in group g and $N = N_1 + N_2 + \ldots + N_G$ is the total sample size; $\mathbf{S}_g$ and $\mathbf{\Sigma}_g$ are the sample and population covariance matrices in group g, and $\mathbf{W}^{(g)}$ is the weight matrix for group g. When $G = 1$, (9.1) reduces to the fit function 1.20 defined in Section 1.11.

Initial estimates are first computed by IV and TSLS for each group separately, as before, ignoring all equality constraints between groups. Parameters which are specified to be equal across groups are then replaced by their mean value.

As before, the χ^2 goodness-of-fit measure is defined as N times the minimum of F. This is a measure of the fit of all LISREL models in all groups, including all constraints, to the data from all groups. The degrees of freedom are

$$d = \frac{1}{2} G(p + q)(p + q + 1) - t \ , \tag{9.2}$$

where t is the total number of independent parameters estimated in all groups. Thus, in a multi-sample analysis, only one χ^2 goodness-of-fit measure is given, whereas the GFI, AGFI, and RMR measures are given for each group.

9.2 Input Data for Multi-Sample Analysis

The input data for each group are stacked after each other. The data for each group are set up as described in Chapter 2, with the following additional rules:

- NG must be defined on the DA line for the first group

- For each group $g, g = 2, 3, ..., G$, every input parameter which has the same value as in the previous group may be omitted

- Pattern matrices and non-zero fixed values as well as starting values are defined as before. A matrix element such as BE(4,3), with one or two indices, refers to the element in the current group. To refer to an element in another group one must use three indices where the first one refers to the group number. For example, BE(2,4,3) refers to β_{43} in $\mathbf{B}^{(2)}$

- To define equality constraints between groups, one specifies the constrained elements as free for the first group, and equality constraints in each of the other groups. For example, if β_{43} is to be invariant over groups, one specifies

    in group 1: FR BE(4,3)
    in group 2: EQ BE(1,4,3) BE(4,3)
    in group 3: EQ BE(1,4,3) BE(4,3), etc.

- If a matrix is specified as ID or ZE in group 1, it must not be specified as DI, FU or SY in subsequent groups. Similarly, if a matrix is specified as DI in group 1, it must not be specified as FU or SY in any subsequent group

- In addition to the matrix specifications described in Section 2.6, the following specifications are possible on the MO line for groups 2, 3, ..., G:

    SP means that the matrix has the *same pattern* of fixed and free elements as the corresponding matrix in the previous group

    SS means that the matrix will be given the *same starting values* as the corresponding matrix in the previous group

    PS means *same pattern and starting values* as the corresponding matrix in the previous group

    IN means that the matrix is *invariant* over groups, i.e., all parameter matrices have the same pattern of fixed and free elements, and all elements which are defined as free in group 1 are supposed to be equal across groups.

In principle, NY, NX, NE, and NK must all be the same in all groups. However, if the numbers of variables are different in different groups, it is possible to introduce pseudo-variables (observed or latent) so as to make the number of variables equal in all groups; see Jöreskog (1971) or Allison (1987), see also Example 10.3. These pseudo-variables are artificial variables which, if chosen properly, have no effects on anything.

Important Note: The number of variables and the form (ZE, ID, DI, SY, FU) of each parameter matrix is specified on the MO line for the first group. These specifications must not be contradicted by a different specification on the MO line for subsequent groups. This does not refer to the specification of a fixed or free matrix.

Example 9.1: Testing Equality of Factor Structures

Sörbom (1976) gave the covariance matrices in Table 9.1. These are based on scores on the ETS Sequential Test of Educational Progress (STEP) for two groups of boys who took the test in both Grade 5 and Grade 7. The two groups were defined according to whether or not they were in the academic curriculum in Grade 12.

- *A : Test the hypothesis $H_\Sigma : \Sigma^{(1)} = \Sigma^{(2)}$*

- *B : Assuming that a measurement (factor analysis) model of the form $\mathbf{x} = \Lambda_x \xi + \delta$ holds in both groups, test the hypothesis that there are two correlated common factors in both groups with a factor pattern of the form*

$$\Lambda_x = \begin{pmatrix} x & 0 \\ x & 0 \\ 0 & x \\ 0 & x \end{pmatrix}$$

- *C : Assuming B, test the hypothesis $H_\Lambda : \Lambda_x^{(1)} = \Lambda_x^{(2)}$*

- *D : Assuming C, test the hypothesis $H_{\Lambda\Theta} : \Theta_\delta^{(1)} = \Theta_\delta^{(2)}$*

- *E : Assuming D, test the hypothesis $H_{\Lambda\Phi\Theta} : \Phi^{(1)} = \Phi^{(2)}$*

Table 9.1: Covariance Matrices for STEP Reading and Writing (Sörbom, 1976)

Boys Academic ($N = 373$)				
STEP Reading, Grade 5	281.349			
STEP Writing, Grade 5	184.219	182.821		
STEP Reading, Grade 7	216.739	171.699	283.289	
STEP Writing, Grade 7	198.376	153.201	208.837	246.069

Boys Non-Academic ($N = 249$)				
STEP Reading, Grade 5	174.485			
STEP Writing, Grade 5	134.468	161.869		
STEP Reading, Grade 7	129.840	118.836	228.449	
STEP Writing, Grade 7	102.194	97.767	136.058	180.460

The data file EX91.DAT contains both labels and covariance matrices. It looks like this

```
READ-GR5 WRIT-GR5 READ-GR7 WRIT-GR7
281.349
184.219 182.821
216.739 171.699 283.289
198.376 153.201 208.837 246.069
READ-GR5 WRIT-GR5 READ-GR7 WRIT-GR7
174.485
134.468 161.869
129.840 118.836 228.449
102.194  97.767 136.058 180.460
```

All five problems A-E can be solved by using a LISREL Submodel 1, i.e.,

$$\mathbf{x} = \mathbf{\Lambda}_x \boldsymbol{\xi} + \boldsymbol{\delta} \ .$$

In problem A, we set $\mathbf{\Lambda}_x^{(1)} = \mathbf{\Lambda}_x^{(2)} = \mathbf{I}$ and $\mathbf{\Theta}_\delta^{(1)} = \mathbf{\Theta}_\delta^{(2} = \mathbf{0}$. This means that $\mathbf{x} \equiv \boldsymbol{\xi}$ so that $\mathbf{\Sigma}^{(g)} = \mathbf{\Phi}^{(g)}$ for $g = 1, 2$. The hypothesis $\mathbf{\Sigma}^{(1)} = \mathbf{\Sigma}^{(2)}$ is therefore the same as $\mathbf{\Phi}^{(1)} = \mathbf{\Phi}^{(2)}$. The input is extremely simple as follows:

```
TESTING EQUALITY OF FACTOR STRUCTURES. HYPOTHESIS A.    GROUP BA
GROUP: BOYS ACADEMIC
DA NG=2 NI=4 NO=373
LA FI=EX91.DAT; CM FI=EX91.DAT
MO NX=4 NK=4 LX=ID TD=ZE
OU
TESTING EQUALITY OF FACTOR STRUCTURES. HYPOTHESIS A.    GROUP BNA
GROUP: BOYS NON-ACADEMIC
DA NO=249
LA FI=EX91.DAT; CM FI=EX91.DAT
MO PH=IN
OU
```

In group 1, $\mathbf{\Phi}$ is free by default. In group 2, $\mathbf{\Phi}$ is declared invariant (PH=IN). Note that on the MO line for the second group, the parameters NX, NK, LX and TD need not be given since they are the same as for group 1. The labels and the covariance matrices are read from a file EX91.DAT.

In problem B, we assume a common factor model with two common factors and leave $\mathbf{\Phi}(2 \times 2)$ to be a free covariance matrix in both groups. To fix the scale for the two factors ξ_1 and ξ_2, we fix the elements λ_{11} and λ_{32} of $\mathbf{\Lambda}_x$ equal to one for both groups. The other elements λ_{21} and λ_{42} and the diagonal elements of $\mathbf{\Theta}_\delta$ are free in both groups. The hypothesis in problem B does not impose any equality constraints on parameters; it only states that the *number* of factors is the same for both groups. The input for the problem B is

```
TESTING EQUALITY OF FACTOR STRUCTURES.    HYPOTHESIS B. GROUP BA
GROUP: BOYS ACADEMIC
DA NG=2 NI=4 NO=373
LA FI=EX91.DAT; CM FI=EX91.DAT
MO NX=4 NK=2
FR LX 2 1 LX 4 2
VA 1 LX 1 1 LX 3 2
OU
TESTING EQUALITY OF FACTOR STRUCTURES.    HYPOTHESIS B. GROUP BNA
GROUP: BOYS NON-ACADEMIC
DA NO=249
LA FI=EX91.DAT; CM FI=EX91.DAT
MO LX=PS
OU
```

The matrices $\Phi^{(1)}$ and $\Phi^{(2)}$ are both free by default. The matrices $\Theta_\delta^{(1)}$ and $\Theta_\delta^{(2)}$ are diagonal and free, also by default. The elements λ_{21} and λ_{42} are declared free in group one. Starting values for these are estimated by the program using two-stage least-squares. In group 2, Λ_x is specified to have the same pattern and the same starting values as for group 1 (LX=PS).

As no equality constraints across groups are imposed, the overall χ^2-value obtained in problem B is the sum of the two χ^2's that would be obtained if the two groups were analyzed separately.

In problems C, D, and E, the input for group 1 is the same as in problem B. In problem C, the input for group 2 differs from that of problem B only in that Λ_x is declared invariant, i.e., LX=IN instead of only LX=PS. In problem D, TD=IN in addition and in problem E, PH=IN in addition. The input for problems C, D and E is as follows:

```
TESTING EQUALITY OF FACTOR STRUCTURES.    HYPOTHESIS C. GROUP BA
GROUP: BOYS ACADEMIC
DA NG=2 NI=4 NO=373
LA FI=EX91.DAT; CM FI=EX91.DAT
MO NX=4 NK=2
FR LX 2 1 LX 4 2
VA 1 LX 1 1 LX 3 2
OU
TESTING EQUALITY OF FACTOR STRUCTURES.    HYPOTHESIS C. GROUP BNA
GROUP: BOYS NON-ACADEMIC
DA NO=249
LA FI=EX91.DAT; CM FI=EX91.DAT
MO LX=IN
OU
TESTING EQUALITY OF FACTOR STRUCTURES.    HYPOTHESIS D. GROUP BA
GROUP: BOYS ACADEMIC
DA NG=2 NI=4 NO=373
LA FI=EX91.DAT; CM FI=EX91.DAT
MO NX=4 NK=2
FR LX 2 1 LX 4 2
VA 1 LX 1 1 LX 3 2
OU
```

```
TESTING EQUALITY OF FACTOR STRUCTURES.    HYPOTHESIS D. GROUP BNA
GROUP: BOYS NON-ACADEMIC
DA NO=249
LA FI=EX91.DAT; CM FI=EX91.DAT
MO LX=IN TD=IN
OU
TESTING EQUALITY OF FACTOR STRUCTURES.    HYPOTHESIS E. GROUP BA
GROUP: BOYS ACADEMIC
DA NG=2 NI=4 NO=373
LA FI=EX91.DAT; CM FI=EX91.DAT
MO NX=4 NK=2
FR LX 2 1 LX 4 2
VA 1 LX 1 1 LX 3 2
OU
TESTING EQUALITY OF FACTOR STRUCTURES.    HYPOTHESIS E. GROUP BNA
GROUP: BOYS NON-ACADEMIC
DA NO=249
LA FI=EX91.DAT; CM FI=EX91.DAT
MO LX=IN TD=IN PH=IN
OU
```

In the output file from a multi-sample analysis, all requested parts of the output are given for each group. Note that the GFI and the RMR are given for each group, but the χ^2 measure is only given for the last group. This χ^2 is a measure of the overall fit of *all* models in *all* groups.

The results of the tests are given in Table 9.2. The most reasonable hypothesis to retain is H_Λ. The two groups have an invariant factor pattern but there is some evidence that they differ in error variances and in factor covariance matrices.

Table 9.2: Summary of Results for Example 9.1

Problem	Hypothesis	χ^2	Degrees of Freedom	P-value	Decision
A	H_Σ	38.08	10	0.000	Rejected
B	$H_{n=2}$	1.52	2	0.468	Accepted
C	H_Λ	8.77	4	0.067	Accepted
D	$H_{\Lambda\Theta}$	21.55	8	0.006	Rejected
E	$H_{\Lambda\Phi\Theta}$	38.22	11	0.000	Rejected

Example 9.2: Testing Equality of Factor Correlation Matrices

Table 9.3 gives observed covariance matrices for two random samples ($N_1 = 865$, $N_2 = 900$, respectively) of candidates who took the Scholastic Aptitude Test in January 1971. The four measures are, in order, x_1 = a 40-item verbal aptitude section, x_2 = a separately timed 50-item verbal aptitude section, x_3 = a 35-item math aptitude section, and x_4 = a separately timed 25-item math aptitude section.

Werts, Linn, and Jöreskog (1976a) used these data to test various assumptions about the psychometric properties of the tests both within and between groups. Werts, Linn, and Jöreskog (1977) showed how to compare correlations, variances, covariances and regression coefficients between groups. Here we use the data to illustrate how one can test equality of factor correlations in a confirmatory factor analysis model.

The model is a LISREL Submodel 1 with

$$\Lambda_x = \begin{pmatrix} x & 0 \\ x & 0 \\ 0 & x \\ 0 & x \end{pmatrix} \quad \Phi = \begin{pmatrix} 1 & \\ x & 1 \end{pmatrix} \quad \Theta_\delta = diag \begin{pmatrix} x \\ x \\ x \\ x \end{pmatrix}$$

and the test is $\phi_{21}^{(1)} = \phi_{21}^{(2)}$.

In problem D of the previous example, it was postulated that factor patterns in Λ_x and error variances in Θ_δ are invariant over groups. This means that differences between groups, if any, must manifest themselves in different factor covariance matrices Φ. By contrast, in this example, we allow Λ_x and Θ_δ to vary over groups and test the hypothesis that the correlation between the two factors is the same in both groups.

Table 9.3: Covariance Matrices for SAT Verbal and Math Sections

Covariance Matrix for Group 1

Tests	x_1	x_2	x_3	x_4
x_1 = a 40-item verbal aptitude section	63.382			
x_2 = a separately timed 50-item verbal aptitude section	70.984	110.237		
x_3 = a 35-item math aptitude section	41.710	52.747	60.584	
x_4 = a separately timed 25-item math aptitude section	30.218	37.489	36.392	32.295

Covariance Matrix for Group 2

Tests	x_1	x_2	x_3	x_4
x_1 = a 40-item verbal aptitude section	67.898			
x_2 = a separately timed 50-item verbal aptitude section	72.301	107.330		
x_3 = a 35-item math aptitude section	40.549	55.347	63.203	
x_4 = a separately timed 25-item math aptitude section	28.976	38.896	39.261	35.403

The input file is

```
TESTING EQUALITY OF FACTOR CORRELATIONS    GROUP 1
DA NG=2 NI=4 NO=865
CM FI=EX92.COV
MO NX=4 NK=2 PH=FI
VA 1 PH 1 1 PH 2 2
FR LX 1 1 LX 2 1 LX 3 2 LX 4 2 PH 2 1
OU
TESTING EQUALITY OF FACTOR CORRELATIONS    GROUP 2
DA NI=4 NO=900
CM FI=EX92.COV
MO PH=IN
FR LX 1 1 LX 2 1 LX 3 2 LX 4 2
OU
```

The overall goodness-of-fit measure for the model with the equality constraint imposed is $\chi^2=4.03$ with 3 degrees of freedom. When the equality constraint is relaxed χ^2 drops to 2.18, so obviously the model is good and the hypothesis of equal factor correlations is tenable. The common correlation is estimated at 0.765.

Example 9.3: Son's and Parents' Reports of Parental Socioeconomic Characteristics

An interesting example of multi-sample analyses is given by Mare and Mason (1981). They report the covariance matrices in Table 9.4 for six variables and three populations. The variables are

SOFED = Son's report of father's education

SOMED = Son's report of mother's education

SOFOC = Son's report of father's occupation

FAFED = Father's report of his own education

MOMED = Mother's report of her own education

FAFOC = Father's report of his own occupation.

The three populations are

Group 1: White Sixth Graders

Group 2: White Ninth Graders

Group 3. White Twelfth Graders

The model is shown in Figure 9.1, where the latent variables TRFED, TRMED, and TRFOC represent the true father's education, mother's education and father's occupation, respectively. This model can be specified as a LISREL Submodel 1 with

$$
\Lambda_x = \begin{pmatrix} x & 0 & 0 \\ 0 & x & 0 \\ 0 & 0 & x \\ 1 & 0 & 0 \\ 0 & 1 & 0 \\ 0 & 0 & 1 \end{pmatrix} \quad \Phi = \begin{pmatrix} x & & \\ x & x & \\ x & x & x \end{pmatrix} \quad \Theta_\delta = \begin{pmatrix} x & & & & & \\ x & x & & & & \\ 0 & 0 & x & & & \\ 0 & 0 & 0 & x & & \\ 0 & 0 & 0 & 0 & x & \\ 0 & 0 & 0 & 0 & 0 & x \end{pmatrix}
$$

Table 9.4: Covariance Matrices for White Sixth, Ninth, and Twelfth Grade. Son's and Parent's Reports of Parental Socioeconomic Characteristics

	1.	2.	3.	4.	5.	6.
			Sixth Grade			
1. SOFED	5.86					
2. SOMED	3.12	3.32				
3. SOFOC	35.28	23.85	622.09			
4. FAFED	4.02	2.14	29.42	5.33		
5. MOMED	2.99	2.55	19.20	3.17	4.64	
6. FAFOC	35.30	26.91	465.62	31.22	23.38	546.01
			Ninth Grade			
1. SOFED	8.20					
2. SOMED	3.47	4.36				
3. SOFOC	45.65	22.58	611.63			
4. FAFED	6.39	3.16	44.62	7.32		
5. MOMED	3.22	3.77	23.47	3.33	4.02	
6. FAFOC	45.58	22.01	548.00	40.99	21.43	585.14
			Twelfth Grade			
1. SOFED	5.74					
2. SOMED	1.35	2.49				
3. SOFOC	39.24	12.73	535.30			
4. FAFED	4.94	1.65	37.36	5.39		
5. MOMED	1.67	2.32	15.71	1.85	3.06	
6. FAFOC	40.11	12.94	496.86	38.09	14.91	538.76

Mare and Mason (1981) considered many models. One of them was that Φ and $\theta_{44}^{(\delta)}$, $\theta_{55}^{(\delta)}$, and $\theta_{66}^{(\delta)}$, are invariant over groups and that $\theta_{21}^{(\delta)}$ is zero in Group 3 (but not in the other groups). A LISREL input file for this model will be

```
SON'S AND PARENTS' REPORTS OF PARENTAL SOCIOECONOMIC CHARACTERISTICS  GRADE 6
DA NI=6 NO=80 NG=3
CM
5.86 3.12 3.32 35.28 23.85 622.09 4.02 2.14 29.42 5.33 2.99 2.55 19.20 3.17
4.64 35.30 26.91 465.62 31.22 23.38 546.01
LA
'SOFED' 'SOMED' 'SOFOC' 'FAFED' 'MOMED' 'FAFOC'
MO NX=6 NK=3 TD=SY
LK
'TRFED' 'TRMED' 'TRFOC'
FR LX 1 1 LX 2 2 LX 3 3 TD 2 1
VA 1 LX 4 1 LX 5 2 LX 6 3
OU SE TV MI ND=2
```

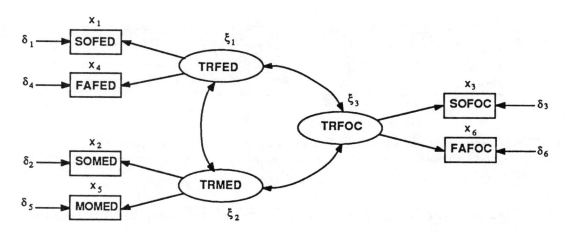

Figure 9.1: Path Diagram for Reports of Parental Socioeconomic Characteristics

```
SON'S AND PARENTS' REPORTS OF PARENTAL SOCIOECONOMIC CHARACTERISTICS  GRADE 9
DA
CM
8.20 3.47 4.36 45.65 22.58 611.63 6.39 3.16 44.62 7.32 3.22 3.77 23.47 3.33
4.02 45.58 22.01 548.00 40.99 21.43 585.14
LA
'SOFED' 'SOMED' 'SOFOC' 'FAFED' 'MOMED' 'FAFOC'
MO LX=PS PH=IN TD=SY
LK
'TRFED' 'TRMED' 'TRFOC'
FR TD 2 1
EQ TD 1 4 4 TD 4 4
EQ TD 1 5 5 TD 5 5
EQ TD 1 6 6 TD 6 6
OU
SON'S AND PARENTS' REPORTS OF PARENTAL SOCIOECONOMIC CHARACTERISTICS  GRADE 12
DA
CM
5.74 1.35 2.49 39.24 12.73 535.30 4.94 1.65 37.36 5.39 1.67 2.32 15.71 1.85
3.06 40.11 12.94 496.86 38.09 14.91 538.76
LA
'SOFED' 'SOMED' 'SOFOC' 'FAFED' 'MOMED' 'FAFOC'
MO LX=PS PH=IN TD=SY
LK
'TRFED' 'TRMED' 'TRFOC'
EQ TD 1 4 4 TD 4 4
EQ TD 1 5 5 TD 5 5
EQ TD 1 6 6 TD 6 6
OU
```

The output file reveals the following reliabilities (squared multiple correlations):

	SOFED	SOMED	SOFOC	FAFED	MOMED	FAFOC
Grade 6	.62	.38	.71	.87	.93	.90
Grade 9	.76	.86	.92	.87	.93	.90
Grade 12	.91	.81	.95	.87	.93	.90

This is a somewhat remarkable result because in grade 12, the sons' reports of their fathers' education and occupation are more reliable than the fathers' reports of their own education and occupation.

9.3   Standardized Solutions in Multi-Sample Analysis

It is important to understand that in a multi-sample analysis with constraints across groups, one must not standardize the variables within each group. Neither the observed nor the latent variables should be standardized. To compare parameters across groups, the variables must be measured in a common metric for all groups. For example, if Λ_x is invariant over groups when $\mathbf{x}$ and ξ are in a common metric, the Λ_x-matrices will not be equal when the $\mathbf{x}$ and/or ξ is standardized within each group if the variances of $\mathbf{x}$ and/or ξ are different over groups. This means that sample covariance matrices must be analyzed and the scales of the latent variables must be set by fixing non-zero elements in Λ_y and Λ_x in such a way that the latent variables are on a common scale.

For reasons just stated, the meaning of *standardized solution* (SS) in multi-sample analysis is not what some people might think. This has been misunderstood in the literature; see Acock and Fuller (1986). If SS is requested on the OU line, the program scales the latent variables so that a *weighted average* of their covariance matrix is a correlation matrix thereby *retaining a scale common to all groups.*

The computation of these standardized solutions is as follows. Let $\hat{\Phi}^{(g)}$ and $\hat{\Omega}^{(g)}$ be the covariance matrices of ξ and η in group g, where

$$\hat{\Omega}^{(g)} = (\mathbf{I} - \hat{\mathbf{B}}^{(g)})^{-1}(\hat{\Gamma}^{(g)}\hat{\Phi}^{(g)}\hat{\Gamma}^{\prime(g)} + \hat{\Psi}^{(g)})(\mathbf{I} - \hat{\mathbf{B}}^{\prime(g)})^{-1} \qquad (9.3)$$

Compute

$$\hat{\Phi} = (1/n)\sum_{g=1}^{G} n_g \hat{\Phi}^{(g)} \, , \qquad (9.4)$$

$$\hat{\Omega} = (1/n)\sum_{g=1}^{G} n_g \hat{\Omega}^{(g)} \, , \qquad (9.5)$$

where $n_g = N_g - 1$, $n = n_1 + n_2 + \cdots + n_G = N - G$. The scale factors for the common metric are then defined as

$$\mathbf{D}_\xi = (diag\,\hat{\Phi})^{\frac{1}{2}} \, , \qquad (9.6)$$

$$\mathbf{D}_\eta = (diag\,\hat{\Omega})^{\frac{1}{2}} \, . \qquad (9.7)$$

The standardized solution for each group is then computed by formulas given in Table 1.6, left column.

This standardized solution *is not* such that the covariance matrix of the latent variables is a correlation matrix in *each* group. Instead, a weighted average of these covariance matrices is a correlation matrix. By computing the standardized solution in this way, we achieve the property that if $\hat{\Lambda}_y$ and/or $\hat{\Lambda}_x$ are invariant in the unstandardized solution they will be so also in the standardized solution.

In LISREL output, the standardized solution defined in this way is called SOLUTION STANDARDIZED TO A COMMON METRIC.

To illustrate this, consider the output obtained from Example 9.1, Problem C by adding SS on the OU line.

```
TESTING EQUALITY OF FACTOR STRUCTURES.   HYPOTHESIS C. GROUP BA
SOLUTION STANDARDIZED TO A COMMON METRIC
        LAMBDA X
                 KSI 1        KSI 2
READ-GR5         14.057        .000
WRIT-GR5         11.580        .000
READ-GR7          .000        14.290
WRIT-GR7          .000        12.575
        PHI
                 KSI 1        KSI 2
    KSI 1        1.134
    KSI 2        1.071        1.157
TESTING EQUALITY OF FACTOR STRUCTURES.   HYPOTHESIS C. GROUP BNA
SOLUTION STANDARDIZED TO A COMMON METRIC
        LAMBDA X
                 KSI 1        KSI 2
READ-GR5         14.057        .000
WRIT-GR5         11.580        .000
READ-GR7          .000        14.290
WRIT-GR7          .000        12.575
        PHI
                 KSI 1        KSI 2
    KSI 1         .799
    KSI 2         .638         .764
```

The $\hat{\Lambda}_x$-matrices in these solutions are the same for both groups and the corresponding $\hat{\Phi}$-matrices are such that

$$\frac{372\hat{\Phi}_1 + 248\hat{\Phi}_2}{620}$$

is a correlation matrix.

By popular demand, we have also introduced in LISREL 7 a solution standardized *within* group corresponding to Section 1.18. This standardizes the latent variables to unit variance *for each group*. As before, it does *not* standardize the observed variables. For Example 9.1, Problem C, this WITHIN GROUP STANDARDIZED SOLUTION looks like this:

TESTING EQUALITY OF FACTOR STRUCTURES.   HYPOTHESIS C. GROUP BA
WITHIN GROUP STANDARDIZED SOLUTION
        LAMBDA X

	KSI 1	KSI 2
READ-GR5	14.969	.000
WRIT-GR5	12.331	.000
READ-GR7	.000	15.373
WRIT-GR7	.000	13.528

        PHI

	KSI 1	KSI 2
KSI 1	1.000	
KSI 2	.935	1.000

TESTING EQUALITY OF FACTOR STRUCTURES.   HYPOTHESIS C. GROUP BNA
WITHIN GROUP STANDARDIZED SOLUTION
        LAMBDA X

	KSI 1	KSI 2
READ-GR5	12.567	.000
WRIT-GR5	10.353	.000
READ-GR7	.000	12.491
WRIT-GR7	.000	10.992

        PHI

	KSI 1	KSI 2
KSI 1	1.000	
KSI 2	.816	1.000

Here each $\hat{\mathbf{\Phi}}$ matrix is a correlation matrix but the $\hat{\mathbf{\Lambda}}_x$ matrices are no longer the same.

As in the case of a single sample, in these SS solutions, *neither* the solution standardized to a common metric *nor* the within group standardized solution will scale the observed variables; *they are still retained in their original metric.*

To standardize the observed variables, one must put SC on the OU line. Even in this case, there are two standardized solutions: the WITHIN GROUP COMPLETELY STANDARD-IZED SOLUTION and the COMMON METRIC COMPLETELY STANDARDIZED SOLU-TION. The first simply standardizes the observed and latent variables within each group as is done for a single group. Equality constraints within and between groups are usually lost. The second SC solution standardizes the observed variables to a common correlation metric, by computing

$$\hat{\mathbf{\Sigma}} = (1/n) \sum_{g=1}^{G} n_g \hat{\mathbf{\Sigma}}^{(g)} \, , \tag{9.8}$$

where $\hat{\mathbf{\Sigma}}^{(g)}$ is the fitted covariance matrix in each group. Let

$$\mathbf{D}_z = (diag \ \hat{\mathbf{\Sigma}})^{\frac{1}{2}} \, , \tag{9.9}$$

and let $\mathbf{D}_y$ and $\mathbf{D}_x$ be the diagonal matrices formed by the first p and the last q elements of $\mathbf{D}_z$, respectively. Then, for each group the common metric completely standardized solution is computed by the formulas in the right column of Table 1.6.

For Example 9.1c, the within group completely standardized solution is

```
TESTING EQUALITY OF FACTOR STRUCTURES.   HYPOTHESIS C. GROUP: BA
WITHIN GROUP COMPLETELY STANDARDIZED SOLUTION
         LAMBDA X
              KSI 1      KSI 2
READ-GR5      .906       .000
WRIT-GR5      .897       .000
READ-GR7      .000       .907
WRIT-GR7      .000       .871
         THETA DELTA
         READ-GR5   WRIT-GR5   READ-GR7   WRIT-GR7
            .180       .195       .178       .242
         PHI
              KSI 1      KSI 2
     KSI 1    1.000
     KSI 2    .935       1.000
TESTING EQUALITY OF FACTOR STRUCTURES.   HYPOTHESIS C. GROUP: BNA
WITHIN GROUP COMPLETELY STANDARDIZED SOLUTION
         LAMBDA X
              KSI 1      KSI 2
READ-GR5      .937       .000
WRIT-GR5      .843       .000
READ-GR7      .000       .841
WRIT-GR7      .000       .800
         THETA DELTA
         READ-GR5   WRIT-GR5   READ-GR7   WRIT-GR7
            .122       .290       .293       .360
         PHI
              KSI 1      KSI 2
     KSI 1    1.000
     KSI 2    .816       1.000
```

and the common metric completely standardized solution is

```
TESTING EQUALITY OF FACTOR STRUCTURES.   HYPOTHESIS C. GROUP: BA
COMMON METRIC COMPLETELY STANDARDIZED SOLUTION
         LAMBDA X
              KSI 1      KSI 2
READ-GR5      .915       .000
WRIT-GR5      .879       .000
READ-GR7      .000       .885
WRIT-GR7      .000       .847
         PHI
              KSI 1      KSI 2
     KSI 1    1.134
     KSI 2    1.071      1.157
```

```
TESTING EQUALITY OF FACTOR STRUCTURES.   HYPOTHESIS C. GROUP: BNA
COMMON METRIC COMPLETELY STANDARDIZED SOLUTION
        LAMBDA X
                  KSI 1        KSI 2
READ-GR5           .915         .000
WRIT-GR5           .879         .000
READ-GR7           .000         .885
WRIT-GR7           .000         .847
        PHI
                  KSI 1        KSI 2
      KSI 1        .799
      KSI 2        .638         .764
```

In this solution both observed and latent variables are standardized to a common metric and Λ_x is still invariant. Such a common metric facilitates comparison of factor variances and covariances. Note that the factor variances and covariances are larger in group 1 than in group 2.

Example 9.4: Subjective and Objective Social Class

Sörbom and Jöreskog (1981) analyzed data on subjective and objective social class previously published by Kluegel, Singleton, and Starnes (1977). One of their models is shown in Figure 9.2. The data are given in Table 9.5.

There are three variables measuring objective status and four measuring subjective status. The objective status measures are:

- *education – indicated by five categories ranging from less than ninth grade to college graduate.*

- *occupation – indicated by the two-digit Duncan SEI score.*

- *income – indicated by the total yearly family income before taxes in 1967, coded in units of $2,000 and ranging from under $2,000 to $16,000 or more.*

All subjective class indicators were structured questions asking respondents to place themselves in one of four class categories: lower, working, middle, or upper. The questions asked the respondents to indicate which social class they felt their occupation, income, way of life, and influence were most like. The criteria, in terms of which class self-placements were made, correspond directly to the Weberian dimensions of economic class (occupation and income), status (lifestyle), and power (influence).

The data file EX94.DAT contains labels, correlations and standard deviations for the two groups.

For the present purpose we consider the model of Figure 9.2. We want to test whether the relationship between objective and subjective class is the same for whites and blacks. We do this by testing the equality of the structural parameter γ.

The analysis reveals that the model fits very badly; $\chi^2 = 121.76$ with 27 degrees of freedom. The modification index for $\theta_{21}^{(\epsilon)}$ is large for both groups. This indicates that the objective class measures are not congeneric. Education and occupation correlate more than can be accounted for by objective class. Allowing ϵ_1 and ϵ_2 to correlate freely in both groups gives $\chi^2 = 86.93$ with 25 degrees of freedom. Relaxing the equality constraint on γ gives $\chi^2 = 76.90$ with 24 degrees of freedom. The drop in χ^2 is 10.03 which is significant at the 0.5% level, so the hypothesis of equal γ must be rejected. The estimates of γ, with standard errors in parenthesis, are:

Whites: $\hat{\gamma} = 1.345(0.210)$

Blacks: $\hat{\gamma} = 0.631(0.119)$

The input file for the last model is:

```
LISREL MODEL FOR SUBJECTIVE AND OBJECTIVE SOCIAL CLASS    WHITES
DA NG=2 NI=7 NO=432
LA FI=EX94.DAT;KM FI=EX94.DAT;SD FI=EX94.DAT
MO NY=3 NX=4 NE=1 NK=1 LY=FR LX=FR TE=SY
LE;OBJCLASS
LK;SBJCLASS
FR TE 2 1; FI LY 1 LX 1; VA 1 LY 1 LX 1
OU MI
LISREL MODEL FOR SUBJECTIVE AND OBJECTIVE SOCIAL CLASS    BLACKS
DA NI=7 NO=368
LA FI=EX94.DAT;KM FI=EX94.DAT;SD FI=EX94.DAT
MO
LE;OBJCLASS
LK;SBJCLASS
FR TE 2 1; FI LY 1 LX 1; VA 1 LY 1 LX 1
OU
```

See Sörbom and Jöreskog (1981) for several other models and hypotheses that may be considered for these data.

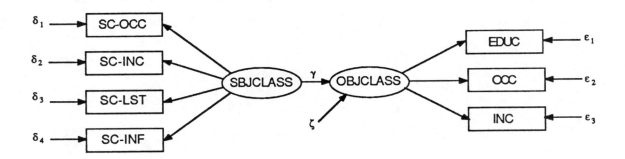

Figure 9.2: Path Diagram for Subjective and Objective Social Class

Table 9.5: Correlations, Means and Standard Deviations for Indicators of Objective Class and Subjective Class. Correlations for Whites Below Diagonal and for Blacks Above Diagonal. N(Whites) = 432; N(Blacks) = 368.

Variables	y_1	y_2	y_3	x_1	x_2	x_3	x_4	Mean (s.d.)
EDUC	—	.404	.268	.216	.233	.211	.207	1.274 (1.106)
OCC	.495	—	.220	.277	.183	.270	.157	2.347 (1.622)
INC	.398	.292	—	.268	.424	.325	.282	4.041 (2.097)
SC-OCC	.218	.282	.184	—	.550	.574	.482	1.288 (0.747)
SC-INC	.299	.166	.383	.386	—	.647	.517	1.129 (0.814)
SC-LST	.272	.161	.321	.396	.553	—	.647	1.235 (0.786)
SC-INF	.269	.169	.191	.382	.456	.534	—	1.318 (0.859)
Mean (s.d.)	1.655 (1.203)	3.670 (2.128)	5.040 (2.198)	1.543 (0.640)	1.548 (0.670)	1.542 (0.623)	1.601 (0.624)	

Chapter 10

LISREL WITH MEAN STRUCTURES

10.1 The Extended LISREL Model

In Chapter 1 the LISREL model was defined by (1.1), (1.2) and (1.3) in which all random variables were assumed to have zero means. This assumption will now be relaxed and the model will be extended to include four new parameter matrices in addition to the previous eight. These new parameter matrices contain intercept terms in the relationships and mean values of the latent variables.

The LISREL model is now defined by the following three equations corresponding to (1.1), (1.2) and (1.3), respectively:

$$\boldsymbol{\eta} = \boldsymbol{\alpha} + \mathbf{B}\boldsymbol{\eta} + \boldsymbol{\Gamma}\boldsymbol{\xi} + \boldsymbol{\zeta} \,, \tag{10.1}$$

$$\mathbf{y} = \boldsymbol{\tau}_y + \boldsymbol{\Lambda}_y \boldsymbol{\eta} + \boldsymbol{\epsilon} \,, \tag{10.2}$$

$$\mathbf{x} = \boldsymbol{\tau}_x + \boldsymbol{\Lambda}_x \boldsymbol{\xi} + \boldsymbol{\delta} \,, \tag{10.3}$$

where $\boldsymbol{\alpha}$, $\boldsymbol{\tau}_y$, and $\boldsymbol{\tau}_x$ are vectors of constant intercept terms. As before, we assume that $\boldsymbol{\zeta}$ is uncorrelated with $\boldsymbol{\xi}$, $\boldsymbol{\epsilon}$ is uncorrelated with $\boldsymbol{\eta}$ and that $\boldsymbol{\delta}$ is uncorrelated with $\boldsymbol{\xi}$. We also assume, as before, that $E(\boldsymbol{\zeta}) = \mathbf{0}$, $E(\boldsymbol{\epsilon}) = \mathbf{0}$ and $E(\boldsymbol{\delta}) = \mathbf{0}$, but it is not assumed that $E(\boldsymbol{\xi})$ and $E(\boldsymbol{\eta})$ are zero (E is the expected value operator). The mean of $\boldsymbol{\xi}$, $E(\boldsymbol{\xi})$, will be a parameter denoted by $\boldsymbol{\kappa}$. The mean of $\boldsymbol{\eta}$, $E(\boldsymbol{\eta})$, is obtained by taking the expectation of (10.1):

$$E(\boldsymbol{\eta}) = (\mathbf{I} - \mathbf{B})^{-1}(\boldsymbol{\alpha} + \boldsymbol{\Gamma}\boldsymbol{\kappa}) \,. \tag{10.4}$$

By taking the expectations of (10.2) and (10.3), we find the mean vectors of the observed variables to be

$$\boldsymbol{\mu}_y = \boldsymbol{\tau}_y + \boldsymbol{\Lambda}_y(\mathbf{I} - \mathbf{B})^{-1}(\boldsymbol{\alpha} + \boldsymbol{\Gamma}\boldsymbol{\kappa}) \,, \tag{10.5}$$

$$\boldsymbol{\mu}_x = \boldsymbol{\tau}_x + \boldsymbol{\Lambda}_x \boldsymbol{\kappa} \,. \tag{10.6}$$

245

Table 10.1: Additional Parameter Matrices in LISREL

Name	Notation	Order	LISREL Name	Default Form	Default Mode
TAU-Y	τ_y	NYx1	TY	ZE	FI
TAU-X	τ_x	NXx1	TX	ZE	FI
ALPHA	α	NEx1	AL	ZE	FI
KAPPA	κ	NKx1	KA	ZE	FI

In general, in a single population, all the mean parameters τ_y, τ_x, α, and κ will not be identified without further conditions imposed. However, in simultaneous analysis of data from several groups, simple conditions (see Jöreskog and Sörbom, 1985) can be imposed to make all the mean parameters identified.

The LISREL model with mean structures introduces four new parameter matrices (actually vectors): τ_y, τ_x, α, and κ. These parameter matrices can be referred to in the same way as with the other parameter matrices in LISREL. The LISREL notation and default forms for these are shown in Table 10.1. Each of these parameter matrices is fixed at zero (ZE) by default. They will be included in the model as soon as they are explicitly mentioned on the MO line. They can be declared either fixed (FI), free (FR), or invariant (IN).

The fit function for the extended LISREL model with mean parameters is defined as

$$F = \sum_{g=1}^{G} \frac{N_g}{N} F_g ,$$ (10.7)

where

$$F_g = \frac{1}{2}(\mathbf{s}^{(g)} - \boldsymbol{\sigma}^{(g)})'\mathbf{W}_{(g)}^{-1}(\mathbf{s}^{(g)} - \boldsymbol{\sigma}^{(g)}) + \frac{1}{2}(\bar{\mathbf{z}}^{(g)} - \boldsymbol{\mu}^{(g)})'\mathbf{V}_{(g)}^{-1}(\bar{\mathbf{z}}^{(g)} - \boldsymbol{\mu}^{(g)})$$ (10.8)

and $\boldsymbol{\mu}^{(g)} = (\boldsymbol{\mu}_y^{(g)}, \boldsymbol{\mu}_x^{(g)})'$.

The first term in (10.8) is the same as (1.20). The second term involves the sample mean vector $\bar{\mathbf{z}}^{(g)}$, the population mean vector $\boldsymbol{\mu}^{(g)}$, a function of parameters by (10.5) and (10.6), and the weight matrix $\mathbf{V}_{(g)}$ defined as

- $\mathbf{V}_{(g)} = \mathbf{S}^{(g)}$ for ULS

- $\mathbf{V}_{(g)} = \mathbf{S}^{(g)}$ for GLS

- $\mathbf{V}_{(g)} = \hat{\boldsymbol{\Sigma}}^{(g)}$ for ML

- $\mathbf{V}_{(g)} = \mathbf{S}^{(g)}$ for DWLS

- $\mathbf{V}_{(g)} = \mathbf{S}^{(g)}$ for WLS

It should be noted that if τ_y, τ_x, α, and κ are all default, the second term in (10.8) is a constant independent of parameters, in which case the problem reduces to that described in Chapter 9 and no mean structures are needed. One can also specify SP, SS, PS, or IN for these matrices as in Section 9.2.

If the observed variables have a multivariate normal distribution it will be shown in Volume II that the ML case defined above yields maximum likelihood estimates in the sense of maximizing the multinormal likelihood function. Under the same assumption, ML and GLS give asymptotically efficient estimators. The fit function (10.7) may be justified under the more general assumption that $\bar{z}^{(g)}$ and $\mathbf{S}^{(g)}$ are asymptotically uncorrelated. This holds, in particular, if the observed variables have no skewness.

10.2 Estimation of Factor Means

Although the mean of a latent variable is undefined (not identified) in a single group, group differences in the means of latent variables can be estimated if the latent variables are on the same scale in all groups. Sörbom (1974) extended the classical model of factorial invariance (Meredith, 1964; Jöreskog, 1971a) so that factor means could also be estimated. Sörbom's model is a LISREL Submodel 1 with mean structures defined as follows

$$\mathbf{x}^{(g)} = \boldsymbol{\tau}_x + \boldsymbol{\Lambda}_x \boldsymbol{\xi}^{(g)} + \boldsymbol{\delta}^{(g)}, g = 1, 2, \ldots, G \,,$$

with the mean of $\boldsymbol{\xi}^{(g)} = \boldsymbol{\kappa}^{(g)}$. To define the origins and the units of measurement of the ξ-factors, one can set $\boldsymbol{\kappa}^{(G)} = \mathbf{0}$ and fix one non-zero value in each column of $\boldsymbol{\Lambda}_x$. The parameters to be estimated are

- $\boldsymbol{\tau}_x, \boldsymbol{\Lambda}_x$ assumed to be invariant over groups
- $\boldsymbol{\kappa}^{(1)}, \boldsymbol{\kappa}^{(2)}, \ldots, \boldsymbol{\kappa}^{(G-1)}$ mean vectors of $\boldsymbol{\xi}$
- $\boldsymbol{\Phi}^{(1)}, \boldsymbol{\Phi}^{(2)}, \ldots, \boldsymbol{\Phi}^{(G)}$ covariance matrices of $\boldsymbol{\xi}$
- $\boldsymbol{\Theta}_\delta{}^{(1)}, \boldsymbol{\Theta}_\delta{}^{(2)}, \ldots, \boldsymbol{\Theta}_\delta{}^{(G)}$ error covariance matrices

The error covariance matrices in $\boldsymbol{\Theta}_\delta$ may be postulated to be invariant over groups, if desired. In most cases these matrices are diagonal.

Example 10.1: Nine Psychological Variables with Factor Means

Sörbom (1974) used nine selected variables from the classical study of Holzinger and Swineford (1939) to illustrate his methodology. The nine variables were selected to measure three latent factors: Space, Verbal, and Memory. The groups consist of eighth-grade children from two schools in Chicago: the Pasteur and the Grant-White schools. The children from each school were divided into two groups according to whether they scored above or below the median on a speeded addition test. Thus the groups are:

1. Pasteur Low ($N_1 = 77$)

2. Pasteur High ($N_2 = 79$)

3. Grant-White Low ($N_3 = 74$)

4. Grant-White High ($N_4 = 71$).

The variables, correlations, standard deviations, and means are given in Table 10.2. The standard deviations and means have been scaled so that the weighted estimate (9.8) of the within groups covariance matrix is a correlation matrix.

Table 10.2: Nine Psychological Variables: Correlations, Means and Standard Deviations

Correlations

| | | | | | Group 1 above main diagonal | | | | |
| | | | | | Group 2 below main diagonal | | | | |
	1	2	3	4	5	6	7	8	9
Visual Perception	—	.32	.48	.28	.26	.40	.42	.12	.23
Cubes	.24	—	.33	.01	.01	.26	.32	.05	-.04
Paper Form Board	.23	.22	—	.06	.01	.10	.22	.03	.01
General Information	.32	.05	.23	—	.75	.60	.15	-.08	-.05
Sentence Completion	.35	.23	.18	.68	—	.63	.07	.06	.10
Word Classification	.36	.10	.11	.59	.66	—	.36	.19	.24
Figure Recognition	.22	.01	-.07	.09	.11	.12	—	.29	.19
Object-Number	-.02	-.01	-.13	.05	.08	.03	.19	—	.38
Number-Figure	.09	-.14	-.06	.16	.02	.12	.15	.29	—

| | | | | | Group 3 above main diagonal | | | | |
| | | | | | Group 4 below main diagonal | | | | |
	1	2	3	4	5	6	7	8	9
Visual Perception	—	.34	.41	.38	.40	.42	.35	.16	.35
Cubes	.32	—	.21	.32	.16	.13	.27	.01	.27
Paper Form Board	.34	.18	—	.31	.24	.35	.30	.09	.09
General Information	.31	.24	.31	—	.69	.55	.17	.31	.34
Sentence Completion	.22	.16	.29	.62	—	.65	.20	.30	.27
Word Classification	.27	.20	.32	.57	.61	—	.31	.34	.27
Figure Recognition	.48	.31	.32	.18	.20	.29	—	.31	.38
Object-Number	.20	.01	.15	.06	.19	.15	.36	—	.38
Number-Figure	.42	.28	.40	.11	.07	.18	.35	.44	—

| | Standard Deviations | | | | Means | | | |
	1	2	3	4	1	2	3	4
Visual Perception	1.06	0.96	0.95	1.03	4.20	4.30	4.29	4.21
Cubes	1.20	0.86	1.03	0.86	5.25	5.03	5.32	5.33
Paper Form Board	1.02	0.99	0.92	1.06	4.96	5.06	5.02	5.09
General Information	1.03	0.96	0.99	1.01	2.98	3.41	3.72	4.15
Sentence Completion	1.08	1.06	0.96	0.91	3.20	3.38	3.78	3.88
Word Classification	0.99	1.01	0.95	1.05	4.45	4.76	5.17	5.59
Figure Recognition	1.17	1.01	0.81	0.98	13.42	13.62	13.70	13.72
Object-Number	1.00	1.10	0.83	1.04	1.74	2.14	1.30	1.78
Number-Figure	1.04	1.00	0.88	1.07	2.10	2.16	1.87	2.44

The nine labels are stored in the file EX101.LAB (note the blank spaces):

```
(9A8) Labels for Nine Psychological Variables
Vis PercCubes   Pap F B Gen InfoSent ComWord ClaFig Rec Obj Num Num Fig
```

All the remaining data are stored in the file EX101.DAT in the order: correlations for group 1, standard deviations for group 1, means for group 1, correlations for group 2, standard deviations for group 2, etc. In the labels file above and the data file below, we use FORTRAN formats to record the data. Each group of data begins with a format line. After the last right parenthesis in the format, one can write any text. This can be used to identify the particular part of the data for which the format is intended. After the format follows the data. The file EX101.DAT looks like this:

```
(9F3.2) Group 1: Pasteur low : Correlations
100
 32100
 48 33100
 28 01 06100
 26 01 01 75100
 40 26 10 60 63100
 42 32 22 15 07 36100
 12 05 03-08 06 19 29100
 23-04 01-05 10 24 19 38100
(9F3.2) Group 1: Pasteur low : Standard deviations
106120102103108 99117100104
(9F4.2) Group 1: Pasteur low : Means
 420 525 496 298 320 4451342 174 210
(9F3.2) Group 2: Pasteur high : Correlations
100
 24100
 23 22100
 32 05 23100
 35 23 18 68100
 36 10 11 59 66100
 22 01-07 09 11 12100
-02-01-13 05 08 03 19100
 09-14-06 16 02 12 15 29100
(9F3.2) Group 2: Pasteur high : Standard deviations
 96 86 99 96106101101110100
(9F4.2) Group 2: Pasteur high : Means
 430 503 506 341 338 4761362 214 216
```

```
(9F3.2) Group 3: Grant-White low : Correlations
100
 34100
 41 21100
 38 32 31100
 40 16 24 69100
 42 13 35 55 65100
 35 27 30 17 20 31100
 16 01 09 31 30 34 31100
 35 27 09 34 27 27 38 38100
(9F3.2) Group 3: Grant-White low : Standard deviations
 95103 92 99 96 95 81 83 88
(9F4.2) Group 3: Grant-White low : Means
 429 532 502 372 378 5171370 130 187
(9F3.2) Group 4: Grant-White high : Correlations
100
 32100
 34 18100
 31 24 31100
 22 16 29 62100
 27 20 32 57 61100
 48 31 32 18 20 29100
 20 01 15 06 19 15 36100
 42 28 40 11 07 18 35 44100
(9F3.2) Group 4: Grant-White high : Standard deviations
103 86106101 91105 98104107
(9F4.2) Group 4: Grant-White high : Means
 421 533 509 415 388 5591372 178 244
```

The model used here is that outlined previously with Λ_x and Θ_δ invariant over groups. The input file is shown on the next page. The first line for each group is a title line. The DA line for the first group specifies the number of groups by NG=4. The next line actually contains 4 control lines; see Section 2.1. These lines tell the program to read the correlations (KM), the standard deviations (SD), the means (ME), and the labels (LA) in that order. As the correlation matrix in the data file has been recorded with one row per line, the keyword SY on the KM line is essential; otherwise, the program would expect the correlations as one long line. The file EX101.LAB will be rewound after it has been read, so that the same labels can be read again for the next group. Note that the Rewind command only applies to the file EX101.LAB not to the file EX101.DAT.

The next five lines specify the model for the first group. The model includes the parameter matrices τ_x, κ, Λ_x, Φ, and Θ_δ. LX, PH, and TD are default, TX is declared free for the first group and is declared invariant for the other groups, and KA is specified as fixed for the first group and free for the others. The OU line for the first group requests t-values (TV), standardized solution (SS), and 2 decimals (ND=2). Note that this information is automatically carried onto the OU line for groups 2 - 4. Similarly, the information on the MO line for the second group is automatically carried onto the MO lines for groups 3 and 4. For the same reason, only the NO parameter needs to be specified on the DA line for groups 2, 3, and 4. The general rule is that all parameters which have the same value as in the previous group need not be specified. However, labels should be given for each group even if they are the same.

```
Holzinger-Swineford Data : LX and TD invariant : PASTEUR Low
DA NI=9 NG=4 NO=77
KM SY FI=EX101.DAT;SD FI=EX101.DAT;ME FI=EX101.DAT;LA FI=EX101.LAB Rewind
MO NX=9 NK=3 TX=FR KA=FI
LK
Space Verbal Memory
PA LX
3(1 0 0) 3(0 1 0) 3(0 0 1)
FI LX 1 1 LX 4 2 LX 7 3
VA 1 LX 1 1 LX 4 2 LX 7 3
OU TV SS ND=2
Holzinger-Swineford Data : LX and TD invariant : PASTEUR High
DA NO=79
KM SY FI=EX101.DAT;SD FI=EX101.DAT;ME FI=EX101.DAT;LA FI=EX101.LAB Rewind
MO LX=IN TX=IN KA=FR TD=IN
LK
Space Verbal Memory
OU
Holzinger-Swineford Data : LX and TD invariant : GRANT-WHITE Low
DA NO=74
KM SY FI=EX101.DAT;SD FI=EX101.DAT;ME FI=EX101.DAT;LA FI=EX101.LAB Rewind
MO
LK
Space Verbal Memory
OU
Holzinger-Swineford Data : LX and TD invariant : GRANT-WHITE High
DA NO=71
KM SY FI=EX101.DAT;SD FI=EX101.DAT;ME FI=EX101.DAT;LA FI=EX101.LAB Rewind
MO
LK
Space Verbal Memory
OU
```

The maximum likelihood solution is shown in Table 10.3. The scaled factor means have been computed such that the weighted mean (weighted by sample size) over the groups is zero for each factor. Mean profiles are given in Figure 10.1.

It is seen that the profiles are similar within schools, with those scoring high on the addition test at a higher level. The spatial ability does not differentiate the groups. For verbal ability, there is a difference between schools, with students from Grant-White being superior. This reflects the fact that the Pasteur school "enrolls children of factory workers, a large percentage of whom were foreign-born and the Grant-White school enrolls children in a middle-class suburban area" (Meredith, 1964). With regard to the memory factor, both groups of the Pasteur school seem superior to the groups of the Grant-White school, although the difference between the high groups is small.

Table 10.3: Maximum Likelihood Estimates for Nine Psychological Variables with Factor Means

Solution Standardized to Common Metric
Factor Loadings

Test	Space	Verbal	Memory	Error Variance	Intercept
Visual Perception	0.72	0	0	0.48	4.20
Cubes	0.43	0	0	0.82	5.20
Paper Form Board	0.52	0	0	0.73	5.00
General Information	0	0.83	0	0.34	3.06
Sentence Completion	0	0.79	0	0.32	3.08
Word Classification	0	0.79	0	0.43	4.51
Figure Recognition	0	0	0.47	0.75	13.56
Object-Number	0	0	0.57	0.70	1.68
Number- Figure	0	0	0.61	0.63	2.07

Factor Covariance Matrices

School	Low Level			High Level		
Pasteur	1.37			0.72		
	0.44	1.12		0.51	1.03	
	0.58	0.24	1.16	0.04	0.20	0.93
Grant-White	0.90			1.02		
	0.63	0.92		0.54	0.92	
	0.54	0.52	0.59	0.96	0.33	1.33

Factor Means / Scaled Factor Means

	Factor Means			Scaled Factor Means		
	Space	Verbal	Memory	Space	Verbal	Memory
Pasteur Low	0.00	0.00	0.00	-0.05	-0.49	-0.06
Pasteur High	0.05	0.32	0.18	0.00	-0.17	0.12
Grant-White Low	0.09	0.70	-0.14	0.04	0.21	-0.20
Grant-White High	0.06	1.01	0.19	0.01	0.52	0.13

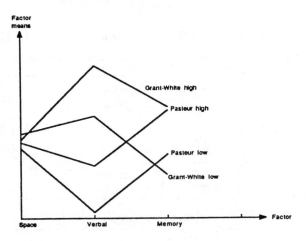

Figure 10.1: Factor Mean Profiles

Example 10.2: Head Start Summer Program

Sörbom (1981) reanalyzed some data from the Head Start summer program previously reanalyzed by Magidson (1977). Sörbom used data on 303 white children consisting of a Head Start sample (N = 148) and a matched Control sample (N = 155). The correlations, standard deviations and means are given in Table 10.4. The children were matched on sex and kindergarten attendance but no attempt had been made to match on social status variables. The variables used in Sörbom's reanalysis were

$x_1 =$ *Mother's education*

$x_2 =$ *Father's education*

$x_3 =$ *Father's occupation*

$x_4 =$ *Family income*

$y_1 =$ *Score on the Metropolitan Readiness Test*

$y_2 =$ *Score on the Illinois Test of Psycholinguistic Abilities*

We want to do the following:

A *Test whether x_1, x_2, x_3 and x_4 can be regarded as indicators of a single construct, $\xi =$ "Socioeconomic status," for both groups. Is the measurement model the same for both groups? Is there a difference in the mean of ξ between groups?*

B *Assuming that y_1 and y_2 can be used as indicators of another construct $\eta =$ "cognitive ability," test whether the same measurement model applies to both groups. Test the hypothesis of no difference in the mean of η between groups.*

C *Estimate the structural equation*

$$\eta = \alpha + \gamma \xi + \zeta .$$

Is γ the same for the two groups? Test the hypothesis $\alpha = 0$. Interpret the results.

Table 10.4: Correlations, Standard Deviations and Means for the Head Start Data

							St. Dev.	Means
Head Start Group								
Variable			Correlations				St. Dev.	Means
x_1	1.000						1.332	3.520
x_2	.441	1.000					1.281	3.081
x_3	.220	.203	1.000				1.075	2.088
x_4	.304	.182	.377	1.000			2.648	5.358
y_1	.274	.265	.208	.084	1.000		3.764	19.672
y_2	.270	.122	.251	.198	.664	1.000	2.677	9.562
Control Group								
Variable			Correlations				St. Dev.	Means
x_1	1.000						1.360	3.839
x_2	.484	1.000					1.195	3.290
x_3	.224	.342	1.000				1.193	2.600
x_4	.268	.215	.387	1.000			3.239	6.435
y_1	.230	.215	.196	.115	1.000		3.900	20.415
y_2	.265	.297	.234	.162	.635	1.000	2.719	10.070

The data file EX102.DAT is

```
1 .441 1 .22 .203 1 .304 .182 .377 1 .274 .265 .208 .084 1
.27 .122 .251 .198 .664 1
1.332 1.281 1.075 2.648 3.764 2.677
3.52 3.081 2.088 5.358 19.672 9.562
MOTHEDUC FATHEDUC FATHOCCU FAMILINC MRT ITPA
5 6 1 2 3 4
1 .484 1 .224 .342 1 .268 .215 .387 1 .23 .215 .196 .115 1
.265 .297 .234 .162 .635 1
1.36 1.195 1.193 3.239 3.9 2.719
3.839 3.29 2.6 6.435 20.415 10.070
MOTHEDUC FATHEDUC FATHOCCU FAMILINC MRT ITPA
5 6 1 2 3 4
```

Consider the measurement model for the four social status indicators x_1, x_2, x_3, and x_4. The model assumes that the x-variables can be accounted for by a single common factor ξ:

$$x_i^{(g)} = \tau_i + \lambda_i \xi^{(g)} + \delta_i^{(g)}, i = 1, 2, 3, 4 .$$

The superscript, g, is running over the two groups, g = 1 for Head Start children and g = 2 for control children. There is no superscript for τ and λ, since we are using the same observed variables in the two groups. Our main interest is in the mean κ of ξ. Assuming $E(\delta_i^{(g)}) = 0$, we find

$$E(x_i^{(g)}) = \tau_i + \lambda_i \kappa \ .$$

If we add a constant, c say, to κ this can be compensated for by subtracting $\lambda_i c$ from τ_i. This means that κ and τ_i cannot be identified simultaneously or phrased in other words: there is no definite origin for the construct ξ. All we can do is to estimate differences among groups, i.e., we can specify the mean of ξ to be zero in the control group, and then κ is the mean difference in social status between the experiment group and the control group.

The input file for problem A can be patterned after the previous example. We leave it as an exercise.

For problem A we get an overall χ^2 measure of goodness-of-fit of the model equal to 35.9 with 10 degrees of freedom, indicating that the fit of the model is not very good. An examination of the modification indices reveals that there might be a correlation between the errors δ_1 and δ_2, i.e., when the correlation among the observed variables caused by the construct ξ has been accounted for, there seems to be a correlation left between x_1 and x_2. This correlation can be interpreted as an indication that parents' education levels correlate more than can be explained by social status. By adding the covariance θ_{21} we get a model with an acceptable fit, χ^2 with 8 degrees of freedom equals 6.5. The difference in degrees of freedom from the previous model is 2, since we have added two parameters, namely the covariances $\theta_{21}^{(1)}$ and $\theta_{21}^{(2)}$ in the two groups. The estimates and their estimated standard errors are given in Table 10.5. It is seen that the groups differ significantly in social status, the difference is 0.340 with a standard error equal to 0.096. λ_1 has been fixed to 1 in order to specify the scale of ξ.

As criteria, Magidson (1977), used two cognitive ability tests—the Metropolitan Readiness Test (MRT) and the Illinois Test of Psycholinguistic Abilities (ITPA). Magidson made separate analyses for the two tests, but here, as suggested by Bentler and Woodward (1978), we will use the two tests to define the construct cognitive ability. This model is the same as before, except that there are only two x-variables. As a matter of fact, the model has no degrees of freedom, so one can compute the estimates simply by equating the first and second order moments implied by the model to their observed counterparts. Also in cognitive ability the Head Start group is inferior to the Control group in the sense that the estimated mean difference is negative (-0.743). However, the difference is not significant, having a standard error equal to 0.440.

For problem C we use the combined model as depicted in Figure 10.2 where the main focus is on the structural equation

$$\eta^{(g)} = \alpha^{(g)} + \gamma^{(g)}\xi^{(g)} + \zeta^{(g)}.$$

Here ξ is "social status" and η is "cognitive ability." Just as we could not previously find an absolute origin for ξ there is no way to find an absolute origin for η either. All we can do is to compare groups and look at differences. For example, we could fix α in the Control group to be zero, and then α in the Head Start group could be interpreted as the effect of the Head Start program when social status has been controlled for.

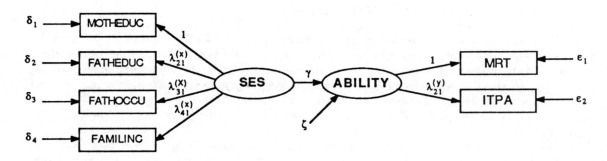

Figure 10.2: Head Start: Model for Problem C

Table 10.5: Head Start: Estimates for the Measurement Model for Social Status

	Head Start Group	Common Parameters	Control Group
$\tau_1^{(x)}$		3.848 (0.092)	
$\tau_2^{(x)}$		3.326 (0.082)	
$\tau_3^{(x)}$		2.579 (0.091)	
$\tau_4^{(x)}$		6.463 (0.236)	
$\lambda_{21}^{(x)}$		0.864 (0.163)	
$\lambda_{31}^{(x)}$		1.384 (0.290)	
$\lambda_{41}^{(x)}$		3.305 (0.684)	
$\theta_{11}^{(\delta)}$	1.494 (0.190)		1.554 (0.200)
$\theta_{22}^{(\delta)}$	1.473 (0.183)		1.154 (0.149)
$\theta_{33}^{(\delta)}$	0.715 (0.137)		0.789 (0.164)
$\theta_{44}^{(\delta)}$	4.305 (0.799)		6.942 (1.127)
$\theta_{21}^{(\delta)}$	0.534 (0.143)		0.500 (0.134)
κ	-0.340 (0.096)		0.0
ϕ	0.242 (0.092)		0.329 (0.121)

Standard Error Estimates within Parentheses

The input for problem C is

```
HEAD START SUMMER PROGRAM: EXPERIMENTALS
DA NI=6 NOBS=149 NG=2
KM FI=EX102.DAT;SD FI=EX102.DAT;ME FI=EX102.DAT
LA FI=EX102.DAT
SE FI=EX102.DAT
MO NX=4 NK=1 NY=2 NE=1 LX=FR LY=FR TY=FR TX=FR AL=FR KA=FR TD=SY
LE
ABILITY
LK
STATUS
FR TD 2 1
FI LX 1 LY 1
VA 1 LX 1 LY 1
OU SE TV MI
HEAD START SUMMER PROGRAM:  CONTROLS
DA NOBS=156
KM FI=EX102.DAT;SD FI=EX102.DAT;ME FI=EX102.DAT
LA FI=EX102.DAT
SE FI=EX102.DAT
MO LX=IN TX=IN LY=IN TY=IN GA=IN TD=SP AL=FI KA=FI
LE
ABILITY
LK
STATUS
OU
```

The χ^2 for the combined model equals 27.52 with 22 degrees of freedom so the fit of the model is acceptable. An examination of the γ parameters in the two groups shows that they are probably equal, since $\hat{\gamma}^{(1)} = 2.296$ and $\hat{\gamma}^{(2)} = 2.027$ with estimated standard errors equal to 0.741 and 0.625, respectively. Thus, the final model is a model with the γ's constrained to be equal. The χ^2 for this model is 27.64 with 23 degrees of freedom. The difference in χ^2 for the last two models can be used as a test of the hypothesis that the γ's are equal. χ^2 with 1 degree of freedom is 0.12 and thus we can treat the γ's as equal. As the slopes are parallel, it is meaningful to talk about α as a measure of the effect of Head Start. The estimates of the model are given in Table 10.6. There seems to be no significant effect for the Head Start program when controlling for social status, although the inclusion of social class has changed the negative effect to be positive. The estimate of α is 0.183 with a standard error equal to 0.377.

In the more general case, when there are more than two groups and/or more than one dependent variable, one can test the hypothesis of no effect by re-estimation of the model with the restriction $\alpha^{(g)} = 0$ added, and then compare the χ^2's. In the above case we obtain χ^2 equal to 27.87 with 24 degrees of freedom. Thus the test of no effect results in a χ^2 with 1 degree of freedom equal to 0.23, which in this case is the same as the square of the estimate of α divided by its standard error.

Table 10.6: Head Start: Estimates for the Combined Model

	Head Start Group	Common Parameters	Control Group
$\tau_1^{(x)}$		3.869 (0.094)	
$\tau_2^{(x)}$		3.339 (0.083)	
$\tau_3^{(x)}$		2.573 (0.090)	
$\tau_4^{(x)}$		6.420 (0.228)	
$\tau_1^{(y)}$		20.357 (0.286)	
$\tau_2^{(y)}$		10.085 (0.216)	
$\lambda_{21}^{(x)}$		0.853 (0.143)	
$\lambda_{31}^{(x)}$		1.207 (0.221)	
$\lambda_{41}^{(x)}$		2.756 (0.515)	
$\lambda_{21}^{(y)}$		0.850 (0.141)	
$\theta_{11}^{(\delta)}$	1.417 (0.186)		1.467 (0.194)
$\theta_{22}^{(\delta)}$	1.438 (0.182)		1.085 (0.144)
$\theta_{33}^{(\delta)}$	0.714 (0.125)		0.839 (0.147)
$\theta_{44}^{(\delta)}$	4.619 (0.736)		7.448 (1.059)
$\theta_{11}^{(\epsilon)}$	6.308 (1.527)		7.321 (1.593)
$\theta_{22}^{(\epsilon)}$	1.471 (0.983)		1.645 (0.999)
$\theta_{21}^{(\delta)}$	0.481 (0.140)		0.422 (0.129)
γ		2.136 (0.549)	
α	0.183 (0.377)		0.0
ϕ	0.315 (0.106)		0.405(0.131)
ψ	6.347 (1.474)		6.185(1.465)
κ	-0.382 (0.103)		0.0

Standard Error Estimates within Parentheses

10.3 Incomplete Data Problems

Incomplete data is a common problem in social science investigations; see Rubin (1976) for the basic statistical issues involved and Afifi and Elashoff (1966) for various procedures for dealing with missing observations. In estimating models, researchers often need to combine data from two or more samples or subsamples, each with a somewhat different set of variables. Werts, Rock and Grandy (1979), Muthén and Jöreskog (1983), Muthén, Kaplan, and Hollis (1987), and Allison (1987), among others, have considered using LISREL's multisample option to deal with incomplete data problems. The following interesting example was provided by Allison (1987).

Table 10.7: Means and Covariance Matrices for Measures of Father's Occupation and Education

	Father's Occupation		Father's Education	
	x_1	x_2	x_3	x_4
Complete Data Subsample				
x_1	180.90			
x_2	126.77	217.56		
x_3	23.96	30.20	16.24	
x_4	22.86	30.47	14.36	15.13
Mean	16.62	17.39	6.65	6.75
Incomplete Data Subsample				
x_1	217.27			
x_2	0.00	1.00		
x_3	25.57	0.00	16.16	
x_4	0.00	0.00	0.00	1.00
Mean	16.98	0.00	6.83	0.00

Data on y_2 and y_4 are missing
in the incomplete data sample

Example 10.3: Estimating a Correlation From Incomplete Data

"Suppose the aim is to estimate the correlation between father's occupational status (FAOC) and father's educational attainment (FAED) for black men in the U.S. Using a sample 2020, Bielby et al. (1977a) estimated that correlation to be 0.433. They recognized, however, that this correlation may be attenuated by random measurement error. To estimate and possibly correct for this error, they took a random subsample of 348 black males from the original sample of 2020 and reinterviewed them approximately three weeks later. Consequently, their original sample can be divided into two groups: a small subsample of 348 with complete data and a larger subsample 1672 with incomplete data" (Allison, 1987, p.84). Therefore, the complete data sample has two indicators x_1 and x_2 of FAOC and two indicators x_3 and x_4 of FAED, whereas the incomplete data sample has only data on x_1 and x_3. The design of the study suggests that the missing data are missing at random.

Table 10.7 gives sample variances, covariances, and means for the two groups. For the missing variables, pseudo values of 1 have been entered for the variances and pseudo values of 0 for the covariances and the means. The use of such pseudo values was suggested originally by Jöreskog (1971a). Allison (1987) showed that, when combined with pseudo values for appropriate parameters, such pseudo values still produce correct ML estimates in LISREL. Allison used LISREL 6 and analyzed moment matrices as described in the next section. Here we use the extended LISREL model as this is much easier.

The model is a Submodel 1 with parameters τ_x, Λ_x, Φ, and Θ_δ:

$$\tau_x = \begin{pmatrix} x \\ x \\ x \\ x \end{pmatrix} \quad \Lambda_x = \begin{pmatrix} 1 & 0 \\ x & 0 \\ 0 & 1 \\ 0 & x \end{pmatrix} \quad \Phi = \begin{pmatrix} x & \\ x & x \end{pmatrix} \quad \Theta_\delta = diag \begin{pmatrix} x \\ x \\ x \\ x \end{pmatrix}$$

The two latent variables ξ_1 and ξ_2 represent true FAOC and FAED, respectively. The two 1's in Λ_x define the scales for these. For the incomplete sample, we set $\tau_2^{(x)}$, $\tau_4^{(x)}$, $\lambda_{21}^{(x)}$ and $\lambda_{42}^{(x)}$ equal to 0 and $\theta_2^{(\delta)}$ and $\theta_4^{(\delta)}$ equal to 1. All free parameters are constrained to be equal across subsamples.

The input file is:

```
FATHER SES    COMPLETE DATA
DA NG=2 NI=4 NO=348
CM FI=EX103.DAT
ME FI=EX103.DAT
MO NX=4 NK=2 TX=FR
VA 1 LX 1 1 LX 3 2
FR LX 2 1 LX 4 2
MA PH
100 25 10
MA TX
16 16 6 6
OU SE SS
FATHERS SES      INCOMPLETE DATA
DA NO=1672
CM FI=EX103.DAT
ME FI=EX103.DAT
MO PH=IN
FI TX 2 TX 4 TD 2 TD 4
VA 1 LX 1 1 LX 3 2 TD 2 TD 4
EQ TX 1 1 1 TX 1
EQ TX 1 3 3 TX 3
EQ TD 1 1 1 TD 1
EQ TD 1 3 3 TD 3
MA TX
16 0 6 0
OU
```

As this is a somewhat unusual model, LISREL has problems generating good starting values. Starting values are therefore given for τ_x and Φ.

The results agree almost exactly with those reported by Allison (1987). The goodness-of-fit χ^2 is 7.74 with 15 degrees of freedom. However, the degrees of freedom are certainly incorrect because LISREL has counted the 9 pseudo values in the data as real data values. The correct degrees of freedom are 6. The value of χ^2 still represents a very good fit.

The estimated covariance between true FAOC and true FAED is 25.18 with a standard error of 1.41. This should be compared with the estimate 23.31 with a standard error of 3.13 obtained from the complete data sample alone. By using the incomplete data sample, the standard error is reduced to less than half. Thus, there is a major gain in precision by using all available data.

We may also compare estimated correlations between true FAOC and true FAED. Based on both samples, this is 0.62. This may be compared with the attenuated estimate of 0.43 reported by Bielby et al. (1977a).

10.4 Growth Curves

A general form of *the multivariate linear model* may be formulated as follows, see, e.g., Potthoff and Roy (1964). Rows of the data matrix $\mathbf{Y}$ of order $N \times p$ are independently distributed with the same covariance matrix $\mathbf{\Sigma}$ and with means of the form

$$E(\mathbf{Y}) = \mathbf{X\Xi P} \,, \tag{10.9}$$

where $\mathbf{X}(N \times q)$ and $\mathbf{P}(r \times p)$ are fixed design matrices of ranks q and r, respectively, and $\Xi(q \times r)$ is a matrix of parameters. If $r = p$ and $\mathbf{P}$ is nonsingular, this is a multivariate regression model with regression matrix $\mathbf{P}'\Xi'$, with elements which are linear functions of the parameters in Ξ.

This model can be specified in LISREL as a submodel 3A in the form of (10.1) and (10.2) with Fixed-x. Put $\mathbf{\Lambda}_y = \mathbf{P}'$, $\mathbf{\Gamma} = \Xi'$, $\mathbf{\Psi} = \mathbf{\Sigma}$ and leave $\boldsymbol{\tau}_y$, $\boldsymbol{\alpha}$, $\boldsymbol{\kappa}$, and $\mathbf{B}$ default.

This model is often used to estimate growth curves from panel data or longitudinal data in which the outcome variable is measured repeatedly on the same persons over several periods of time.

Consider a response variable y being measured on N individuals at T points in time $t_1, t_2, \ldots, t_T$. The raw data take the form of a data matrix $\mathbf{Y}$ of order $N \times T$, where y_{ij} is the observed measurement on individual i at time t_j. It is assumed that the rows of $\mathbf{Y}$ are independently distributed with the same covariance matrix $\mathbf{\Sigma}$. Also, the mean vectors of the rows are assumed to be the same, namely $\boldsymbol{\mu}' = (\mu_1, \mu_2, \ldots, \mu_T)$.

However, here we focus attention on the mean μ_t as a function of t. This gives a growth curve describing how the mean of y changes over time.

We consider polynomial growth curves of the form

$$\mu_t = \kappa_0 + \kappa_1 t + \kappa_2 t^2 + \cdots + \kappa_h t^h$$

or

$$\boldsymbol{\mu} = \begin{pmatrix} 1 & t_1 & t_1^2 & \cdots & t_1^h \\ 1 & t_2 & t_2^2 & \cdots & t_2^h \\ \vdots & \vdots & \vdots & \ddots & \vdots \\ 1 & t_T & t_T^2 & \cdots & t_T^h \end{pmatrix} \begin{pmatrix} \kappa_0 \\ \kappa_1 \\ \vdots \\ \kappa_h \end{pmatrix} . \tag{10.10}$$

The degree of the polynomial h is assumed to be less than or equal to $T - 1$. When $h < T - 1$, the mean vector $\boldsymbol{\mu}$ is constrained and there is not a one-to-one correspondence between μ_1, μ_2, $\ldots$, μ_T and the polynomial coefficients κ_0, κ_1, $\ldots$, κ_h. In this section we consider the estimation of these polynomial coefficients.

The above generalizes easily to the case of several groups of individuals with possibly different mean vectors. Suppose, for example, that there are two groups with n_1 and n_2 individuals in each group. Let the first n_1 rows of $\mathbf{Y}$ be the measurements on individuals in Group 1 and let the last n_2 rows be the measurements on individuals in Group 2. The growth curves for the two groups may differ, so we assume that there are two distinct growth curves to be estimated, that is,

$$E(y_{it}^{(g)}) = \kappa_0^{(g)} + \kappa_1^{(g)} t + \cdots + \kappa_h^{(g)} t^h, \qquad g = 1, 2 \,.$$

In multiple-group comparisons one may be interested in the following type of questions:

- Should the growth curves be represented by third-degree polynomials, say, or are quadratic or linear growth curves adequate?

- Should separate growth curves be used for different groups or do all groups have the same growth curve?

Often we conceive of the effect of treatment as represented by a parallel displacement of the whole growth curve for one group in relation to another. This cannot be taken for granted, however, but must be tested by means of data. In addition, growth curves can differ in terms of the degree of the polynomial but also in the shape for the same degree of polynomial. The covariance matrices Σ may be the same in different groups, or the correlation matrices may be the same and the standard deviations different, or the covariance matrices may be all different. The covariance matrices may also be structured in various ways.

Growth curves can be estimated more efficiently and tests about the growth curves will be more powerful if the covariance structure, which arises naturally in repeated measurements, is taken into account. This covariance structure very often has an autoregressive nature. Therefore, we focus attention to the deviation $e_t = y_t - \mu_t$ of y_t from its mean value μ_t on the growth curve and consider various autoregressive models for this.

The first-order autoregressive model is

$$e_t = \beta_t e_{t-1} + z_t \ , t = 2, 3, \ldots, T \ ,$$

where the residual z_t is uncorrelated with e_{t-1}. It is also assumed that $z_2, z_3, \ldots, z_T$ are all uncorrelated.

It is readily verified that

$$Cov(y_t, y_{t-1}) = E(e_t e_{t-1}) = \beta_t \sigma_{t-1}^2 \ ,$$

where

$$\sigma_{t-1}^2 = Var(y_{t-1}) = E(e_{t-1}^2) \ ,$$

and that

$$Cov(y_t, y_{t-k}) = \beta_t \beta_{t-1} \cdots \beta_{t-k+1} \sigma_{t-k}^2, \ k = 1, 2, \ldots$$

Hence, the covariance matrix of $\mathbf{y}$ is (in the case of $T = 4$)

$$\Sigma = \begin{pmatrix} \sigma_1^2 & & & \\ \beta_2 \sigma_1^2 & \sigma_2^2 & & \\ \beta_3 \beta_2 \sigma_1^2 & \beta_3 \sigma_2^2 & \sigma_3^2 & \\ \beta_4 \beta_3 \beta_2 \sigma_1^2 & \beta_4 \beta_3 \sigma_2^2 & \beta_4 \sigma_3^2 & \sigma_4^2 \end{pmatrix}$$

It is seen that Σ is constrained; its 10 variances are functions of only seven parameters. Since the variances are free parameters, it is the six covariances that are functions of the three parameters β_2, β_3, and β_4.

This model is the perfect Markov simplex mentioned in Section 6.6. If all $\beta_i = 1$, we have the perfect Wiener simplex, see Jöreskog (1970b). Higher-order autoregressive models may also be considered. For example, a second-order model has

$$e_t = \beta_{t,t-1} e_{t-1} + \beta_{t,t-2} e_{t-2} + z_t \ , \ t = 3, 4, \ldots, T \ .$$

The model can be estimated directly with LISREL using the following specification corresponding to (10.1) and (10.2):

$$\begin{pmatrix} e \\ \eta \end{pmatrix} = \begin{pmatrix} 0 \\ \kappa \end{pmatrix} + \begin{pmatrix} \mathbf{T}_\beta & 0 \\ 0 & 0 \end{pmatrix} \begin{pmatrix} e \\ \eta \end{pmatrix} + \begin{pmatrix} z \\ 0 \end{pmatrix} \qquad (10.11)$$

$$y = \begin{pmatrix} \mathbf{I} & \mathbf{P} \end{pmatrix} \begin{pmatrix} e \\ \eta \end{pmatrix} + 0 \,, \qquad (10.12)$$

where $\mathbf{T}_\beta$, in the case of a second-order autoregressive model, is a square matrix whose non-zero elements are the subdiagonal elements:

$$\beta_{21}, \beta_{31}, \beta_{32}, \beta_{42}, \beta_{43}, \beta_{53}, \beta_{54}, \ldots, \beta_{T,T-2}, \beta_{T,T-1} \,.$$

The matrix $\mathbf{P}$ is the fixed matrix of order $T \times (h+1)$ given in (10.10). When $\mathbf{T}_\beta$ is present in (10.11), the covariance matrix of z should be diagonal. The case of an unstructured Σ is obtained by setting $\mathbf{T}_\beta$ to zero and letting the covariance matrix of z be free.

Example 10.4: Berkeley Guidance Study

As an illustration of growth curve estimation, we use data on stature for boys and girls aged 3–7 ($T = 5$) from Tuddenham and Snyder (1954). The means, variances and covariances of the stature measurements for the two groups are given in Table 10.8.

We begin by testing the hypothesis that the covariance matrix of the measured variables are equal for boys and girls. This is done as in Example 9.1A. The means are not involved. The likelihood ratio test statistics gives $\chi^2 = 21.59$ with 15 degrees of freedom. The P-value is 0.12, so the hypothesis is not rejected.

Next, we test the hypothesis of equal mean vectors for boys and girls without assuming equal covariance matrices. For this we use Submodel 1 in the form of (10.3). Take $\Lambda_x = \mathbf{I}$ and $\Theta_\delta = \mathbf{0}$. Then the mean vector is τ_x and the covariance matrix is Φ. The input file for this is as follows.

```
Testing Equality of Mean Vectors. Input for Girls
DA NG=2 NI=5 NO=70
CM FI=GIRLS.COV
ME FI=GIRLS.MEA
MO NX=5 NK=5 TX=FR LX=ID TD=ZE
OU SE TV MI
Testing Equality of Mean Vectors. Input for Boys
DA NO=66
CM FI=BOYS.COV
ME FI=BOYS.MEA
MO TX=IN
OU
```

The test gives $\chi^2 = 25.87$ with 5 degrees of freedom, so the hypothesis is rejected. Boys and girls have different mean vectors.

We proceed by estimating a growth curve for boys and girls under the assumption that the covariance matrices are equal. The model is the one defined in (10.11) and (10.12) with $\mathbf{T}_\beta = 0$ and $Cov(z)$ equal in the two groups but otherwise unconstrained. We assume that the growth

Table 10.8: Berkeley Guidance Study

| | Observed and Fitted Means | | | | |
| | Age | | | | |
	3	4	5	6	7
Girls					
Observed	95.45	102.99	110.26	117.25	123.41
Fitted	95.46	102.95	110.27	117.18	123.39
Boys					
Observed	96.71	104.27	111.13	117.47	124.01
Fitted	96.70	104.32	111.11	117.54	124.03

Observed (Above) and Fitted (Below) Covariance Matrices

Girls

3	12.110				
	12.628				
4	12.454	15.132			
	12.570	14.504			
5	13.491	16.074	18.148		
	13.270	14.963	16.423		
6	14.061	16.424	18.567	20.612	
	14.134	15.757	17.379	19.793	
7	14.822	17.133	19.587	21.534	23.426
	15.051	16.592	18.408	20.663	22.461

Boys

3	13.177				
	12.628				
4	12.693	13.838			
	12.570	14.504			
5	13.055	13.784	14.592		
	13.270	14.963	16.423		
6	14.211	15.049	16.118	18.923	
	14.134	15.757	17.379	19.793	
7	15.294	16.018	17.156	19.738	21.437
	15.051	16.592	18.408	20.663	22.461

curves are cubic, i. e., $h = 3$. Measuring time as $age - 5$, the matrix $\mathbf{P}$ is (one can of course use orthogonal polynomials instead):

$$\mathbf{P} = \begin{pmatrix} 1 & -2 & 4 & -8 \\ 1 & -1 & 1 & -1 \\ 1 & 0 & 0 & 0 \\ 1 & 1 & 1 & 1 \\ 1 & 2 & 4 & 8 \end{pmatrix}$$

In LISREL we take $p=5$, $m=9$, $\Lambda_y = (\begin{array}{cc} \mathbf{I} & \mathbf{P} \end{array})$, $\Theta_\epsilon = 0$, $\alpha = $ a (9×1) vector, where the last four elements are the coefficients of the growth curve polynomial, $\mathbf{B}$ (9×9) $= 0$, and Ψ a 9×9 symmetric matrix where the last four rows are fixed zeros.

```
Estimating Third Degree Growth Curve for Girls
Assuming Sigma(Girls) = Sigma(Boys)
DA NG=2 NI=5 NO=70
CM FI=GIRLS.COV
ME FI=GIRLS.MEA
MO NY=5 NE=9 AL=FR PS=FI TE=ZE
MA LY
1 0 0 0 0 1 -2 4 -8
0 1 0 0 0 1 -1 1 -1
0 0 1 0 0 1  0 0  0
0 0 0 1 0 1  1 1  1
0 0 0 0 1 1  2 4  8
FI AL 1 - AL 5
FR PS 1 1 - PS 5 5
MA PS
12.110
12.454      15.132
13.491      16.074      18.148
14.061      16.424      18.567      20.612
14.822      17.133      19.587      21.534      23.426 /
OU NS SE TV RS AD=OFF
Estimating Third Degree Growth Curve for Boys
Assuming Sigma(Girls) = Sigma(Boys)
DA NO=66
CM FI=BOYS.COV
ME FI=BOYS.MEA
MO AL=PS LY=PS PS=IN
OU
```

Since NE is larger than NY, starting values must be provided and NS must be entered on the OU line. It is sufficient to provide starting values for the first five rows of Ψ for the first group. These starting values are taken to be the covariance matrix for girls. Note that the slash is necessary because Ψ is actually of order 9×9. Λ_y is the same fixed matrix in both groups. Ψ is specified to be invariant. The joint covariance matrix of boys and girls is in the upper left 5×5 submatrix of Ψ. All other elements of Ψ are fixed zeros. The polynomial coefficients are the last 4 elements of α. The first 5 elements of α are fixed zeros. AD is set off because Λ_y does not have full column rank and Ψ is not positive definite.

This model gives an overall χ^2 of 23.13 with 17 degrees of freedom. The P-value is 0.145. The polynomial growth curves are estimated as

$$\text{Girls}: \quad \mu_t = 110.278(0.487) + 7.165(0.119)t - 0.214(0.030)t^2 - 0.046(0.025)t^3 \qquad (10.13)$$

$$\text{Boys}: \quad \mu_t = 111.112(0.502) + 6.537(0.123)t - 0.186(0.031)t^2 + 0.074(0.025)t^3 \qquad (10.14)$$

The quantities in parentheses are the standard errors of the polynomial coefficients. Table 10.8 presents the observed and fitted means and the observed and fitted variances and covariances. It is seen that the differences between the observed and the fitted quantities are generally small so the overall fit of the model can be regarded as good.

Do boys and girls have the same growth curves? We can test this hypothesis by re-estimating the model under the constraint that the polynomial coefficients are the same and calculating the difference in χ^2-values. This gives $\chi^2 = 24.46$ with 4 degrees of freedom so the hypothesis is rejected. Inspection of the polynomial coefficients in (10.13) and (10.14) in relation to their standard errors suggest that each coefficient is different for boys and girls. Also, the coefficient κ_3 for girls is not significant. So a quatratic curve would be sufficient for girls. It looks like the two growth curves are entirely different. However, in the range of t from -2 to $+2$ ($t = \text{age} - 5$), the two curves are in fact close to each other.

Further analysis can be done by including $\mathbf{T}_\beta$ in (10.11) and letting $\boldsymbol{\Psi}$ be diagonal. A test of the Wiener simplex structure gives an overall $\chi^2 = 59.63$ with 27 degrees of freedom. Although the Wiener simplex is fairly consistent with the observed covariance matrices, the fit is not sufficiently good. A test of the Markov simplex gives $\chi^2 = 46.93$ with 23 degrees of freedom. This model does not fit the data either. For this data it seems best to retain the model with a joint but unstructured covariance matrix.

Chapter 11

TECHNICAL PARAMETERS IN LISREL

11.1 Technical Parameters

In addition to the parameters TM and IT (see Section 2.15) which limit the computer time and the *number of iterations*, respectively, several technical parameters are available in LISREL 7 to control the *minimization algorithm* used to obtain the LISREL solution (ULS, GLS, ML, WLS, and DWLS). The default values for these parameters have been chosen after considerable experimentation so as to optimize the algorithm. *Most users of* LISREL *do not have a reason to change these parameters.* However, they *can* be changed and users may do so at their own risk. The technical parameters and their default values are

Parameter	Default Value
IT	3 × number of parameters
EPS	0.000001
IM	2
IS	2
IC	5×10^{-11}
MT	20

To change any of these parameters, simply assign a new value on the OU line. For example, to change MT to 15, write

```
OU  ....  MT=15 ....
```

11.2 Iteration Algorithm

To describe the function of each of these technical parameters we will briefly describe the minimization algorithm. Let $\theta(t \times 1)$ be the vector of independent model parameters to be estimated and let $F(\theta)$ be the general fit function (1.20). Let $\theta^{(0)}$ represent the initial estimates obtained by IV, TSLS or specified by the user. The minimization algorithm generates successive points $\theta^{(1)}$, $\theta^{(2)}$, ..., in the parameter space such that

$$F[\theta^{(s+1)}] < F[\theta^{(s)}] .$$

267

The process ends when the convergence criterion (defined in Section 11.4) is satisfied or when s = IT, whichever occurs first. For s = 0, 1, 2,..., let $\mathbf{g}^{(s)}$ be the gradient vector at $\theta=\theta^{(s)}$, let $\alpha^{(s)}$ be a sequence of positive scalars, and let $\mathbf{E}^{(s)}$ be a sequence of positive definite matrices. Then the minimization algorithm is

$$\theta^{(s+1)} = \theta^{(s)} - \alpha^{(s)}\mathbf{E}^{(s)} .\tag{11.1}$$

The parameter IS controls the choice of $\alpha^{(s)}$ and the parameter IM controls the choice of $\mathbf{E}^{(s)}$ as follows:

IS = 1 $\alpha^{(s)} = 1$ if $F[\theta^{(s+1)}] < F[\theta^{(s)}]$, otherwise $\alpha^{(s)}$ is determined by *line search*; see Section 11.5.

IS = 2 $\alpha^{(s)}$ is determined by line search; see Section 11.5.

IM = 1 $\mathbf{E}^{(s+1)} = \mathbf{E}^{(s)}$, i.e., $\mathbf{E}^{(s)}$ is held constant.

IM = 2 $\mathbf{E}^{(s+1)}$ is determined from $\mathbf{E}^{(s)}$ by the method of Davidon-Fletcher-Powell; see Fletcher and Powell (1963).

IM = 3 $\mathbf{E}^{(s+1)}$ = The inverse of the information matrix (defined below) evaluated at $\theta = \theta^{(s+1)}$.

In all three cases of IM, $\mathbf{E}^{(0)}$ equals the inverse of the *information matrix* evaluated at $\theta= \theta^{(0)}$; see Section 11.3.

Combinations of IS and IM give rise to six alternative minimization algorithms that can be used. The combination IS=2 and IM=2 is the Davidon-Fletcher-Powell algorithm. This is used by default. The combination IS=1 and IM=3 is the Fisher's Scoring algorithm. This requires the fewest iterations but takes more time in each iteration due to the computation and inversion of the information matrix. The combination IM=1 with IS=1 takes the least time per iteration but usually requires more iterations. Our experience is that no combination is optimal for all problems. The behavior of the iterative procedure depends strongly on how good or bad the initial estimates are and on how well-behaved the data are.

11.3   Information Matrix

The *information matrix* is defined as

$$\mathbf{E} = plim\partial^2 F/\partial\theta\partial\theta' .\tag{11.2}$$

For the ML fit function which is the negative of the logarithm of a likelihood function, this corresponds to Fisher's information matrix (see Silvey, 1970, p.41). We will use the term information matrix also for the other methods. If the model is identified, i.e., if all its parameters are identified, the information matrix is positive definite. This is a mathematical statement. In practice, the information matrix must be evaluated at a point in the parameter space estimated from the data, and the positive definiteness of $\mathbf{E}$ can only be assessed within the numerical accuracy by which computations are performed. In the program, $\mathbf{E}$ is inverted using an ingenious variant of the square root method due to Dickman and Kaiser (1961). In this method successive pivotal quantities $\|\mathbf{E}_{11}\|, \|\mathbf{E}_{22}\|, \|\mathbf{E}_{33}\|, \ldots, \|\mathbf{E}_{tt}\|$ are computed, where $\mathbf{E}_{ii}$ is the submatrix of

$\mathbf{E}$ formed by the first i rows and columns and $\|\mathbf{E}_{ii}\|$ is the determinant of $\mathbf{E}_{ii}$. If $\mathbf{E}$ is positive definite all the pivotal quantities are positive. In the program, the parameter IC, with default value 5×10^{-11}, has the following function. If $\|\mathbf{E}_{i-1,i-1}\| \geq$ IC and $\|\mathbf{E}_{ii}\| <$ IC, then the matrix $\mathbf{E}_{i-1,i-1}$ is considered positive definite, $\mathbf{E}_{ii}$ is considered singular, and the program prints a message suggesting that the parameter θ_i may not be identified. This is usually an indication that θ_i is involved in an indeterminacy with one or more of the parameters $\theta_1, \theta_2, \ldots, \theta_{i-1}$ and it may well be that some of the parameters involved in this indeterminacy are not identified. For an example of how the program behaves when the model is not identified see Section 6.6.

11.4 Convergence Criterion

The convergence criterion is satisfied if for all $i = 1, 2, \ldots, t$

$$|\partial F/\partial \theta_i| < \text{ EPS } if \ |\theta_i| \leq 1 \tag{11.3}$$

and

$$|(\partial F/\partial \theta_i)/\theta_i| < \text{ EPS } if \ |\theta_i| > 1 , \tag{11.4}$$

where the bars indicate absolute values. The default value, 0.000005, of EPS has been chosen so that the solution is usually accurate to three significant digits. However, this cannot be guaranteed to hold for all problems. If a less accurate solution is sufficient, EPS may be increased and if a more accurate solution is required, EPS should be decreased. This does not necessarily mean, however, that EPS $= 0.00005$ gives a solution with two correct digits, nor that EPS $= 0.0000005$ gives a solution correct to four digits.

11.5 Line Search

Let θ be a given point in the parameter space and let $\mathbf{g}$ and $\mathbf{E}$ be the corresponding gradient vector and positive definite weight matrix, respectively. In this section we consider the problem of minimizing $F(\theta)$ along the line

$$\theta - \alpha\mathbf{E}\mathbf{g}, \ \ \alpha \geq 0 .$$

Along this line the function $F(\theta)$ may be regarded as a function $f(\alpha)$, of the distance α from the point θ, i.e.,

$$f(\alpha) = F(\theta - \alpha\mathbf{E}\mathbf{g}), \ \ \alpha \geq 0 . \tag{11.5}$$

The slope of $f(\alpha)$ at any point α is given by

$$s(\alpha) = -\mathbf{g}'\mathbf{E}\mathbf{g}_\alpha , \tag{11.6}$$

where $\mathbf{g}_\alpha$ is the gradient vector of $F(\theta)$ at $\theta - \alpha\mathbf{E}\mathbf{g}$. In particular, the slope at $\alpha = 0$ is $s(0) = -\mathbf{g}'\mathbf{E}\mathbf{g}$, which is negative unless $\mathbf{g} = \mathbf{0}$. If $\mathbf{g} = \mathbf{0}$, the minimum of $F(\theta)$ is located at θ. If $s(0) < 0$, $f(\alpha)$ has a minimum for some $\alpha > 0$, since $F(\theta)$ is continuous and non-negative. Figure 11.1 shows a typical example of $f(\alpha)$ and $s(\alpha)$. In most cases the fit function $F(\theta)$ is convex at least in a region around the minimum, so that $f(\alpha)$ will be as in Figure 11.1. However, convexity may not hold for all data and models at all points in the parameter space. In fact, situations like Figure 11.2 have occurred. The procedure to be described is capable of handling such cases as well.

The minimizing α may be approximated by various interpolation and extrapolation procedures. For example, one takes a trial value α^* of α and determines $f(\alpha^*)$ and $s(\alpha^*)$. If $s(\alpha^*)$ is positive, one interpolates cubically for the minimum, using function values and slope values at $\alpha = 0$ and $\alpha = \alpha^*$. If $s(\alpha^*)$ is negative, one extrapolates linearly for the zero of $s(\alpha)$ using only slope values at $\alpha = 0$ and $\alpha = \alpha^*$. Although this procedure is satisfactory in most cases, a more complicated procedure is necessary if a very accurate determination of the minimum is required or if $f(\alpha)$ and $s(\alpha)$ have more irregular forms than those of Figure 11.1. The following procedure is capable of locating the minimum to any desired degree of accuracy, within machine capacity, and it can also deal with various irregular shapes of the curves $f(\alpha)$ and $s(\alpha)$.

The behavior of $f(\alpha)$ is investigated at a sequence of test points $P^* = [\alpha^*, s(\alpha^*), f(\alpha^*)]$. There triples $P_1 = [\alpha_1, s(\alpha_1), f(\alpha_1)]$, $P_2 = [\alpha_2, s(\alpha_2), f(\alpha_2)]$ and $P_3 = [\alpha_3, s(\alpha_3), f(\alpha_3)]$ are used to save information about the function. The value α_3 is the smallest value for which $s(\alpha_3) > 0$, α_2 is the largest value with $s(\alpha_2) < 0$, and α_1 is the second largest value with $s(\alpha_1) < 0$. If only one point with negative slope is known, P_1 and P_2 are assumed to be the same point. By these definitions, $\alpha_1 \leq \alpha_2 < \alpha_3$ and α_1 and α_2 cannot decrease and α_3 cannot increase. At the beginning only one point is known namely $P_0 = [0, s(0), f(0)]$, where $s(0) < 0$, so that P_1 and P_2 are both equal to P_0 and no point P_3 is known.

Each test point $P^* = [\alpha^*, s(\alpha^*), f(\alpha^*)]$ is examined as follows. First the truth values of each of the following five logical statements are determined:

- B_1: $s(\alpha^*) < cs(0)$, where c is a small positive constant

- B_2: $f(\alpha^*) > f(0)$

- B_3: $s(\alpha^*) > 0$

- B_4: $(B_1.OR..NOT.B_3).AND.B_2$

- B_5: $[s(\alpha^*) > s(\alpha_2)].AND.[s(\alpha_2) \geq s(\alpha_1)]$

Statements B_1, B_2, and B_3 involve relations between P^* and P_0 only, B_4 is a function of B_1, B_2, and B_3, and B_5 involves P^*, P_1, and P_2 only. The eight possible outcomes of B_1, B_2 and B_3 and the consequent outcome of B_4 are shown in Table 11.1.

Table 11.1: All Possible Truth Values of B1, B2, B3, and B4

T = True		F = False		
line	B1	B2	B3	B4
1	T	T	T	T
2	T	T	F	T
3	T	F	T	F
4	T	F	F	F
5	F	T	T	F
6	F	T	F	T
7	F	F	T	F
8	F	F	F	F

Statement B_4 is examined first. If B_4 is true (lines 1, 2 and 6) it means that P^* is in a region "too far out" as shown by region CD in Figure 11.2. The trial step α^* is therefore decreased by multiplying by a constant scale factor $b < 1$ and starting anew with the decreased α^*, disregarding information from previous test points, if any. If B_4 is false, B_1 is examined. If B_1 is true (lines 3 and 4), the minimum is at P^* as illustrated by region AB in Figure 11.2. If B_1 is false, B_3 is examined. If B_3 is true (lines 5 and 7), the test point P^* has positive slope, yielding a P_3, and a new test point is determined by cubic interpolation using the information provided by P_2 and P_3. This is illustrated by region BC in Figure 11.2. The interpolation formulas are given in Section 11.6. If B_3 is false (line 8), the test point P^* has negative slope (region OA), yielding a P_2. Then, if a previous P_3 is available, a new test point is interpolated between P_2 and P_3, as above; otherwise B_5 is examined. If B_5 is true, a new test point is obtained by extrapolation using P_1 and P_2. Otherwise, the step size α^* is increased by multiplying by a constant scale factor $a > 1$. Figures 11.3a-b illustrate the two cases when B_5 is true and B_5 is false.

Figure 11.4 shows a flow diagram of how test points are examined. Successive test points are taken in this way until B_4 is false and B_1 is true. This usually occurs after two test points but, if the search is done in a region far away from the minimum of $F(\theta)$, more test points may be required. If a point where B_1 is true is found, this is the new point $\theta^{(s+1)}$. The information matrix is then updated to $\mathbf{E}^{(s+1)}$ as explained in Section 11.2.

During the line search, the point with the smallest function value is saved. At most MT (default value = 20) test points are permitted in each direction. After MT test points, the program examines the smallest function value obtained. If this is smaller than $f(0)$, the point with the smallest function value is taken as the new point $\theta^{(s+1)}$ and $\mathbf{E}^{s+1}$ is computed by inverting the information matrix at that point.

If no test point with function value smaller than $f(0)$ is found, the program changes the direction of search to the steepest descent direction represented by the line $\theta - \alpha g$. If the line search along this direction is successful this yields a new point $\theta^{(s+1)}$. If no point with function value smaller than $f(0)$ is found along the steepest descent direction, the program gives up and prints the message:

W_A_R_N_I N_G: Serious problems encountered during minimization.
            Unable to continue iterations. Check your data and model.

In most cases, the problem is in the data or the model. However, it can also occur in ill-conditioned problems (model being nearly non-identified, information matrix being nearly singular), where it is impossible to obtain the accuracy required by the convergence criterion due to insufficient arithmetic precision. The latter case is often characterized by a solution which is very close to the minimum—sufficiently close for most practical purposes. This can be evaluated by putting the parameter FD (for First Derivatives) on the OU line and inspecting these derivatives in the output file.

The constants a, b and c referred to in this section are fixed in the program at 2.0, 0.75, and 0.1, respectively.

Users of LISREL who are interested in studying the behavior of the iterative procedure should request the technical output (PT) where the values of α, $s(\alpha)$ and $f(\alpha)$ are given at each test point. The parameter PT is given on the OU line.

11.6 Interpolation and Extrapolation Formulas

Interpolation is used whenever two points $P_2 = [\alpha_2, s(\alpha_2), f(\alpha_2)]$, with negative slope $s(\alpha_2)$, and $P_3 = [\alpha_3, s(\alpha_3), f(\alpha_3)]$, with positive slope $s(\alpha_3)$, $\alpha_2 < \alpha_3$, are known. Extrapolation is used whenever two points $P_1 = [\alpha_1, s(\alpha_1), f(\alpha_1)]$ and $P_2[\alpha_2, s(\alpha_2), f(\alpha_2)]$, both with negative slopes and with $s(\alpha_2) > s(\alpha_1)$, $\alpha_1 < \alpha_2$, are known. In both cases we determine the "smoothest" curve $f^*(\alpha)$ satisfying the four boundary conditions and approximate the minimum of $f(\alpha)$ by an appropriate minimum of $f^*(\alpha)$.

Let $A = [a, s_a, f_a]$ and $B = [b, s_b, f_b]$ be two points with $a < b$. The curve $f^*(\alpha)$ is defined as the one which minimizes

$$\int (d^2 f^* / d\alpha^2)^2 d\alpha$$

and satisfies $f^*(a) = f_a$, $s^*(a) = s_a$, $f^*(b) = f_b$ and $s^*(b) = s_b$. By means of calculus of variations it can be shown that the resulting curve is a cubic, whose slope at any point α, $a \leq \alpha \leq b$, is given by

$$s^*(\alpha) = s_a - 2[(\alpha - a)/\lambda](s_a + z) + [(\alpha - a)/\lambda]^2(s_a + s_b + 2z) , \tag{11.7}$$

where

$$\lambda = b - a , \tag{11.8}$$

and

$$z = (3/\lambda)(f_a - f_b) + s_a + s_b . \tag{11.9}$$

If $s_a + s_b + 2z = 0$, $s^*(\alpha)$ degenerates into a linear function, whose zero is located at

$$\alpha = a - \frac{s_a}{s_b - s_a}(b - a) . \tag{11.10}$$

Otherwise, $s^*(\alpha)$ has the two roots

$$\alpha_1 = a + \frac{s_a + z + \sqrt{Q}}{s_a + s_b + 2z}(b - a) , \tag{11.11}$$

$$\alpha_2 = a + \frac{s_a + z - \sqrt{Q}}{s_a + s_b + 2z}(b - a) , \tag{11.12}$$

where

$$Q = z^2 - s_a s_b . \tag{11.13}$$

If s_a and s_b have different signs, Q is positive. If s_a and s_b are both negative, Q may be positive or negative. If Q is negative, the two roots (11.11) and (11.12) are complex and cannot be used. In this case the linear slope formula (11.10) is used. This yields a value $\alpha > b$.

If Q is positive, both roots are real. Then if $s_a + s_b + 2z > 0$, the largest of the two roots, which is α_1, corresponds to a minimum of $f^*(\alpha)$. On the other hand, if $s_a + s_b + 2z < 0$, the smallest of the two roots, which is α_1 corresponds to the minimum. Thus, in both cases, α_1 is the root of interest. It is readily verified that α_1 is between a and b if $s_a < 0$ and $s_b > 0$ and larger than b if $s_b < s_a < 0$.

If $s_b \approx -s_a$, the form (11.11) of α_1 is not suitable for computation since considerable accuracy may be lost in taking the difference of nearly equal quantities. For this reason, the following mathematically equivalent form is used in the computations:

$$\alpha = a + \left[1 - \frac{s_b + \sqrt{Q} - z}{s_b - s_a + 2\sqrt{Q}}\right] . \tag{11.14}$$

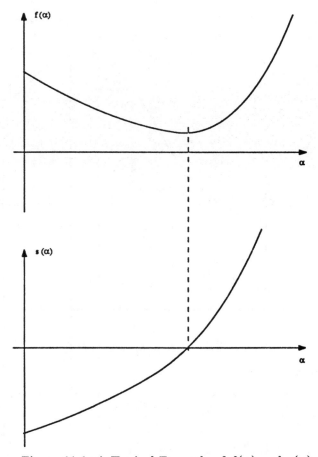

Figure 11.1: A Typical Example of $f(\alpha)$ and $s(\alpha)$

11.7 Alternative Scaling Option for Latent Variables

By default, LISREL 7 assumes that users will define the unit of measurement in η-variables by assigning a non-zero fixed value in each column of Λ_y and in ξ-variables by either fixing the diagonal of Φ (by PH=ST or otherwise) or by fixing a non-zero value in each column of Λ_x. In fact, LISREL 7 will check this and stop if no scale has been defined for a latent variable.

A mathematically inclined user may want to define the scales for latent variables in some other way. To be able to do so, the check done by LISREL 7 must be turned off. This can be done by the parameter SO on the OU line.

11.8 Hints on Resolving Problem Cases

LISREL works well when the model is right for the data. In such cases, the program produces good initial estimates and converges after a few iterations to an admissible solution. However, in practice many different deviations from this ideal situation may occur

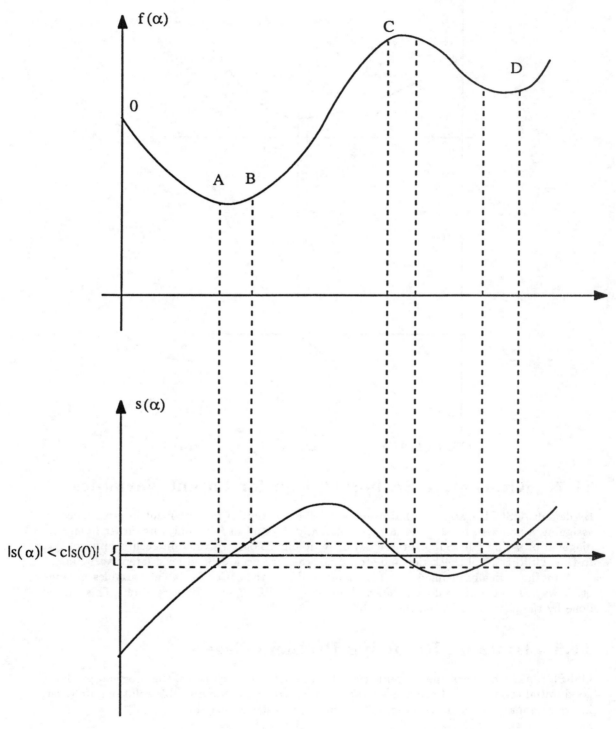

Figure 11.2: Various Regions of $f(\alpha)$ and $s(\alpha)$ Curves

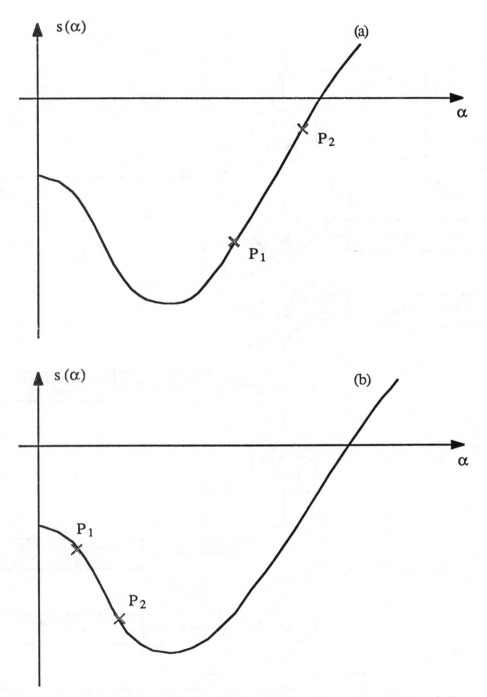

Figure 11.3: Two Slope Curves Showing Different Locations of P_1 and P_2

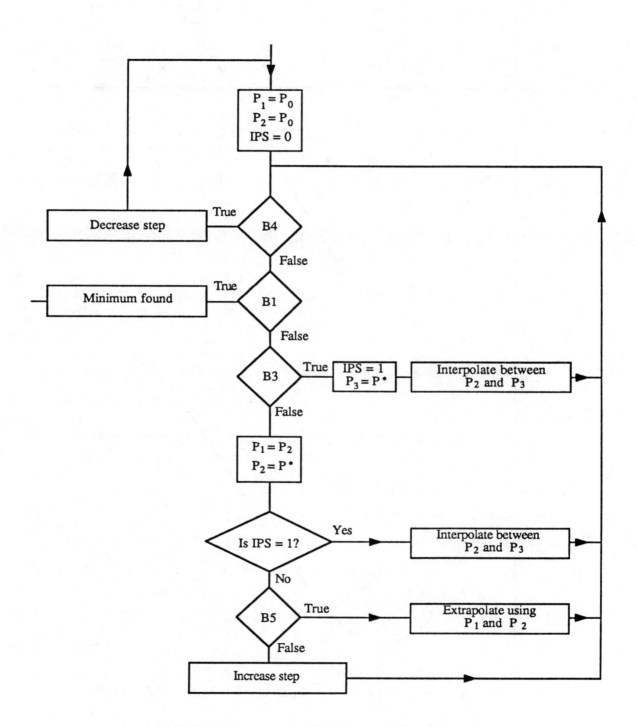

Figure 11.4: Flow Diagram Showing How Test Points are Examined

- because the proposed model is wrong for the data or the data are inadequate for the model, or

- because mistakes are made in the input file or the data so that in fact a model or data different from the intended are analyzed

This section explains how LISREL behaves in such cases and gives some hints on how to resolve problem cases.

Our basic philosophy in writing the program is to try to detect most errors and inconsistencies as early as possible and stop the program. However, it is not possible to check everything and it is of course impossible to reject a bad but otherwise formally correct model without running it through. Such models are therefore not detected until after some computation.

LISREL will detect most syntax errors in the input file. For example, LISREL will detect

- invalid line names and parameter names as well as invalid parameter values

- missing DA, MO, and OU lines

- logical errors on MO, FR, FI, VA, and ST lines, such as references to LY when NY and/or NE has not been defined

It is harder to detect errors in data (labels, raw data, covariance matrices, etc.) To help the program detect errors in the data, we recommend that all data be read from external files. *Do not put the data in the input file. Put different kinds of data in different files.* See Example 7.2. If these recommendations are followed, the program will detect if there are too few elements in the data and if there are illegal characters in the data. The program cannot detect if there are too many elements in the data file or if an element has an unreasonable (but legal) value. *Always check the matrix to be analyzed in the output file to see if it is correct.*

Erroneous values in covariance or correlation matrices often lead to matrices that are not positive definite. This will result in one of the following error messages:

```
W_A_R_N_I_N_G : Matrix to be analyzed is not positive definite,
               ridge option taken with ridge constant =   1.000
```

```
F_A_T_A_L  E_R_R_O_R : Matrix to be analyzed is not positive definite.
```

The value of the ridge constant reported in the error message may differ from the value 1.000 reported here.

Suppose the problem has passed the syntax and data checks without errors. Things can still go wrong because either the model defined in the input file is not the one intended or simply because the model is wrong or bad for the data. LISREL "protests violently" against bad models in the following ways:

- Bad initial estimates are produced. In some cases these may be so bad that iterations cannot begin because the matrix Σ estimated at the initial estimates of parameters is not positive definite. This produces the following error message:

```
F_A_T_A_L  E_R_R_O_R : Unable to start iterations because matrix SIGMA is
                       not positive definite.
                       Provide better starting values.
```

- After iterations have started, a bad model may be detected at the admissibility check (see Section 1.11.4), which occurs after the tenth iteration, unless some other value of AD is specified on the OU line. *Do not set the admissibility check off unless the model has fixed zero diagonal elements in Φ, Ψ, Θ_ϵ, or Θ_δ by intention.* The admissibility check has been included as a result of critique from users of earlier versions of LISREL, which could run for many iterations without producing any useful results. Although there may be exceptions, our experience suggests that if a solution is not admissible after 10 iterations, it will remain non-admissible if the program is allowed to continue to iterate. The error message which stops the program when the model is not admissible is

  `F_A_T_A_L  E_R_R_O_R : Admissibility test failed.`

  There will also be warning messages in the output file indicating for which parameter matrix the test fails.

  If this message occurs, one should check the data and the model carefully to see if they are as intended. If they are and the admissibility test still fails after 10 iterations, one can set AD to some large value such as 20 or 30. *Do not set AD = OFF.*

- If a model passes the admissibility test, there could still be something wrong with the model specification. This will most likely result in non-convergence of iterations after IT iterations which produce the following message:

  `W_A_R_N_I_N_G : The number of iterations exceeded  51`

  or the following message:

  `W_A_R_N_I_N_G : Serious problems were encountered during minimization.`
  `               Unable to continue iterations. Check your model and data.`

In both cases, the program stops iterating and writes the "solution" at that point to the output file. This solution usually indicates what is wrong in the model.

If the data and the model specification are correct and the "problem" still does not converge in IT iterations, one can set IT to a larger value to allow more iterations, or one can use a different minimization method by changing IM and/or IS; see Section 11.1. It may also be a good idea to put FD (first derivatives) on the OU line in case the program will produce the second warning above. The first derivatives give an indication of how "close" the "solution" is.

The most likely explanation for the occurrence of the second warning is that the model is empirically non-identified, in the sense that the information matrix is nearly singular. This can be checked by asking for PC (for print correlations of estimates) on the OU line, which produces a correlation matrix of order $t \times t$, where t is the number of parameters estimated. This correlation matrix is an estimate of the asymptotic covariance matrix of the parameter estimates scaled to a correlation matrix. Very large correlations in this matrix indicate that the fit function is nearly flat and that it is impossible to obtain sufficiently good parameter estimates.

This problem can usually be resolved by imposing more constraints on the model. For example, one could fix off-diagonal elements of Ψ or one could set more elements of Λ_y or Λ_x to zero.

BIBLIOGRAPHY OF LISREL-RELATED LITERATURE

Aaker, D.A., Bagozzi, R.P., and Carman, J.M. (1980) On using response latency to measure preference. *Journal of Marketing Research*, 17, 237-244.

Abbey, A., and Andrews, F. (1985) Modeling psychological determinants of life quality. *Social Indicators Research*, 16, 1-34.

Achen, C.H. (1987) As statisticians see us: Comments on Freedman's paper "As other see us... ." *Journal of Educational Statistics*, 12, 148- 150.

Acito, F., and Anderson, R.D. (1984) On simulation methods for investigating structural modeling. *Journal of Marketing Research*, 21, 107-112.

Acock, A., and Fuller, T.D. (1986) Standardized solutions using LISREL on multiple populations. *Sociological Methods and Research*, 13, 551-557.

Afifi, A.A., and Elashoff, R.M. (1966) Missing observations in multivariate statistics. 1. Review of the literature. *Journal of the American Statistical Association*, 61, 595-604.

Aigner, D.J., Hsiao, C., Kapteyn, A., and Wansbeek, T. (1984) Latent variable models in econometrics. In Z. Griliches and M.D. Intriligator (Eds.): *Handbook of Econometrics*, Volume 2. Amsterdam: North-Holland.

Aigner, D.J., and Goldberger, A.S., Eds. (1977) *Latent variables in socioeconomic models.* Amsterdam: North-Holland Publishing Co.

Aigner, D.J., Hsiao, C., Kapteyn, A., and Wansbeek, T. (1984) Latent variable models in econometrics. In Z. Griliches and M.D. Intriligator (Eds.): *Handbook of econometrics*, vol. 2. Amsterdam: North-Holland Publishing Co.

Aish, A.M., Fuchs, D., Jöreskog, K.G. and Schmidt, P. (1989) Political efficacy and responsiveness in the United States, the Netherlands, and West Germany: A cross-national panel analysis. In preparation

Aish, A.M., and Jöreskog, K.G. (1989) A panel model for political efficacy and responsiveness. *Quality and Quantity*, 23, in press.

Aitken, A.C. (1934-35) On least squares and the linear combination of observations. *Proceedings of the Royal Society of Edinburgh*, 55, 42- 48.

Akaike, H. (1987) Factor analysis and AIC. *Psychometrika*, 52, 317-332.

Algina, J. (1980) A note on identification in the oblique and orthogonal factor analysis models. *Psychometrika*, 45, 393-396.

Allison, P.D. (1977) Testing for interaction in multiple regression. *American Journal of Sociology*, 83, 144-153.

Allison, P.D. (1987) Estimation of linear models with incomplete data. Pp. 71-103 in C. Clogg (Ed.): *Sociological Methodology 1987*. San Francisco: Jossey Bass.

Alwin, D.F., and Hauser, R.M. (1975) The decomposition of effects in path analysis. *American Sociological Review*, 40, 37-47.

Alwin, D.F., and Jackson, D.J. (1980) Measurement models for response errors in surveys: Issues and applications. Pp 68-199 in K.F. Schuessler (Ed.): *Sociological Methodology 1980*. San Francisco: Jossey-Bass.

Alwin, D.F., and Jackson, D.J. (1981) Applications of simultaneous factor analysis to issues of factorial invariance. Pp 249-279 in D. Jackson and E. Borgatta (Eds.): *Factor analysis and measurement in sociological research: A Multi-Dimensional Perspective*. Beverly Hills: Sage.

Alwin, D.F., and Tessler, R.C. (1974) Causal models, unobserved variables, and experimental data. *American Journal of Sociology*, 80, 1, 58-86.

Alwin, D.F., and Thornton, A. (1984) Family origins and the schooling process: Early versus late influence of parental characteristics. *American Sociological Review*, 49, 784-802.

Amemiya, Y., Fuller, W.A., and Pantula, S.G. (1987) The covariance matrix of estimators for the factor model. *Journal of Multivariate Analysis*, 22, 51-64.

Amemiya, Y., and Anderson, T.W. (1985) Asymptotic chi-square tests for a large class of factor analysis models. Technical Report No. 13, Econometric Workshop, Stanford University.

Anderson, J.C. (1985) A measurement model to assess measure-specific factors in multiple-informant research. *Journal of Marketing Research*, 22, 86-92.

Anderson, J.C., and Gerbing, D.W. (1982) Some methods for respecifying measurement models to obtain unidimensional construct measurement. *Journal of Marketing Research*, 19, 453-460.

Anderson, J.C., and Gerbing, D.W. (1984) The effect of sampling error on convergence, improper solutions, and goodness of fit indices for maximum likelihood confirmatory factor analysis. *Psychometrika*, 49, 155-173.

Anderson, J.G. (1987) Structural equation models in the social and behaviour sciences: Model building. *Child Development*, 58, 49-64.

Anderson, R.G., Engledow, J.L., and Becker, H. (1979) Evaluating the relationships among attitude toward business, product satisfaction, experience, and search effort. *Journal of Marketing Research*, 16, 394- 400.

Anderson, S.B., and Maier, M.H. (1963) 34000 pupils and how they grew. *Journal of Teacher Education*, 14, 212-216.

Anderson, T.W. (1957) Maximum likelihood estimates for a multivariate normal distribution when some observations are missing. *Journal of the American Statistical Association*, 52, 200-203.

Anderson, T.W. (1959) *An introduction to multivariate statistical analysis*. New York: Wiley.

Anderson, T.W. (1969) Statistical inference for covariance matrices with linear structure. *In P.R. Krishnaiah (Ed.): Multivariate Analysis II*. New York: Academic Press.

Anderson, T.W. (1973) Asymptotically efficient estimation of covariance matrices with linear structure. *Annals of Statistics*, 1, 135-141.

Anderson, T.W. (1984) Estimating linear statistical relationships. *Annals of Statistics*, 1-45.

Anderson, T.W., and Amemiya, Y. (1985) The asymptotic normal distribution of estimators in factor analysis under general conditions. Technical Report No. 12, Econometric Workshop, Stanford University.

Anderson, T.W., and Amemiya, Y. (1986) Asymptotic distributions in factor analysis and linear structural relations. Technical Report No. 18, Econometric Workshop, Stanford University.

Anderson, T.W., and Rubin, H. (1956) Statistical inference in factor analysis. In *Proceedings of the Third Berkeley Symposium*, Volume V. Berkeley: University of California Press.

Andrews, D.F., Gnanadesikan, R., and Warner, J.L. (1973) Methods of assessing multivariate normality. Pp 95-116 in P.R. Krishnaiah (Ed.): *Multivariate analysis III*. New York: Academic Press.

Andrews, F.M., and McKennell, A.C. (1980) Measures of self-reported well-being: Their affective, cognitive and other components. *Social Indicators Research*, 8. 127-155.

Arminger, G. (1986) Linear stochastic differential equation models for panel data with unobserved variables. *Sociological Methodology*, 187- 212.

Arminger, G. (1987) Misspecification, asymptotic stability, and ordinal variables in the analysis of panel data. *Sociological Methods and Research*, 15, 336-348.

Arora, R. (1982) Validation of an S-O-R model for situation, enduring, and response components of involvement. *Journal of Marketing Research*, 19, 505-516.

Asher, H.B. (1983) *Causal modeling* (2nd ed.): Beverly Hills: Sage.

Babakus, E. (1985) *The sensitivity of maximum likelihood factor analysis given violations of interval scale and multivariate normality assumptions.* Unpublished doctoral dissertation, University of Alabama, Tuscaloosa.

Babakus, E., Ferguson, C.E. Jr., and Jöreskog, K.G. (1987) The sensitivity of confirmatory maximum likelihood factor analysis to violations of measurement scale and distributional assumptions. *Journal of Marketing Research*, 24, 222-228.

Baer, D.E., and Curtis, J.E. (1984) French Canadian-English Canadian differences in values: National survey findings. *Canadian Journal of Sociology*, 9, 405-427.

Bagozzi, R.P. (1977) Structural equation models in experimental research. *Journal of Marketing Research*, 14, 209-226.

Bagozzi, R.P. (1978) The construct validity of the affective, behavioral, and cognitive components of attitude by analysis of covariance structures. *Multivariate Behavioral Research*, 13, 9-31.

Bagozzi, R.P. (1979) The role of measurement in theory construction and hypothesis testing: Toward a holistic model. *Proceedings of the American Marketing Association, 1979*, 15-33.

Bagozzi, R.P. (1980a) *Causal models in marketing*. New York: Wiley.

Bagozzi, R.P. (1980b) Attitudes, intentions, and behavior: A test of some key hypotheses. *Journal of Personality and Social Psychology*, 41, 607-627.

Bagozzi, R.P. (1980c) Performance and satisfaction in an industrial sales force: An examination of their antecedents and simultaneity. *Journal of Marketing*, 44, 65-77.

Bagozzi, R.P. (1980d) The nature and causes of self-esteem, performance, and satisfaction in the sales force: A structural equation approach. *Journal of Business*, 53, 315-331.

Bagozzi, R.P. (1981a) An examination of the validity of two models of attitude. *Multivariate Behavioral Research*, 16, 323-359.

Bagozzi, R.P. (1981b) Causal modeling: A general method for developing and testing theories in consumer research. *Advances in Consumer Research*, 3, 195-202.

Bagozzi, R.P. (1981c) Evaluating structural equation models with unobservable variables and measurement error: A comment. *Journal of Marketing Research*, 18, 375-381.

Bagozzi, R.P. (1982) A field investigation of causal relations among cognitions, affect, intentions, and behavior. *Journal of Marketing Research*, 19, 562-584.

Bagozzi, R.P. (1983) Issues in the application of covariance structure analysis: A further comment. *Journal of Consumer Research*, 9, 449- 450.

Bagozzi, R.P. (1984) A prospectus for theory construction in marketing. *Journal of Marketing*, 48, 11-29.

Bagozzi, R.P., Tybout, A.M., and Craig, C.S. (1979) The construct validity of the tripartite classification of attitudes. *Journal of Marketing Research*, 16, 88-95.

Bagozzi, R.P., and Burnkrant, R.E. (1979) Attitude organisation and the attitude-behaviour relationship. *Journal of Personality and Social Psychology*, 37, 913-929.

Bagozzi, R.P., and Phillips, L.W. (1982) Representing and testing organizational theories: A holistic construal. *Administrative Science Quarterly*, 27, 459-489.

Bagozzi, R.P., Fornell, C., and Larcker, D.F. (1981) Canonical correlation analysis as a special case of a structural relations model. *Multivariate Behavioral Research*, 16, 437-454.

Baker, R.L., Mednick, B., and Brock, W. (1984) An application of causal modeling techniques to prospective longitudinal data bases. Pp 106- 132 in S.A. Mednick, M. Harway and K.M. Finello (Eds.): *Handbook of longitudinal research*, volume 1. New York: Praeger.

Balderjahn, I. (1985) The robustness of LISREL unweighted least squares estimation against small sample size in confirmatory factor analysis models. Pp. 3-10 in W. Gaul and M. Schader (Eds.): Classification as a tool of research. Amsterdam: Elsevier Science Publishers.

Bartholomew, D.J. (1980a) Factor analysis for categorical data (with discussion). *Journal of the Royal Statistical Society*, Series B, 42, 293-321.

Bartholomew, D.J. (1980b) Factor analysis for categorical data. *Journal of the Royal Statistical Society*, Series B, 42, 293-312.

Bartholomew, D.J. (1984) The foundations of factor analysis. *Biometrika*, 71, 221-232.

Bartholomew, D.J. (1985) Foundations of factor analysis: Some practical implications. *British Journal of Mathematical and Statistical Psychology*, 38, 1-10.

Bartholomew, D.J. (1987) *Latent variable models and factor analysis.* Oxford, U.K.: Oxford University Press.

Baumrind, D. (1983) Specious causal attributions in the social sciences: The reformulated stepping-stone theory of heroin use as exemplar. *Journal of Personality and Social Psychology*, 45, 1289-1298.

Beale, E.M.L., and Little, R.J.A. (1975) Missing values in multivariate analysis. *Journal of the Royal Statistical Society*, series B, 37, 129- 145.

Bearden W.O., and Teel, J.E. (1983) Selected determinants of consumer satisfaction and complaint reports. *Journal of Marketing Research*, 20, 21-28.

Bearden, W.O., Sharma, S., and Teel, J.E. (1982) Sample size effects on chi-square and other statistics used in evaluating causal models. *Journal of Marketing Research*, 19, 425-430.

Bearden, W.O., and Mason, J.B. (1980) Determinants of physician and pharmacist support of generic drugs. *Journal of Consumer Research*, 7, 121-130.

Bearden, W.O., and Shimp, T.A. (1982) The use of extrinsic cues to facilitate product adoption. *Journal of Marketing Research*, 19, 229- 239.

Bekker, P.A. (1986) *Essays on identification in linear models with latent variables.* Ph.D. Dissertation, Catholic University of Tilburg, Holland.

Bekker, P.A. (1986) Comment on identification in the linear errors in variables model. *Econometrica*, 54, 215-217.

Bentler, P.M. (1976) Multistructure statistical model applied to factor analysis. *Multivariate Behavioral Research*, 11, 3-25.

Bentler, P.M. (1978) The interdependence of theory, methodology, and empirical data. Causal modeling as an approach to construct validation. Pp. 267-302 in D.B. Kandel (Ed.): *Longitudinal Drug Research.* New York: John Wiley.

Bentler, P.M. (1980) Multivariate analysis with latent variables. Causal models. *Annual Review of Psychology*, 31, 419-456.

Bentler, P.M. (1982a) Confirmatory factor analysis via noniterative estimation: A fast, inexpensive method. *Journal of Marketing Research*, 19, 417-424.

Bentler, P.M. (1982b) Linear systems with multiple levels and types of latent variables. Pp 101-130 in K.G. Jöreskog and H. Wold (Eds.): *Systems under indirect observation: Causality, structure, prediction.* Part I. Amsterdam: North-Holland.

Bentler, P.M. (1983a) Simultaneous equations as moment structure models: With an introduction to latent variable models. *Journal of Econometrics*, 22, 13-42.

Bentler, P.M. (1983b) Some contributions to efficient statistics for structural models: Specification and estimation of moment structures. *Psychometrika*, 48, 493-517.

Bentler, P.M. (1984a) Causal modeling via structural equation system. In J. Nesselroade and R.B. Cattell (Eds.): *Handbook of multivariate experimental psychology.* New York: Plenum, in press.

Bentler, P.M. (1984b) Structural equation models in longitudinal research. Pp 88-105 in S.A. Mednick, M. Harway, and K.M. Finello (Eds.): *Handbook of longitudinal Research*, Volume 1. New York: Praeger.

Bentler, P.M. (1985) *Theory and implementation of EQS: A structural equations program.* Los Angeles: BMDP Statistical Software, Inc.

Bentler, P.M. (1986) Structural modeling and Psychometrika: An historical perspective on growth and achievements. *Psychometrika*, 51, 35-51.

Bentler, P.M. (1987a) Drug use and personality in adolescence and young adulthood: Structural models with nonnormal variables. *Child Development*, 58, 65-79.

Bentler, P.M. (1987b) Structural modeling and the scientific method: Comments on Freedman's critique. *Journal of Educational Statistics*, 12, 151-157.

Bentler, P.M., and Bonett, D.G. (1980) Significance tests and goodness of fit in the analysis of covariance structures. *Psychological Bulletin*, 88, 588-606.

Bentler, P.M., and Chou, C-P. (1987) Practical issues in structural modeling. *Sociological Methods and Research*, 16.

Bentler, P.M., and Dijkstra, T. (1985) Efficient estimation via linearization in structural models. Pp 9-24 in P.R. Krishnaiah (Ed.): *Multivariate analysis VI*. Amsterdam: North-Holland.

Bentler, P.M., and Freeman, E.H. (1983) Tests for stability in linear structural equation systems. *Psychometrika*, 48, 143-145.

Bentler, P.M., and Huba, G.J. (1979) Simple minitheories of love. *Journal of Personality and Social Psychology*, 37, 124-130.

Bentler, P.M., and Lee, S-Y. (1983) Covariance structures under polynomial constraints: Applications to correlation and alpha-type structural models. *Journal of Educational Statistics*, 8, 207-222, 315-317.

Bentler, P.M., and Speckart, G. (1979) Models of attitude-behaviour relations. *Psychological Review*, 86, 452-464.

Bentler, P.M., and Speckart, G. (1981) Attitudes "cause" behaviors: A structural equation analysis. *Journal of Personality and Social Psychology*, 40, 226-238.

Bentler, P.M., and Tanaka, J.S. (1983) Problems with EM algorithms for ML factor analysis. *Psychometrika*, 48, 247-251.

Bentler, P.M., and Weeks, D.G. (1979) Interrelations among models for the analysis of moment structures. *Multivariate Behavioral Research*, 14, 169-186.

Bentler, P.M., and Weeks, D.G. (1980) Linear structural equations with latent variables. *Psychometrika*, 45, 289-308.

Bentler, P.M., and Weeks, D.G. (1981) Multivariate analysis with latent variables. In P.R. Krishnaiah and L. Kanal, (Eds.): *Handbook of Statistics*, Volume 2. Amsterdam: North-Holland Publishing Co.

Bentler, P.M., and Weeks, D.G. (1985) Some comments on structural equation models. *British Journal of Mathematical and Statistical Psychology*, 38, 120-121.

Bentler, P.M., and Woodward, J.A. (1978) A Head Start reevaluation: Positive effects are not yet demonstrable. *Evaluation Quarterly*, 2, 493-510.

Beran, R. (1979) Testing for ellipsoidal symmetry of a multivariate density. *The Annals of Statistics*, 7, 150-162.

Berk, R.A. (1983) An introduction to sample selection bias in sociological data. *American Sociological Review*, 48, 386-398.

Berkson, J. (1980) Minimum chi-square, not maximum likelihood! *The Annals of Statistics*, 8, 457-487.

Berry, W.D. (1984) *Nonrecursive causal models*. Beverly Hills: Sage.

Biddle, B.J., and Marlin, M.M. (1987) Causality, confirmation, credulity, and structural equation modeling. *Child Development*, 58, 4- 17.

Bielby, D., del Vento, and Bielby, W.T. (1984) Work commitment, sex- role attitudes, and women's employment. *American Sociological Rewiew*, 49, 234-247.

Bielby, W.T. (1981) Neighborhood effects: A LISREL model for clustered samples. *Sociological Methods and Research*, 10, 82-111.

Bielby, W.T., and Hauser, R.M. (1977) Structural equation models. *Annual Review of Sociology*, 3, 137-161.

Bielby, W.T., Hauser, R.M., and Featherman, D.L. (1977a) Response errors of black and nonblack males in models of the intergenerational transmission of socioeconomic status. *American Journal of Sociology*, 82, 1242-1288.

Bielby, W.T., Hauser, R.M., and Featherman, D.L. (1977b) Response errors of nonblack males in models of the stratification process. *Journal of the American Statistical Association*, 72, 723-735.

Billings, R.S., and Wroten, S.P. (1978) Use of path analysis in industrial organizational psychology: Criticisms and suggestions. *Journal of Applied Psychology*, 63, 677-688.

Birnbaum, M.H., and Mellers, B.A. (1979) One-mediator model of exposure effects is still viable. *Journal of Personality and Social Psychology*, 37, 1090-1096.

Bishop, Y.M.M., Fienberg, S.E., and Holland, P.W. (1975) *Discrete multivariate analysis: Theory and Practice*. Cambridge, Mass.: MIT.

Blalock, H.M., Jr., (Ed.) (1971) *Causal models in the social sciences*. Chicago: Aldine Publishing Co.

Blalock, H.M., Jr., (Ed.) (1974) *Measurement in the social sciences*. Chicago: Aldine Publishing Co.

Blalock, H.M., Jr. (1979) Measurement and conceptualization problems: the major obstacle to integrating theory and research. *American Sociological Review*, 44, 881-894.

Blalock, H.M., Jr. (1982) *Conceptualization and measurement in the social sciences*. Beverly Hills: Sage.

Blalock, H.M., Jr., (Ed.) (1985a) *Causal models in panel and experimental designs*. New York: Aldine Publishing Co.

Blalock, H.M., Jr., (Ed.) (1985b) *Causal models in the social sciences*. Second Edition. New York: Aldine Publishing Co.

Blau, P., and Duncan, O.D. (1967) *The American occupational structure*. New York: Wiley.

Blok, H., and Saris, W.E. (1983) Using longitudinal data to estimate reliability. *Applied Psychological Measurement*, 7, 285-301.

Blåfield, E. (1981) Covariance structures and multicollinearity. University of Jyväskylä, Reports on Statistics 3/81.

Bock, R.D. (1960) Components of variance analysis as a structural and discriminal analysis for psychological tests. *British Journal of Statistical Psychology*, 13, 151-163.

Bock, R.D., and Aitkin, M. (1981) Marginal maximum likelihood estimation of item parameters: Applications of an EM algorithm. *Psychometrika*, 46, 443-459.

Bock, R.D., and Bargmann, R.E. (1966) Analysis of covariance structures. *Psychometrika*, 31, 507-534.

Bock, R.D., and Lieberman, M. (1970) Fitting a response model for n dichotomously scored items. *Psychometrika*, 35, 179-197.

Bohrnstedt, G.W. (1969) Observations on the measurement of change. In E.F. Borgatta (Ed.): *Sociological Methodology 1969*. San Francisco: Jossey-Bass, 113-133.

Bohrnstedt, G.W. (1970) Reliability and validity assessment in attitude measurement. Pp. 80-99 in G.F. Summers: *Attitude measurement*.

Bohrnstedt, G.W. (1983) Measurement. Pp 69-121 in P. Rossi, J. Wright, and A. Anderson (Eds.): *Handbook of survey research*. New York: Academic Press.

Bohrnstedt, G.W., and Borgatta, E.F. (Eds.): (1981) *Social measurement: Current issues*. Beverly Hills: Sage.

Bohrnstedt, G.W., and Felson, R.B. (1983) Explaining the relations among children's actual and perceived performances and self-esteem. *Journal of Personality and Social Psychology*, 45, 43-56.

Bollen, K.A. (1980) Issues in the comparative measurement of political democracy. *American Sociological Review*, 45, 370-390.

Bollen, K.A. (1984) Multiple indicators: internal consistency or no necessary relationship? *Quality and Quantity*, 18, 377-385.

Bollen, K.A. (1986) Sample size and Bentler and Bonett's nonnormed fit index. *Psychometrika*, 51, 375-377.

Bollen, K.A. (1987a) Outliers and improper solutions: A confirmatory factor analysis example. *Sociological Methods and Research*, 15, 375- 384.

Bollen, K.A. (1987b) Total, direct, and indirect effects in structural equation models. In C. Clogg (Ed.): *Sociological Methodology 1987*. San Francisco: Jossey Bass.

Bollen, K.A. (1989) *Structural equations with latent variables*. New York: Wiley.

Bollen, K.A., and Jöreskog, K.G. (1985) Uniqueness does not imply identification. A note on confirmatory factor analysis. *Sociological Methods and Research*, 14, 155-163.

Bollen, K.A., and Schwing, R.C. (1987) Air pollution-morality models: A demonstration of the effects of random measurement error. *Quality and Quantity*, 21, 37-48.

Boomsma, A. (1982) The robustness of LISREL against small sample sizes in factor analysis models. In K.G. Jöreskog and H. Wold (Eds.): *Systems under indirect observation: causality, structure, prediction* Part 1. Amsterdam: North-Holland Publishing Co.

Boomsma, A. (1983) *On the robustness of LISREL (maximum likelihood estimation) against small sample size and non- normality*. Unpublished doctoral dissertation, University of Groningen, Groningen, The Netherlands.

Boomsma, A. (1985) Nonconvergence, improper solutions, and starting values in LISREL maximum likelihood estimation. *Psychometrika*, 50, 229-242.

Brown, C.H. (1983) Asymptotic comparison of missing data procedures for estimating factor loadings. *Psychometrika*, 48, 269-291.

Browne, M.W. (1970) Analysis of covariance structures. Paper presented at the annual conference of the South African Statistical Association.

Browne, M.W. (1974) Generalized least squares estimators in the analysis of covariance structures. *South African Statistical Journal*, 8, 1-24.

Browne, M.W. (1977a) Generalized least squares estimators in the analysis of covariance structures. Pp 205-226 in D.J. Aigner and A.S. Goldberger (Eds.): *Latent variables in socio-economic models*. Amsterdam: North-Holland.

Browne, M.W. (1977b) The analysis of patterned correlation matrices by generalized least squares. *British Journal of Mathematical and Statistical Psychology*, 30, 113-124.

Browne, M.W. (1977) The decomposition of multitrait-multimethod matrices. *British Journal of Mathematical and Statistical Psychology*, 37, 1-21.

Browne, M.W. (1982) Covariance structures. Pp 72-141 in D. M. Hawkins (Ed.): *Topics in applied multivariate analysis*. Cambridge: Cambridge University Press.

Browne, M.W. (1984) Asymptotically distribution-free methods for the analysis of covariance structures. *British Journal of Mathematical and Statistical Psychology*, 37, 62-83.

Browne, M.W. (1987) Robustness of statistical inference in factor analysis and related models. *Biometrika*, 74, 375-384.

Burnkrant, R.E., and Page, T.J., Jr. (1982) An examination of the convergent discriminant, and predictive validity of Fishbein's behavioral intention model. *Journal of Marketing Research*, 19, 550-561.

Burt, R.S. (1973) Confirmatory factor-analytic structures and the theory construction process (plus corrigenda). *Sociological Methods and Research*, 2, 131-190.

Burt, R.S. (1976) Interpretational confounding of unobserved variables in structural equation models. *Sociological Methods and Research*, 5, 3- 51.

Burt, R.S. (1981) A note on interpretational confounding of unobserved variables in structural equation models. Pp 299-318 in P.V. Marsden (Ed.): *Linear models in social research.* Beverly Hills: Sage.

Burt, R.S., Fisher, M.G., and Christman, K.P. (1979) Structures of well-being. *Sociological Methods and Research*, 8, 111-120.

Burt, R.S., Wiley, J.A., Minos, M.J., and Murray, J.R. (1978) Structure of well-being: Form, content and stability over time. *Sociological Methods and Research*, 6,365-407.

Buse, A. (1982) The likelihood ratio, Wald and Lagrange multiplier tests: An expository note. *The American Statistician*, 36, 153-157.

Busemeyer, J.R., and Jones, L.E. (1983) Analysis of multiplicative combination rules when the causal variables are measured with error. *Psychological Bulletin*, 93, 549-562.

Bye, B.V., Gallicchio, S.J., and Dykacz, J.M. (1985) Multiple indicator, multiple-cause models for a single latent variable with ordinal indicators. *Sociological Methods and Research*, 13, 487-509.

Bynner, J. (1982) Use of LISREL in the solution to a higher-order factor problem in a study of adolescent self images. *Quality and Quantity*, 15, 523-540.

Bynner, J.M., and Romney, D.M. (1985) LISREL for beginners. *Canadian Psychology*, 26, 43-49.

Bynner, J.M., and Romney, D.M. (1986) Intelligence, fact or artifact: Alternative structures for cognitive abilities. *British Journal of Educational Psychology*, 56, 13-23.

Calder, B.J., Phillips, L.W., and Tybout, A.M. (1982) The concept of external validity. *Journal of Consumer Research*, 9, 240-244.

Calder, B.J., Phillips, L.W., and Tybout, A.M. (1983) Beyond external validity. *Journal of Consumer Research*, 9, 112-114.

Calsyn, J.R., and Kenny, D.A. (1977) Self-concept of ability and perceived evaluation of others: Cause or effect of academic achievement? *Journal of Educational Psychology*, 69, 136-145.

Cambanis, S., Huang, S., and Simons, G. (1981) On the theory of elliptically contoured distributions. *Journal of Multivariate Analysis*, 11, 368-385.

Campbell, D.T. (1960) Recommendations for APA test standards regarding construct, trait, or discriminant validity. *American Psychologist*, 15, 546-53.

Campbell, D.T., and Fiske, D.W. (1959) Convergent and discriminant validation by the multitrait-multimethod matrix. *Psychological Bulletin*, 56, 81-105

Campbell, D.T., and Stanley, J.C. (1963) *Experimental and Quasiexperimental designs for research.* Chicago: Rand McNally.

Campbell, R.C., and Mutran, E. (1982) Analyzing panel data in studies of aging. *Research on Aging*, 4, 3-41.

Campbell, R.T. (1983) Status attainment research: End of the beginning or beginning of the end. *Sociology of Education*, 56, 47-62.

Carmines, E. G., and McIver, J. P. (1981) Analysing models with unobservable variables. Pp 65 - 115 in G.W. Bohrnstedt and E.F. Borgatta (Eds.): *Social Measurement: Current Issues*. Beverly Hills: Sage.

Carroll, J.B. (1945) The effect of difficulty and chance success on correlations between items and between tests. *Psychometrika*, 26, 347- 372.

Carroll, J.B. (1983) The difficulty of a test and its factor composition revisited. In H. Wainer and S. Messick (Eds.): *Principles of modern psychological measurement*. Hillsdale, N.J: Erlbaum.

Carroll, J.D., Pruzansky, S., and Kruskal, J.B. (1980) Candeling: A general approach to multidimensional analysis of many-way arrays with linear constraints on parameters. *Psychometrika*, 45, 3-24.

Cattell, R.B. (1978) *The scientific use of factor analysis in behavioral and life sciences*. New York: Plenum Press.

Cattell, R.B. (1973) *Personality and mood by questionnaire*. San Francisco: Jossey-Bass.

Chamberlain, G. (1977) An instrumental variable interpretation of identification in variance-components and MIMIC models. In P. Taubman (Ed.): *The determinants of socio-economic success within and between families*. Amsterdam: North-Holland Publishing. Co.

Chen, H-T. (1983) Flowgraph analysis of effect decomposition: Use in recursive and nonrecursive models. *Sociological Methods and Research*, 12, 3-29.

Christoffersson, A. (1975) Factor analysis of dichotomized variables. *Psychometrika*, 40, 5-32.

Churchill, G.A., Jr., and Pecotich, A. (1982) A structural equation investigation of the pay satisfaction-valence relationship among salespeople. *Journal of Marketing*, 46, 114-124.

Churchill, G.A.Jr., and Suprenant, C. (1982) An investigation into the determinants of customer satisfaction. *Journal of Marketing Research*, 19, 491-504.

Cliff, N. (1983) Some cautions concerning the application of causal modeling methods. *Multivariate Behavioral Research*, 18, 115-126.

Cliff, N. (1987) Comments on Professor Freedman's paper. *Journal of Educational Statistics*, 12, 158-160.

Cliff, N., and Krus, D.J. (1976) Interpretation of canonical analysis: Rotated vs. unrotated solutions. *Psychometrika*, 41, 35-42.

Clogg, C. (1981) Latent structure models of mobility. *American Journal of Sociology*, 86,836-868.

Cole, D.A., Howard, G.S., and Maxwell, S.E. (1981) Effects of nomo-versus multiple-operationalization in construct validation efforts. *Journal of Consulting and Clinical Psychology*, 49, 395-405.

Comrey, A.L. (1985) A method for removing outliers to improve factor analytic results. *Multivariate Behavioral Research*, 20, 273-281.

Connell, J.P. (1987) Structural equation modeling and the study of child development: A question of goodness of fit. *Child Development*, 58, 167-175.

Connell, J.P., and J.S. Tanaka (1987) Introduction to the special section on structural equation modeling. *Child Development*, 58, 2-3.

Cooley, W. W. (1979) Structural equations and explanatory observational studies. Pp XV-XXIIX in K.G. Jöreskog and D. Sörbom. *Advances in factor analysis and structural equation models*. Cambridge, Massachusetts: Abt Books.

Cooley, W.W., and Lohnes, P.R. (1976) *Evaluation research in education*. New York: Wiley.

Corcoran, M. (1980) Sex differences in measurement error in status attainment models. *Sociological Methods and Research*, 9, 199-217.

Cornelius, S.W., Willis, S.L., Nesselroade, J.R., and Baltes, P.B. (1983) Convergence between attention variables and factors of psychometric intelligence in older adults. *Intelligence*, 7, 253-269.

Costner, H.L. (1971) Utilizing causal models to discover flaws in experiments. *Sociometry*, 34, 398-410.

Costner, H.L., and Schoenberg, R. (1973) Diagnosing indicator ills in multiple indicator models. Pp 167-199 in A.S. Goldberger and O. D. Duncan (Eds.): *Structural equation models in the social sciences*. New York: Seminar Press.

Crano, W.D., and Mendoza, J.L. (1987) Maternal factors that influence children's positive behaviour: Demonstration of a structural equation analysis of selected data from the Berkeley growth study. *Child Development*, 58, 38-48.

Cronbach, L.J., and Meehl, P.E. (1955) Construct validity in psychological tests. *Psychological Bulletin*, 52, 281-302.

Cudeck, R. (1976) A note on structural models for the circumplex. *Psychometrika*, 51, 143-147.

Cudeck, R. (1989) The analysis of correlation matrices using covariance structure models. *Psychological Bulletin*, 96, in press.

Cudeck, R., and Browne, M. W. (1983) Cross-validation of covariance structures. *Multivariate Behavioral Research*, 18, 147-157.

Cunningham, W.R. (1980) Age comparative factor analysis of ability variables in adulthood and old age. *Intelligence*, 4, 133-149.

Cuttance, P., and Ecob, R. (1987) *Structural modelling by example: Applications in Educational, Behavioral, and Social Research*. Cambridge, U.K.: Cambridge University Press.

Dalton, R.J. (1980) Reassessing parental socialization: Indicator unreliability versus generational transfer. *The American Political Science Review*, 74, 421-431.

Davidon, W.C. (1959) Variable metric method for minimization. A.E.C. *Research and Development Report*, ANL5990, Argonne National Laboratory.

Davies, M., and Kandel, D.B. (1981) Parental and peer influences on adolescents' educational plans: Some further evidence. *American Journal of Sociology*, 87, 363-387.

De Leeuw, J. (1983) Models and methods for the analysis of correlation coefficients. *Journal of Econometrics*, 22, 113-137.

DeSarbo, W.S., Hausman, R.E., Shen, L., and Thompson, W. (1982) Constrained canonical correlation. *Psychometrika*, 47, 489-516.

Dempster, A.P., Laird, N.M., and Rubin, D.B. (1977) Maximum likelihood from incomplete data via the EM algorithm. *Journal of the Royal Statistical Society*, series B, 39, 1-22.

Denison, D.R. (1982) Multidimensional scaling and structural equation modeling: A comparison of multivariate techniques for theory testing. *Multivariate Behavioral Research*, 17, 447-470.

Devlin, S.J., Gnanadesikan, R., and Kettenring, J.R., (1975) Robust estimation and outlier detection with correlation coefficients. *Biometrika*, 62, 531-545.

Dickman, K., and Kaiser, H.F. (1961) Program for inverting a Gramian matrix. *Educational and Psychological Measurement*, 21, 721-727.

Dijkstra, T. (1981) *Latent variables in linear stochastic models*. Ph.D. thesis, University of Groningen.

Dijkstra, T. (1983) Some comments on maximum likelihood and partial least squares methods. *Journal of Econometrics*, 22, 67-90.

Dijkstra, T. (1984) *Latent variables in linear models: Reflections on 'Maximum likelihood' and 'Partial least squares' methods*. Amsterdam: Sociometric Research Foundation.

Dillon, W.R. (1910) Investigating causal systems with qualitative variables: Goodman's wonderful world of logits. *Advances in Consumer Research*, 8, 209-219.

Dillon, W.R., and Goldstein, M. (1984) *Multivariate analysis: Methods and applications*. New York: Wiley.

Dillon, W.R., Kumar, A., and Mulani, N. (1987) Offending estimates in covariance structure analysis: Comments on the causes of and solutions to Heywood cases. *Psychological Bulletin*, 101, 126-135.

Divgi, D.R. (1979) Calculation of the tetrachoric correlation coefficient. *Psychometrika*, 44, 169-172.

Dixon, W.J. (1981) *BMDP Statistical software*. Berkeley: University of California Press.

Donaldson, G. (1983) Confirmatory factor analysis models of information processing stages: An alternative to different scores. *Psychological Bulletin*, 94, 143-151.

Donner, A., and Rosner, B. (1982) Missing values in multiple linear regression with two independent variables. *Communications in Statistics - Theory and Methods*, 11, 127-140.

Draper, N.S., and Smith, H. (1966) *Applied regression analysis*. New York: Wiley

Driel, O.P. van (1978) On various causes of improper solutions in maximum likelihood factor analysis. *Psychometrika*, 43, 225-243.

Duncan, O.D. (1966) Path analysis: Sociological examples. *American Journal of Sociology*, 72, 1-16.

Duncan, O.D. (1969) Some linear models for two-wave, two-variable panel analysis. *Psychological Bulletin*, 72, 177-182.

Duncan, O.D. (1972) Unmeasured variables in linear models for panel analysis. In H.L. Costner (Ed.): *Sociological Methodology 1972*. San Francisco: Jossey-Bass, 36-82.

Duncan, O.D. (1975) *Introduction to structural equation models*. New York: Academic Press.

Duncan, O.D., Haller, A.O., and Portes, A. (1968) Peer influence on aspiration: A reinterpretation. *American Journal of Sociology*, 74, 119-137.

Dunn, J.E. (1973) A note on a sufficiency condition for uniqueness of a restricted factor matrix. *Psychometrika*, 38, 141-143.

Dwyer, J.H. (1983) *Statistical models for the social and behavioral sciences*. Oxford: Oxford University Press.

Eiting, M.H., and Mellenbergh, G.J. (1980) Testing covariance matrix hypotheses: An example from the measurement of musical abilities. *Multivariate Behavioral Research*, 15, 203-223.

Elder, G.H., and Liker, J.K. (1982) Hard times in women's lives: Historical influences across forty years. *American Journal of Sociology*, 88, 241-269.

Entwisle, D.R., and Hayduk, L.A. (1981) Academic expectations and the school attainment of young children. *Sociology of Education*, 54, 34- 50.

Entwisle, D.R., and Hayduk, L.A. (1982) *Early schooling: Cognitive and affective outcomes*. Baltimore: Johns Hopkins University Press.

Etezadi-Amoli, J., and McDonald, R.P. (1983) A second generation nonlinear factor analysis. *Psychometrika*, 48, 315-342.

Ethington, C.A., and Wolfle, L.M. (1986) A structural model of mathematics achievement for men and women. *American Educational Research Journal*, 23, 65-75.

Everitt, B. S. (1984) *An introduction to latent variable models*. London: Chapman and Hall.

Faulbaum, F. (1987) Intergroup comparisons of latent means across waves. *Sociological Methods and Research*, 15, 317-335.

Ferguson, T.S. (1958) A method of generating best asymptotically normal estimates with application to the estimation of bacterial densities. *Annals of Mathematical Statistics*, 29, 1046-1062.

Fink, E.L., and Mabee, T.I. (1978) Linear equations and nonlinear estimation. *Sociological Methods and Research*, 7, 107-120.

Fink, E.L., and Mabee, T.I. (1978) Linear equations and nonlinear estimation: A lesson from a nonrecursive example. *Sociological Methods and Research*, 7, 107-120.

Finkbeiner, C. (1979) Estimation for the multiple factor model when data are missing. *Psychometrika*, 44, 409-420.

Finn, J.D. (1974) *A general model for multivariate analysis.* New York: Holt, Reinhart and Winston.

Finney, J.M. (1972) Indirect effects in path analysis. *Sociological Methods and Research*, 1, 175-186.

Fisher, F.M. (1966) *The identification problem in econometrics.* New York: McGraw-Hill.

Fisher, F.M. (1970) A correspondence principle for simultaneous equation models. *Econometrica*, 38, 73-92.

Fiske, S.T., Kenny, D.A., and Taylor, S.E. (1982) Structural models for the mediation of salience effects on attribution. *Journal of Experimental Social Psychology*, 18, 105-127.

Fleishman, J., and Benson, J. (1987) Using LISREL to evaluate measurement models and scale reliability. *Educational and Psychological Measurement*, 47, 925-939.

Fletcher, R., and Powell, M.J.D. (1963) A rapidly convergent des cent method for minimization. *Computer Journal*, 6, 163- 168.

Folmer, H. (1981) Measurement of the effects of regional policy instruments by means of linear structural equation models and panel data. *Environment and Planning*, A, 13, 1435-1448.

Fornell, C. (1979) External single-set components analysis of multiple- criterion multiple-predictor analysis. *Multivariate Behavioral Research*, 14, 323-338.

Fornell, C. (Ed.): (1982) *A second generation of multivariate analysis*, Volume 1 and 2. New York: Praeger.

Fornell, C. (1983) Issues in the application of covariance structure analysis: A comment. *Journal of Consumer Research*, 9, 443-448.

Fornell, C., and Bookstein, F.L. (1982) Two structural equation models: LISREL and PLS applied to consumer exit-voice theory. *Journal of Marketing Research*, 19, 440-452.

Fornell, C., and Larcker, D.F. (1981a) Evaluating structural equation models with unobservable variables and measurement error. *Journal of Marketing Research*, 18, 39-50.

Fornell, C., and Larcker, D.F. (1981b) Structural equation models with unobservable variables and measurement error: Algebra and statistics. *Journal of Marketing Research*, 18, 382-388.

Fornell, C., and Larcker, D.F. (1984) Misapplications of simulations in structural equation models. Reply to Acito and Anderson. *Journal of Marketing Research*, 21, 113-117.

Fornell, C., and Robinson, W.T. (1983) Industrial organization and consumer satisfaction/dissatisfaction. *Journal of Consumer Research*, 9, 403-412.

Fox, J. (1980) Effect analysis in structural equation models: Extensions and simplified methods of computation. *Sociological Methods and Research*, 9, 3-28.

Fox, J. (1985) Effect analysis in structural-equation models II: Calculation of specific indirect effects. *Sociological Methods and Research*, 14, 81-95.

Fox, J. (1987) Statistical models for nonexperimental data: A comment on Freedman. *Journal of Educational Statistics*, 12, 161-164.

Frederiksen, C.R. (1974) Models for the analysis of alternative sources of growth in correlated stochastic variables. *Psychometrika*, 39, 223- 245.

Fredricks, A.J., and Dossett, D.L. (1983) Attitude-behavior relations: A comparison of the Fishbein-Ajzen and the Bentler-Speckart models. *Journal of Personality and Social Psychology*, 45, 501-512.

Fredricks, A.J., and Dossett, D.L. (1983) Attitude-behavior relations: A comparison of the Fischbein-Ajzen and Bentler-Speckart models. *Journal of Personality and Social Psychology*, 45, 501-512.

Freedman, D.A. (1987) A rejoinder on models, metaphors, and fables. *Journal of Educational Statistics*, 12, 206-223.

Freedman, D.A. (1987) As other see us: A case study in path analysis. *Journal of Educational Statistics*, 12, 101-128.

Freeman, E.H. (1982) The implementation of effect decomposition methods for two general structural covariance modeling systems. Unpublished dissertation. University of California, Los Angeles.

French, J.V. (1951) The description of aptitude and achievement tests in terms of rotated factors. *Psychometric Monographs*, 5.

Frey, B.S., and Weck-Hanneman, H. (1984) The hidden economy as an 'unobserved' variable. *European Economic Review*, 26, 33-53.

Fritz, W. (1986) The LISREL-approach of causal analysis as an instrument of critical theory comparison within management science. Pp. 145-152 in W. Gaul, and M. Schader (Eds.): *Classification as a Tool of Research*. North-Holland: Elsevier Science Publishers B.V.

Fuchs, C. (1982) Maximum likelihood estimation and model selection in contingency tables with missing data. *Journal of the American Statistical Association*, 77, 270-278.

Fulker, D.W., Baker, L.A., and Bock, R.D. (1983) Estimating components of covariance using LISREL. *Data Analyst* (Scientific Software, Inc.) 1, 5-8.

Fuller, W.A. (1986) Estimators of the factor model for survey data. In I.B. MacNeill, and G.J. Umphrey (Eds.): *Proceedings of the symposia in statistics and festschrift in honour of V.M. Joshi*. Boston: Reidel.

Fuller, W.A. (1987) *Measurement error models*. New York: John Wiley and Sons.

Gallini, J. (1983) Misspecifications that can result in path analysis structures. *Applied Psychological Measurement*, 7, 125-137.

Gallini, J.K., and Mandeville, G.K. (1984) An investigation of the effect of sample size and specification error on the fit of structural equation models. *Journal of Experimental Education*, 53, 9-19.

Gardner, R.C., Lalonde, R.N., and Moorcroft, R. (1987) Second language attrition: The role of motivation and USE. *Journal of Language and Social Psychology*, 6, 29-47.

Gardner, R.C., and Lalonde, R.N. (1983) The socio-educational model of second language acquisition: An investigation using LISREL causal modeling. *Journal of Language and Social Psychology*, 2, 1-15.

Geraci, V.J. (1976) Identification of simultaneous equation models with measurement error. *Journal of Econometrics*, 4, 263-283.

Geraci, V.J. (1977) Estimation of simultaneous equation models with measurement error. *Econometrica*, 45, 1243-1255.

Gerbing, D.W., and Anderson, J.C. (1984) On the meaning of within- factor correlated measurement errors. *Journal of Consumer Research*, 11, 572-580.

Gerbing, D.W., and Anderson, J.C. (1985) The effects of sampling error and model characteristics on parameter estimation for maximum likelihood confirmatory factor analysis. *Multivariate Behavioral Research*, 20, 255-271.

Gerbing, D.W., and Anderson, J.C. (1987) Improper solutions in the analysis of covariance structures: Their interpretability and a comparison of alternate respecifications. *Psychometrika*, 52, 99-111.

Gerbing, D.W., and Hunter, J.E. (1982) The metric of the latent variables in the LISREL-IV analysis. *Educational and Psychological Measurement*, 42, 423-427.

Gerbing, D.W., and Hunter, J.E. (1986) *ITAN: A statistical package for ITem ANalysis including multiple groups factor analysis*. Revision E. Waco, TX: Baylor University Computation Center.

Geweke, J.F., and Singleton, K.J. (1980) Interpreting the likelihood ratio statistic in factor models when sample size is small. *Journal of the American Statistical Association*, 75, 133-137.

Glasser, M. (1964) Linear regression analysis with missing observations among the independent variables. *Journal of the American Statistical Association*, 59, 834-844.

Gleser, L.J. (1981) Estimation in a multivariate 'errors in variables' regression model: large sample results. *Annals of Statistics*, 9, 24-44.

Gnanadesikan R., and Kettenring J.R. (1972) Robust estimates, residuals, and outlier detection with multiresponse data. *Biometrics*, 28, 81-124.

Gnanadesikan, R. (1977) *Methods for statistical data analysis of multivariate observations*. New York: Wiley.

Goldberger, A.S. (1964) *Econometric theory*. New York: Wiley.

Goldberger, A.S. (1971) Econometrics and psychometrics: A survey of communalities. *Psychometrika*, 36, 83-107.

Goldberger, A.S. (1972) Structural equation methods in the social sciences. *Econometrica*, 40, 979-1001.

Goldberger, A.S. (1973) Structural equation models: An overview. In A.S. Goldberger and O.D. Duncan (Eds.): *Structural equation models in the social sciences*. New York: Seminar Press.

Goldberger, A.S., and Duncan, O.D., Eds. (1973) *Structural equation models in the social sciences*. New York: Seminar Press.

Gollob, H.F., and Reichardt, C.S. (1987) Taking account of time lags in causal models. *Child Development*, 58, 80-92.

Gottfredson, D.C. (1982) Personality and persistence in education: A longitudinal study. *Journal of Personality and Social Psychology*, 43, 532-545.

Graff, J., and Schmidt, P. (1982) A general model for decomposition of effects. In K.G. Jöreskog and H. Wold (Eds.): *Systems under indirect observation: Causality, structure and prediction*. Amsterdam: North- Holland Publishing Co.

Greenberg, D., and Kessler, R.C. (1982) Equilibrium and identification in linear panel models. *Sociological Methodology and Research*, 10, 435-451.

Greene, V.L. (1977) An algorithm for total and indirect causal effects. *Political Methodology*, 44, 369-381.

Greenlees, J.S., Reece, W.S., and Zieschang, K.D. (1982) Imputation of missing values when the probability of response depends on the variable being imputed. *Journal of the American Statistical Association*, 77, 251-261.

Griliches, Z. (1974) Errors in variables and other unobservables. *Econometrica*, 42, 971-998.

Guilford, J.P. (1956) The structure of intellect. *Psychological Bulletin*, 53, 267-293.

Guttman, L.A. (1954) A new approach to factor analysis: The radix. In P.F. Lazarsfeld (Ed.): *Mathematical thinking in the social sciences*. New York: Columbia University Press.

Hambleton, R., and Cook, L.L. (1977) Latent trait models and their use in the analysis of educational test data. *Journal of Educational Measurement*, 14, 75-96.

Hargens, L.L., Reskin, B.F., and Allison, P.D. (1976) Problems in estimating measurement error from panel data. *Sociological Methods and Research*, 4, 439-458.

Harlow, L.L. (1985) *Behavior of some elliptical theory estimators with nonnormal data in a covariance structures framework: A Monte Carlo study*, Ph.D. Thesis. University of California, Los Angeles.

Harman, H.H. (1967) *Modern factor analysis* (3rd ed.) Chicago: University of Chicago Press.

Hart, B., and Spearman, C. (1913) General ability, its existence and nature. *British Journal of Psychology*, 5, 51-84.

Hartley, H.O., and Hocking, R.R. (1971) The analysis of incomplete data. *Biometrics*, 27, 783-823.

Hasselrot, T., and Lernberg, L.O. (Eds.) (1980) *Tonåringen och livet*. Vällingby, Sweden:Liber förlag (In Swedish).

Hattie, J. (1985) Methodology review: Assessing unidimensionality of tests and items. *Applied Psychological Measurement*, 9, 139-164.

Hauser, R.M. (1984) Some cross-population comparisons of family bias in the effects of schooling on occupational status. *Social Science Research*, 13, 159-187.

Hauser, R.M. (1986) Family effects in simple models of education, occupational status, and earnings: Findings from the Wisconsin and Kalamazoo studies. *Journal of Labor Economics*, 4, 83-115.

Hauser, R.M., and Goldberger, A.S. (1971) The treatment of unobservable variables in path analysis. Pp. 81-117 in Costner, H.L.: *Sociological Methodology*.

Hauser, R.M., and Mossel, P.A. (1985) Fraternal resemblance in educational attainment and occupational status. *The American Journal of Sociology*, 91, 650-673.

Hauser, R.M., and Mossel, P.A. (1987) Some structural equation models of sibling resemblance in educational attainment and occupational status. In P. Cuttance and R. Ecob (Eds.): *Structural modelling by example: Applications in educational, behavioral, and social research*. Cambridge, U.K.: Cambridge University Press.

Hauser, R.M., Tsai, S.L., and Sewell, W.H. (1981) A model of stratification with response error in social and psychological variables. University of Wisconsin Madison: Center for Demography and Ecology Working Paper 81-16.

Hayduk, L.A. (1985) Personal space: The conceptual and measurement implications of structural equation models. *Canadian Journal of Behavioural Science*, 17, 140-149.

Hayduk, L.A. (1987) *Structural equation modelling with* LISREL: *Essentials and advances*. Baltimore: The Johns Hopkins University Press.

Hayduk, L.A., and Wonnacott, T. (1980) Effect equations or effect coefficients: a note on the visual and verbal presentation of multiple regression interactions. *Canadian Journal of Sociology*, 5, 399-404.

Haynam, G.E., Govindarajulu, A., and Leone, F.C. (1970) Tables of the cumulative noncentral chi square distribution. Pp. 1-78 in H.L. Harter and D.B. Owen (Eds.): *Selected Tables of Mathematical Statistics*. Providence: American Mathematical Society.

Heckman, J.J. (1979) Sample selection bias as a specification error. *Econometrica*, 45, 153-161.

Heise, D.R. (1969) Separating reliability and stability in test-retest correlation. *American Sociological Review*, 34, 93-101.

Heise, D.R. (1970) Causal inference from panel data. In E.F. Borgatta and G.W. Bohrnstedt (Eds.): *Sociological Methodology 1970*. San Francisco: Jossey-Bass,3-27.

Heise, D.R. (1972) Employing nominal variables, induced variables, and block variables in path analysis. *Sociological Methods and Research*, 1, 147-173.

Heise, D.R. (1975) *Causal analysis*. New York: Wiley.

Heise, D.R., and Simmons, R.G. (1985) Some computer-based developments in sociology. *Science*, 228, 428-33.

Hemelrijk, J. (1966) Underlining random variables. *Statistika Neerlandika*, 20, 1-8.

Hertel, B.R. (1976) Minimizing error variance introduced by missing data routines in survey analysis. *Sociological Methods and Research*, 4, 459-474.

Herting, J.R. (1985) Multiple indicator models using LISREL. In H.M. Blalock, Jr. (Ed.): *Causal models in the social sciences*, (2nd ed). New York: Aldine.

Hertzog, C., and Nesselroade, J.R. (1987) Beyond autoregressive models: Some implications of the trait-state distinction for the structural modeling of developmental change. *Child Development*, 58, 93-109.

Hill, P.W., and McGaw, B. (1981) Testing the assumptions underlying Bloom's taxonomy. *American Educational Research Journal*, 18, 93- 101.

Hilton, T.L. (1969) Growth study annotated bibliography. Progress Report 69-11. Princeton, N.J.: Educational Testing Service.

Hocking, R.R., and Marx, D.L. (1979) Estimation with incomplete data. An improved computational method and the analysis of nested data. *Communications in Statistics - Theory and Methods*, 8, 1155-1181.

Hocking, R.R., and Smith, W.B. (1968) Estimation of parameters in the multivariate normal distribution with missing observations. *Journal of the American Statistical Association*, 63, 159-173.

Hodapp, V. (1984) *Analyse linearer kausalmodelle*. Bern, Switzerland: Verlag Hans Huber. (In German)

Hodge, R.W., and Treiman, D.J. (1968) Social participation and social status. *American Sociological Review*, 33, 723-740.

Hoelter, J.W. (1983) Factorial invariance and self-esteem: Reassessing race and sex differences. *Social Forces*, 61, 834-46.

Hoelter, J.W. (1983) The analysis of covariance structures: Goodness-of- fit indices. *Sociological Methods and Research*, 11, 325-344.

Hoelter, J. (1984) Relative effects of significant others on self- education. *Social Psychology Quarterly*, 47, 255-262.

Holbrook, M.B. (1978) Beyond attitude structure: Toward the informational determinants of attitude. *Journal of Marketing Research*, 15, 545-556.

Holzinger, K., and Swineford, F. (1939) *A study in factor analysis: The stability of a bifactor solution*. Supplementary Educational Monograph no. 48. Chicago: University of Chicago Press.

Hope, K. (1987) Barren theory or pretty craft: A response to Professor Freedman. *Journal of Educational Statistics*, 12, 129-147.

Hoppe, H-H. (1980) On how not to make inferences about measurement error. *Quality and Quantity*, 14, 503-510.

Horn, J.L., and McArdle, J.J. (1980) Perspectives on mathematical/statistical model building (MASMOB) in aging research. Pp 503-541 in L.W. Poon (Ed.): *Aging in the 1980's*. Washington, D.C.: American Psychological Association.

Howe, H.G. (1955) Some contributions to factor analysis. Report ORNL-1919. Oak Ridge, Tenn.: Oak Ridge National Laboratory.

Huba, G.J., Wingard, J.A., and Bentler, P.M. (1981) A comparison of two latent variable causal models for adolescent drug use. *Journal of Personality and Social Psychology*, 40, 180-193.

Huba, G.J., and Bentler, P.M. (1982) On the usefulness of latent variable causal modeling testing theories of naturally occurring events. *Journal of Personality and Social Psychology*, 43, 604-611.

Huba, G.J., and Bentler, P.M. (1983) Test of a drug use causal model using asymptotically distribution free methods. *Journal of Drug Education*, 13, 3-14.

Huba, G.J., and Harlow, L.L. (1987) Robust structural equation models: Implications for developmental psychology. *Child Development*, 58, 147-166.

Huba, G.J., and Palisoc, A.L. (1983) Computerized path diagrams on a line printer. *Computational Statistics and Data Analysis*, 1, 137-140.

Hughes, M.A., Price, R.L., and Marrs, D.W. (1986) Linking theory construction and theory testing: Models with multiple indicators of latent variables. *Academy of Management Review*, 11, 128-144.

Huitema, B.H. (1980) *The analysis of covariance and alternatives*. New York: Wiley.

Hultsch, D.F., Hertzog, C., and Dixon, R.A. (1984) Text recall in adulthood: The role of intellectual abilities. *Developmental Psychology*, 20, 1193-1209.

Humphreys, L.G. (1968) The fleeting nature of college academic success. *Journal of Educational Psychology*, 59, 375-380.

Hunter, J.E, Gerbing, D.W., and Boster, F.J. (1982) Machiavellian beliefs and personality: Construct validity of the Machiavellianism dimension. *Journal of Personality and Social Psychology*, 43, 1293- 1305.

Hunter, J.E. (1973) Methods or reordering the correlation matrix to facilitate visual inspection and preliminary cluster analysis. *Journal of Educational Measurement*, 10, 51-61.

Hunter, J.E., and Gerbing, D.W. (1982) Unidimensional measurement, second-order factor analysis, and causal models. In B.M. Staw and L.L. Cummings (Eds): *Research in Organizational Behavior* (Vol. 4, pp. 267-299). JAI Press.

Hägglund, G. (1982) Factor analysis by instrumental variable methods. *Psychometrika*, 47, 209-222.

Hägglund, G. (1986) *Factor analysis by instrumental variables methods*. Acta Universitatis Upsaliensis (Ph.D. Dissertation). University of Uppsala.

Härnqvist, K. (1962) *Manaul till DBA* (Manual for DBA). Stockholm: Skandinaviska Testförlaget (In Swedish).

Jackson, D.N., and Chan, D.W. (1980) Maximum-likelihood estimation in common factor analysis: A cautionary note. *Psychological Bulletin*, 88, 502-508.

Jagodzinski, W. (1984) The overestimation of stability coefficients in LISREL applications: some problems in the correction for attenuation. (In German) *Zeitschrift für Soziologie*, 13, 225-242.

Jagodzinski, W., Kühnel, S.M., and Schmidt, P. (1987) Is there a "Socratic effect" in nonexperimental panel studies? *Sociological Methods and Research*, 15, 259-302.

Jagodzinski, W., and Kühnel, S.M. (1987) Estimation of reliability and stability in single-indicator multiple-wave models. *Sociological Methods and Research*, 15, 219-258.

Jagpal, H.S. (1982) Multicollinearity in structural equation models with unobservable variables. *Journal of Marketing Research*, 19, 431-439.

James, L.R., Mulaik, S.A., and Brett, J.M. (1982) *Causal analysis: Assumptions, models, and data.* Beverly Hills: Sage.

Jennrich, R.I. (1978) Rotational equivalence of factor loading matrices with specified values. *Psychometrika*, 43, 421-426.

Jennrich, R.I. (1987) Tableau algorithms for factor analysis by instrumental variables. *Psychometrika*, 52, 469-476.

Jennrich, R.I., and Robinson, S.M. (1969) A Newton-Raphson algorithm for maximum likelihood factor analysis. *Psychometrika*, 34, 111-123.

Jensema, C. (1976) A simple technique for estimating latent trait mental test parameters. *Educational and Psychological Measurement*, 36, 705- 715.

John, G., and Reve, T. (1982) The reliability and validity of key informant data from dyadic relationships in marketing channels. *Journal of Marketing Research*, 19, 517-524.

Johnson, D.R., and Creech, J.C. (1983) Ordinal measures in multiple indicator models: A simulation study of categorization errors. *American Sociological Review*, 48, 398-407.

Johnston, J. (1972) *Econometric methods.* New York: McGraw- Hill.

Judd, C.M., and Krosnick, J.A. (1982) Attitude centrality, organization, and measurement. *Journal of Personality and Social Psychology*, 42, 436-447.

Jöreskog, K.G. (1966) Testing a simple structure hypothesis in factor analysis. *Psychometrika*, 32, 165-178.

Jöreskog, K.G. (1967) Some contributions to maximum likelihood factor analysis. *Psychometrika*, 32, 443-482.

Jöreskog, K.G. (1969) A general approach to confirmatory maximum likelihood factor analysis. *Psychometrika*, 34, 183-202.

Jöreskog, K.G. (1970a) A general method for analysis of covariance structures. *Biometrika*, 57, 239-251.

Jöreskog, K.G. (1970b) Estimation and testing of simplex models. *British Journal of Mathematical and Statistical Psychology*, 23, 121- 145.

Jöreskog, K.G. (1970c) Factoring the multitest-multioccasion correlation matrix. In C. E. Lunneborg (Ed.): *Current problems and techniques in multivariate psychology.* Proceedings of a conference honoring Professor Paul Horst. Seattle: University of Washington.

Jöreskog, K.G. (1971a) Simultaneous factor analysis in several populations. *Psychometrika*, 57, 409-426.

Jöreskog, K.G. (1971b) Statistical analysis of sets of congeneric tests. *Psychometrika*, 36, 109-133.

Jöreskog, K.G. (1973a) A general method for estimating a linear structural equation system. In A.S. Goldberger and O.D. Duncan (Eds.): *Structural equation models in the social sciences.* New York: Seminar Press, 85-112.

Jöreskog, K.G. (1973b) Analysis of covariance structures. In P.R. Krishnaiah (Ed.): *Multivariate Analysis - III*. New York:Academic Press, 263-285.

Jöreskog, K.G. (1974) Analyzing psychological data by structural analysis of covariance matrices. In R.C. Atkinson et al. (Eds.): *Contemporary developments in mathematical psychology*- Volume II. San Francisco: W.H. Freeman, 1-56.

Jöreskog, K.G. (1976) Causal models in the social sciences: The need for methodological research. *In Uppsala University 500 years*, Volume 7. Stockholm: Almqvist & Wiksell International.

Jöreskog, K.G. (1977a) Factor analysis by least-squares and maximum-likelihood methods. Pp. 125-153 in K. Enslein, A. Ralston, and H.S. Wilf (Eds.): *Statistical methods for digital computers*. New York: Wiley.

Jöreskog, K.G. (1977b) Structural equation models in the social sciences: Specification, estimation and testing. In P.R. Krishnaiah (Ed.): *Applications of statistics*. Amsterdam: North-Holland Publishing Co., 265-287.

Jöreskog, K.G. (1978a) An econometric model for multivariate panel data. *Annales de l'INSEE*, 30-31, 355-366.

Jöreskog, K.G. (1978b) Structural analysis of covariance and correlation matrices. *Psychometrika*, 43, 443-477.

Jöreskog, K.G. (1979a) Author's addendum, February, 1979. Pp. 40- 43 in K.G. Jöreskog and D. Sörbom: *Advances in factor analysis and structural equation models*. Cambridge, Mass.: Abt Books.

Jöreskog, K.G. (1979b) Basic ideas of factor and component analysis. In K.G. Jöreskog and D. Sörbom: *Advances in factor analysis and structural equation models*. Cambridge, Mass.: Abt Books, 5-20.

Jöreskog, K.G. (1979c) Statistical estimation of structural models in longitudinal developmental investigations. In J.R. Nesselroade and P.B. Baltes (Eds.): *Longitudinal research in the study of behavior and development*. New York: Academic Press.

Jöreskog, K.G. (1981a) Analysis of covariance structures. *Scandinavian Journal of Statistics*, 8, 65-92.

Jöreskog, K.G. (1981b) Basic issues in the application of LISREL. *Data*, 1:1, 1-6.

Jöreskog, K.G. (1981c) Introduction to LISREL V. *Data*, 1:2,1-6.

Jöreskog, K.G. (1982) The LISREL approach to causal model building in the social sciences. Pp 81-99 in K.G. Jöreskog and H. Wold (Eds.): *Systems under indirect observation*: Part I. Amsterdam: North-Holland Publishing.

Jöreskog, K.G. (1983) Factor analysis as an errors-in-variables model. In H. Wainer and S. Messick (Eds.): *Principals of Modern Psychological Measurement: A Festschrift in Honor of Frederic M. Lord*. Hillsdale, N.J.: Lawrence Erlbaum Publishers. Pp. 185 -196.

Jöreskog, K.G. (1986a) Analysis of Longitudinal Data with LISREL. Im W. Lehmacher und A. Hörmann (Hrsg.) *Statistik- Software. 3. Konferenz über die wissenschaftliche Anwendung von Statistik-Software, 1985*. Stuttgart: Gustav Fischer Verlag.

Jöreskog, K.G. (1986b) Estimation of the polyserial correlation from summary statistics. Research Report 86-2. University of Uppsala, Department of Statistics.

Jöreskog, K.G., and Goldberger, A.S. (1972) Factor analysis by generalized least squares. *Psychometrika*, 37, 243-250.

Jöreskog, K.G., and Goldberger, A.S. (1975) Estimation of a model with multiple indicators and multiple causes of a single latent variable. *Journal of the American Statistical Association*, 10, 631-639.

Jöreskog, K.G., and Lawley D.N. (1968) New methods in maximum likelihood factor analysis. *British Journal of Mathematical and Statistical Psychology*, 21: 85-96.

Jöreskog, K.G., and Sörbom, D. (1976) Statistical models and methods for test-retest situations. In D.N.M. deGruijter and L.J.Th. van der Kamp (Eds.): *Advances in psychological and educational measurement*. New York: Wiley, 285-325.

Jöreskog, K.G., and Sörbom, D. (1977) Statistical models and methods for analysis of longitudinal data. In D.J. Aigner and A.S. Goldberger (Eds.): *Latent variables in socio-economic models*. Amsterdam: North- Holland Publishing Co.,285-325.

Jöreskog, K.G., and Sörbom, D. (1979) *Advances in factor analysis and structural equation models*. Cambridge, Mass.: Abt Books.

Jöreskog, K.G., and Sörbom, D. (1980a) EFAP II: *Exploratory factor analysis program* (Computer program). Chicago: International Educational Services.

Jöreskog, K.G., and Sörbom, D. (1980b) Simultaneous analysis of longitudinal data from several cohorts. Research Report 80-5. University of Uppsala, Department of Statistics.

Jöreskog, K.G., and Sörbom, D. (1982) Recent developments in structural equation modeling. *Journal of Marketing Research*, 19, 404 -416.

Jöreskog, K.G., and Sörbom, D. (1985) Simultaneous analysis of longitudinal data from several cohorts. Pp. 323-341 in W.M. Mason and S.E. Fienberg (Eds.): *Cohort analysis in social research: Beyond the identification problem*. New York: Springer-Verlag.

Jöreskog, K.G., and Sörbom, D. (1986a) PRELIS *A program for multivariate data screening and data summarization. A preprocessor for* LISREL. Mooresville, Indiana: Scientific Software, Inc.

Jöreskog, K.G., and Sörbom, D. (1986b) SIMPLIS - *A fast and simple version of* LISREL. Mooresville, Indiana: Scientific Software, Inc.

Jöreskog, K.G., and Sörbom, D. (1986c) Zur simultanen analyse von längsschnittdaten aus mehreren kohorten. Im C. Möbus und W. Schneider (Hrsg.): *Strukturmodelle für Längsschnittdaten und zeitreihen:* LISREL, *Pfad- und Varianzanalyse*. Bern, Switzerland: Verlag Hans Huber. (In German)

Jöreskog, K.G., and Wold, H. (Eds.) (1982) *Systems under indirect observation: Causality, structure, prediction*. Amsterdam: North- Holland Publishing Co.

Kaiser, H.F., and Dickman, K. (1960) Sample and population score matrices and sample correlation matrices from an arbitrary population correlation matrix. *Psychometrika*, 27, 179-182.

Kalleberg, A.L. (1974) A causal approach to the measurement of job satisfaction. *Social Science Research*, 3, 299-322.

Karlin, S. (1987) Path analysis in genetic epidemiology and alternatives. *Journal of Educational Statistics*, 12, 165-177.

Keeves, J.P. (1972) *Educational environment and student achievement.* Stockholm Studies in Educational Psychology No. 20. Stockholm: Almqvist & Wiksell.

Kelderman, H., Mellenbergh, G.J., and Elshout, J.J. (1981) Guilford's facet theory of intelligence: An empirical comparison of models. *Multivariate Behavioral Research* 16, 37-62.

Kennedy, P.H., Starrfield, S.L., and Baffi, C. (1983) Using LISREL analysis for drug research. *Journal of School Health*, 53, 277-281.

Kenny, D.A. (1979) *Correlation and causality.* New York: Wiley.

Kenny, D.A., and Judd, C.M. (1984) Estimating the nonlinear and interactive effects of latent variables. *Psychological Bulletin*, 96, 201- 210.

Kerchoff, A.C. (1974) *Ambition and attainment.* Rose Monograph Series.

Kerlinger, F.N. (1980) Analysis of covariance structure tests of a criterion-referenced theory of attitudes. *Multivariate Behavioral Research*, 15, 403-422.

Kessler, R.C., and Greenberg, D.F. (1981) *Linear panel analysis: Models of quantitative change.* New York: Academic Press.

Kiiveri, H.T. (1987) An incomplete data approach to the analysis of covariance structures. *Psychometrika* , 52, 539-554.

Kim, J.O., and Mueller, C.W. (1978) *Introduction to factor analysis: What it is and how to do it.* Beverly Hills: Sage.

Klein, L.R. (1950) *Economic fluctuations in the United States 1921- 1941.* Cowles Commission Monograph No. 11. New York: Wiley.

Kluegel, J.R., Singleton, R., and Starnes, C.E. (1977) Subjective class identification: A multiple indicators approach. *American Sociological Review*, 42, 599-611.

Kmenta, J. (1971) *Elements of econometrics.* New York: MacMillan.

Kohn, M.L., and Schooler, C.L. (1981) Job conditions and intellectual flexibility: a longitudinal assessment of their reciprocal effects. Pp 281-313 in D.J. Jackson and E.F. Borgotta (Eds.): *Factor analysis and measurement in sociological research.* Beverly Hills: Sage.

Kohn, M.L., and Schooler, C.L. (1982) Job conditions and personality: A longitudinal assessment of their reciprocal effects. *American Journal of Sociology*, 87, 1257-1286.

Kohn, M.L., and Schooler, C.L. (1983) Work and Personality: *An inquiry into the impact of social stratification.* Norwood, N.J.: Ablex.

Krane, W.R., and McDonald, R.P. (1978) Scale invariance and the factor analysis of covariance matrices. *British Journal of Mathematical and Statistical Psychology*, 31, 218-228.

Krause, M. (1987) Chronic financial strain, social support, and depressive symptoms among older adults. *Psychology and Aging*, 2, 185-191.

Kristof, W. (1971) On the theory of a set of tests which differ in length. *Psychometrika*, 36, 207-255.

Kroonenberg, P.M., and Lewis, C. (1982) Methodological issues in the search for a factor model: Exploration through confirmation. *Journal of Educational Statistics*, 7, 69-89.

Laake , P. (1987) *Studies of performance in models with non-linear covariance structure: A non-robust and a robust approach.* Unpublished Ph.D. Dissertation, University of Oslo, Norway.

Lalonde, R.N., and Gardner, R.C. (1984) Investigating a causal model of second language acquisition: Where does personality fit? *Canadian Journal of Behavioural Science*, 16, 224-237.

Land, K.C., and Felson, M. (1978) Sensitivity analysis of arbitrarily identified simultaneous-equation models. *Sociological Methods and Research*, 6, 283-307.

Lansman, M., Donaldson, G., Hunt, E., Yantis, S. (1982) Ability factors and cognitive processes. *Intelligence*, 6, 347-386.

Lau, R.R. (1982) Origins of health locus of control beliefs. *Journal of Personality and Social Psychology*, 42, 322-334.

Laumann, E.O., Knoke D., and Kim, Y-H. (1985) An organizational approach to state policy formation: A comparative study of energy and health domains. *American Sociological Review*, 50, 1-19.

Lawley, D.N. (1940) The estimation of factor loadings by the method of maximum likelihood. *Proceedings of the Royal Society Edinburgh*, 60, 64-82.

Lawley, D.N. (1943) On problems connected with item selection and test construction. *Proceedings of the Royal Society of Edinburgh*, 61-A, 273-287.

Lawley, D.N. (1944) The factorial analysis of multiple item tests. *Proceedings of the Royal Society of Edinburgh*, 62-A. 74-82.

Lawley, D.N., and Maxwell, A.E. (1971) *Factor analysis as a statistical method*, (2nd edition). London: Butterworths.

Leamer, E.E. (1978) *Specification searches: Ad hoc inference with non-experimental data.* New York: Wiley.

Lee, S-Y. (1980) Estimation of covariance structure models with parameters subject to functional restraints. *Psychometrika*, 45, 309- 324.

Lee, S-Y. (1981) A. Bayesian approach to confirmatory factor analysis. *Psychometrika.* 46, 153-160.

Lee, S-Y. (1985) Analysis of covariance and correlation structures. *Computational Statistics and Data Analysis*, 2, 279-295.

Lee, S-Y. (1986) Estimation for structural equation models with missing data. *Psychometrika*, 51, 93-99.

Lee, S-Y., and Bentler, P.M. (1980) Some asymptotic properties of constrained generalized least squares estimation in covariance structure models. *South African Statistical Journal*, 14, 121-136.

Lee, S-Y., and Fong, W.K. (1983) A scale invariant model for three- mode factor analysis. *British Journal of Mathematical and Statistical Psychology*, 36, 217-223.

Lee, S-Y., and Jennrich, R.I. (1979) A study of algorithms for covariance structure analysis with specific comparisons using factor analysis. *Psychometrika*, 44, 99-113.

Lee, S-Y., and Jennrich, R.I. (1984) The analysis of structural equation models by means of derivative free nonlinear least squares. *Psychometrika*, 49, 521-528.

Lee, S-Y., and Poon, W-Y. (1986) Maximum likelihood estimation of polyserial correlations. *Psychometrika* , 51, 113-121.

Lee, S-Y., and Tsui, K.L (1982) Covariance structure analysis in several populations. *Psychometrika*, 47, 297-308.

Lei, H., and Skinner, H.A. (1982) What difference does language make? Structural analysis of the personality research form. *Multivariate Behavioral Research*, 17, 33-46.

Levin, M.E. (1979) On theory-change and meaning-change. *Philosophy of Science*, 46, 407-424.

Lewis-Beck, M.S., and Mohr, L.B. (1976) Evaluating effects of independent variables. *Political Methodology*, 3, 27-47.

Li, C.C. (1975) *Path analysis: A primer*. Pacific Grove: Boxwood.

Liang, J. (1984) Dimensions of the life satisfaction index: A structural formulation. *Journal of Gerontology*, 39, 613-622.

Lindsay, P., and Knox, W.E. (1984) Continuity and change in work values among young adults: A longitudinal study. *American Journal of Sociology*, 89, 918-931.

Lingoes, J.C., and Borg, I. (1983) A quasi-statistical model for choosing between alternative configurations derived from ordinally constrained data. *British Journal of Mathematical and Statistical Psychology*, 36, 36-53.

Linn, R.L., and Werts, C.E. (1982) Measurement error in regression. Pp. 131-154 in G. Keren (Ed): *Statistical and methodological issues in psychology and social science research*. Hillsdale, NJ: Erlbaum.

Liska, A.E., and Reed, M.D. (1985) Ties to conventional institutions and delinquency: Estimating reciprocal effects. *American Sociological Review*, 50, 547-560.

Little, R.J.A. (1982) Models for nonresponse in sample surveys. *Journal of the American Statistical Association*, 77, 237-250.

Little, R.J.A. (1983) Superpopulation models for nonresponse: The nonignorable case. Pp. 383-416 in W.G. Madow, I. Olkin and D.B. Rubin (Eds.): *Incomplete data in sample surveys*, vol 2. New York: Academic Press.

Little, R.J.A., and Schluchter, M.D. (1985) Maximum likelihood estimation for mixed continuous and categorical data with missing values. *Biometrika*, 72, 497-512.

Lohnes, P.R. (1979) Factorial modeling in support of causal inference. *American Educational Research Journal*, 16, 323-340.

Lomax, R. G. (1982) A guide to LISREL-type structural equation modelling. *Behaviour Research Methods and Instrumentation*, 14, 1-8.

Lomax, R.G. (1983) A guide to multiple-sample structural equation modeling. *Behavior Research Methods and Instrumentation*, 15, 580- 584.

Long, J. S. (1976) Estimation and hypothesis testing in linear models containing measurement error. *Sociological Methods and Research*, 5, 157-206.

Long, J.S. (1981) Estimation and hypothesis testing in linear models containing measurement error: A review of Jöreskog's model for the analysis of covariance structures. Pp 209-256 in P.V. Marsden (Ed.): *Linear models in social research*. Beverly Hills: Sage.

Long, J.S. (1983a) *Confirmatory factor analysis: A preface to* LISREL. Beverly Hills: Sage Publications.

Long, J.S. (1983b) *Covariance structure models: An introduction to* LISREL. Beverly Hills: Sage Publications.

Lord, F.M. (1952) *A theory of test scores.* (Psychometric Monograph No 7). Psychometric Society.

Lord, F.M. (1956) A study of speed factors and academic grades. *Psychometrika*, 21, 31-50.

Lord, F.M. (1957) A significance test for the hypothesis that two variables measure the same trait except for errors of measurement. *Psychometrika*, 22, 207-220.

Lord, F.M. (1980) *Applications of item response theory to practical testing problems.* Hillsdale, NJ: Erlbaum.

Lord, F.M., and Novick, M.E. (1968). *Statistical theories of mental test scores.* Reading: Addison-Wesley Publishing Co.

Lorens, C.S. (1964) *Flowgraphs for the modeling and analysis of linear systems.* New York: McGraw Hill.

Luenberger, D.G. (1979) *Introduction to dynamic systems.* New York: Wiley.

Lunneborg, C.E., and Abbott, R.D. (1983) *Elementary multivariate analysis for the behavioral sciences.* Amsterdam: North-Holland.

Luoma, M. (1981) On the use of LISREL in the analysis of investment equations. Proceedings of the University of Vaasa, Discussion Paper 28.

Lutz, R.J. (1975) An experimental investigation of causal relations among cognitions, affect and behavioral intention. *Journal of Consumer Research*, 3, 197-208.

Lynch, J.G., Jr. (1982) On the external validity of experiments in consumer research. *Journal of Consumer Research*, 9, 225-244.

MacCallum, R. (1986) Specification searches in covariance structure modeling. *Psychological Bulletin*, 100, 107-120.

MacLeod, C.M., Jackson, R.A., and Palmer, J. (1986) On the relation between spatial ability and field dependence. *Intelligence*, 10, 141-151.

Madansky, A. (1964) Instrumental variables in factor analysis. *Psychometrika*, 29, 105-113.

Madden, T.J., and Dillon, W.R. (1982) Causal analysis and latent class models: An application to a communication hierarchy of effects model. *Journal of Marketing Research*, 19, 472-490.

Magidson, J. (1977) Toward a causal model approach for adjusting for pre-existing differences in the non-equivalent control group situation. *Evaluation Quarterly*, 1, 399-420.

Magidson, J. (1982) Some common pitfalls in causal analysis of categorical data. *Journal of Marketing Research*, 19, 461-471.

Malamuth, N.M. Factors associated with rape as predictors of laboratory aggression against women. *Journal of Personality and Social Psychology*, 45, 432-442.

Mardia, K.V. (1970) Measures of multivariate skewness and kurtosis with applications. *Biometrika*. 57, 519-530.

Mardia, K.V. (1974) Applications of some measures of multivariate skewness and kurtosis in testing normality and robustness studies. *Sankhya*, B36, 115-128.

Mare, R.D., and Mason, W.M. (1981) Children's report of parental socioeconomic status. In G.W. Bohrnstedt and E.F. Borgatta (Eds.): *Social Measurement: Current Issues*. Beverly Hills: Sage Publications.

Marini, M.M., Olsen, A.R., and Rubin, D.B. (1979) Maximum likelihood estimation in panel studies with missing data. Pp. 314-357 in K.F. Schuessler (Ed.): *Sociological methodology 1980*. San Francisco: Jossey-Bass.

Marsden, P.V. (1983) On interaction effects involving block variables. *Sociological Methods and Research*, 11, 305-232.

Marsden, P.V. (1983) On interaction involving block variables. *Sociological Methods and Research*, 11, 305-323.

Marsh, H.W., and Hocevar, D. (1983) Confirmatory factor analysis of multitrait-multimethod matrices. *Journal of Educational Measurement*, 20, 231-248.

Marsh, H.W., and Hocevar, D. (1985) Application of confirmatory factor analysis to the study of self-concept: First- and higher-order factor models and their invariance across groups. *Psychological Bulletin*, 97, 562-582.

Martens, P.L. (1981) Socioeconomic status, family structure and socialization of early adolescent children. Project Metropolitan Research Report No. 16. University of Stockholm, Department of Sociology.

Martin, J.A. (1982) Application of structural modeling with latent variables to adolescent drug use: A reply to Huba, Wingard, and Bentler. *Journal of Personality and Social Psychology*, 43, 598-603.

Martin, J.A. (1987) Structural equation modeling: A guide for the perplexed. *Child Development*, 58, 33-37.

Martin, J.K., and McDonald, R.P. (1975) Bayes estimates in restricted factor analysis: A treatment of Heywood cases. *Psychometrika*, 40, 505-517.

Martin, N.G., Eaves, L.J., and Loesch, D.Z. (1982) A genetic analysis of covariation between finger ridge counts. *Annals of Human Biology*, 9, 539-552.

Maruyama, G., Rubin, R.A., and Kingsbury, G.G. (1981) Self-esteem and educational achievement: Independent constructs with a common cause. *Journal of Personality and Social Psychology*, 40, 962-975.

Maruyama, G., and McGarvey, B. (1980) Evaluating causal models: An application of maximum-likelihood analysis of structural equations. *Psychological Bulletin*, 87, 502-512.

Matsueda, R.L., and Bielby, W.T. (1986) Statistical power in covariance structure models. Pp. 120-158 in N.B. Tuma (Ed.): *Sociological Methodology 1986*. San Francisco: Jossey Bass.

McAlister, A.L., Krosnick, J.A., and Milburn, M.A. (1984) Causes of adolescent cigarette smoking: Tests of a structural equation model. *Social Psychology Quarterly*, 47, 24-36.

McArdle, J.J. (1980) Causal modeling applied to psychonomic systems simulation. *Behavior Research Methods and Instrumentation*, 12, 193- 209.

McArdle, J.J., and Epstein, D. (1987) Latent growth curves within developmental structural equation models. *Child Development*, 58, 110-133.

McArdle, J.J., and McDonald, R.P. (1984) Some algebraic properties of the reticular action model for moment structures. *British Journal of Mathematical and Statistical Psychology*, 37, 234-251.

McCarthy, J.D., and Hoge, D.R. (1984) The dynamics of self-esteem and delinquency. *American Journal of Sociology*, 90, 396-410.

McDonald, R.P. (1974) Testing pattern hypothesis for covariance matrices. *Psychometrika*, 39, 189-200.

McDonald, R.P. (1975) Testing pattern hypotheses for correlation matrices. *Psychometrika*, 40, 253-255.

McDonald, R.P. (1978) A simple comprehensive model of the analysis of covariance structures. *British Journal of Mathematical and Statistical Psychology*, 31, 59-72.

McDonald, R.P. (1979) The structural analysis of multivariate data: A sketch of a general theory. *Multivariate Behavioral Research*, 14, 21- 28.

McDonald, R.P. (1980) A simple comprehensive model for the analysis of covariance structures: Some remarks on applications. *British Journal of Mathematical and Statistical Psychology*, 33, 161-183.

McDonald, R.P. (1981) The dimensionality of tests and items. *British Journal of Mathematical and Statistical Psychology*, 34, 100-117.

McDonald, R.P. (1982) A note on the investigation of local and global identifiability. *Psychometrika*, 47, 101-103

McDonald, R.P., and Ahlawat, K.S. (1974) Difficulty factors in binary data. *British Journal of Mathematical and Statistical Psychology*, 27, 82-99.

McDonald, R.P., and Krane, W.R. (1977) A note on local identifiability and degrees of freedom in the asymptotic likelihood ratio test. *British Journal of Mathematical and Statistical Psychology*, 30, 198-203.

McDonald, R.P., and Krane, W.R. (1979) A Monte Carlo study of local identifiability and degrees of freedom in the asymptotic likelihood ratio test. *British Journal of Mathematical and Statistical Psychology*, 32, 121- 132.

McDonald, R.P., and Mulaik, S.A. (1979) Determinacy of common factors: A nontechnical review. *Psychological Bulletin*, 86, 297-308.

McGaw, B., Sörbom, D., and Cumming, J. (1986) Analysis of linear structural relations. *International Journal of Educational Research*, 10, 173-181.

McGaw, B., and Jöreskog, K.G. (1971) Factorial invariance of ability measures in groups differing in intelligence and socio-economic status. *British Journal of Mathematical and Statistical Psychology*, 24, 154-168.

McKennell, A.C. (1978) Cognition and affect in perceptions of well- being. *Social Indicators Research*, 5, 389-426.

McKennell, A.C., and Andrews, F.M. (1980) Models of cognition and affect in perceptions of well-being. *Social Indicators Research*, 8, 257- 298.

McKennell, A.C., Atkinson, T., and Andrews, F.M. (1980) Structural constancies in surveys of perceived well-being. In A. Szalai and F.M. Andrews (Eds.): *The Quality of Life:Comparative Studies*. Beverly Hills: Sage.

McPherson, J.M., Welch, S., and Clark, C. (1977) The stability and reliability of political efficacy: Using path analysis to test alternative models. *American Political Science Review*, 71, 509-521.

Mellenbergh, G.J., Kelderman, H., Stijlen, J.G., and Zondag, E. (1979) Linear models for the analysis and construction of instruments in a facet design. *Psychological Bulletin*, 86, 766-776.

Meredith, W. (1964) Rotation to achieve factorial invariance. *Psychometrika*, 29, 187-206.

Miller, K.A., Kohn, M.L., and Schooler, C.L. (1985) Educational self- direction and the cognitive functioning of students. *Social Forces*, 63, 923-944.

Mislevy, R. (1986) Recent developments in the factor analysis of categorical variables. *Journal of Educational Statistics*, 11, 3-31.

Mislevy, R.J. (1984) Estimating latent distributions. *Psychometrika*, 49, 359-381.

Molenaar, P.C.M. (1985) A dynamic factor model for the analysis of multivariate time series. *Psychometrika*, *50*, 181-202.

Monfort, A. (1978) First-order identification in linear models. *Journal of Economics*, 7, 333-350.

Mooijaart, A. (1983) Two kinds of factor analysis for ordered categorical variables. *Multivariate Behavioral Research*, 18, 423-441.

Mooijaart, A., and Bentler, P.M. (1985) The weight matrix in asymptotically distribution-free methods. *British Journal of Mathematical and Statistical Psychology*, 38, 190-196.

Moreland, R.L., and Zajonc, R.B. (1979) Exposure effects may not depend on stimulus recognition. *Journal of Personality and Social Psychology*, 37, 1085-1089.

Muirhead, R.J. (1982) *Aspects of multivariate statistical theory*. New York: Wiley.

Mukherjee, B.N. (1970) Likelihood ratio tests of statistical hypotheses associated with patterned covariance matrices in psychology. *Brittish Journal of Mathematical and Statistical Psychology*, 23, 120.

Mulaik, S.A. (1972) *The foundation of factor analysis*. New York: McGraw-Hill.

Mulaik, S.A. (1987) Toward a conception of causality applicable to experimentation and causal modeling. *Child Development*, 58, 18-32.

Munck, I.M.E. (1979) *Model building in comparative education: Applications of the* LISREL *method to cross-national survey data*. IEA Monograph Studies No. 10. Stockholm: Almqvist & Wiksell International.

Muthén, B. (1978) Contributions to factor analysis of dichotomous variables. *Psychometrika*, 43, 551-560.

Muthén, B. (1979) A structural probit model with latent variables. *Journal of the American Statistical Association*, 74, 807-811.

Muthén, B. (1980) Factor analysis of dichotomous variables: American attitudes towards abortion. In D.J. Jackson and E.F. Borgatta (Eds.): *Factor analysis and measurement in sociological research*. Beverley Hills: Sage.

Muthén, B. (1981) Some categorical response models with continuous latent variables. In K.G. Jöreskog and H. Wold (Eds.): *Systems under indirect observation: Causality, structure, and prediction*. Amsterdam: North-Holland Publishing Co.

Muthén, B. (1983) Latent variable structural equation modeling with categorical data. *Journal of Econometrics*, 22, 43-65.

Muthén, B. (1984) A general structural equation model with dichotomous, ordered categorical, and continuous latent variable indicators. *Psychometrika*, 49, 115-132.

Muthén, B. (1987) Response to Freedman's critique of path analysis: Improve credibility by better methodological training. *Journal of Educational Statistics*, 12, 178-184.

Muthén, B., Kaplan, D., and Hollis, M. (1987) On structural equation modeling with data that are not missing completely at random. *Psychometrika*, 52, 431-462.

Muthén, B., and Christoffersson, A. (1981) Simultaneous factor analysis of dichotomous variables in several groups. *Psychometrika*, 46, 407-419.

Muthén, B., and Jöreskog, K.G. (1983) Selectivity problems in quasi-experimental studies. *Evaluation Review*, 7, 139-174.

Muthén, B., and Kaplan, D. (1985) A comparison of some methodologies for the factor analysis of non-normal Likert variables. *British Journal of Mathematical and Statistical Psychology*, 38, 171-189.

Möbus, C., and Schneider, W. (1986) *Strukturmodelle für längsschnittdaten und zeitreihen: LISREL, Pfad- und Varianzanalyse.* Bern, Switzerland: Verlag Hans Huber. (In German)

Nelson, F.H., Lomax, R.G., and Perlman, R. (1984) A structural equation model of second language acquisition for adult learners. *Journal of Experimental Education*, 53, 29-29.

Newton, R.R., Komaeoka, V.A., Hoelter, J.W., and Tanaka-Matsumi, J. (1984) Maximum likelihood estimation of factor structures of anxiety measures: A multiple group comparison. *Education and Psychological Measurement*, 44, 179-193.

Norström, T. (1981) *Studies in the causation and prevention of traffic crime.* Stockholm: Almqvist & Wiksell International.

Nunnally, J.C. (1978) *Psychometric theory* (2nd ed). New York: McGraw-Hill.

O'Grady, K.E. (1983) A confirmatory maximum likelihood factor analysis of the WAIS-R. *Journal of Consulting and Clinical Psychology*, 51, 826-831.

Okamoto, M., and Ihara, M. (1983) A new algorithm for the least squares solution in factor analysis. *Psychometrika*, 48, 597-605.

Okamoto, M., and Ihara, M. (1984) Partial Gauss-Newton algorithm for least-squares and maximum likelihood methods in factor analysis. *Journal of Japan's Statistical Society*, 14, 137-144.

Olsson, U. (1979a) Maximum likelihood estimation of the polychoric correlation coefficient. *Psychometrika*, 44, 443-460.

Olsson, U. (1979b) On the robustness of factor analysis against crude classification of the observations. *Multivariate Behavioral Research*, 14, 485-500.

Olsson, U., and Bergman, L.R. (1977) A longitudinal factor model for studying change in ability structure. *Multivariate Behavioral Research*, 12, 221-242.

Olsson, U., Drasgow, F., and Dorans, N.J. (1982) The polyserial correlation coefficient. *Psychometrika*, 47, 337-347.

Orchard, T., and Woodbury, M.A. (1972) A missing information principle: Theory and applications. *Proceedings of the Sixth Berkeley Symposium on Mathematical Statistics*, 1, 697-715.

Parkerson, J.A., Lomax, R.G., Schiller, D.P., and Walberg, H.J. (1984) Exploring causal models of educational achievement. *Journal of Educational Psychology*, 76, 638-646.

Paulhus, D.L. (1983) Sphere-specific measures of perceived control. *Journal of Personality and Social Psychology*, 44, 1253-1265.

Paulhus, D.L. (1984) Two-component models of socially desirable responding. *Journal of Personality and Social Psychology*, 46, 598- 609.

Pearson, K. (1900) On the correlation of characters not quantitatively measurable. *Royal Society Philosophical Transactions*, series A, 195, 1-47.

Peter, J.P. (1979) Reliability: A review of psychometric basics and recent marketing practices. *Journal of Marketing Research*, 16, 6-17.

Pfeifer, A., and Schmidt, P. (1987) LISREL*: Die Analyse komplexer strukturgleichungsmodelle*. Stuttgart, West Germany: Gustav Fischer Verlag. (In German)

Phillips, L.W., Chang, D.R., and Buzzel, R.D. (1983) Product quality, cost position and business performance: A test of some key hypothesis. *Journal of Marketing*, 47, 26-43.

Phillips, L.W. (1981) Assessing measurement error in key informant reports: A methodological note on organizational analysis in marketing. *Journal of Marketing Research*, 18, 395-415.

Phillips, L.W. (1982) Explaining control losses in corporate marketing channels: An organizational analysis. *Journal of Marketing Research*, 19, 525-549.

Poon, W-Y., and Lee, S-Y. (1987) Maximum likelihood estimation of multivariate polyserial and polychoric correlation coefficients. *Psychometrika*, 52, 409-430.

Porst, R., Schmidt, P., and Zeifang, K. (1987) Comparisons of subgroups by models with multiple indicators. *Sociological Methods and Research*, 15, 303-315.

Potthoff, R.F., and Roy, S.N. (1964) A generalized multivariate analysis of variance model useful especially for growth curve problems. *Biometrika*, 51, 313-326.

Punj, G.N., and Staelin, R. (1983) A model of consumer information search behavior for new automobiles. *Journal of Consumer Research*, 9, 366-380.

Raaijmakers, J.G.W., and Pieters, J.P.M. (1987) Measurement error and ancova: Functional and structural relationship approaches. *Psychometrika* , 52, 521-538.

Rao, C.R. (1967) Least square theory using an estimated dispersion matrix and its application to the measurement of signals. *5th Berkeley Symposium on Probability and Mathematical Statistics*. Berkeley: Univ of California Press,355-372.

Rao, C.R. (1973) *Linear statistical inference and its applications*. New York: Wiley.

Reilly, M.D. (1982) Working wives and convenience consumption. *Journal of Consumer Research*, 8, 407-418.

Rindskopf, D.M. (1981) Structural equation models in analyses of nonexperimental data. In R.F. Boruch, P.M. Wortman, D.S. Cardroy, and Associates: *Reanalysing program evaluations*. San Franscisco:Jossey- Bass.

Rindskopf, D.M. (1983a) Parameterizing inequality constraints on unique variances in linear structural equation models. *Psychometrika*, 48, 73- 83.

Rindskopf, D.M. (1983b) Using inequality constraints to prevent Heywood cases: The LISREL parameterization. *Data Analyst*, 1, 1-3.

Rindskopf, D.M. (1984a) Structural equation models: Empirical identification, Heywood cases, and related problems. *Sociological Methods and Research*, 13, 109-119.

Rindskopf, D.M. (1984b) Using phantom and imaginary latent variables to parameterize constraints in linear structural models. *Psychometrika*, 49, 37-47.

Robins, P.K., and West, R. (1977) Measurement errors in the estimation of home value. *Journal of the American Statistical Association*, 72, 290-294.

Robinson, P.M. (1974) Identification, estimation and large-sample theory for regressions containing unobservable variables. *International Economic Review*, 15, 680-692.

Rock, D.A., Werts, C.E., Linn, R.L., and Jöreskog, K.G. (1977) A maximum likelihood solution to the errors in variables and errors in equation models. *Journal of Multivariate Behavioral Research*, 12, 187-197.

Rock, D.A., Werts, C.E., and Flaugher, R.L. (1978) The use of analysis of covariance structures for comparing the psychometric properties of multiple variables across populations. *Multivariate Behavioral Research*, 13, 403-418.

Rogosa, D. (1987) Casual models do not support scientific conclusions: A comment in support of Freedman. *Journal of Educational Statistics*, 12, 185-195.

Romer, D. (1981) A person situated causal analysis of self-reports of attitudes. *Journal of Personality and Social Psychology*, 41, 562-576.

Rosenbaum, P.R. (1984) Testing the conditional independence and monotonicity assumptions of item response theory. *Psychometrika*, 49, 425-435.

Rothenberg, T.J. (1987) Comments on Freeman's paper. *Journal of Educational Statistics*, 12, 196-197.

Rubin, D.B (1974) Characterizing the estimation of parameters in incomplete data problems. *Journal of the American Statistical Association*, 69, 467-474.

Rubin, D.B. (1976) Inference and missing data. *Biometrika*, 63, 581-592.

Rubin, D.B. (1977). Formalizing subjective notions about the effect of nonrespondents in sample surveys. *Journal of the American Statistical Association*, 72, 538-543.

Rubin, D.B., and Thayer, D.T. (1982) EM algorithms for ML factor analysis. *Psychometrika*, 47, 69-76.

Rubin, D.B., and Thayer, D.T. (1983) More on EM for ML factor analysis. *Psychometrika*, 48, 253-257.

Ryan, M.J. (1980) Psychobiology and consumer research: A problem of construct validity. *Journal of Consumer Research*, 7, 92-96.

Ryan, M.J. (1982) Behavioral intention formation: The interdependency of attitudinal and social influence variables. *Journal of Consumer Research*, 9, 263-278.

Saris, W. (1980) Linear structural relationships. *Quality and Quantity*, 14, 205-224.

Saris, W.E and Stronkhorst, L.H. (1984) *Causal modelling in non- experimental research*. Amsterdam: Sociometric Research Foundation.

Saris, W.E and Stronkhorst, L.H. (1984) *Titles of articles for secondary analysis: An appendix to 'Causal modelling in non-experimental research'*. Amsterdam: Sociometric Research Foundation.

Saris, W.E., Satorra, A. and Sörbom, D. (1987) The detection and correction of specification errors in structural equation models. In C. Clogg (Ed.): *Sociological Methodology 1987*. San Francisco: Jossey. Bass.

Saris, W.E., de Pijper, M., and Mulder, J. (1978) Optimal procedures for estimation of factor scores. *Sociological Methods and Research*, 7, 85- 106.

Saris, W.E., de Pijper, W.M., and Zegwaart, P. (1979) Detection of specification errors in linear structural equation models. Pp. 151-171 in K.F. Schuessler (Ed.): *Sociological Methodology 1979*. San Fracisco: Jossey Bass.

Sato, M. (1987) Pragmatic treatment of improper solutions in factor analysis. *Annals of the Institute of Statistical Mathematics*, 39, 443- 455.

Satorra, A. (1987) Alternative test criteria in covariance structure analysis: A unified approach. *Psychometrika*, in press.

Satorra, A., and Saris, W.E. (1985) Power of the likelihood ratio test in covariance structure analysis. *Psychometrika*, 50, 83-90.

Scheifley, V.M., and Schmidt, W.H. (1978) Analysis of repeated measures data: A simulation study. *Multivariate Behavioral Research*, 13, 347-362.

Schmitt, N. (1982) The use of analysis of covariance structures to assess beta and gamma change. *Multivariate Behavioral Research*, 17, 343- 358.

Schneeweiss, H. (1985) Estimating linear relations with errors in the variables: The merging of two approaches. Pp 207-221 in H. Schneeweiss, and H. Strecker (Eds.): *Contributions to Econometrics and Statistics Today*. Berlin, Heidelberg: Springer-Verlag.

Schoenberg, R. (1972) Strategies for meaningful comparison. Pp 1-35 in H. L. Costner (Ed.) *Sociological Methodology 1972*. San Francisco: Jossey-Bass.

Schoenberg, R. (1982) Multiple indicator models: Estimation of unconstrained construct means and their standard errors. *Sociological Methods and Research*, 10: 421-433.

Schoenberg, R., and Richtand, C. (1984) Application of the EM method: A study of maximum likelihood estimation of multiple indicator and factor analysis models. *Sociological Methods and Research*, 13, 127-150.

Schul, P.L., Pride, W.M., and Little, T.L. (1983) The impact of channel leadership behavior on interchannel conflict. *Journal of Marketing*, 3, 21-34.

Schwab, D.P. (1980) Construct validity in organizational behavior. *Research in Organizational Behavior*, 2, 3-43.

Searle, S.R. (1982) *Matrix algebra useful for statistics*. New York: Wiley.

Seneta, E. (1987) Discussion of D.A. Freedman's "As other see us... ." *Journal of Educational Statistics*, 12, 198-201.

Sewell, W.H., Haller, A.O., and Ohlendorf, G.W. (1970) The educational and early occupational status attainment process: Revisions and replications. *American Sociological Review*, 35, 1014-1027.

Shapiro, A. (1982) Weighted minimum trace factor analysis. *Psychometrika*, 47, 243-264.

Shapiro, A. (1983) Asymptotic distribution theory in the analysis of covariance structures (a unified approach). *South African Statistical Journal*, 17, 33-81.

Shapiro, A. (1985a) Asymptotic distribution of test statistics in the analysis of moment strucures under inequality constraints. *Biometrika*, 72, 133-144.

Shapiro, A. (1985b) Asymptotic equivalence of minimum discrepancy function estimators to GLS estimators. *South African Statistical Journal*, *19*, 73-81.

Shapiro, A. (1986) Asymptotic theory of overparameterized structural models. *Journal of the American Statistical Association*, 81, 142-149.

Shapiro, A. (1987) Robustness properties of the MDF analysis of moment structures. *South African Journal*, 21, 39-62.

Shapiro, A., and Browne, M.W. (1983) On the investigation of local identifiability: A counterexample. *Psychometrika*, 48, 303-304.

Shapiro, A., and Browne, M.W. (1987) Analysis of covariance structures under elliptical distributions. *Journal of the Amarican Statistical Association*, 82, 1092-1097.

Shultz, N.R., Kaye, D.B., Hoyer, W.J. (1980) Intelligence and spontaneous flexibility in adulthood and old age. *Intelligence*, 4, 219- 231.

Silverman, R.A., and Kennedy, L.W. (1985) Loneliness, satisfaction and fear of crime: A test for nonrecursive effects. *Canadian Journal of Criminology*, 27, 1-12.

Silvey, S.D. (1970) *Statistical inference*. Middlesex, U.K.: Penguin Books.

Smith, D.A., and Patterson, E.B. (1984) Applications and generalization of MIMIC models to criminological research. *Journal of Research in Crime and Delinquency*, 21, 333-352.

Smith, E.R. (1982) Beliefs, attributions, and evaluations: Nonhierarchical models of mediation in social cognition. *Journal of Personality and Social Psychology*, 43, 248-259.

Smith, E.R. (1982) Beliefs, attributions, and evaluations: Nonhierarchical models of meditation in social cognition. *Journal of Personality and Social Psychology*, 43, 248-259.

Sobel, M. (1982) Asymptotic confidence intervals for indirect effects in structural equation models. In S. Leinhardt (Ed.): *Sociological Methodology 1982*. San Francisco: Jossey Bass.

Sobel, M.E., and Bohrnstedt, G.W. (1985) Use of null models in evaluating the fit of covariance structure models. Pp 152-178 in N. B. Tuma (Ed.): *Sociological Methodology 1985*. San Francisco: Jossey-Bass.

Spearman, C. (1914) Theory of two factors. *Psychological Review*, 21, 105-115.

Spearman, C., and Holzinger, K. (1924) The sampling error in the theory of two factors. *British Journal of Psychology*, 15, 17-19.

Speckart, G., and Bentler, P.M. (1982) Application of attitude behavior models to varied content domains. *Academic Psychology Bulletin*, 4, 453-466.

Stavig, G.R., and Acock, A.C. (1981) Applying the semistandardized regression coefficient to factor, canonical, and path analysis. *Multivariate Behavioral Research*, 16, 207-213.

Stegelmann, W. (1983) Expanding the Rasch model to a general model having more than one dimension. *Psychometrika*, 48, 259-267.

Steiger, J.H., and Browne, M.W. (1984) The comparison of interdependent correlations between optional linear composites. *Psychometrika*, 49, 11-24.

Steiger, J.H., Shapiro, A., and Browne, M.W. (1985) On the multivariate asymptotic distribution of sequential chi-square statistics. *Psychometrika*, 50, 253-264.

Stelzl, I. (1986) Changing causal relationships without changing the fit: Some rules for generating equivalent LISREL models. *Multivariate Behavioral Research*, 21, 309-331.

Stolzenberg, R.M. (1980) The measurement and decomposition of causal berg, R.M. (1980) The measurement and decomposition of causal effects in nonlinear and nonadditive models. Pp 459-88 in K.F. Schueller (Ed.): *Sociological Methodology, 1980*. San Francisco: Jossey-Bass.

Stolzenberg, R.M., and Land, K.C. (1983) Causal modeling and survey research. Pp 613-675 in P. Rossi, J. Wright and A. Anderson (Eds.): *Handbook of Survey Research*. New York: Academic Press.

Stroud, A.H., and Sechrest, D. (1966) *Gaussian quadrature formulas*. Englewood Cliffs, NJ: Prentice Hall.

Swain, A.J. (1975) A class of factor analysis estimation procedures with common asymptotic sampling properties. *Psychometrika*, 40, 315- 335.

Sörbom, D. (1974) A general method for studying differences in factor means and factor structures between groups. *British Journal of Mathematical and Statistical Psychology*, 27, 229-239.

Sörbom, D. (1975) Detection of correlated errors in longitudinal data. *British Journal of Mathematical and Statistical Psychology*, 28, 138- 151.

Sörbom, D. (1976) A statistical model for the measurement of change in true scores. In D.N.M. de Gruijter and J.L.Th. van der Kamp (Eds.): *Advances in psychological and educational measurement*. New York: Wiley. 159-169.

Sörbom, D. (1978) An alternative to the methodology for analysis of covariance. *Psychometrika*, 43, 381-396.

Sörbom, D. (1981) Stuctural equation models with structured means. In K.G. Jöreskog and H. Wold (Eds.): *Systems under indirect observation: Causality, structure and prediction*. Amsterdam: North- Holland Publishing Co.

Sörbom, D. (1989) Model modification. *Psychometrika*, in press.

Sörbom, D., and Jöreskog, K.G. (1981) The use of LISREL in sociological model building. In E. Borgatta and D.J. Jackson (Eds.) *Factor analysis and measurement in sociolgical research: A multidimensional perspective*. Beverly Hills: Sage.

Sörbom, D., and Jöreskog, K.G. (1982) The use of structural equation models in evaluation research. Pp 381-418 in C. Fornell (Ed.): *A second generation of multivariate analysis*, volume 2. 1985. New York: Praeger.

Sörbom, D., and Jöreskog, K.G. (1986). Strukturgleichungsmodelle in der Evaluationsforschung. In C. Möbus und W. Schneider (Hrsg.): *Strukturmodelle für Längsschnittdaten und Zeitreihen:* LISREL, *Pfad- und Varianzanalyse.* Bern, Switzerland: Verlag Hans Huber.

Tanaka, J. S., and Huba, G. J. (1985) A fit index for covariance structure models under arbitrary GLS estimation. *British Journal of Mathematical and Statistical Psychology*, *38*, 197-201.

Tanaka, J.S. (1984) *Some results on the estimation of covariance structure models.* Ph.D. Thesis, University of California, Los Angeles.

Tanaka, J.S. (1987) "How big is enough?": Sample size and goodness of fit in structural equation models with latent variables. *Child Development*, 58, 134-146.

Tanaka, J.S., and Bentler, P.M. (1983) Factor invariance of premorbid social competence across multiple populations of schizophrenics. *Multivariate Behavioral Research*, 18, 135-146.

Tanaka, J.S., and Huba, G.J. (1984) Confirmatory hierarchical factor analyses of psychological distress measures. *Journal of Personality and Social Psychology*, 46, 621-635.

Taubman, P. (Ed.) (1977) *Kinometrics: Determinants of socioeconomic success within and between families.* Amsterdam: North- Holland.

Theil, H. (1971) *Principles of econometrics.* New York: Wiley.

Thomson, E., and Williams, R. (1982) Beyond wives family sociology: A method for analyzing couple data. *Journal of Marriage and the Family*, 44, 999-1008.

Thornberry, T.P., and Christenson, R.L. (1984) Unemployment and criminal involvement: An investigation of reciprocal causal structures. *American Sociological Review*, 49, 389-411.

Thornton, A., Alwin, D.F., and Camburn, D. (1983) Causes and consequences of sex-role attitudes and attitude change. *American Sociological Review*, 48, 211-227.

Thurstone, L.L. (1938) Primary mental abilities. *Psychometric Monographs*, 1.

Thurstone, L.L. (1947) *Multiple factor analysis.* Chicago: University of Chicago Press.

Tuddenham, R.D., and Snyder, M.M. (1954) *Physical growth of boys and girls from birth to eighteen years.* Berkeley: University of California Press.

Turner, M.E., and Stevens, C.D. (1959) The regression analysis of causal paths. *Biometrics*, 15, 236-258.

Tyler, T.R., and Rasinski, K. (1984) Comparing psychological images of the social perceiver: Role of perceived informativness, memorability, and affect. *Journal of Personality and Social Psychology*, 46, 308-329.

Van de Ven, W.P.M.M., and Van der Gaag, J. (1982) Health as an unobservable: A MIMIC model of demand for health care. *Journal of Health Economics*, 1, 157-183.

Van Praag, B.M.S., Dijkstra, T.K., and Van Velzen, J. (1985) Least-squares theory based on general distributional assumptions with an application to the incomplete observations problem. *Psychometrika*, 50, 25-36.

Votaw, D.F.Jr. (1948) Testing compound symmetry in a normal multivariate distribution. *Annals of Mathematical Statistics*, 19, 447-473.

Warren, R.D., White, J.K., and Fuller, W.A. (1974) An errors in variables analysis of managerial role performance. *Journal of the American Statistical Association*, 69, 886-893.

Weeks, D.G., Michela, J.L., and Peplau, L.A. (1981) Relations between loneliness and depression: A structural equation analysis. *Journal of Personality and Social Psychology*, 39, 1238-1244.

Weeks, D.G.A. (1980) A second-order longitudinal model of ability structure. *Multivariate Behavioral Research*, 15, 353-365.

Weisberg, S. (1985) *Applied linear regression* (2nd ed). New York: Wiley.

Werts, C.E, Rock, D.A., Linn, R.L., and Jöreskog, K.G. (1978) A general method of estimating the reliability of a composite. *Educational and Psychological Measurment*, 38, 933-938.

Werts, C.E., Breland, H.M., Grandy, J., and Rock, D.R. (1980) Using longitudinal data to estimate reliability in the presence of correlated measurement errors. *Educational and Psychological Measurement*, 40, 19-28.

Werts, C.E., Jöreskog, K.G., and Linn, R.L. (1973) Identification and estimation in path analysis with unmeasured variables. *American Journal of Sociology*, 78, 1469-1484.

Werts, C.E., Jöreskog, K.G., and Linn, R.L. (1985) Comment on the estimation of measurement error in panel data. Pp 145-150 in H.M. Blalock Jr. (Ed.): *Causal models in panel and experimental designs*. New York: Aldine.

Werts, C.E., Linn, R.L., and Jöreskog, K.G. (1971) Estimating the parameters of path models involving unmeasured variables. In H.M Blalock (Ed.): *Causal models in the social sciences*. Chicago: Aldine-Atherton.

Werts, C.E., Linn, R.L., and Jöreskog, K.G. (1972) A multitrait- multimethod model for studying growth. *Educational and Psychological Measurement*, 32, 655-678.

Werts, C.E., Linn, R.L., and Jöreskog, K.G. (1973a) A congeneric model for platonic true scores. *Educational and Psychological Measurement*, 33, 311-318.

Werts, C.E., Linn, R.L., and Jöreskog, K.G. (1973b) Another perspective on 'Linear regression, structural relations, and measurement error.' *Educational and Psychological Measurement*, 33, 327-332.

Werts, C.E., Linn, R.L., and Jöreskog, K.G. (1974a) Quantifying unmeasured variables. In H.M Blalock (Ed.): *Measurement in the social sciences: Theories and Strategies*. Chicago: Aldine-Atherton.

Werts, C.E., Linn, R.L., and Jöreskog, K.G. (1974b) Intraclass reliability estimates: Testing structural assumptions. *Educational and Psychological Measurement*, 34, 25-33.

Werts, C.E., Linn, R.L., and Jöreskog, K.G. (1976) Analyzing ratings with correlated intrajudge measurement errors. *Educational and Psychological Measurement*, 36, 319-328.

Werts, C.E., Linn, R.L., and Jöreskog, K.G. (1977) A simplex model for analyzing academic growth. *Educational and Psychological Measurement*, 37, 745-756.

Werts, C.E., Linn, R.L., and Jöreskog, K.G. (1978) Reliability of college grades from longitudinal data. *Educational and Psychological Measurement*, 38, 89-95.

Werts, C.E., Rock, D.A., Linn, R.L., and Jöreskog, K.G. (1976a) A comparison of correlations, variances, covariances and regression weights with or without measurement errors. *Psychological Bulletin*, 83, 1007-1013.

Werts, C.E., Rock, D.A., Linn, R.L., and Jöreskog, K.G. (1976b) Testing the equality of partial correlations. *American Scientist*, 30, 101-102.

Werts, C.E., Rock, D.A., Linn, R.L., and Jöreskog, K.G. (1977) Validating psychometric assumptions within and between populations. *Educational and Psychological Measurement*, 37, 863-871.

Werts, C.E., Rock, D.A., and Grandy, J. (1979) Confirmatory factor analysis applications: Missing data problems and comparison of path models between populations. *Multivariate Behavioral Research*, 14, 199-213.

Werts, C.E., and Linn, R.L. (1970) Path analysis: Psychological examples. *Psychological Bulletin*, 67, 193-212.

Wheaton, B. (1978) The sociogenisis of psychological disorder. *American Sociological Review*, 43, 383-403.

Wheaton, B. (1987) Assessment of fit in overidentified models with latent variables. *Sociological Methods and Research*, 16, 118-154.

Wheaton, B., Muthén, B., Alwin, D., and Summers, G. (1977) Assessing reliability and stability in panel models. In D.R. Heise (Ed.): *Sociological Methodology 1977*. San Francisco: Jossey-Bass.

Wiley, D.E. (1973) The identification problem for structural equation models with unmeasured variables. In A.S. Goldberger and O.D. Duncan (Eds.): *Structural equation models in the social sciences*. New York: Seminar Press, 69-83.

Wiley, D.E., Schmidt, W.H., and Bramble, W.J. (1973) Studies of a class of covariance structure models. *Journal of the American Statistical Association*, 68, 317-323.

Wilks, S.S. (1932) Moments and distribution of estimates of population parameters from fragmentary samples. *Annals of Mathematical Statistics*, 3, 163-195.

Willassen, Y. (1978) An analysis of the effect of transitory income on consumption. *The Scandinavian Journal of Economics*, 80, 299-310.

Winship, C., and Mare, R.D. (1983) Structural equations and path analysis for discrete data. *American Journal of Sociology*, 89, 54-110.

Wold, H. (1982) Soft modeling: The basic design and some extentions. Pp 1-54 in K.G. Jöreskog and H. Wold (Eds.): *Systems under indirect observation: Causality, structure, prediction, Part II*. Amsterdam: North Holland Publishing.

Wold, H. (1987) Response to D.A. Freedman. *Journal of Educational Statistics*, 12, 202-205.

Wolfle, L.M. (1982) Causal models with unmeasured variables: An introduction to LISREL. *Multiple Linear Regression Viewpoints*, 11, 9-54.

Wolfle, L.M., and Ethington, C.A. (1985) SEINE: Standard errors of indirect effects. *Educational and Psychological Measurement*, 45, 161- 166.

Wolfle, L.M., and Ethington, C.A. (1986) Within-variable, between- occasion error covariance in models of educational achievement. *Educational and Psychological Measurement*, 46, 571-583.

Wothke, W., and Browne, M.W. (1989) The direct product model for the MTMM matrix parameterized as a second order factor analysis model. *Psychometrika*, in press.

Wright, S. (1934) The method of path coefficients. *Annals of Mathematical Statistics*, 5, 161-215.

Wright, S. (1954) The interpretation of multivariate systems. In O. Kempthorne et al. (Eds.): *Statistics and mathematics in biology*. Ames: Iowa State College Press.

Wright, S. (1960) Path coefficiants and path regressions: Alternative or complementary concepts? *Biometrics*, 16, 189-202.

Yanai, H., and Mukherjee, B.N. (1987) A generalized method of image analysis from an intercorrelation matrix which may be singular. *Psychometrika* , 52, 555-564.

Subject Index

A-format, see format
AC line 54, 60, 71, 195
AD (ADmissibility test) 72, 211, 214, 278
AD = OFF 72, 136, 141, 214, 278
ADF, see asymptotically distribution free
adjusted goodness-of-fit index, see AGFI
admissibility test 24, 72, 211, 278
admissible
    parameter space 24
    solution 211, 214, 215, 277
AGFI 42, 43, 49, 229
AL (ALpha vector) 110, 246
algorithm
    Davidon-Fletcher-Powell 268
    Fisher's scoring 268
ALL
    print everything 72
    starting values 68
alternative
    hypothesis 216
    scaling option 273, see also SO
AM (Automatic Model modification) 70,
    111, see also MA = AM
analysis
    of covariance (ANCOVA) 112, 114, 116
    of variance (ANOVA) 112, 114, 115
assessment of fit 40, 97, see also goodness
    of fit
assumptions
    of LISREL model 4
    of regression analysis 108
asymptotic
    covariance matrix 20, 48, 54, 60, 193,
        194, 195, 197, 200, 203, 206, 207,
        209, see also AC line
    normality 103
    standard error 31
    theory 101, 191
    variances 20, 54, 61, see also AV line

asymptotically
    distribution free 20
    efficient estimators 247
    uncorrelated parameters 247
asymptotically correct
    chi-square measure 22, 47, 48
    standard error 22, 47, 48
attenuated coefficient 133, 259, 261
augmented moment matrix 18, 54, 59, 261,
    see also MA = AM
autocorrelated errors 183, 202
autocorrelation 129, 181
automatic model modification 70, 111, see
    also AM
autoregressive model 262
AV line 61, 71

bad model 278
BE (BEta matrix) 63, 72
behavioral equations 128
bias 133, 134
binomial distribution 205
biserial correlation 18, 193
bivariate regression 116
blank lines 156
blank spaces 55, 58, 85

canonical correlation 18
case 57
causal inference 221
cause variables 119
censored variables 193
character parameter values 51
    AM (Augmented moment Matrix), see
        MA = AM
    CM (Covariance Matrix), see MA =
        CM
    DI (DIagonal), see DI

Author Index